Comparison
and Universal Grammar

For Trudy

Comparison
and Universal Grammar

LEON STASSEN

Basil Blackwell

© Leon Stassen 1985

First published 1985

Basil Blackwell Ltd
108 Cowley Road, Oxford OX4 1JF, UK

Basil Blackwell Inc
432 Park Avenue South, Suite 1505,
New York, NY 10016, USA

British Library Cataloguing in Publication Data

Stassen, Leon
Comparison and universal grammar: an essay in universal grammar.
1. Grammar, Comparative and general
I. Title
415   P201

ISBN 0–631–14058–1

Library of Congress Cataloging in Publication Data

Stassen, Leon.
Comparison and universal grammar.

Bibliography: p.
Includes index.
1. Comparison (Grammar)   2. Grammar, Comparative and general.   I. Title.
P255.S73   1985   415   84–28247

ISBN 0–631–14058–1 (lib. bdg.)

Typeset by Freeman Graphic, Tonbridge, Kent
Printed in Great Britain by T.J. Press Ltd, Padstow, Cornwall

Contents

Acknowledgements

This book is a revised version of my doctoral dissertation, which was presented at the University of Nijmegen in November 1984. Part of the research contained in it was conducted during a stay at the Netherlands Institute of Advanced Study in the Humanities and Social Sciences (NIAS) in Wassenaar, The Netherlands.

My dissertation was supervised by Pieter Seuren, who played an active part in the development of my ideas, and who possessed the priceless quality of insisting on those changes which he knew would be for the better. I am also indebted to Melissa Bowerman, Joan Bybee, Herbert Clark, Bernard Comrie, John Hawkins, Remmert Kraak and Lachlan McKenzie, for their valuable comments on the manuscript at various stages of its completion. This does not imply, of course, that any of these kind people can be held responsible for the facts or the fiction put forward in this study.

I hope that this book, whatever its further merits may be, will be accepted as a tribute to those linguists who, far from the turmoil of theoretical debate, devote their lives to a minute description of the facts in what is called 'exotic' languages. Writing a book like this simply would not have been possible if these specialists had not been willing to share their knowledge with me. In the course of my investigation, I have also become deeply impressed by the profundity of the insights of older, often long-forgotten, descriptivist grammarians. Hanoteau (1896), Hoffmann (1903), Taylor (1921), Lafitte (1944) or Lukas (1953) are not exactly household names in current linguistics; but they have become my friends, and their work has an enduring value, to which this essay may bear testimony.

Abbreviations

In the glosses of the example sentences the following abbreviations have been used:

ABL	ablative case	EMPH	emphasis marker
ABSTR	abstract form	ERG	ergative case
ACC	accusative case	FEM	feminine gender
ADESS	adessive case	FUT	future tense
ADHORT	adhortative mood	GEN	genitive case
ADV	adverbial marker	GER	gerundial marker
AG	agentive case	GOAL	goal case
AOR	aorist tense	HAB	habitual aspect
ART	article	INAN	inanimate marker
ASS	assertive marker	IMP	imperative mood
CAUS	causative marker	IND	indicative mood
CLASS	classifier	INDEF	indefinite marker
COMPLET	completive aspect	INESS	inessive case
CONCESS	concessive mood	INF	infinitive
COND	conditional mood	LOC	locative case
CONJ	conjunctive mood	MASC	masculine gender
CONT	continuative aspect	MED	mediative case
CONV	converb	MOMENT	momentanous aspect
COP	copula	NARR	narrative mood
DAT	dative case	NEG	negative marker
DEM	demonstrative	NOM	nominative case
DEP	dependent mood	NONFUT	non-future tense
DET	determiner	NOUN	nominalization marker
DISJ	disjunctive mood	PASS	passive voice
DUAL	dual	PAST	past tense
DUR	durative aspect	PCP	participial marker
ELAT	elative case	PERF	perfect marker

1PL., 2PL, 3PL	1st, 2nd, 3rd person plural	SER. MARK	serial marker
		SUBJ	subject marker
POSS	Possessive	SUBJCT	subjunctive marker
PRES	Present tense	SUBORD	subordination marker
PROG	Progressive aspect	SUP	supplementary element
PRT	Particle (unspecified function)	TEMP	temporal mood
		TOP	topic marker
Q	question marker	TNS	tense marker
REFL	reflexive	TRANS	transitive marker
REL	relative marker	UNSPEC	marker of non-specificity
REM	remote past tense		
1SG, 2SG, 3SG	1st, 2nd, 3rd person singular	VN	verbal noun

Part One

A Cross-linguistic Typology of Comparatives

1
Introduction

1.1 General background

The present essay must be placed within the framework of Typological Universal Grammar, a trend in linguistic investigation which is relatively young, but which constantly increased in importance throughout the seventies. Taking the pioneering research on word-order by Greenberg (1963, 1966) as a starting point, universalist authors have begun to tackle a variety of topics, such as coordinate ellipsis (Sanders, 1976; Harries, 1978), relative-clause formation (Keenan and Comrie, 1977, 1979; Downing, 1978; C. Lehmann, 1984), reflexivity (Faltz, 1977), causative formation (Comrie, 1975, Shibatani, 1975), the expression of grammatical functions and the phenomenon of ergativity (Keenan, 1976a, 1976b; Schachter, 1977; Comrie, 1978a; Plank, 1979; Hopper and Thompson, 1982), verbal aspect (Comrie, 1976) and word-order variation (W. Lehmann, 1973; Vennemann, 1974; Steele, 1978; Hawkins, 1979, 1980, 1984); in all these cases, new discoveries and illuminating insights into the nature of human language have been brought to light. The history of this new universalist trend has been documented in Ferguson (1978). Basic principles of the approach, and discussions of the results in some of the better-known areas of universalist research, can be found in the textbooks by Comrie (1981) and Mallinson and Blake (1981).

As I see it, the goals of Typological Universal Grammar do not differ essentially from those of other forms of linguistic inquiry. Universal Grammar, too, tries to contribute to a solution of the problem of how to define the notion 'human language' in terms of a set of restrictive principles; that is, like any other approach in theoretical linguistics, Universal Grammar is in search of the essential features of the rule system (or rule systems) known as 'natural human language'. The differences between Universal Grammar and other schools within the field of theoretical linguistics are, in my opinion, mainly a matter of method and perspective. I think it is safe to say that most of the recent research in theoretical linguistics (e.g., the research conducted within the framework of the Extended Standard Theory; see Chomsky, 1981) has tried to arrive at the underlying basic principles of human language by means of an in-depth investigation of a very small set of languages; usually, English is the sole language which is taken into consideration. While universalist authors do not deny the validity of this type of 'narrow' approach, they nevertheless feel that a broadening of the scope of linguistic investigation is in order; therefore, Universal Grammar bases its inquiries on data from an extensive sample of (preferably unrelated) languages. It is expected that, by a comparison of the structural properties of a large variety of languages, new generalizations as to the nature of human language may come to be formulated. These generalizations may then be used as a supplement (or, as the case may be, as an evaluation measure) of the regularities which have been discovered in the study of single instances of natural language.

It will be obvious that the broad, survey-type perspective adopted by Typological Universal Grammar calls for a specific type of methodology, which differs from established linguistic practice in a significant number of respects. Therefore, the remaining part of this chapter will be devoted to an exposition of the way in which a universalist linguistic investigation is conducted, and a discussion of a number of methodological problems which may be raised in connection with this type of research. Throughout this chapter, it should be kept in mind that universalist methodology is still in its infancy, and that therefore no hard-and-fast rules of proper conduct can be prescribed. However, notwithstanding this rather early stage of development, there are a number of issues which must be clarified before any universalist research project can be undertaken; and the least that can be asked of any universalist grammarian is that he state explicitly what solutions he has adopted towards these preliminary methodological questions.

1.2 Stages in a universalist research project

From a methodological point of view, the conduct of a universalist research project can be split up in a number of successive stages. As a first step, one must establish a *language sample*, which forms the empirical basis of the research project at issue. The choice of an adequate language sample for a given descriptive purpose is not without its problems; I will say more about this point in section 1.3.1. For the moment, however, I will assume that we can succeed in setting up a language sample which meets at least some general requirements of representativity.

Once a more or less adequate language sample has been assembled, one arrives at the stage of *typology*. At this stage, the languages in the sample are investigated for one or several structural features, which form the *parameter* of the typology, and which must have been defined beforehand in a language-independent fashion (see section 1.3.2). When this basic feature has been attested and documented in all of the languages in the sample, a number of different situations may arise. On the one hand, it may turn out that none of the languages under investigation has the features for which the survey was undertaken. In that case (given that the sample which is used has some degree of representativity), one may formulate one's findings in a statement of the following general form:

No human language exhibits feature/property X.

Statements of this form are known in the literature as *absolute negative universals of language*.

The opposite situation may also be encountered. That is, it is also possible that all languages in the sample exhibit the feature upon which the typological survey was based. In such a case, the results of the investigation may be summarized in a statement of the following general form, a so-called *absolute positive universal of language*:

All human languages exhibit feature/property X.

It will be obvious that absolute universals, whether they be positive or negative, tell us something about the restrictions on the notion 'possible human language' in a very straightforward way; they formulate conditions which any rule system must meet if it is to be called a natural language, and as such they can be viewed as the ultimate and optimal research result for any form of linguistic inquiry. Recently advanced instances of absolute universals include, among others, the island constraints established by Ross (1967), the Subjacency Condition proposed by Chomsky (1973), and the Noun Phrase Accessibility Hierarchy put forward by Keenan and Comrie (1977). All of these are abstract principles which are meant to constrain the structural possibilities of natural language systems in a non-trivial way.

Absolute universals, however, are not the only kind of results to be produced by universalist inquiries, nor are they necessarily the most interesting ones. When searching for absolute universals, one deliberately abstracts from the highly characteristic and significant phenomenon of *variation* among languages, and it is, more often than not, this variation which is particularly revealing as to the restrictions that are imposed on natural language systems. It is for this reason that, at least up to now, some of the more exciting results of universalist research have come from cases in which a 'real' typology could be established, that is, cases in which the parameter X had been defined in such a way that the following descriptive result could be obtained:

Feature/property X is exhibited by natural languages in *n* different ways.

In cases where such a situation holds, the linguistic manifestations of the parameter X across languages can be *classified* into a number of different *types*; these types represent the possible *options* which languages may select in the formal expression (or *encoding*) of the parameter X. Related to the classification of (construction) types, the *languages* in the sample can also be classified into a number of *categories*, on the basis of difference and similarity in the ways in which various groups of languages select their options for the encoding of the parameter X. In short, a cross-linguistic typology consists of two related categorizations, viz. the typology of a certain construction type and the classification of the sampled languages in relation to the types attested in the typology of the parameter.

Typologies, in the sense defined above, are interesting for a number of linguistic and non-linguistic reasons. Their main linguistic importance lies in the fact that such typologies can be used as data for a further exploration into the *non-randomness of linguistic encoding*. That natural languages show variation in their encoding properties is an irrefutable empirical fact; but it is a basic assumption in all universalist work that languages do not vary in unpredictable ways and that, therefore, typological variation can be subject to explanation. Of course, this point of view is a matter of faith; it cannot be refuted by single counter-examples, and it will be abandoned only if the research which is based on it does not yield sufficient results. In other words, the assumption that typological variation among languages is non-random belongs to the core of the research programme[1] of Universal Grammar, and is therefore immune to direct falsification.

If we accept the basic premise that linguistic encoding across languages is (at least in principle) non-random, we may conclude (following Sanders, 1976: 15) that the major function of typologies is 'to serve as the raw materials for explanation, the most refined and manageable raw materials that are available concerning the nature of the objects they typologize'. Thus, typologies are adequate to the extent that they 'generate significant questions that are clear, explicit and likely to be productively answerable' (Sanders, ibid.). Now, given that our data-sampling results in a typology in which the languages in the sample are classified into a number of different categories, the explanatory questions that can be asked are at least of the following two distinct types.

The first explanatory question with regard to a typology concerns the question of *the occurrence of attested and non-attested categories*. When a typology has been established, it will generally be the case that it is not immediately clear why that typology contains just these attested types, instead of other, non-attested but also imaginable, alternatives. Thus, it is perfectly justifiable to ask the question: 'Why is the typology as a whole the way it is' (Sanders, 1976: 15). Clearly, a principled answer to this question will lead to a further understanding of the restrictions which delineate the concept of 'possible human language'.

The second, and related explanatory question concerns *the attested distribution of languages over the types in the typology*; that is, it is a question about the explanation of type-membership. One might phrase this question in the following form: why should it be that certain languages in the sample are members of category X, and not of category Y? In other words, typological analysis assumes that the grouping of languages in the typology reflects a division into *natural classes*, and attempts to formulate a basis for the explanation of this naturalness.

In summary, then, we may say that Typological Universal Grammar will try to discover a set of statements which predict attested and non-attested types, and which can account for the attested distribution of languages over these typological variants.

Among the strategies which are employed in Universal Grammar to solve the explanatory problems posed by a multi-categorial typology, a natural and widely used strategy involves the identification of a determining 'outside' factor, that is 'some additional common distinguishing property or set of properties of all members of a given type' (Sanders, 1976: 15). In practice, this strategy leads to the formation of *a second typology*, which is based on a new parameter; this additional typology should be set up in such a way that its categorizations provide a match for the distinctions which were attested in the original typology. If such a new parameter (or set of parameters) can be identified, it should be possible to formulate so-called *implicational universals of language*, which have the following general form:

> If a language belongs to category X in typology A, it belongs to category Y in typology B.

In statements of this form, one of the properties mentioned refers to the 'outside factor' or 'determinant', which is used as the basis for the prediction of the other typological property; this latter property commonly refers to the category in the original typology to which the language in question belongs. In this way, various typologically relevant structural properties of languages can be brought together in a cluster of implicational relations.

It should be pointed out immediately that implicational universals cannot, in themselves, count as an *explanation* of the attested facts in the first typology. As they stand, universals of this kind merely state a *correlation* between two different typological options for a given category of natural languages. In other words, such universals are the expression of a *descriptive* research result of typological linguistic analysis. Now, it goes without saying that the statement of this kind of research result is certainly a valuable contribution to the progress of linguistic theory, and one of the most urgent tasks of Universal Grammar is to state such clusters of properties as precisely as possible, and for as many properties as is feasible. However, it will also be clear that, if such implicational statements are to transcend the level of pure description, some further requirements should be imposed on them, in order to ensure their status as an *explanatory framework*.

The concept of explanation is far from clear in linguistics in general, and even less so in a relatively young field such as Universal Grammar. As I see it, linguists commonly employ a more or less intuitive notion of explanation; they would say that a certain analysis explains a body of facts if that analysis leads to a deeper and hitherto unformulated insight, which establishes regularity in a seemingly irregular phenomenon. Thus, explanation presupposes the demonstration of a non-randomness, or regularity, in the data, by means of principles which are, in some intuitive sense, viewed as the causal factor of that regularity. Now, if we apply this intuitive notion of explanation to the version of Universal Grammar which is adopted in this study, we can single out at least three conditions which the second typology in (a set of) implicational universals must meet if it is to be rated as the *explanans* of the first typology, the *explanandum*.

The first condition on explanatory typologies which I would like to advance is the following. In order for a typology A to count as an explanation of a correlated typology B, it should be the case that the categories in typology A *exhaust* the theoretically possible variations in the expression of the linguistic parameter upon which it is based. That is, if A is to count as an explanation of B, it should be the case that the categories of which A consists can, in some explicit way, be shown to cover all the possible categories for this typology. (An example of a typology which is exhaustive in this sense would be a typology in which languages are classified on the basis of whether or not they have the possibility of Equi-NP-Deletion.[2] Given this particular parameter, it will be clear that such a typology will maximally consist of only two categories, one containing the languages which do have Equi-NP-Deletion, and another which contains the languages without Equi-NP-Deletion. Thus, a two-category typology is exhaustive of the theoretical possibilities of variation for this particular parameter.) I take it to be a defensible conclusion that, if a certain typology B is correlated with a typology A which is exhaustive in this sense, we can say that typology A *explains* typology B. In such a situation, the attested occurrence of types in B is no longer a matter of chance; it can now be shown to be non-random, by virtue of the fact that these types in B are in correlation with a typology which contains all possible variations of its parameter, and is therefore by definition non-random.

Apart from this notion of exhaustiveness, there is a second condition which, if met, will increase the credibility of a certain typology as an explanans for another typology. This condition has to do not so much with the explanans-typology itself, but rather with the kind of correlation which exists between the two typologies at issue. I think it is justifiable to say that a typology A will stand a better chance of being accepted as the explanation of a correlated typology B if *the match between the categories in the two typologies is optimal.* That is, it should not be the case that only some categories in A can be correlated to categories in B, while other categories in A do not have their match in B; conversely, one may require that all, and not just some, categories in B have their counterpart in some category (or categories) in A. If such an optimal match between the two typologies can be demonstrated, we are in a position to say that the facts in the explanandum-typology B are *fully and exhaustively predictable* from the facts in A. In other words, in such a situation there is a sense in which we can say that typology B is the way it is *because* typology A is the way it is, and this formulation corresponds largely to the intuitive notion of explanation outlined above.

The two conditions on explanatory adequacy discussed so far can both be regarded as *formal requirements on explanans-typologies;* they involve properties of typologies which are independent of the actual parameters on which these typologies are based. In addition, there is also a *conceptual factor* which determines the explanatory value of additional typologies. In order for a typology A to count as the explanation of a typology B, one will generally require that the parameter of A represent some 'deeper-lying', 'more elementary' or 'more fundamental' linguistic property than the parameter upon which typology B is based. Of course, the notion of 'degree of fundamentality' which is involved here is very hard to operationalize; moreover, any claim as to the 'fundamentality' of one linguistic feature over another is bound to meet with controversy, since such a claim will inevitably be tied up with a priori ideas about the aims and methods of linguistics in general. Nevertheless, there are at least some areas of linguistic theory where the fundamentality of certain concepts over others has been explicitly advocated. To be specific, grammarians of the so-called 'localist' school have claimed that various types of constructions in natural languages (such as possessive constructions, existentials, aspectual expressions and types of case marking) can be shown to be derived from the expression of *spatio-temporal relations.* Accordingly, this latter type of relations may be advanced as a candidate for the status of 'fundamental linguistic feature'.[3] As will become clear in the following chapters, my own approach to the explanation of the implicational universals which I will propose can be said to be sympathetic to the localist viewpoint. It must be understood, however, that I do not necessarily adhere to all the opinions and analyses that have been put forward by authors who work within a localist framework.

Needless to say, the above three conditions are not intended to provide a full and explicit account of the concept of explanation in Typological Universal Grammar. They are meant as a first approximation, which should give us at least some foothold in deciding upon the explanatory value of implicational universals. If one or more of these conditions are met by an additional typology, I think we have some extent of justification for the claim that this second typology is more than just a correlate of the first; it can now be viewed as the *determinant* of that first typology, that is, as a deeper-lying causal principle by which the non-randomness of variation in the original typology can be predicted and explained.

Naturally, implicational universals of the kind discussed above cannot be the last word on the subject of human language, even if some degree of explanatory validity can be attached to them. As is the case in any worthwhile form of scientific investigation, the statement of regularities of the kind that are laid down in implicational universals gives rise to further problems of explanation. Clearly, in pursuing these problems one will inevitably reach a point where the investigation must transcend the boundaries of linguistics proper; the ultimate explanation of linguistic universals, if it can ever be reached at all, will have to be found by a combination of efforts from various scientific branches, such as linguistics, psychology, neurology, biology and perhaps even physics. Therefore, to require of Universal Grammar that it have a definitive explanation for all the regularities it discovers would be too much to ask. What can be asked, though, is that Universal Grammar make a thorough and exact inventory of these regularities, and that it play an active role in the interdisciplinary efforts to find principled explanations for them.

In the following chapters, I will apply the methods of Typological Universal Grammar to the description of one structural feature of human language, viz. the various possibilities which languages possess to express *comparison of inequality*. I will present a typology of comparative constructions which is based on a sample of 110 languages, and following that I will propose a set of implicational universals from which the typological variation in the encoding of comparison can be predicted. However, before presenting the actual typological data I would like to point out a number of methodological considerations which determine the framework within which the cross-linguistic investigation of comparative constructions is going to be conducted.

1.3   Issues in universalist methodology

The above sketch of the conduct of a universalist research project is of course very much an idealization. In reality, every stage in the process will confront the researcher with specific problems, both of a theoretical and a practical nature. Now, as I pointed out earlier, the methodology of universalist linguistic research has not yet reached a state of such maturity that generally applicable guide-lines for the proper conduct of an investigation can be derived from it. As a matter of fact, I think it can be said that the methodology of recent universalist grammar, in as far as it exists at all, is a by-product of actual descriptive work, rather than a preliminary framework in which all research has to be fitted; universalist methodology is developed 'along the way', so to speak. This is not necessarily a bad thing. In my opinion, a new development in a science should not be stifled beforehand by all too rigorous requirements on method. As long as some general conditions on representativity and repeatability are met, I think it is best to give universalist grammar, at least for the time being, a generous amount of freedom to develop its own standards. In the end, of course, it is always the significance of the research results which makes a specific branch of science worthwhile; nobody needs a type of linguistics which, for all its methodological impeccability, comes up with conclusions that are ultimately boring.

All this, however, must not be taken to imply that universalist researchers should be totally free to make any methodological decision which happens to suit them, nor that they should be absolved from the obligation to provide ample justification for such decisions. The very least one may expect is that a universalist grammarian be willing to state explicitly the pros and cons of the solutions he has adopted, so that the potential strength or weakness of his approach can be assessed from the outset. In the following sections, I intend to meet this minimal requirement: I will deal with a number of methodological problems which I have encountered in the course of my project, and I will discuss the solutions which appeared to me to be the most appropriate.

1.3.1   *The construction of the language sample*

A first problem which is certain to be raised in connection with any kind of universalist linguistic research concerns the construction of the sample upon which the typology is to be based. Given the fact that there are presumably more than 4000 languages in the world, it will be evident that, for practical reasons alone, any universalist project will have to limit itself to a selected subset of languages. It is also obvious that one will have to make efforts to make this selected subset as representative as possible, and that known sources of bias should be eliminated from the sample. Unfortunately, however, at the present time the requirements which an adequate language sample must fulfil are still far from clear; there is not even general agreement among linguists about the size which typological samples should have.

For some types of universalist projects, the choice of the sample is dictated beforehand by the theoretical question which the typology is expected to elucidate. To give but one example, a linguist who is interested in the variation in the distribution of labio-dental consonants across languages would be well advised to exclude languages which do not have such consonants from his sample. In survey-type universalist studies like the present one, however, no such a priori guide-line is given. Such studies are of an exploratory nature: it is their very purpose to trace the limits on possibilities of linguistic encoding, so that an a priori delineation of the languages to be considered would be detrimental to their utility.

Notwithstanding the considerable amount of uncertainty as to what constitutes a good sample, there are some rules-of-thumb that have become generally accepted in recent Universal Grammar. For one thing, it is commonly taken as a prerequisite of language samples that they be as free from *genetic and areal bias* as possible; that is, the languages in the sample should be distributed evenly among the language families and linguistic areas in the world. If this requirement is met, and the sample is constructed on the basis of genetic affiliation, this procedure will lead automatically to certain conditions on the size of the sample. If all the major linguistic families in the world are to be represented in the sample by at least one member, one arrives at samples which have a size that is not below 80 languages. The examples of samples given in Bell (1978) all vary in size between 80 and 140 languages; samples which exceed this size are generally considered to be unwieldy.

It should be remarked here that the criterion of genetic affiliation in the construction of language samples can only provide a guide-line, and that it should not be taken too absolutely. For one thing, it is not clear whether this criterion provides the only, or even the most important, factor to eliminate sources of bias from the sample. In the present state of universalist research, all kinds of different typological studies are based on samples which have genetic affiliation as their defining term. This practice can be explained from the fact that, of all possible sources of bias, genetic bias has the advantage of at least being known, so that it is a wise move to eliminate at least this factor from the sampling procedure. It may very well be the case, however, that by using genetic affiliation as a criterion for the stratification of samples other significant factors in this stratification are overlooked; one may very well imagine a universalist study in which the sample has been stratified according to, say, the distribution of word-order types instead of genetic affiliation. As Universal Grammar proceeds, it is easy to imagine that the criterion of genetic affiliation will come to be supplemented, or even superseded, by other criteria that provide a basis of sample construction.

Apart from this matter of principle, there are also practical factors which tend to diminish the importance of genetic affiliation as a criterion of sample stratification. In practice, the major sources of information on the various languages in the sample are written grammatical descriptions and texts; only in a few cases can these data be supplemented by the use of native speakers as informants. Now, as every universalist grammarian is bound to discover, grammatical descriptions of various languages (if one is lucky enough to find them at all) differ enormously in their degree of explicitness and sophistication. Therefore, the sample in most survey-type universalist studies is, from sheer necessity, heavily influenced by considerations of convenience; one must simply make do with whatever data are available, however scanty and unreliable they may be. It should be added that the specific subject to be investigated may have its own effect upon the construction of the sample. Quite often, one finds that grammars which are excellent in some areas of grammatical structure are insufficient in others; thus, for instance, many grammatical descriptions are very informative as far as morphology is concerned, but fail to state explicitly the finer points of syntax. I assume that every universalist researcher will have encountered the frustrating situation that a grammar fails to state some detailed pieces of information which are vital to the problem under investigation; in such a case, there is no other choice than to cancel that language from the sample. In this connection, the 'centrality' of the information one looks for may also be a factor. Thus, for example, one will find that information on basic word order can be derived from almost any grammatical description, no matter how general or amateuristic it may be. On the other hand, information on a rather 'marginal' construction type such as the comparative construction is often not to be found in even the most minute grammars. One may conclude, then, that the construction of typological samples will, at least for the time being, always involve a certain degree of compromise and arbitrariness.

In view of this general situation, I have constructed my sample on the following guide-lines. I have tried to meet the requirements of genetic spreading and size by selecting a sample of 110 languages, which are chosen from all the important language families listed in Voegelin and Voegelin (1977). An alphabetical list of the languages in my sample is presented in Appendix A; also, I have indicated there the source or sources from which information about these languages has been gained. A grouping of the languages in the sample on the basis of their genetic affiliation is given in Appendix B.

I am quite prepared to admit that the sample used in this study has various weak points. There remains some degree of genetic bias in my sample in that it contains 12 languages of the Indo-European family. This may be judged to be a case of over-representation; I have tried to minimize this instance of bias by choosing Indo-European languages from all the sub-branches of this family. Furthermore, one could say that the Amerind languages are somewhat under-represented; for the 150 groups of Amerind languages, a total of 26 languages is a meagre choice, even given our restriction to a sample of this size. I can only agree to this objection, and add that it is a familiar difficulty which, at least for now, is unsolvable. Despite the large efforts, made in the thirties and afterwards, to document American Indian languages, one has to observe that the structural information contained in the grammars of these languages is very often incomplete, or else is made irretrievable by the idiosyncratic and tedious predilection for tagmemic notations. Especially in the case of Amerind languages one often despairs of the fact that two days of deciphering a grammatical text has not resulted in finding one good and clear example of the comparative construction.

All in all, though, while the sample used in this essay is far from perfect, I am of the opinion that it does not compare too unfavourably with samples employed in other case studies in Universal Grammar. As long as a standardization of survey samples is still out of reach, the practice followed in previous research must be one's primary guide-line; in this respect, I feel that the sample used in this study is reasonably adequate.[4]

1.3.2 The definition of the typological basis

At the very start of the actual execution of a typological linguistic investigation, the researcher is bound to be confronted with a major methodological issue, viz. *the problem of cross-linguistic identification*. An example may help to illustrate the nature of this problem. Suppose that a universalist linguist wants to set up a typology of the ways in which the concept of possession is expressed in natural languages. This linguist will then be immediately faced with the problem of how to decide which structural configurations in each of the languages in his sample must be considered to constitute the primary expression of possessivity. In other words, the linguist will need some criterion for the cross-linguistic identification of possessive structures, so that he will not compare incomparable items.

With regard to this problem, it is clear that a purely formal definition of the notion 'possessive structure' cannot be completely satisfactory here. If one were to define the criterion for the notion 'possessive structure in a natural language' in purely formal terms, one would identify only those possessive constructions which have a specified formal manifestation, while leaving out all those instances of natural languages in which a different formal way of encoding possessivity has been chosen. In short, the use of purely formal criteria for the identification of comparable constructions across languages makes this identification unsolvable for all those cases in which it is not trivial.

The reason why purely formal criteria do not work as a method of cross-linguistic identification lies in the fact that such criteria are, by their very nature, language-dependent. However, it is not the aim of Typological Universal Grammar to single out those languages in which a construction type has a specific formal expression; Typological Universal Grammar attempts to present a survey of all the different ways in which natural languages may encode some linguistically relevant property. Hence, it must be concluded that the definition of this property (that is, the basic feature which is to serve as the parameter of the typology) should be stated in terms which are *independent of the characteristics of single languages or groups of languages*.

In recent universalist studies which deal with morphological or syntactic variation among languages, the common strategy has been to employ *semantic* (or perhaps better: *cognitive*) definitions for the parameter of the typology. That is, the feature upon which the typology is to be based is defined in terms of its semantic content or function, rather than in terms of its alleged structural characteristics. This semantic solution to the problem of cross-linguistic identification has been used in a number of prestigious universalist publications, such as Keenan and Comrie (1977), where the typology of relativization is based upon a semantic definition of the notion 'relative clause'. The semantic strategy is even – though somewhat less explicitly – adhered to in the early word-order studies by Greenberg (1963, 1966). It can be observed that Greenberg's universals refer to notions like 'verb', 'subject' and 'direct object', terms which cannot (or at least not exhaustively) be defined cross-linguistically by invoking formal characteristics alone.

In conformity with this strategy currently favoured among universalist linguists, I have chosen to use a cognitive criterion for identifying cases of the comparative construction across the languages in my sample. Stating, for the moment, the definition somewhat loosely and informally, I will say that

> a construction counts as a comparative construction (and will there-fore be taken into account in the typology), if that construction has the semantic function of assigning a graded (i.e. non-identical) position on a predicative scale to two (possibly complex) objects.

Thus, typical instances of the comparative in the languages of my sample will include those expressions which have a semantic function of the type exemplified by English expressions like *John is taller than Bill* or *Harry is more cunning than brave*. Fortunately, it turns out that a semantic definition of this kind can be used in practice without serious difficulties; there is a considerable amount of unanimity among grammarians of various languages with respect to the question of what counts as a comparative in their respective subject-languages.

In this connection, let me add that a semantic or cognitive definition will be employed in this study not only in the definition of the notion 'comparative construction', but also in referring to several other notions, such as 'separative construction' (chapter 2), 'temporal chaining' (chapter 3) and 'consecutive chain' (chapter 4). The term 'separative construction', for instance, must always be taken to refer to any type of construction in a natural language which has the semantic function of indicating the source of a movement, regardless of whether this function is expressed formally by means of a preposition, a postposition, a case affix or some other syntactic or morphological device. It would, of course, be perfectly feasible to set up a typology of the various ways in which this 'separative' meaning is formally encoded in natural languages. However, such a typology, interesting though it may be in its own right, lies beyond the descriptive scope of the present investigation.

1.3.3   The construction of a typology

Once the relevant data have been established across the sample by means of some language-independent criterion of identification, one is in a position to start the actual work of typological investigation, viz. the construction of a typology. At this stage, the languages in the sample are classified into a number of categories, on the basis of differences and similarities in the way in which the parameter of the typology is formally expressed by them. Accordingly, the typology reflects the attested variation of linguistic encoding among languages with respect to the basic linguistic property under discussion.

Now, it might be thought that, once the set of relevant data has been assembled, the construction of a typology can be a fairly straightforward procedure. One might argue that the classification of languages into categories, and the classification of constructions into types, should be the result of a mechanical application of a series of decisions, which are motivated by empirically attested differences and similarities in the encoding properties of the languages under observation. In reality, however, such a 'blind', mechanical procedure seldom yields interesting results. It must be kept in mind that the construction of a typology is not a goal in itself; the whole business of constructing typologies derives its theoretical significance from the fact that these typologies function as 'the raw material for principled inquiry and explanation' (Sanders, 1976: 15). Thus, the adequacy of a typology depends on the extent to which it 'generates significant questions that are clear, explicit and likely to be productively answerable' (Sanders, ibid.). In other words, the categorization in which a typology results should be theoretically fertile.

Given this central function of typologies, it will be clear that a typological categorization of languages or construction types must necessarily involve an evaluation of the theoretical significance and relevance of the criteria on which the division rests. In particular, it will be the case that not every observable formal difference between languages or construction types is of equal importance in the typology; the researcher will always be forced to assign relative weight to the various differences which can be objectively observed in his data. In some cases, a blind application of a division procedure on the basis of observable formal differences can result in a typology which is too detailed for the purpose for which it was constructed in the first place. To give an example, suppose that our data show a difference among languages with respect to the fact that some languages use prepositions in their constructions, whereas other languages prefer postpositions. Now, whether this observable formal difference is a significant fact that must be reflected in a typological distinction depends entirely on the use one wants to make of the typology for explanatory purposes. If, for instance, the typology is supposed to elucidate various regularities which are linked up with word-order variation, the difference between prepositional and postpositional languages might be judged to be a central fact, which may give rise to a division of languages into two separate categories. In other cases, however, one might decide that this observed difference in word order is only a concomitant fact which has nothing to do with the central explanatory question at issue. In that case, the researcher may choose to ignore this difference, and hence he will (other things being equal) lump prepositional and postpositional languages together into one single typological category.

While in some cases 'blind' application of formal division procedures can lead to typologies that are too detailed for our explanatory purpose, the opposite situation may also be encountered. That is, one may also arrive at a situation in which a typology that is based on formal distinctions is not informative enough. Again, an example may help to illustrate this case. Suppose that our cross-linguistic data on a certain construction type give rise to a division of constructions into two groups with formally distinct characteristics: in one group, a certain relevant NP in the construction is in the nominative case, whereas in other constructions this same NP is put into an oblique case, marked by some adposition. Now, it is conceivable that a categorization on the basis of this observable formal difference does not go far enough for our explanatory purposes; it might be the case that it is of theoretical significance for us to know whether the adposition in the second group of constructions is a locative marker, an ablative marker, a dative marker, an instrumental marker, and so on. In such a case, purely formal differences are no longer of any use, since notions like 'locative' or 'ablative' can be defined cross-linguistically only in semantic terms. In other words, it is not only the case that observable formal differences are not always relevant to our division of languages and construction types; there are also cases in which such differences are not sufficient, and where they must be supplemented by further divisional criteria of a semantic nature.

Thus, in the end, typologies must be looked upon as data of an explanatory linguistic theory. Since it is a well-known fact of general methodology that, in all branches of science, data-gathering is a procedure which is at least partially influenced by theoretical considerations, it will come as no surprise that the construction of linguistic typologies will necessarily be guided by judgements (or premonitions) of theoretical relevance and significance.

Apart from this major methodological issue in the construction of typologies, there are a few other points which need comment here. One question concerns *the admissibility of diachronic and etymological data* in the construction of a typology. For a number of languages, it can be established that changes in their encoding properties have occurred in the course of their history; in such cases, one may argue about the 'true' typological status of those languages. One way to settle such a dispute is simply to banish all references to diachronic data from the typology; usually, such a strategy is motivated on the grounds that diachronic data are available for only a small subset of natural languages, so that no systematic use of this type of data can be made. Moreover, a decision to exclude all diachronic data is in line with the strict separation of synchronic and diachronic linguistics, which was advocated by de Saussure and has been a longstanding article of faith in structuralist linguistic theory.

In my opinion, there is not much to be gained from an a priori rejection of diachronic data in typological linguistic research. On the contrary, I think that one might argue that such a rejection could even have harmful effects on the overall adequacy of a typology. In recent Universal Grammar, the insight has gained ground that natural languages are, with regard to their structural properties, often compromises between various interfering strategies, the balance between which may vary from language to language, and from one developmental stage of a language to another.[5] Diachronic change is one of the results of such a change in balance; another phenomenon which may be explained by taking this point of view is the fact that many construction types in natural languages have 'hybrid' features, and can therefore be subject to 'multiple analyses' (Hankamer, 1977). If we accept this perspective, diachronic data are a valuable clue in finding explanations for typological distinctions; they illustrate areas of linguistic structure where categories may blend into one another, and they can, therefore, be seen as indications of the underlying principles which are assumed to determine the distribution of attested and non-attested language types.

Related with this point is a second problem in the construction of typologies, which has to do with *the indeterminacy of categorization* which one may encounter for some languages. I think we can safely assume that, in any linguistic typology, one will come across at least a few instances of languages which cannot be categorized into one single class in a fully straightforward fashion. One of the causes of this indeterminacy may be the fact that the language in question has undergone (or is in the process of undergoing) diachronic change; another possibility is that the language, in its synchronic encoding procedure, turns out to be a 'mix' of two or more encoding possibilities. In such cases, I think the best way to act is to accept this indeterminacy as an empirical fact, rather than to try forcing the language into one single category. Cases of indeterminate category status should, I feel, be treated as data in the same way as cases where the category status is straight-forward; and the explanation one has for the typology as a whole should be able to handle not only the clear cases, but should also indicate why indeterminacy is possible. In this respect, I think there is a parallel with the view on idiolect variation which is put forward by Eliott, Legum and Thompson (1969). These authors claim that idiolect variation among native speakers (and, as a result of this, divergence of judgements of grammaticality) should be looked upon as a primary concern for linguistic theory, rather than as a mere nuisance factor. In their view, cases of indeterminate grammaticality are empirical facts, which deserve explanation as much as those cases in which such indeterminacy is absent.

1.3.4   *The evaluation of universals*

As I stated earlier, a first step in explaining the data which a linguistic typology offers us involves the formulation of implicational universals. In implicational statements, the defining characteristics of a particular typological option are linked causally or functionally to some independent characteristic of the languages in question; in this way, a correlation is formulated between the typological properties of a set of languages and some additional property, which serves as the basis of prediction for the observed typological features. As is generally the case in scientific inquiry, no sure-fire rules can be given as to the way in which such linguistic correlations are to be discovered. It is true that one may invoke a number of discovery techniques in this process (such as the use of a computer in testing a broad range of correlational possibilities); but, at least for the time being, one is forced to conclude that the procedure for discovering implicational universals is, in the words of Popper (1934), still very much a matter of 'art, not science'.

Therefore, let us assume without further elaboration that the research project has resulted in the establishment of a set of implicational universals, which are intended to predict the typological variation that we have encountered in the sample. Obviously, such universals are, at this stage, nothing more than hypotheses about assumed regularities; they should be validated by testing them against the facts of each separate language. At this point, we need to answer an important question: *what are the criteria of falsification for a universal?* Or, to phrase this problem in a slightly different way: how many counterexamples are we allowed to tolerate, before we must reject a universal as false?

Regrettably, I think we have to admit that, for the moment, there is no final and generally applicable answer to this question. Practice in recent Universal Grammar has shown that practically no universal of any significance is completely free of exceptions; by their very nature, *linguistic universals formulate tendencies rather than laws.* From this general fact, it follows that universals, if they are to have any theoretical function at all, should not be rejected on the basis of single instances of falsification. If one were to impose the strict requirement that universals be exceptionless, Typological Universal Grammar would simply cease to exist as a valid perspective in linguistic inquiry; and, given the number of significant results that Typological Grammar has produced in recent years, this would be too high a price to pay for methodological purity. One can agree with Comrie (1981: 20), who writes: 'To say that the universal has no validity because there are counterexamples to it, and to leave the discussion at that, would be to abrogate one's responsibility as a linguist to deal with significant patterns in language.'

Nevertheless, even if we grant it that a universal may have at least some exceptions, we are still faced with the problem of the extent to which such a universal may be in conflict with the facts. It may be useful to point out here that statistical evaluation measures, such as employed in physics and social science, seem to be of very limited use in current linguistic typological research. Given the fact that there is no generally accepted evaluation metric for the representativity of the language samples from which the data in typological linguistic studies are drawn, the computation of exact p-values for linguistic universals would be a fruitless, and even pompous, thing to do. Obviously, if a universal were to be verified in, say, only 50 per cent of all cases, nobody would reasonably maintain that this universal should be considered to be correct; the point is, however, that we lack the tools in typological linguistics to determine exactly what the maximum of counterexamples to a particular universal may be in relation to the total number of cases which it is supposed to cover.

All in all, then, we are left with the uncomfortable, but nonetheless very real situation that there is in fact no straightforward procedure to evaluate the validity of proposed linguistic universals. Whether a universal will be accepted as a correct generalization depends on a number of considerations which are hard to weigh exactly, and which are interwoven in ways that are as yet largely unclear. Among these considerations, we may list at least the following:

(a) The number of counterexamples in relation to the total number of cases covered by the universal. In order for a universal to stand a chance, counterexamples should be intuitively rated as 'incidental' deviations, which do not distort a clear over-all picture.

(b) The extent to which a universal is significant, that is, the extent to which a principled explanation for it is available. A universal stands a better chance of surviving falsifications if it can be fitted into a general explanatory theory.

(c) The extent to which a universal has proven to be theoretically fertile. An example of such a universalist research result is the Noun Phrase Accessibility Hierarchy in Relative Clause Formation, formulated by Keenan and Comrie (1977). Since this hierarchy has turned out to be applicable in a number of different areas of grammatical structure, its immunity to falsification by single counterexamples has undoubtedly increased.

In summary, we may state that it is futile to think that linguistic universals can ever be proven to be correct. Typological linguistic analysis should set itself a more modest goal: the best we can hope for is to arrive at a certain degree of plausibility for our universals, to the effect that other researchers in the field are willing to accept them as a working hypothesis in their own investigations.

1.3.5   Model-neutrality

As a last methodological remark, I would like to comment briefly on the overall theoretical perspective which will be adopted in this study. In particular, I want to make it clear from the outset that my general approach should be conceived of as being *model-neutral*. I am of the opinion that cross-linguistic work should not affiliate itself outright with any of the theoretical frameworks currently in favour, such as Chomskyan GB-theory or Relational Grammar. For this reason, I have taken care to state my findings in terms which are largely uncontroversial, and which belong to the common stock of traditional grammatical theory. Of some terms it should be understood that they are used here in a very general, almost metaphorical sense, and that no specific theoretical relevance should be attached to them. For example, when I use the term 'deletion', it should not be inferred that I claim that a specific procedure of string-derivation by means of deletion rules should be part of a grammar (let alone universal grammar). The term 'deletion' will be used as a matter of convenience, and must 'be taken as merely a recognition of the consistent syntactic and semantic relationships between . . . sentence types, not as an acknowledgement that one type does derive from the other (or, to be more exact, shares an underlying structure)' (Mallinson and Blake, 1981: 36).[6] Of course, it may turn out later that my results are more in line with certain theoretical alternatives than with others, but it is not my aim here to bring such decisions about. What I want to do is to establish some characteristics of the comparative construction which must be incorporated into any theory of grammatical structure. This attitude, which has been practised in the majority of recent universalist studies, is a healthy one, I think; it is the best possible guard against theoretical myopia, and it frees the empirical work from the dogmatism which has marred quite a large amount of recent theoretical linguistic discussion.

It goes without saying, of course, that I do not want to advocate the position that universalist grammar should be opposed to the formulation of theories, and that it should confine itself to mere data-gathering. Like all other forms of scientific activity, typological linguistic studies are a waste of time if they do not lead to theoretical progress, and the only way to achieve this goal is by means of the testing of theories. I do feel, however, that linguistic theories have of late reached the point of near-sterility, due to the fact that their empirical basis is kept too narrow. Therefore, I agree wholeheartedly with Comrie's (1978b) dictum that, first and foremost, 'linguistics is about languages,' instead of being mainly about the technicalities of grammatical models.

1.4   Outline of the following chapters

In the following chapters, I will present the results of a typological investigation of the ways in which the concept of *comparison of inequality* is encoded in natural languages. Chapter 2 contains a discussion of the criteria which have been employed in establishing a typology of comparative constructions, and presents the actual *typology of comparative options* which results from the application of these criteria. In chapter 3, three candidates for the function of *determinant* of the typology of comparative constructions are considered; the conclusion is that, of these three parameters, the parameter of *temporal chaining* is the most promising. Consequently, chapter 4 deals with the construction of *a new typology*, in which the various ways of codifying temporal chaining are laid down. In chapter 5, *a set of implicational universals* is defined, in which the categories in the second typology are explicitly matched with the categories that have been attested in the typology of comparative constructions.

The chapters in part two of this study (i.e., chapter 6 to chapter 10) contain *the empirical data* upon which the investigation rests. In each of these chapters, one of the universals which have been formulated in chapter 5 is examined for its empirical validity, by testing it against the actual facts of the relevant languages in the sample. As a general conclusion, it can be said that the set of proposed implicational universals can be shown to be confirmed to such a degree that they may rightfully be considered to express valid correlations.

Finally, in part three we take a closer look at *the explanatory value* of the proposed set of universals. Since this set of universals is found to be wanting in this respect, *a new model for the explanation of comparative-type choice* is developed, in which the original set of universals has been incorporated. In the final chapter of part three, the empirical and explanatory adequacy of this new model is put to the test, and found to be superior to the earlier model of comparative-type choice developed in chapter 5.

2

The Typology of Comparative Constructions

In this chapter, I will apply the methods of Typological Universal Grammar in the construction of a cross-linguistic typology of comparative constructions. First, I will discuss the definition of the concept 'comparative construction', and deal with some practical limitations and decisions which I have made in my investigation. Next, I will present an outline of the criteria which have been used in the categorization of comparative constructions into types. The last sections of this chapter will be devoted to a discussion of each of the individual categories that have been established in the typology, and a presentation of a few cases in which such a categorization seems to be indeterminate.

2.1   The definition of the concept 'comparative construction'

In the preceding chapter (see section 1.3.2), the conclusion was reached that the basis of a cross-linguistic syntactic typology should be defined in language-independent terms. Accordingly, I proposed a semantic definition of the notion 'comparative construction', which I repeat here for convenience:

> *Definition:* a construction in a natural language counts as a comparative construction (and will therefore be taken into account in the typology) if that construction has the semantic function of assigning a graded (i.e. non-identical) position on a predicative scale to two (possibly complex) objects.

Thus, a case of comparison of inequality minimally involves three things: *a gradable predicative scale*, which represents the property on which the comparison is made, and *two concepts*, one of which represents the standard against which the other is measured and found to be unequal. The conceptual content of a comparative construction is elegantly phrased by Small (1929: 12–13), who writes:

the speaker who uses comparison as a means of indicating the intensity of a given quality in an object casts about in his mind for a second object well known to the hearer which has that same quality, perhaps in a greater or lesser degree. If he is fortunate enough to hit upon a second object that, to the best of his judgement, has the quality in exactly the *same* degree as the object he is discussing, he may indicate the intensity of the quality by equating the first object with the second, thus: John is as tall as the gate-post, or, The dog runs as rapidly as the bird flies. Instead of a second *object* of comparison the speaker may also refer to a second *condition* of the first object itself, thus: John is just as accurate as he was in the rifle match a year ago. This way of pointing out the intensity of a given attribute may be termed the *comparison of equality*.

Should the hypothetical speaker be unable to hit upon a second object or condition that exactly matches the first in the quality observed, or should he desire to contrast the first object with the second, he will call up to the attention of the hearer another object having the same quality, but either in a higher or a lower degree of intensity. Thus: John is taller than Mary; Dogs are friendlier than cats; The patient *is* now weaker than he *was*; The poet *wrote* more vividly than the artist *painted*. This sort of thing may best be referred to as the *comparison of inequality*.

In what follows, we will be concerned exclusively with cases of the comparison of inequality. Hence, I will use the term 'comparative construction' or 'comparative' for the more accurate, but also more cumbersome term 'construction which represents the comparison of inequality'.

Given this semantic definition of the comparative, we should be able to identify the cross-linguistic codification of this concept, thereby establishing the data base of the typology. However, before I can present an exposition of the attested typological variants of the comparative construction, I must first point out a number of complications which are connected with the definition of the notion 'comparative construction', and mention several practical decisions which further restrict the scope of the inquiry.

First, I have found it useful to confine my typology to those cases of comparative constructions in which *two objects or individuals (typically expressed in the form of NPs)* are being graded against each other. The reason for this decision is entirely practical; whereas all grammars of the languages in the sample indicate the way in which NP-comparatives are formed, they do not, in general, provide for sufficiently reliable data on constructions in which other elements (say, adjectives, verbs or clauses) are involved. Thus, the prototypical sentence for our investigation will be a sentence along the lines of those in *(1)*, and not of those in *(2)*:

(1) ENGLISH:
a.   *The tree is taller than the house*
b.   *I like Pamela better than Lucy*

(2) ENGLISH:
a.   *The general was more cunning than brave*
b.   *The team plays better than last year*
c.   *The president is smarter than you think*

Constructions like those in *(2)* will be taken into account only when we look at some languages in detail. In particular, they will provide evidence for our analysis of the comparative constructions in English and Dutch (see chapter 9).

Given this limitation to cases of NP-comparison, the following terminology will be adopted throughout the discussion. The linguistic codification of the predicative scale in a comparative construction will be termed *the comparative predicate* or simply *the predicate*; in the majority of examples, the comparative predicate will have the form of a predicatively used adjective. Of the two NPs in the construction, the NP which indicates the object that serves as a yardstick for the comparison (that is, to use Small's terms, 'the second object') will be referred to as *the standard NP*. The other NP in the construction, which refers to the objective of the mental operation of comparison, will be called *the comparee NP*. Thus, in a sentence like *(3)*, the NP *Mary* is the standard NP, and the NP *John* the comparee NP:

(3) ENGLISH:
     John is taller than Mary

The predicative adjective *tall*, which names the scale on which the comparison takes place, is the comparative predicate in this particular comparative construction.

As a second preliminary point, it must be realized from the outset that my typology of comparatives may suggest a division among languages which looks more definite and neat than it actually is. For one thing, I must concede that a number of languages in my sample have comparatives which do not seem to fit neatly into one of the established categories. These languages appear to have a 'mixed comparative', that is, a comparative in which the fundamental characteristics of two typological variants are combined; I will say more about these cases in section 2.5. Another phenomenon which weakens the strictness of the typology is the fact that quite a few languages appear to have more than one alternative to express NP-comparison. An example of a language in which this is the case is Latin. In this language, the grading of two objects against each other is typically expressed by means of a construction like the one in *(4)*, which contains the comparative particle *quam*:

(4) LATIN:
Cato   est eloquentior   quam Cicero
C.-NOM is   more-eloquent than   C.-NOM
'Cato is more eloquent than Cicero'

However, as is noted in Kühner–Gerth (1955), Latin has also the possibility of a comparative like the one in *(5)*. In this case, the particle *quam* is no longer present, and the standard NP is put into the ablative case:

(5) LATIN:
Cato   Cicero-ne   eloquentior   est
C.-NOM C.   -ABL more-eloquent is
'Cato is more eloquent than Cicero'

Faced with this double option for comparative-type choice, I have chosen to categorize the languages in my sample in two different ways. I take it that for each language there is a *primary comparative construction*, which is somehow more 'natural' or 'unmarked' than its possible alternatives. In the typical case, this primary comparative can be used more widely than any of its alternative options;[1] thus, for example, we will see in section 9.4.1 that the ablative comparative in Latin is restricted in its use by certain specific conditions, whereas the *quam*-comparative is not. For this reason, Latin will be classified primarily as a language of Type 6 (a so-called Particle Comparative), and the ablative comparative will be rated as a *secondary* comparative option for this language. Later on, I will argue that a language is not completely free in the choice of its secondary comparative(s); this choice can be shown to be governed by the same principles which determine the selection of its primary comparative form.

To conclude these preliminary remarks, one final point needs to be mentioned. As can be easily observed, it would be possible to split up the languages in the sample into two groups, on the basis of the fact that some languages require an overt marking of the predicate in their comparative constructions, whereas other languages do not. Restricting ourselves to predicative adjectives, we find that a majority of the languages under investigation do not use such an overt marking; in these languages, predicative adjectives in comparatives retain their unmarked, 'positive' form. Some languages, however, mark a predicative adjective in a comparative construction by means of a special affix (e.g., *-er* in English, German and Dutch, *-ior* in Latin, *-bb* in Hungarian, *-ago* in

Basque) or a special adverb (*more* in English, *plus* in French). I have not been able to find a principled way to account for this phenomenon of morphological marking; that is, I have not succeeded in finding an explanatory principle on the basis of which the presence or absence of this marking can be predicted.[2] Hence, I will assume that the phenomenon of comparative-marking is irrelevant to our typology of comparative constructions, and that it must be explained eventually in terms of (as yet unknown) regularities which are independent of those that determine the choice of a particular type of comparative construction. Therefore, I will not indicate systematically whether or not a given language requires morphological marking of the comparative predicate; I will, however, refer to the comparative morpheme of individual languages at various points in the discussion.

2.2   Parameters in the typology of comparatives

In the following sections, I will discuss the parameters of my typology of comparatives, that is, those features of comparative constructions which constitute the basis of a categorization into types. As I observed in section 1.3.3, the choice of such parameters is not completely theory-independent: objectively possible parameters will always have to be weighed against one another for their theoretical relevance and utility. In my case, this evaluation of possible starting points for a cross-linguistic typology of comparatives has led to a categorization in which *the encoding of the standard NP* (and the variation which can be observed in that encoding) is taken to constitute a highly significant factor.

2.2.1   *Case assignment of the standard NP*

With regard to the encoding of the standard NP in comparatives, a first dichotomy involves a split between *derived-case comparatives* and *fixed-case comparatives*. The parameter upon which this first distinction is based has to with the procedure by which *grammatical case* is assigned to standard NPs. In one group of constructions, this case assignment appears to be non-unique; that is, the standard NP *is not put into one single case* in all the instances of the comparative construction. Instead, the standard NP appeares to derive its case assignment from the case into which the comparee NP in the construction has been put. Thus, if the comparee NP in the construction happens to function as a subject, and is therefore put into the nominative case, the standard NP in that construction will also have nominative case; if the comparee NP is in the accusative case, they standard NP will also be marked for accusative, and so on. In short, we can observe here a parallelism in case assignment to the two NPs in the construction, to the effect that the case assignment of the comparee NP appears to determine the case assignment of the standard NP. Comparative constructions in which this situation obtains will be termed instances of *derived case*.

In contrast to this, other comparative constructions are more single-minded, in that they employ one particular case form for the standard NP. That is, these constructions put the standard NP into *one and the same oblique case form* in all instances of comparison, no matter what the case form of the comparee NP in the construction may be. In other words, the case assignment to the standard NP is independent of the case assignment to the comparee NP in this type of construction. Comparatives which exhibit this feature will be called instances of *fixed case*.

The opposition between instances of derived case and fixed case can be illustrated by the two comparative constructions in Latin, which we briefly mentioned above. The Latin *quam*-comparative can be shown to be an instance of derived case. Thus, in sentence (6) the standard NP (that is, the NP following *quam*) is marked for nominative case, whereas in (7) the standard NP has received accusative marking:

(6) LATIN:
 Brutum ego   non minus amo   quam tu
 B.-ACC I-NOM not less   love-1SG than you-NOM
 'I love Brutus no less than you (love Brutus)'

(7) LATIN:
 Brutum ego   non minus amo   quam te
 B.-ACC I-NOM not less   love-1SG than you-ACC
 'I love Brutus no less than (I love) you'

The variation in case marking of the standard NP in these two Latin sentences corresponds with a difference in interpretation. The first sentence in the pair must be translated as 'I love Brutus no less than *you love Brutus*', while the other sentence means 'I love Brutus no less than *I love you*'. Thus, in the first sentence it is the subject NP *ego* (marked by nominative case) which must be interpreted as the comparee NP, and the scale on which the comparison is based can be phrased as 'the various degrees of intensity with which people love Brutus'. In the second sentence, the direct object NP *Brutum* (marked for accusative case) functions as the comparee NP; here the scale of comparison might be described as 'the various degrees of intensity with which I love various individuals'. We can see, then, that in this Latin comparative the case form of the standard NP must be parallel to the case form which has been assigned to the comparee NP.

In addition to its *quam*-comparative, Latin has also a comparative which must be looked upon as an instance of fixed case. In this construction, the standard NP is invariably put into the ablative case, regardless of the case form of the comparee NP. As a result, a sentence like *(8)*, which is the fixed-case counterpart of the sentence *(6)* and *(7)*, is ambiguous, due to the fact that it can be either the subject NP *ego* or the object NP *Brutum* which may be taken as the comparee NP; the fixed ablative form of the standard NP does not give us any clue as to the right choice of the comparee NP for this construction. In other words, sentence *(8)* may have either the reading which we assigned to *(6)* or the reading of *(7)*:

> *(8) LATIN:*
> Brutum   ego   non minus te   amo
> B.-ACC I-NOM not less   you-ABL love-1SG

According to Kühner–Gerth (1955: vol. 2, 466), it is because of this ambiguity that the ablative comparative is avoided in Latin constructions where there are two possible candidates for the function of comparee NP.

2.2.2   *Subcategorization of fixed-case comparatives*

Within the category of fixed-case comparatives, there is a further typological criterion which readily presents itself. Given the fact that all these constructions share the feature that they encode the standard NP in a fixed-case form, one may try out a further division of these constructions, which is based on *the particular type of case form employed*. As it turns out, the question of the nature of this case assignment to the standard NP provides us with a useful typological parameter, in that it gives rise to a number of comparative types which can be defined in a relatively straightforward fashion.

A first dichotomy in the category of fixed-case comparatives concerns a distinction between constructions in which the standard NP is encoded as *a direct object*, and constructions in which the standard NP is a constituent of *an adverbial phrase*. In the first group, the standard NP is encoded in the structural form which the language employs to codify the direct object of a transitive verb; formal means to achieve this may include accusative case marking, word order conditions, special types of verbal agreement, or combinations of these alternatives. Now, it is clear that, in order for this codification to be viable, the comparative constructions at issue must contain a transitive predicate by which the standard

NP can be governed; this requirement becomes particularly pressing if the comparative predicate itself is not a transitive verb, but, say, an intransitive predicative adjective. The typical solution to this problem of government is the inclusion of *a special transitive verb in the comparative construction*, which has the general meaning of 'to surpass', 'to excel', 'to exceed' or 'to be more than', and which may be looked upon as the signal of a case of comparison of inequality in that particular language.[3] Thus, in comparatives of this type, the surface structure typically contains two predicates, one of which represents the scale of comparison, and another which provides the syntactic means to represent the standard NP as a direct object; the comparee NP in the construction is encoded as the subject of this latter transitive verb. There is, within this type, a certain amount of variation in the way in which these two predicates are formally expressed in surface structure; we will present a global discussion of these variants in section 2.3.4, and postpone a more detailed exposition of this variation to chapter 8. For the moment, I will confine myself to a single illustration of this particular type of comparative, by way of a random example:

(9)   *DUALA:*
      Nin ndabo e kolo buka   nine
      this house it big   exceed that
      'This house is bigger than that'

In opposition to fixed-case comparatives in which the standard NP has the syntactic function of a direct object, a second group of fixed-case constructions represents the standard NP as a constituent of an *adverbial phrase*. Obviously, since adverbial phrases do not impose any structural requirements of government, the addition of a special predicate to the construction is unnecessary here. Hence we find that, in the typical case of this category, the comparative predicate is the only predicative form in the construction, and that it is modified syntactically by the adverbial phrase containing the standard NP. Comparative constructions of this type will be called *adverbial comparatives*.

While direct-object comparatives constitute a terminal category in our typology (i.e., a category that cannot be split up into further subclasses), adverbial comparatives do allow for further subcategorization. The parameters of this subcategorization will be discussed in the next section.

2.2.3   Subcategorization of adverbial comparatives

As it turns out, a large majority of the languages which possess an adverbial comparative choose to represent their standard NPs in the form

of an adverbial phrase which has a clearly recognizable *locational* interpretation. In other words, most languages in this category model the
codification of their standard NPs on one of the options which they have
in the formal expression of *the semantic system of spatial relations*.
Given this fact, it becomes possible to introduce a further typological
division within the category of adverbial comparatives, based upon the
particular locational option which a language selects for the representation
of its standard NP. In order to be able to appreciate in full this
significance of locational parameters for the typology of comparative
constructions, we will first have to make a few general remarks on the
semantics of spatial expressions.

The semantic system of spatial relations (that is, the semantic network
of the ways in which two objects are conceived of as being related to one
another with respect to their location in space) has been a continuous
subject of inquiry for several generations of linguists and psychologists,[4]
and, despite the considerable progress made in this area, it must be
concluded that the stratification of this system is still not fully understood. Evidently, the present study cannot pretend to be a contribution to
this specific field in semantic theory; I will deal with spatial notions only
in as far as they are needed for an understanding of certain typological
decisions which I propose for the classification of adverbial comparatives.

A first major semantic distinction within the kinds of spatial relations
that two objects may maintain concerns the notion of *contact*. Thus, in
one set of spatial relations, the two objects involved are conceived of as
being so closely together in space that they are thought of as forming a
spatial unity. The set of spatial relations which share the semantic feature
of implying that the two objects are in contact will be called *locative
relations*, and the linguistic elements which are used to encode such
locative relations will be referred to as *locative markers*. Languages may
employ different devices for the formal expression of locative relations,
including case affixes, adpositions and verbal infixes; however, as I
pointed our earlier, the exact morphological procedure for the marking
of locative (and other spatial) relations will not concern us here.

Opposed to the set of spatial relations which imply contact between
objects we find a set of spatial relations in which the two objects are
conceived of as being in two different places; that is, these relations imply
a *spatial distance* between the two objects involved. Now, if two objects
are stated to be distant from each other, it is often the case that *a
movement* of one of the objects is implied. If such is the case, a further
classification can be made: on the one hand, relations which imply that
the movement is intended to *extend* the distance between the two objects
and, on the other hand, relations which imply that the movement is

intended to *diminish* that distance. If the movement of one of the objects has the effect of creating a larger distance between the two objects, the second object in the pair can be looked upon as the *source* or *origin* of the movement of the other object. Spatial concepts which imply that one of the objects is moving away from its source will be called *separative relations*, and the formal linguistic means to express them will be termed *separative markers*.

The mirror-image of a separative spatial notion is an *allative* notion. In the case of allative relations, it is understood that the movement of one of the objects has the effect of reducing the distance between the two objects, and, accordingly, the second object can be seen as the *goal* to which the movement of the first object is directed. The formal means which languages employ to encode these allative relations will be referred to as *allative markers*.

Now, if we look at the various ways in which languages with an adverbial comparative encode their standard NPs, we can observe a reflection of the tripartite spatial distinction between locative, separative and allative relations. It turns out that a large majority of the languages at issue selects one of these three semantic options as a model in the codification of its comparative constructions.

If a language chooses to codify its standard NP by means of a *separative* marker, the prototypical choice appears to be a marker with a meaning which is equivalent to that of English *from*. Semantically speaking, one might say that in these languages comparison seems to be 'metaphorized' as a movement in which the object represented by the standard NP is taken as the point of origin. Apparently, a marker with the meaning 'from' is the most unmarked or natural codification of this separative comparative. We do find, however, occasional instances of languages in which a different separative marker has been chosen to encode standard NPs. Thus, for example, there are languages in which the marker at issue has the meaning of 'up from'; in this case, a marker has been chosen which refers explicitly to the vertical dimension of the space in which the separative movement takes place, as opposed to the use of 'from', which is essentially neutral with respect to space dimensionality. Also, we find a few cases where the separative marker on the standard NP must be glossed as 'beyond'. In these cases, it seems that an additional parameter is introduced into the separative relation, namely, the position which the speaker or the observer occupies relative to the two objects involved in the separative relation. Again, this is in contrast with the use of 'from', which is essentially neutral as to the spatial position of the observer. Lastly, we come across one or two examples of separative comparatives where the marker of the standard NP is translated as 'behind' or 'after'. Such cases might be seen as instances of separative relations which include an observer-orientation, but in which the aspect of the separative predicate is perfective rather than imperfective.

Languages which choose an *allative* relation as the metaphor for the expression of comparison typically select a marker with a meaning which is equivalent to that of the English preposition *to*. Thus, the prototypical form of the standard NP in this type of adverbial comparative is that of a *goal-phrase*. As was the case with separative comparatives, a limited amount of diversification may be encountered in the choice of allative comparative markers. A few languages explicitly refer to the vertical dimension of space, encoding their standard NPs by a marker meaning 'up to'. We also find markers of standard NPs which can be translated as 'on this side of', thereby betraying observer-orientation, or markers with the meaning 'in front of' or 'before', which might be judged to be a case of observer-oriented allative movement in perfective aspect.

Lastly, there are languages which model their codification of comparison on the expression of *locative* spatial relations. The unmarked case here is the use of a marker which resembles English *at* or *on* in meaning. Occasionally, however, locative comparative markers are encountered which refer to other possibilities of spatial contact, such as 'on top of', 'beside; next to' or 'against'.

2.2.4　*Problems in the categorization of adverbial comparatives*

In connection with the above classification of adverbial comparatives into three semantically defined types, I must point out a couple of conceptual and practical difficulties. While this classification turns out to be fairly straightforward in the majority of the relevant languages, there are also several languages in which there may arise some uncertainty as to the correct classification of their comparative construction. This uncertainty may be caused by various factors which I will briefly touch upon below.

First, it can be observed that the formal codification of the locational system as a whole shows considerable variation across languages. In particular, languages vary in the degree of explicitness to which semantically distinct locational concepts are mapped onto distinctions in formal (i.e., lexical and/or structural) representations. On one side of the scale of explicitness, we find languages like Ubykh or Finnish, where differences in locational shades of meaning are formally encoded in a very elaborate system of case distinctions. Finnish, for example, has different case forms to represent such locational concepts as illative ('movement within a closed space': *in/inside the house*), elative ('movement out of an enclosed space': *out of the house*), inessive ('position of an object in a closed space': *inside/within the house*), adessive ('position of an object on the surface of another object': *on/upon the table*), ablative ('removal of an object from the surface of another object': *from/off the table*), allative ('movement towards an object': *to the house*), and several more. However, opposed to languages with this kind of very fine-grained system of locational representations, we also find languages in which most, if not all, spatial concepts are represented by one single formal mode of expression. An example of a language in which this situation obtains is Mapuche (see de Augusta, 1903). In this South-American language, the postposition *meu* functions as a very general locational marker, which may be glossed as 'in', 'on', 'at', 'to', 'from' or 'with', depending on the context. It will be clear that, in languages with such a generalized locational encoding, difficulties of classification will arise if they happen to have an adverbial comparative construction; since the standard NP in Mapuche is marked by the postposition *meu*, we are at a loss to decide whether this language should be classified as a language with a locative, an allative or a separative comparative. In my opinion, there is no generally applicable solution to this classificatory problem; the best way to act is to consider these problematic cases one by one. In some cases, we may be able to contrast the general locational marker with other markers in the language, which have a more specialized locational meaning. Thus, for instance, while the postposition *du* in Tubu (which also marks the standard NP in comparatives) is a general locational marker, Tubu also has specific locational markers meaning 'to' and 'from' (see Lukas, 1953). Now, since there is no specialized marker for 'on' or 'at' in this language, one might be justified in deciding that the basic meaning of the postposition *du* is locative, and that, therefore, the comparative construction in Tubu can be classified as an instance of the locative comparative. In a language like Mapuche, however, a solution along these lines cannot be made to work. Faced with such a situation, I think the best one can do is to note the difficulty explicitly, and to concede that the language in question is a case in which our criteria fail to provide for a straightforward categorization.

One might say that in languages like Tubu and Mapuche the locational distinctions 'contact vs. non-contact' and 'separative vs. allative' have both been *neutralized* in the formal expression of spatial relations. As we saw, these two languages are rather radical in their neutralization of spatial concepts and their type is not very frequent. There are, however, fairly common cases of a 'partial' neutralization to be noted in a large number of different languages. For example, in Dutch the semantic distinction between allative location and locative location is neutralized in surface structure in the case of the preposition *in*, which can be used to express both a motion towards an object (*hij viel in de rivier*: 'he fell into the river') and a location of an object inside another object (*hij zwom in de rivier*: 'he swam in the river'). A case of a language in which this particular type of partial neutralization creates indeterminacy as to the correct classification of the comparative construction is Kanuri. In this language, the standard NP in comparatives is marked by a case suffix which has both an allative and a locative interpretation (see Lukas, 1953). Parallel to cases in which general neutralization of locational concepts has taken place, these cases of partial neutralization will be discussed individually, and for each case a specific solution (or, as the case may be, the admission that there is no ready solution) will be stated.

Apart from the more or less practical problem created by cases of neutralization, we should mention one other source of indeterminacy in the classification of adverbial comparatives. This particular difficulty is more of a conceptual nature: it stems from the observation that, in a limited number of languages, the standard NP in the comparative is part of an adverbial phrase which does not have a clearly recognizable locational interpretation. Thus, we find standard NPs marked by elements which are to be glossed as an *instrumental marker* ('by', 'with'), an *agentive* marker ('by'), a *comitative* marker ('with', 'in the company of') or a *benefactive* marker ('to', 'for the sake of'). One obvious way to deal with such cases would be to increase the number of subcategories into which adverbial comparatives can be divided; in addition to the three locationally defined subclasses mentioned above, one would then allow for a proliferation of other subclasses, which are modelled upon the formal expression of non-locational relations. In this study, however, I will adopt a different approach, to the effect that the existence of a few cases of non-locational adverbial comparatives will not be taken to constitute a significant typological factor.

The point of view which will be defended here may be characterized as *localistic*. It rests upon the hypothesis that 'spatial expressions are more basic, grammatically and semantically, than various kinds of non-spatial expressions . . . Spatial expressions are linguistically more basic, according to the localists, in that they serve as structural templates, as it were, for other expressions; and the reason why this should be so, it is plausibly suggested by psychologists, is that spatial organization is of central importance in human cognition' (Lyons, 1977: 718). Thus, the localist position, which has been defended by linguists and psychologists alike, is characterized by the claim that non-spatial expressions must be seen as ultimately derived from spatial expressions, by means of processes of meaning-expansion and abstraction. An obvious point in favour of this position is 'the incontrovertible fact that temporal expressions, in many related languages, are patently derived from local expressions' (Lyons, ibid.). But apart from temporal expressions, there are also less obvious grammatical categories which may be candidates for a localistic analysis, such as tense, and various notions connected with the grammatical category of aspect (see Comrie, 1976). What makes the localistic hypothesis particularly relevant to the subject of the present essay is the claim that, on the one hand, agentive and instrumental phrases can be localistically conceived of as source phrases, and that, on the other hand, indirect objects and benefactive phrases can be seen as the localistic meaning-expansion of goal-phrases (see Anderson, 1971; Anderson and Dubois–Charlier, 1975). If we accept this localistic analysis, we are in a position to categorize comparatives in which the standard NP is encoded in an agentive or instrumental phrase as special instances of the separative comparative. Conversely, comparatives in which the standard NP has the form of an indirect object or a constituent of a benefactive phrase can be classified as special cases of the allative comparative. With respect to adverbial comparatives which have a comitative interpretation, it seems semantically plausible to classify them as a (more or less) non-spatial meaning-expansion of locative comparatives. Like locative phrases, comitative phrases too imply a close contact between objects or individuals. Furthermore, we may point out that comitative phrases are common in the formal expression of the concept of possessivity across languages. As has been argued in a large number of publications,[5] possessive constructions are structurally cognate to locative constructions in many unrelated languages throughout the world.

2.2.5   Subcategorization of derived-case constructions

With the distinction of direct-object comparatives and the three subtypes of adverbial comparatives, we have established the terminal categories of the class of fixed-case comparative constructions. To conclude our discussion of the parameters which we employ in our typology of comparatives, we must now pay attention to the other major class, viz. those comparatives in which the case of the standard NP can be derived or determined from the case of the comparee NP. One might say that, in such constructions, the case of the standard NP is 'parasitic' on the case assignment which the comparee NP has received.

Within the class of derived-case comparatives, we can single out one highly typical subcategory, which can be identified very easily across languages. For this category, a defining characteristic is that the comparative construction consists of *two structurally independent clauses*; one of these clauses contains the comparee NP, whereas the other clause contains the standard NP. Furthermore, the two clauses in question show a *structural parallelism*, to the effect that the grammatical function of the comparee NP is one of the clauses is reduplicated by the grammatical function of the standard NP in the other clause. If, for example, the comparee NP functions as the grammatical subject in its clause, the standard NP will also have subject status in its clause.

Since the comparative construction at issue consists of two independent clauses, it follows that the construction will also have to contain two independent predicates. In other words, a further feature of this type of comparative is that *the comparative predicate is expressed twice.* There are various different ways to formalize this double reference to the scale of comparison; we will say more about this point in section 2.3.5.

As a last point, we should note that the semantic relation between the two independent clauses in this comparative construction is usually to be described as *adversative coordination*; its literal interpretation is something along the lines of 'A is *p*, but B is *q*.' Thus, one might say that, in this type of comparative, there is no direct measuring of the two objects against each other, but the non-equal gradation of the objects involved can be inferred from the fact that they are contrasted in an adversative coordination.

To quote just one example of this type of *conjoined comparative*, consider the following sentence from Samoan:

(10) SAMOAN:
   Ua loa   lenei va'a , ua puupuu lena
   is long this boat   is short   that
   'This boat is longer than that boat'

Conjoined comparatives of the type discussed above form a very typical subclass of derived-case comparatives, but they are by no means the sole representatives of this category. In addition, we find a considerable number of comparative constructions in which the standard NP has derived case, but which cannot be called instances of conjoined comparatives, since in these constructions:

(a) comparee NP and standard NP are not constituents of separate independent clauses in surface structure; and
(b) there is no (or at least no obligatory) double reference to the scale of comparison in surface structure.

In short, these instances of derived-case comparatives do not have the structural form of an (adversative) coordination in surface structure, at least not from the point of view of synchronic syntax.[6] Typically, the standard NP in these comparatives is accompanied by an element which we may call *the comparative particle*. In the typical case, this particle cannot be identified as a case marker, since its presence is independent of the particular case form which the standard NP happens to have. A derived-case comparative construction in which such a comparative particle is present will be called an instance of the *particle comparative*. Examples of particle comparatives which have already been introduced in the foregoing text are the Latin *quam*-comparative and the English *than*-comparative. Some preliminary remarks on this type of comparative will be made in section 2.4. Chapter 9 will be devoted to a detailed discussion of the constructions in which a comparative particle is present.

2.3 Five major types of comparative constructions

If we apply the above criteria to the cross-linguistic data base of our typology of comparatives, we arrive at a classification into five clearly identifiable variants. In this section, I will briefly introduce each of these variants in turn, and list the languages which have a comparative construction of the type at issue as their primary or secondary option. Furthermore, I have included some comments on the basic word order of the languages involved; as will become clear, we can observe some degree of correlation between basic word-order type and choice of comparative type.

2.3.1 *Type 1: The Separative Comparative*

The Separative Comparative is an instance of fixed-case adverbial comparative constructions. NP-comparison is, in this type, expressed in one single surface clause. In this clause the comparee NP can, in principle, have any grammatical function. In contrast, the standard NP is invariably encoded as a constituent part of an adverbial phrase with a (spatial or non-spatial) separative interpretation. Examples of this type of comparative construction are the following:

(11) MUNDARI:
Sadom-ete hati   mananga-i
horse-from elephant big   -PRES. 3SG
'The elephant is bigger than the horse'

(12) JAPANESE:
Nihon-go wa   doits-go yori muzukashi
Japanese TOP German from difficult
'Japanese is more difficult than German'

(13)   CARIB:
Kuliali a   -kuliali kopo apoto-me   mang
canoe   your-canoe from big   -one is
'My canoe is bigger than your canoe'

A list of languages which exhibit this comparative construction as their primary option reads as follows:

Amharic	Eskimo	Manchu
Andoke	Guarani	Mundari
Arabic (Class.)	Hebrew (Biblical)	Nama
Aranda	Hindi	Piro
Aymara	Japanese	Quechua
Bedauye	Jurak	Tajik
Bilin	Kashmiri	Tibetan
Burmese	Khalka	Tupi
Burushaski	Korean	Turkish
Carib	Lamutic	Vayu
Cœur d'Alene	Laz	

A secondary separative comparative can be found in:

Albanian	Finnish	Latin
Basque	Old French	Russian
Old English	Greek (Class.)	Tamil

From this listing, we may conclude that the Separative Comparative is very widely spread indeed; almost 30 per cent of the languages in the sample choose this type as their primary option. A striking characteristic of this category is that the languages which it contains appear to have *a strong preference for SOV word-order*. Of the 32 languages with a primary separative comparative, only four (viz. Arabic (VSO), Cœur d'Alene (VOS), Guarani (SVO) and Biblical Hebrew (VSO) are contradictions to this tendency.

2.3.2   *Type 2: The Allative Comparative*

Like the Separative Comparative, the Allative Comparative is an instance of a fixed-case adverbial comparative type. It can rightly be regarded as the mirror-image of the Separative Comparative. Again, we find NP-comparison expressed in one single clause, with the comparee NP appearing in any grammatical function. The standard NP, however, does not form a part of a source-phrase, but is invariably encoded as a constituent part of a (spatial or non-spatial) goal-phrase. Examples of this type include:

(14) MAASAI:
Sapuk ol -kondi to l -kibulekeny
is-big the-deer   to the-waterbuck
'The deer is bigger than the waterbuck'

(15) BRETON:
Jazo bras-ox wid-on
he   big -PRT for -me
'He is bigger than me'

Listing the primary languages in this class, we get:

Breton	Maasai	Tarascan
Jacaltec	Nuer	
Kanuri	Siuslawan	

An Allative Comparative as a secondary option can be encountered in Mandinka, Mangarayi and Tamil.

We can note here that, at least as far as the primary options are concerned, the Allative Comparative appears to be limited almost exclusively to languages which have *basic verb-initial word-order*. Kanuri, an SOV-language, is the only exception here. Indeed, the relatively small size of the class may well be connected with the fact that a considerable number of verb-initial languages prefer a Conjoined Comparative or a Particle Comparative as their primary option in comparative-type choice; for this, see section 2.3.5 and section 2.4.

2.3.3   Type 3: The Locative Comparative

The third instance of fixed-case adverbial comparatives is the Locative Comparative. In this construction, the standard NP is invariably encoded as a constituent of an adverbial phrase which is marked by an element that indicates spatial or non-spatial contact. Apart from the marking of the standard NP, the Locative Comparative is formally similar to the Separative Comparative and the Allative Comparative in all significant respects. That is, the construction again consists of one single clause, and the comparee NP is free to fulfil any grammatical function.

Examples of this comparative type include the following:

(16) CHUCKCHEE:
Gamga-qla'ul-ik   qetvu -ci   -um
all   -men -on strong-more-1SG
'I am stronger than all men'

(17) SALINAN:
      Ragas-mo in   luwa ti -hek
      surely-you more man on-me
      'You are more of a man than me'

The following 12 languages are primary members of this class:

Chuckchee	(SOV)	Miwok	(VSO)	Tamazight	(VSO)
Cebuano	(VSO)	Naga	(SOV)	Tamil	(SOV)
Mandinka	(SOV)	Navaho	(SOV)	Tubu	(SOV)
Mapuche	(SOV)	Salinan	(VSO)	Ubykh	(SOV)

Secondary Locative Comparatives are documented for:

Basque	(SOV)	Hungarian	(SOV?)	Nama	(SOV)
Dakota	(SOV)	Latvian	(SVO)	Samoan	(VSO)
Gumbainggir	(SOV)	Maori	(VSO)		

As for word order, the absence of SVO-languages in this class is a striking fact, even if we make allowance for the relatively small size of the category. Thus, it seems that a predilection for *either SOV or VSO order* among the languages of this category may be stated with some confidence. This tendency is strengthened even further when the secondary members of this type are taken into account.

2.3.4   Type 4: The Exceed Comparative

The Exceed Comparative is the fourth and final variant of fixed-case comparative constructions. Its main characteristic is that the standard NP is invariably constructed as the direct object of a special transitive verb, the meaning of which can be glossed as 'to exceed' or 'to surpass'. Furthermore, the comparee NP always functions as the subject of this 'exceed'-verb. From a semantic point of view, the Exceed Comparative may be considered as cognate to the Separate Comparative, in that both constructions imply a movement of an object beyond or farther away from another object. Formally, however, the two types of comparatives are definitely distinct.

As to the representation of the comparative predicate in this type, strategies may differ from language to language. Some language prefer a so-called 'serial verb'-construction, in which the comparee NP is constructed as the subject of a verbal complex which contains both the comparative predicate and the exceed-verb. We will discuss this variant in detail in section 8.1. For the moment, the following examples of this *Exceed-1 Comparative* may suffice:

(18)   YORUBA:
O *tobi ju*   *u*
he big exceed him
'He is bigger than him'

(19)   VIETNAMESE:
Vang qui   *hon*   *bac*
gold valuable exceed silver
'Gold is worth more than silver'

In other languages, such as Hausa, we find that the exceed-verb is the only main predicate in the construction. In this variant, which we will call the *Exceed-2 Comparative*, the comparative predicate is expressed in a subordinate form which functions syntactically as an adverbial phrase:

(20)   HAUSA:
Doki ya-fi   *rago girma*
horse it -exceed goat bigness
'A horse is bigger than a goat'

Still other languages construct the comparative predicate as the sole main verb in the construction, while the exceed-verb receives some subordinate form (e.g., the form of a participle, or of an infinitive). An example of this *Exceed-3 Comparative* can be found in Swahili:

(21)   SWAHILI:
Mti huu ni mrefu ku -shinda ule
tree this is big   INF-exceed that
'This tree is taller than that tree'

We should emphasize here that, whatever the strategy in representing the comparative predicate and the exceed-verb may be, the main characteristic of all the variants of the Exceed Comparative is that the construction consists of one single sentence, and that it contains a transitive exceed-verb which takes the standard NP as its direct object.

My sample contains 20 languages which have some variant of the Exceed Comparative as their primary option. These languages are the following:

Banda	Hausa	Swahili
Bari	Igbo	Thai
Cambodian	Jabem	Vietnamese
Dagomba	Kirundi	Wolof
Duala	Mandarin	Yagan
Fulani	Margi	Yoruba
Gbeya	Nguna	

A secondary Exceed Comparative can be found in:

Aymara	Quechua	Sranan
Maasai	Sika	Tamazight

As for word order, we can observe that for this set of languages *SVO order appears to be mandatory*, at least as far as the primary members of this type are concerned.

2.3.5   Type 5: The Conjoined Comparative

The Conjoined Comparative is the most conspicuous manifestation of derived-case comparative constructions. In this type, NP-comparison is typically effected by means of the adversative coordination of two clauses; one of these clauses contains the comparee NP, and the other clause contains the standard NP. Furthermore, there is a structural parallelism between the two clauses, to the effect that the grammatical function which the comparee NP fulfils in its clause is matched by the grammatical function of the standard NP in its clause. As a result, this type of comparative involves two grammatically independent clauses, which are connected in such a way that a gradation between the two objects can be inferred.

Within this category, we can distinguish two subtypes, on the basis of the particular manner in which the double reference to the scale of comparison is effected. These two subtypes are:

- *Type 5A:* conjoined comparatives in which the two clauses contain *antonymous predicates*; and
- *Type 5B:* conjoined comparatives in which the comparative predicates in the two clauses exhibit a *positive–negative polarity*.

An example of the first subtype is the following sentence from Sika:

(22)   SIKA:
       Dzarang tica gahar , dzarang rei kesik
       horse   that big   horse   this small
       'That horse is bigger than this horse'

Subtype 5B can be illustrated by the following example:

(23)   HIXKARYANA:
       Kaw-ohra naha Waraka, kaw naha Kaywerye
       tall -not he-is W.   tall he-is K.
       'Kaywerye is taller than Waraka'

A list of the 20 primary languages in this class reads as follows:

Abipon	(SVO)	Mangarayi	(SOV)	Nahuatl	(SVO)
Cayapo	(OSV)	Maori	(VSO)	Pala	(SVO)
Dakota	(SOV)	Menomini	(SVO)	Samoan	(VSO)
Ekagi	(SOV)	Miskito	(SOV)	Shipibo	(SOV)
Gumbainggir	(SOV)	Mixtec	(VSO)	Sika	(SVO)
Hixkaryana	(OVS)	Motu	(SOV)	Yavapai	(SOV)
Kobon	(SOV)	Monumbo	(SOV)		

A secondary option for a Conjoined Comparative can be found in:

Banda	(SVO)	Ilocano	(VSO)	Nuer	(VSO)
Kirundi	(SVO)	Mapuche	(SOV)	Swahili	(SVO)

A first thing to note about this class is that the languages which it contains appear to exhibit a certain degree of geographical grouping. The primary languages in this class are predominantly Australian, Papuan or Polynesian, or else can be situated on the American continent. It thus looks as if the choice for a Conjoined Comparative is (at least to a certain extent) influenced by the characteristics of certain linguistic areas.

As regards basic word order, no definite statement can be made for this class. Basic word order does not seem to be a determining factor in the choice for or against a Conjoined Comparative; all major word-order patterns are represented in this category and, what is more, they occur in proportions which do not differ greatly from those which one would expect to find in a random[7] selection of languages.

2.4   Particle Comparatives

In the case of the five typological categories which we discussed in the preceding section, classification is fairly straightforward; the languages which are listed under each of the respective headings are easily recognizable as instances of the type in question. However, I have already pointed out that, for a number of languages in my sample, classification is a bit more problematic. In this section, I will deal with one set of such problematic cases, the so-called *Particle Comparatives*. Following that, I will note a number of cases where classification seems to be indeterminate as a result of the 'mixing' of two comparative types.

Under the heading of 'Particle Comparatives' I have lumped together a number of constructions which have in common that the standard NP has derived case. However, these constructions also lack a number of features which characterize the main class of derived-case comparatives, viz. the Conjoined Comparative. For one thing, Particle Comparatives do not (or do not have to) consist of two grammatically independent clauses, at least not in their present synchronic form; in other words, Particle Comparatives do not have the structural form of a coordination of clauses. As a result, the standard NP in this type of comparative functions structurally as a constituent part of a phrase in the clause which also contains the comparee NP. In this respect, Particle Comparatives resemble (again, as far as their synchronic form is concerned) adverbial comparatives rather than conjoined comparatives, where standard NP and comparee NP are constituents of separate and independent clauses.

A typical characteristic of all Particle Comparative is the presence of a specific *comparative particle*, which accompanies the standard NP. In the typical case, this particle cannot be identified as some kind of case marker, since the case form of the standard NP in this type of comparative is derived from the case assignment of the comparee NP.[8] Another feature of Particle Comparatives, which we may note in passing, is that morphological marking of comparative predicates seems to be exceptionally popular with them. Of the 18 languages with a Particle Comparative, there are 13 languages in which morphological comparative-marking of the predicate is obligatory.

While Particle Comparatives share at least one common feature (namely, the fact that they are, or have been, instances of derived case), there are also indications that the Particle Comparative is not a homogeneous category. The internal diversification of this set of comparatives is brought out by the fact that the comparative particles which are involved in the various constructions cannot be shown to have the same origin or categorial status for all of the languages in this class. One gets the impression that the class of Particle Comparatives (in as far as they can rightly be said to form a class at all) has assembled its members from a large variety of sources and that, in languages with a Particle Comparative, the formation of the comparative construction has, so to speak, 'gone wrong along the way'. A full discussion of the various forms which Particle Comparatives may have will be presented in chapter 9.

Examples of languages with a Particle Comparative are Latin and English, and also the following languages:

(24)   *HUNGARIAN:*
     Istvan   magasa-bb   mint Peter
     I.-NOM tall   -PRT than P.-NOM
     'Istvan is taller than Peter'

(25) *JAVANESE:*
      Enak   daging karo iwak
      is-good meat   than fish
      'Meat is better than fish'

(26) *MALAGASY:*
      Lehibe noho ny   zana-ny Rabe
      tall   than the son -his R.
      'Rabe is taller than his son'

A primary Particle Comparative of some type can be attested for the following 18 languages in the sample:

Albanian	(SVO)	Gaelic	(VSO)	Latin	(SOV)
Basque	(SOV)	Goajiro	(VSO)	Latvian	(SVO)
Dutch	(SVO/SOV)	Greek (Cl.)	(SOV)	Malagasy	(VOS)
English	(SVO)	Hungarian	(SOV?)	Russian	(SVO)
French	(SVO)	Ilocano	(VSO)	Sranan	(SVO)
Finnish	(SVO)	Javanese	(SVO/VSO)	Toba Batak	(VOS)

Furthermore, a Particle Comparative occurs as a second option in Bari (SVO) and Classical Nahuatl (SVO).

Looking at the list of languages with a primary Particle Comparative, I think it is safe to say that this comparative type is, to a considerable extent, to be rated as an areal phenomenon. No less than 12 of the 18 languages at issue are members of the European 'Sprachbund', while four others belong to the Austronesian family. As for word order, this list makes it clear that basic word-order patterns do not seem to constitute a determining factor in the choice for a Particle Comparative. As with conjoined comparatives, all major word orders are represented here, in roughly the proportions which one would expect to encounter in a random selection of languages. All in all, then, we may conclude that there is no correlation between derived-case comparison and preference for certain word-order types, while for the various subtypes of fixed-case comparison such a preference can be established with some certainty.

2.5   Mixed cases

As I pointed out earlier, there are certain languages in my sample for which the type of comparative construction is hard to determine uniquely. These languages appear to have a *mixed comparative*, in which the essential features of two different types seem to have been combined.

Now, in section 1.3.3 I adopted the view that such cases of indeterminacy must be conceived of as empirical data, which require explanation as much as cases in which this indeterminacy is absent. A framework in which the phenomenon of type-mixing in comparatives might find a principled explanation will be presented in chapter 15. For the present, I will restrict myself to a brief presentation of the relevant cases.

In the sample we find at least three languages with a comparative which combines features of the Conjoined Comparative and the Exceed Comparative. In all three of these languages, the construction consists of an adversative coordination of two structurally independent sentences; if we take this feature to be the determining factor in the classification of these constructions, we would have to categorize them as instances of the Conjoined Comparative. Unlike the regular case of the Conjoined Comparative, however, in these constructions the second sentence does not contain a negation or an antonymous predicate, nor is there a structural parallelism between the two sentences with respect to the grammatical function of the standard NP and the comparee NP. Instead, the second sentence has an exceed-verb as its predicate, which takes the standard NP as its direct object and the comparee NP as its subject. We find this 'Conjoined Exceed Comparative' in Fulani and Acholi:

(27)   FULANI:
Samba mawi , o   buri   Amadu
S.   is-big , he exceed A.
'Samba is bigger than Amadu'

(28)   ACHOLI:
Gwok mera dit ki   kato   meri
dog   my big and exceed your
'My dog is bigger than yours'

In the above Fulani example, it is the comparee NP which is mentioned explicitly in the first clause of the comparative. We can, however, also find instances of the opposite possibility, that is, cases of a Conjoined Exceed Comparative in which the first sentence has the standard NP as its subject. Examples of this state of affairs are provided by the (secondary) comparatives in Motu, Tamazight and Temne. Cp.:

(29)   MOTU:
Una na namo , ina herea-ia
that is good   this exceeds
'This is better than that'

(30)   *TAMAZIGHT:*
      Aiis   ennek ioularen , oua hin ioufi
      horse your   is-good   that my exceeds
      'My horse is better than your horse'

(31)   *TEMNE:*
      A -seth   ane a fino , kere anan a thas
      the-house this it good but that it exceed
      'That house is better than this house'

Quite a different case of indeterminacy is presented by the classification of the comparative construction in Gaojiro. Part of the difficulty
here is that the two sources on this Arawakan language (Celedon, 1878;
Holmer, 1949) seem to contradict one another on an essential point. If
we follow Holmer (1949: 146), we observe that the Goajiro comparative
obligatorily includes the presence of the item *aulaka*, which in other
contexts must be translated as 'and' or 'too'. Furthermore, the standard
NP in the construction is not only expressed by that NP itself, but is also
referred to by an adverbial phrase which consists of the postposition *-lia*
'from' and a proclitic pronominal element which agrees with the standard
NP in person, number and gender. The following sentences may illustrate
this construction:

(32)   *GOAJIRO:*
a.   *Aulaka Rupeta mulia'u , hu -lia   Rafaela*
       and   R.   big-is   her-from R.
       'Roberto is bigger than Rafaela'

b.   *Aulaka Rafaela ha'u -co , nu -lia   Rupeta*
       and   R.   small-is   him-from R.
       'Rafaela is smaller than Roberto'

Faced with this situation, we may venture the hypothesis that the Goajiro
comparative is a Conjoined Comparative in which, untypically, the
second clause has the form of a separative expression. Accordingly, we
might rate this construction as a case of mixing between the Conjoined
Comparative and the Separative Comparative.

In contrast to this representation of the Goajiro comparative, Celedon
(1878: 20) notes an essentially different state of affairs. For one thing,
Celedon does not mention the presence of the item *aulaka* in this
construction. More importantly, this author states that the standard NP
in Goajiro comparatives is signalled by the presence of the element *nöria*;
it is plausible to view this item as a phonological or orthographical
variant of the element *nu-lia* 'from him/it' mentioned by Holmer.[9] Now,

the essential point is that, according to Celedon's data, the particle *nöria* is an invariable element; it does not show any morphological agreement with the standard NP. Thus, Celedon quotes the following examples of the Goajiro comparative:

(33)   GOAJIRO:
a.   Kauzu -shi   Pedro nöria Juan
       beautiful-MASC P.   than   J.
       'Pedro is more handsome than Juan'

b.   Kauza -se   Maria nöria Juana
       beautiful-FEM M.   than   J.
       'Maria is prettier than Juana'

c.   Ooyor-shi   taya nöria pia
       fat   -MASC I   than   you
       'I am fatter than you'

If Holmer's analysis were followed here, the particle *nöria* in these sentences would have to have the forms *nu-ria* 'from him', *hu-ria* 'from her', and *pu-ria* 'from you', respectively. Since this variation is not attested by Celedon, we must assume that this author takes the item *nöria* to be a comparative particle, which would make Goajiro an instance of a language with a Particle Comparative.

In considering the case of Goajiro, I have decided to follow Celedon's facts, and hence I have classified this language under the heading of the Particle Comparative. I think that the most plausible way to account for the various data on the Goajiro comparative is to assume that, in this construction, the erstwhile separative phrase 'from X' (which has been retained as such in some dialects or by some native speakers) has gradually come to be reanalysed as an invariable adverbial element, in its most neutral form, viz. the form 'from it'. In other words, my suggestion is that Goajiro presents a case in which a Separative Comparative has entered a period of transition into another type, viz. the Particle Comparative; an intermediate stage in this process may be seen in the fact that this construction has at least some features which point to a conjoined analysis. In this connection, it may also be useful to point out that a basic separative interpretation of the particle in a Particle Comparative is by no means uncommon; the comparative particle *asa* in Toba Batak is an adverb with the meaning 'after that', and the same is true for the Dutch comparative particle *dan*. But it must be admitted, of course, that this solution to the problem with which Goajiro confronts us contains a high degree of speculation, and that this language remains a case which seems to resist straightforward classification.

Finally, we must consider one rather peculiar case of mixed NP-comparison. Telugu, a Dravidian language, marks the standard NP in its comparatives by means of the affixes *-kanna* or *-kante*:

(34)   TELUGU:
     I -pandu a   -pandu-kanna tipi -ga   undi
     this-fruit   that-fruit -PRT   sweet-one is
     'This fruit is sweeter than that fruit'

The suffixes *-kanna* and *-kante* are not spatial postpositions in Telugu; they mean neither 'to' nor 'at' nor 'from', nor can they be identified as postpositions which have a meaning that is localistically derivable from such spatial markers. Given this fact, it would seem appropriate to classify Telugu as a language with a Particle Comparative. However, if we look a bit closer at the etymology of the comparative items *-kanna* and *-kante*, we find that these elements are actually non-finite forms of the negative copula *ka-du* 'not to be', a verb which occurs in sentences like the following:

(35)   TELUGU:
a.   *Ramarav podugu-vadu ka -du*
     R.   tall   -one   not-is
     'Ramarav is not tall'

b.   *I -pandu tipi -di ka -du*
     this-fruit   sweet-one   not-is
     'This fruit is not sweet'

To be exact, the element *kanna* is the Infinitive form of this negative copula, a form which is used to represent the predicate of subordinate temporal clauses. The element *kante* must be viewed as the Adverbial Conditional of the negative copula, a form which codifies the predicate of subordinate conditional clauses. Hence, we might say that the comparative construction in (34) has in fact the literal meaning: 'While/if that fruit is not (sweet', this fruit is sweet.' In other words, the Telugu comparative might be taken to be a Conjoined Comparative of the polar subtype; as such, Telugu would be deviant only in that it has reduced one of the conjoined clauses in the construction to a subordinate form, whereas the regular cases of the Conjoined Comparative prefer to keep the structural coordination of the two clauses intact. On the other hand, one might also maintain that Telugu is a language with a Particle Comparative. The fact that the particle(s) in question are verbal forms with the meaning 'not being' cannot be regarded as an argument against this classification, in view of the fact that, apparently, particles in such comparatives are of a heterogeneous origin anyway. Given these alternatives, and the lack of argumentation to make a principled choice between them, I have decided to treat Telugu as an indeterminate case which defies straightforward classification. The comparative construction in Telugu will therefore not figure in the discussion of the various comparative types that will be presented in the following chapters; its occurrence will not be brought up until, in chapter 15, a general framework for the explanation of the occurrence and distribution of comparative-types has been developed.

3

In Search of a Determinant Factor

Now that the description of the data on the comparative constructions in our sample has resulted in the establishment of a cross-linguistic typology, our next task will be to find a principled way to account for the distinctions which this typology offers. As I noted in section 1.2, such a principled account presupposes that we are able to find an explanation for the attested occurrence and non-occurrence of the categories which figure in the typology, and for the attested distribution of languages over the options which the typology offers. A natural way to provide answers to these questions is to search for a second typological parameter which can be identified as the determining outside factor of our original typology of comparatives. That is, we will try to categorize the languages in our sample in an additional typology, in such a way that categorizations in this second typology match the distinctions which we have attested in the typology of comparatives: this matching can be laid down in a set of implicational universals. In as far as the parameter of the second typology can be argued to be more basic or fundamental to language systems than the first (i.e. than comparison), we can call this second typology the *determinant* of the typology of comparative constructions; it serves as the basis upon which the non-randomness of variation in the encoding of comparison can be accounted for, and hence it can, in some sense, be said to constitute an explanation for that variation.

3.1   Word order as a possible determinant

At first glance, it would seem to be evident from our data that basic word-order type is a likely candidate for the function of determinant in our typology of comparatives. As we observed, for at least four of the major categories in the typology a specific choice of word order is a very stringent, if not necessary, condition. We may express the relations which we have found to exist between word-order pattern and choice of comparative type in the following four general statements:

(1) a. *If a language has a Separative Comparative, then its basic word order is SOV.*
   b. *If a language has an Allative Comparative, then its basic word order is verb-initial.*
   c. *If a language has a Locative Comparative, then its basic word order is either SOV or verb-initial.*
   d. *If a language has an Exceed Comparative, then its basic word order is SVO.*

Naturally, these four statements should not be taken as absolute universals of language; they formulate tendencies, in the sense of Comrie (1981: 27). We may say, however, that, as tendencies go, our statements seem to be fairly sound. Restricting ourselves to the primary choices of comparative type, we can observe that statement *(1a)* is contradicted by only four out of 32 languages in the sample (viz. Classical Arabic, Cœur d'Alene, Guarani and Biblical Hebrew); statement *(1b)* is contradicted by one language out of seven (viz. Kanuri); and statements *(1c)* and *(1d)*, which concern 12 and 20 languages, respectively, are not contradicted at all in the sample. There thus seems to be some ground for positioning tentatively a correlation between basic word-order type and choice of comparative type; this correlation is of the kind which is expressed in the above four general statements. In what follows, I will refer to the statements in *(1)* as *word-order-based universals of comparative type choice*.

Now, although the four statements in *(1)* clearly represent valid universal tendencies, one is nevertheless left with the uneasy feeling that, somehow, this set of word-order-based universals does not tell the whole story about the attested occurrence of comparative types. This suspicion is confirmed once we examine to what extent the parameter of word-order variation can be said to provide an *explanatory framework* for the choice of a particular comparative type. If we look at the three requirements for universal explanations (see section 1.2), we can note that the parameter of basic word order will, at its best, fulfil only one of these requirements, namely, the requirement of being the 'more basic' linguistic feature of the two parameters involved. Since the publication of Greenberg (1963), it has become a common assumption in Universal Grammar that word order is a fundamental characteristic of natural languages, from which various other cases of cross-linguistic variation can be deduced (for instance, the order of elements in phrases, the direction of deletion and adjunction procedures, and so on). Hence, it is certainly justifiable to bring up basic word order as a 'deeper-lying' causal factor in the linguistic typology of comparative constructions. On the other two counts, however, the set of word-order-based universals can be shown to fail as an explanatory framework.

For one thing, it can be observed that the set of universals stated in *(1)* does not exhaust all the theoretically possible cases of combinations of word-order types. It is a generally accepted fact in Universal Grammar that natural languages are distributed over three major word-order types, viz. SOV, VSO/VOS and SVO; these three word-order types are correlated to comparative types in the statements *(1a)*, *(1b)* and *(1d)*, respectively. In addition, however, statement *(1c)* claims that a specific comparative type, viz. the Locative Comparative, is correlated with either SOV or VSO word order. Now, given that at least some comparative types can be correlated to two word-order types to the exclusion of the third, we may expect there to be other comparative types for which a correlation with a different combination of word-order types can be attested. As it is, however, our data show that it is only the SOV–VSO combination which correlates with an empirically documented comparative type; there are no comparative types for which a choice for either SOV or SVO, or a choice for either SVO or VSO, is prescribed. As it stands, the set of word-order-based universals formulated above offers no principled account for this empirically attested exclusion of theoretically possible combinations of word-order types, and its explanatory value is considerably weakened by this fact.

As a second point, it can be seen that the set of word-order-based universals covers only four classes of comparative types out of six; for the Conjoined Comparative and the various manifestations of Particle Comparatives no correlation whatsoever with a particular type of basic word order can be established. One might argue here that the Particle Comparative is only a minor class, if a class at all. But even if we grant this, we are still faced with the uncomfortable situation that the correlation of comparative type to word-order type breaks down in more than 35 per cent of our primary cases of comparative constructions; this situation gets even worse once secondary options are taken into account. Moreover, by accepting word order as the primary determinant of the typology of comparatives, one highly typical and important variant in that typology, viz. the Conjoined Comparative, is left without any explanation of its occurrence at all.

Considerations of this kind suggest that the relation between basic word-order types and certain comparative types, while undoubtedly real, should nevertheless be thought of as being of a more indirect nature. They suggest that we should be able to track down a new typological parameter which intermediates between these two typologies. Of this intermediate parameter, it should be required that it lead to a typology in which each category is correlated both to a certain comparative type and, at the same time, to a certain word-order type (c.q. a combination of word-order types, or a lack of definite word-order type). In this way, a word-order-based universal of comparative-type choice such as

> (1a) *If a language has a Separative Comparative, then it has basic SOV word order*

should be replaced by the syllogism (2), which clearly illustrates the concomitant status of word-order type in comparative-type choice:

> (2) a. *Languages with a Separative Comparative belong to type A in the typology of X.*
>   b. *Languages of type A in the typology of X typically have SOV word order.*
>   c. *Therefore: languages with a Separative Comparative typically have SOV word order.*

Thus, the establishment of a new determinant parameter for the typology of comparatives enables us (at least in principle) to maintain the empirically attested correlations between word-order types and certain comparative types, while at the same time the drawbacks of a direct correlation between these two typologies stand a chance of being eliminated. In the new model, the problems with which the set of word-order-based universals confront us are transformed into issues regarding the correlations between word-order types and the variants of the new intermediate typology. Hence, the explanatory value of this new parameter can be examined from two different sides. On the one hand, the new typology should be able to make correct predictions about the attested characteristics of the typology of comparative constructions. In addition, the new parameter should also be able to incorporate the set of word-order-based universals in a principled, unproblematic fashion.

3.2   Spatial relations as a possible determinant

If we accept the line of reasoning outlined in the preceding section, our next problem is of course to find out what this assumed new 'intermediate' parameter might be. At this point, the system of the ways in which spatial relations are encoded in natural languages readily presents itself. As we observed in the foregoing chapter, the relation between spatial expressions and comparatives is most conspicuous in the case of the various types of adverbial comparatives, but there is also a natural way in which the Exceed Comparative can be viewed as spatially derived. In short, one might venture the hypothesis that the typology of comparatives is the way it is because comparative constructions in natural languages tend to borrow their linguistic manifestion from the codification of certain types of spatial notions.

If we investigate this hypothesis for its value as an explanatory framework, we can conclude that it is certainly satisfactory from a conceptual point of view. The idea that spatial relations constitute a more fundamental concept than comparison is not likely to meet with serious disagreement among linguists or psychologists. There are, however, a number of objections against this hypothesis which have to do with the formal way in which the parameters of spatial relations and comparison appear to be connected.

First, it should be observed that the hypothesis, as it stands, does not offer a *full matching* of the types in the two typologies. While a relation between spatial expressions and comparatives is evident in the case of fixed-case comparatives, no such matching can be made in the case of derived-case constructions. Now, it might be argued that this imperfect matching is just a fact of life; one might maintain that, apparently, some languages choose a spatial model in their encoding of comparison, while other languages simply do not. I think one has to admit that there is, at present, no way to prove that such a position is incorrect. I do feel, however, that, as long as the forces behind the phenomenon of linguistic variation are still largely a mystery, one should aim at the formulation of universal theories which cover all the different linguistic manifestations of a given parameter, instead of only a subset.

As a second, and perhaps more damaging, objection, we can note that the hypothesis, in its above formulation at least, falls short of the criterion of *exhaustiveness* which I discussed in section 1.2. Even for those languages in which a direct modelling of comparison on spatial relations is evident, the hypothesis offers no restricted framework: it does not answer the question of why it is that some of these languages select a separative relation as their structural template of comparison, while others prefer an allative or a locative relation. Given the plausible assumption that, in principle, all of these languages have the means to encode all of these different spatial notions, we must conclude that the 'localist' hypothesis advanced above is not constrained enough to enable us to make precise predictions of the choice of comparative type in a given language.

Notwithstanding these objections, however, it remains an undeniable and highly significant fact that there is a close connection between the expression of spatial relations and comparison in a large number of unrelated languages. Faced with this seemingly paradoxical situation, I have adopted the following line of argumentation. I assume that the mental act of comparison is, in its cognitive representation, indeed based upon spatial concepts; a further elaboration of this assumption will be given in section 11.3. However, as far as the linguistic codification of the concept of comparison is concerned, I will defend the position that it is not spatial location which is the determinant factor in this encoding, but rather the notion of *temporal chaining*. Again, I may point out here that localist authors (e.g., Lyons (1977: 719)) have claimed the existence of a progressive degree of abstraction in the order of 'spatial location', 'temporal location' and 'abstract location' (such as grammatical functions, existentiality, possessivity and causativity). Given this framework, the central claim of this study can be phrased as the statement that comparative constructions in natural languages are one more case of 'abstract location'.

3.3   Temporal chaining as the determinant of comparative types

As a cognitive notion, temporal chaining can be defined as the process by which the mind establishes 'the relation between two events, A and B, as overlapping, preceding or following each other' (Traugott, 1975: 208). The result of the mapping of this process onto a language system is a *temporal chain*, i.e., a semantic configuration in which two tensed propositions (representing states or events) are presented successively. We will see in chapter 4 that, semantically, temporal chains can be divided into two classes. In one class of cases, temporal chains must be interpreted as stating that the events or states in question occur at the same point in time; these temporal chains will be referred to as *simultaneous (temporal) chains*. The other class, in which the events or states referred to in the chain must be taken to occur or obtain one after the other will be called *consecutive (temporal) chains*.

In addition, I assume that this semantic or cognitive temporal chaining is mirrored formally by a range of syntactic constructions in which sentences or predicates are linearly ordered with respect to one another. Thus, *syntactic temporal chaining* will be assumed to be the formal linguistic correlate of the semantic chaining of propositions; *syntactic chains* represent the formal ways in which the cognitive process of temporal chaining is encoded in natural language. Natural languages may vary in the ways in which they choose to encode temporal chaining, and hence it is possible to construct *a typology of syntactic chains*. One of the best-known and major ways in which temporal chaining can be formalized in natural languages is the application of the structural procedure of *coordination of sentences or predicates*. However, as we shall see, coordination is by no means the only option in syntactic chaining constructions across languages.

The central aim of this study is to provide evidence for the position that temporal chaining must be identified as the determinant of comparative-type choice in natural languages. Thus, I will argue that the choice of a particular comparative type for a language L can be predicted from the type (or types) of temporal chaining which that language permits, and that the attested occurrence of comparative types across languages is determined by the theoretically possible types of temporal chains in natural languages. As will become clear in chapter 4, the possibility of having certain types of temporal chaining in a given language is in its turn partially constrained by the basic word-order pattern of that language. As a result, the correlations between comparative types and word-order types can be accounted for. Thus, I will argue for universal statements of the following general kind:

(3)   *Languages with a comparative construction of type A must have a temporal chaining construction of type X. Since languages with a temporal chaining construction of type X typically have the word-order option W, languages with a comparative of type A typically have the word-order option W.*

In chapter 4 I shall give a survey of the ways in which temporal chaining is structurally realized in natural languages, and following that I shall present a definitive statement of the universals of comparative-type choice which I defend. Before doing so, however, it may be interesting to advance a number of preliminary reasons for thinking that temporal chaining might be the proper candidate for the intervening parameter in our model. In particular, I want to quote here a number of facts which seem to point to a possible formal relationship between comparatives and coordinations.

3.4   Preliminary data

Preliminary indications that temporal chaining may be the appropriate candidate for the function of determinant factor in comparative-type choice stem from a variety of sources. First, we can note that by postulating temporal chaining as a typological determinant, we can explain the occurrence of at least two of the major classes of comparatives in a natural and direct fashion. These categories of comparative constructions appear as syntactic temporal chains even in surface structure: the Conjoined Comparative is structurally a case of sentential coordination, while at least some cases of the Exceed Comparative have the surface form of a serialization, which is a major syntactic chaining type in these languages.[1] Further preliminary evidence for the crucial role of temporal chaining in the choice of comparative type can be derived from a number of isolated facts about the morphology of the comparative constructions in various languages. At first sight, these facts may appear to be nothing more than oddities, but they fall into a pattern once we assume a relation between comparative formation and the formation of coordinated (i.e., a special type of chaining) constructions.

On the one hand, we can note that, for a number of languages with a Particle Comparative, the comparative particle seems to be a lexical item that is also in use as a marker of (some type of) coordination between sentences. In Javanese, the element *karo* not only marks the standard NP in comparatives, but also occurs freely as the coordinating particle 'and'. Cp.:

(4)   JAVANESE:
a.   *Enak   daging karo iwak*
     is-good meat   than fish
     'Meat is better than fish'

b.   *Bapaq menjang ing-desa karo simboq menjang ing-desa uga*
     father go   to -field and mother go   to -field too
     'Father went to the field, and mother went to the field too'

In Toba Batak, the comparative particle *asa* is also in use as an adverbial consecutive marker, with the meaning 'and after that' or 'too':

(5)   TOBA BATAK:
a.   *Dumejak   utang-na asa   torop di obuk*
     more-many debt -his than crowd of hair
     'He has more debts than hairs on his head'

b.   *Ningon dapot   ho do   i   , asa gabe ho*
     first   have-got you EMPH this   then rich you
     'First you must have this, then you will be rich'

A similar situation as in Toba Batak may be claimed for the English comparative particle *than* (see Small, 1923: 8; see, however, Joly, 1967 for a different opinion), and possibly also for Standard Dutch, where the comparative particle *dan* is homonymous – and perhaps diachronically related – to the sentential consecutive marker *dan* 'then'. Cp.:

(6) STANDARD DUTCH:
a. Jan is groter dan Piet
   J.   is taller   than   P.
   'Jan is taller than Piet'

b. Eerst ga ik , dan gaat Jan
   first   go   I   then goes J.
   'First I will go, then Jan will go'

Furthermore, we observe that in Bari (Spagnolo, 1933: 266) the comparative particle *na gwon* functions as the adversative sentential coordinator 'but':

(7) BARI:
a. Nan kita   bya   na gwon do   yeyeju
   I   work more   than   you think
   'I work harder than you think'

b. Söromundi kata , na gwon kala 'bayin
   groundnuts exist   but   teeth exist-not
   'We have groundnuts, but no appetite'

The situation in Bari is identical to that in Basque and Ilocano, where the comparative particles (*baino* and *ngem*, respectively) also function as the adversative coordinator 'but':[2]

(8) BASQUE:
a. Jakes   baino lodi-ago da
   J.-NOM than   fat -PRT he-is
   'He is fatter than Jakes'

b. Ethorri   da   , bainan ez   gogotik
   come-PCP. PERF he-is   but   not voluntarily
   'He has come, but not out of free will'

(9) ILOCANO:
a. Nainimbag daitoy ngem daita
   good   this   than   that
   'This is better than that'

b. Nasayaat ti porlon -ko, ngem daan   bassiten
   good-one is carriage-my but   already oldish
   'My carriage is fine-looking, but it is already somewhat old'

Lastly, the use of the coordinator *but* as a comparative particle can be attested both in older variants of English and in at least some dialects of modern American English. Sentence *(10)* is a line from a play by William

Shakespeare, and sentence *(11)* is a quote from a song by Southern country-and-western singer Hank Williams:

> *(10)*   RENAISSANCE ENGLISH:
> *Thou knowst no less but all*   (Twelfth Night, 1,4)

> *(11)*   AMERICAN ENGLISH:
> *Ain't no more left but the blues to cry*

In this connection it is also worth noting that, in a number of languages, the comparative particle which marks the standard NP seems to be identical to the disjunctive coordination marker 'or'. Such a language is Classical Greek. Alexandre (1880: 644) cites the following phrases from the works of Plato:

> *(12)*   CLASSICAL GREEK:
> a.   *Chrēsthos ē poneros*
> good   or bad
> 'Good or bad'

> b.   *Sofoteros ē su*
> wiser   than you
> 'Wiser than you'

The same situation seems to have held in Gothic, where the item *thau* represented both comparison and disjunction (Benveniste, 1948: 140). In that same paper, Benveniste mentions the disjunctive and comparative particle *li* in Old Slavonic. Small (1923: 36) states that Swiss and Middle High German dialects employ the disjunctive element *weder* as a marker of standard NPs in NP-comparatives. Bergmans (1982: 78) reports that in several Eastflemish and Westflemish dialects there is a comparative particle *of*, which coincides with the disjunctive element *of* in Standard Dutch and Standard Flemish:

> *(13)*   EASTFLEMISH/WESTFLEMISH:
> a.   *Komt hij vandaag of morgen*
> comes he today   or tomorrow
> 'Will he come today or tomorrow?'

> b.   *Ik ben groter of mijn broer*
> I   am taller or my   brother
> 'I am taller than my brother'

There are also cases in which the comparative particle seems to be identical to the element which represents the negative coordinative particle 'nor'. In his discussion of the English comparative, Joly (1967: 17) states that *nor* used as a comparative particle 'is still alive in modern dialects, from the Shetland Islands to Cornwall, from Ireland to the United States'. Example *(14a)* was observed in a number of West-English dialects, and example *(14b)* in an American dialect:

(14)   NON-STANDARD ENGLISH:
a.   *I know better nor that*
b.   *It's richer nor you'll ever be*

Joly further mentions cases in which the positive disjunctive item *or* is used as a comparative particle in English dialects. The use of *or* as a comparative marker appears to have been widespread in Northern British dialects from about 1250 onwards, and can still be found today in Scottish dialects:

(15)   SCOTTISH ENGLISH:
         Der   no   a thing at   I leek better ir   a rosn   tattie
         there not a thing that   I like better or   a roast (?) potato
         'There is nothing I like better than a roast potato'

Speaking of Scotland, we should mention that Scottish Gaelic uses the negative coordination *na* 'nor' as the particle of comparison, a feature which is normal for Celtic languages. Cp.:

(16)   SCOTTISH GAELIC:
         Is baine Calum na   Seumas
         is fairer C.   than   S.
         'Calum is fairer than Seumas'

(17)   MIDDLE WELSH: (Strachan, 1909: 133)
         Na werthu   na   ellwng
         nor sell-FUT. 1SG nor   release-FUT. 1SG
         'I will neither sell it nor let it go'

Finally, the situation in Latvian's primary comparative is completely parallel to that in Gaelic:

(18)   LATVIAN: (Endzelin, 1922: 233)
a.   *Meitas   vecakas ne   mate*
         daughters older   than   mothers
         'The daughters are older than the mothers'

b.   *Man nau ne tes   ne   mat*
         I   have nor father nor   mother
         'I have neither father nor mother'

Not only do the comparative particles of various languages appear to exhibit relations to sentential coordinative (i.e., chaining) markers, but we also find cases where the obligatory morphological marking on the comparative predicate seems to be related to coordinating items. For instance, in Hindi (which has a Separative Comparative if the standard NP is overtly expressed) the predicate in a comparative construction in which there is no overt standard NP must be preceded by the element *aur*. This item is also commonly employed as the connective element 'and' between clauses and phrases:

(19)   *HINDI:*
a.   *Ap   aur   bare   haim*
     you   PRT   big   are
     'You are bigger'

b.   *Usne   bangla   sikhi   thi   aur   hindi*
     he   Bengali   learning   was   and   Hindi
     'He learned Bengali and Hindi'

A very similar situation is found in Goajiro, a language which we discussed in section 2.5. In Goajiro, the item *aulaka* 'and, too' is reportedly (see Holmer, 1949) very often found accompanying the predicate in comparative constructions:

(20)   *GOAJIRO:*
a.   *Aulaka   Rupeta   mulia'u   hulia   Rafaela*
     PRT   R.   big   than   R.
     'Roberto is taller than Rafaela'

b.   *Aulaka   etka   ci   ta -melei*
     and   dog   this   me-with
     'And this dog is mine'

In Tajik (Rastorgueva, 1963), the conjunction *kham* 'and, too' is at least phonetically identical to the marker of comparative predicates:

(21)   *TAJIK:*
a.   *Ruy-ash   az   barf   kham   safed   ast*
     face-her   from   snow   PRT   white   is
     'Her face is whiter than snow'

b.   *Shumo   na -rafted   man   kham   na -raftam*
     you   not-go-PAST. 2SG   I   and/too   not-go-PAST. 1SG
     'You did not go and neither did I'

An identical situation obtains in Ossetic (Abaev, 1964):

(22) OSSETIC:
a. *Deu-ej   chuyz-der*
   you-from   good -PRT
   'Better than you'

b. *Stalite serttivtoj , mej   der   skasti*
   stars   began-shine moon and/too rose
   'The stars began to shine, and the moon came up'

Lastly, we note that in Tamil (Beythan, 1943; Asher, 1982) the standard NP in comparatives is commonly followed by the suffix *-um*. This suffix is also the connective particle in conjunctions. Cp.:

(23) TAMIL:
a. *Agarar-il -um periyar   antanar*
   kings -from-PRT Brahmans are-great
   'Brahmans are greater than kings'

b. *Agarar-um periyar   -um*
   kings -PRT Brahmans-PRT
   'Kings and Brahmans'

All these facts, then, suggest that it might be worthwhile to take a look at coordinated (and other types of chaining) constructions as a possible determinant of comparative-type choice. But, of course, the actual proof of whether such a determining relation exists must be given by examining the predictions which follow from such an assumption for the languages in the sample. I will turn to this matter in part two of this study, after an exposition of the syntactic types of temporal chaining (chapter 4) and the final statement of the universals which I propose (chapter 5).

4

Types of Syntactic Chaining

4.1 Introduction

As has been noted by theoretical linguists, comparative linguists, and grammarians of single exotic languages, syntactic chaining of a series of event-expressing sentences or predicates can be employed to express two different states of affairs. Such a series can be used to express either *simultaneous action* (in which the events described by the predicates in the series are taken to happen at the same time), or *consecutive action*, which implies that the events described by the predicates occur one after the other. Thus, from a semantic point of view, we may conclude that the semantic notion of temporal chaining, as defined in the preceding chapter, allows for *two semantic subtypes*, one in which the propositions in the semantic representation are ordered with respect to temporal succession, and another in which no such ordering is imposed.

For a number of languages, the semantic distinction between simultaneous and consecutive chaining is matched by a syntactic differentiation at the level of surface structure. Such is the case in Igbo. As is pointed out in Welmers (1973), Igbo has a simultaneous action construction, in which the first verb in the series can be in any tense. All following verbs in the chain, however, must appear in the Incompletive Form, that is, a type of verbal phrase consisting of the particle *nà* followed by a verbal noun. Thus we have:

(1) *IGBO:*
    Ha   no   n'oce nà   èri   nri
    they sat down PRT eating food
    'They sat and ate/They sat eating'

In the consecutive action construction in Igbo, the first verb in the series may again be in any tense, but all following verbs have to be put into the so-called Narrative Form. In the regular case, this form consists of a verb stem with obligatory low tone and a verbal suffix *-é/-á*. Thus we get:

(2) IGBO:
O jiri egbe gbù-é   ago
he took gun kill-NARR leopard
'He took a gun and killed the leopard'

We can conclude, then, that in Igbo simultaneous action and consecutive action are formally kept apart in surface structure. In this particular language, syntactic differentiation between the two chaining types takes place by representing non-first predicates in a chain by means of formally different verbal formations. As we shall see in the following sections, other languages may employ different procedures to mark this differentiation; but since the actual mechanics of syntactic simultaneous and consecutive chaining in specific languages are largely beyond the scope of this study, we will not pursue this matter further here.

Opposed to cases like Igbo, we find other languages in which the semantic distinction between simultaneous and consecutive chaining is not matched by a syntactic opposition in surface structure, at least not in the typical case. For example, the English coordination (3) may be interpreted both as a case of simultaneous action and as a case of consecutive action, depending on whether John and Mary performed as a duo or whether they were two separate acts in some cultural happening:

(3) ENGLISH:
John played the flute and Mary recited a poem by Yeats

Similarly, Amharic (Cohen, 1936: 142) encodes its temporal chains by putting one of the predicates in the chain into the so-called Gerundial Form, while the other predicate is constructed as a main predicate. Gerundial Forms are subordinate but finite forms, which have no tense of their own; their exact temporal interpretation must be inferred from the tense marking on the main verb, and from contextual factors. Hence, in Amharic, the same subordinate form serves as the codification of both simultaneous and consecutive chaining:

(4) AMHARIC:
Talast   sastwo   tamallasna
enemy-NOM flee-GER. 3SG return-PERF. IND. 1PL
'While the enemy fled, we returned' or
'After the enemy had fled, we returned'

As a last example of languages of this sort, let us consider the syntactic chaining construction in Mandarin (Li and Thompson, 1978). In this language, a prominent way to encode cases of temporal chaining is the use of so-called serial verb constructions, in which predicates are strung together in a series without overt coordinative marking. An example of this type of chaining construction is the following:

(5)   MANDARIN:
      Tā kàn diànying chī píngguo
      he see movie   eat apple
      'He saw a movie and ate an apple'

Now, as Li and Thompson (1978: 241) remark, serial verb constructions in Mandarin are essentially indeterminate as to their temporal interpretation (and, for that matter, as to other semantic nuances). Thus, a serial verb construction may, on one case, receive a simultaneous interpretation (see *(6a)*), whereas in other cases this same syntactic construction is naturally interpreted as a consecutive chain:

(6)   MANDARIN:
   a. *Tā xiê   xiâoshuo mài gûdong*
      he write novel   sell antique
      'He writes novels and sells antiques'

   b. *Tā mâi piào jǐnqu*
      he buy ticket go-in
      'He bought a ticket and went in'

With regard to this situation, Li and Thompson (ibid.) state: 'What is evident . . . is that the serial verb construction is used to encode a number of different relationships between predicates in Mandarin. These predicate relationships are structurally distinct in most other languages because of the presence of grammatical markers.' Somewhat further on, they observe:

A good part of the knowledge of possible relationships between clauses in a sentence is acquired by normal people as a result of their experience in the world. This knowledge is language-independent and results from our perception of and experience with the world. Given any two events, there can only be a small, finite number of relationships between them. Language merely reflects and codifies these relationships in various multi-predicate constructions, although different languages employ different strategies in their codification. (p.244–5)

We may say, then, that in cases like English, Amharic and Mandarin the semantic distinction between simultaneous action and consecutive action has been *formally neutralized* in the codification of temporal chaining. As such, these languages are opposed to cases like Igbo, in which this semantic distinction is *mirrored* by two different procedures of syntactic encoding.

It should be remarked in this context that the boundary between neutralizing and mirroring languages is a fluid one, and that there are also cases of syntactic chaining which may be called instances of *partial neutralization*. As an example of such a case, let us consider a type of chain in Latin, the so-called Ablative Absolute construction. The details of this construction will be discussed in chapter 10; for the present purpose, a few general remarks may suffice. First, the Ablative Absolute can be used only for those cases of temporal chaining in which the subjects of the predicates in the chain are not identical. Secondly, in a chain of this type one of the predicates is constructed as a main predicate, while the other predicate receives the form of a non-finite participle; participles are nominal–adjectival forms which, like other nouns and adjectives, are marked for case, number and gender. A third feature of the Ablative Absolute is that the subject of the predicate with the participial form is put into an oblique case form, viz. the ablative case, and that the participle of which it is the subject is made to agree with it in case, gender and number; hence, the participle too is marked for ablative case. Examples of this type of Latin chaining construction are:

(7)   LATIN:
a.   *Domino*   *bibente*
     master-ABL. MASC. SG   drink-PCP. PRES. ABL. MASC. SG
     servae   *cantant*
     slave girls-NOM. PL   sing-PRES. IND. 3PL
     'While the master drinks, the slave girls sing'

b.   *Galliā*   *victā*
     G.-ABL. FEM. SG   conquer-PCP. PERF. PASS. ABL. FEM. SG
     Caesar   revenit
     C.-NOM   return-PERF. IND. 3SG
     'After Gallia had been conquered, Caesar returned'

The examples in (7) make it clear that the Ablative Absolute in Latin can be employed both for cases of simultaneous action and for cases of consecutive action: both types of temporal chaining involve the same syntactic procedure. However, it cannot be said that the Latin Ablative Absolute constitutes a complete neutralization of the semantic contrast at issue. Although the two sentences in (7) are derived by the same syntactic procedure, the participial forms which figure in these sentences are formally distinct: for the codification of simultaneous action by the Ablative Absolute the Present Participle has to be used, whereas the codification of consecutive action in this construction type requires the Perfect Participle. In other words, Latin has a procedure for the codification of temporal chaining which involves the application of one single structural procedure to two formally distinct non-finite predicative forms. We may conclude from this that the Latin Ablative Absolute is neither a case of complete neutralization like the serial verb construction in Mandarin, nor a case of complete diversification as illustrated by the two distinct structural procedures in Igbo. Hence, cases like the Latin Ablative Absolute will be referred to as instances of *partial neutralization*.

In the following sections, I will present a typology of the ways in which the two semantic subtypes of temporal chaining are syntactically encoded in the languages of my sample. Now, the phenomenon of (complete or partial) neutralization is a first indication of the fact that languages often use parallel or even identical procedures to codify simultaneous and consecutive chaining; this tendency will be formulated as a general principle in the final section of this chapter. However, in order to facilitate the exposition I have found it convenient first to deal with each of the semantic subtypes separately. In doing so, I will concentrate largely on the options which languages have in the codification of consecutive action; as it turns out, it is this subtype which is the more complex of the two, and which is therefore more in need of clarification.

4.2   The definition of the notion 'consecutive chain'

Before we can set up a typology of the ways in which consecutive action is syntactically encoded across languages, we will have to formulate a criterion for the cross-linguistic identification of this construction type; in other words, we need a language-independent definition of the notion 'consecutive chain' (or *C-chain* for short). As we saw in section 1.3.2, in typological syntax such language-independent definitions are necessarily of a semantic (or perhaps better: cognitive) nature. Hence, our first task now is to provide a further delineation of the notion 'consecutive chain' in semantic terms. The resulting definition of this notion should at least be tight enough to enable us to isolate the relevant construction in each of the languages of the sample.

As I indicated above, at the centre of the notion 'consecutive chain' lies the concept of *temporal succession of events*. That is, a minimal requirement for a construction to count as a C-chain is that it describes a situation in which events occur one after the other, in a fixed temporal order. By this requirement, consecutive chains are opposed to simultaneous chains *(S-chains)*, in which no such order is implied.

However, although the expression of temporal succession is a necessary condition on consecutive chains, there are reasons to assume that it is not a sufficient condition. As the literature on consecutive chaining shows, various authors state that an additional semantic condition should be imposed: the events in the C-chain should not only be temporally ordered, but in addition they should be conceived of as 'particularly closely related' (Welmers, 1973: 367). The exact nature of this 'close relationship' is hard to pin down, but it seems that, somehow, consecutive ordering implies more than just a mere temporal succession; it must also be the case that the ordered events in the chain should be conceived of as successive stages in the progress of one complex 'total event'. Conclusions to this effect can be derived from statements such as the one in Crazzolara (1933: 136), who states of the so-called Narrative Mood in Nuer: 'it is used for connecting *successive particulars of an event or transaction*' (my italics). Another example of an author who stresses the requirement that the events in a consecutive chain should be taken as the constituent particulars of one complex action is Labouret (1934). In describing the so-called Injunctive Form in Mandinka, this author remarks that the verbal construction at issue 'marks . . . that the performance of the action or the acquisition of the state is subordinated to the performance of another action or the acquisition of another state' (p.202; my translation). In connection with this additional condition of coherence between the successive events in a C-chain, it is also a telling fact that, in many languages, the primary examples of consecutive chaining tend to be constructions in which the first predicate in the chain describes a motion. Apparently, the kind of temporal succession which has the property of being consecutive is typically initiated by a movement, which, so to speak, 'triggers' the sequence of events of which the consecutive series consists. Thus, an initial movement appears to be pre-eminently appropriate to set up a context in which following events can be naturally interpreted as being contingent upon one another; many of the examples of C-chains which we will encounter are of the kind illustrated by the English sentences 'He went out and closed the door' or 'He stood up and left.'

It must be admitted that there remains a certain vagueness in the above definition of consecutive chaining, even if we accept the additional requirement of relationship or coherence between the events in such a chain. Therefore, in addition to postulating positive conditions, we may also employ a negative strategy to get a clearer picture of what must be counted as a consecutive chain in a given language. We may contrast consecutive chains with other types of constructions which also express a temporal ordering between events, and which can therefore be assumed to be semantically cognate to C-chains.

A first construction which comes readily to mind in this connection is the *final* or *purposive* construction. From a semantic point of view, constructions of this type are meant to express that, of two successive events, the first event is/was performed with the purpose of bringing about the second event. Typical English examples of this final construction include sentences in which the second event in the chain is encoded in the form of an infinitive, preceded by the conjunction *to* or *in order to*. Cp.:

(8)   ENGLISH:
a.   *John stood up to close the window*
b.   *John told that story in order to embarrass me*

Semantically speaking, final constructions are cognate to C-chains in that both construction types imply a successive ordering between events, and also an intimate relationship between the events in that succession. There is, however, also a clear semantic difference, which can be stated in terms of the *truth values* of consecutive and final assertions. Informally speaking, we can say that a final chain like *(8a)* is true even if the second event did not take place in reality; all that is needed for this assertion to be true is that the first event took place, and that there was some intention on John's part to perform the second action. In contrast, a C-chain like

(9)   ENGLISH:
      John stood up and closed the window

can only be said to be true if the closing of the window by John actually happened.

Notwithstanding this semantic difference, the dividing line between consecutive and final constructions is a diffuse one. This relative indeterminacy is at least partially due to the fact that, in consecutive constructions too, a purpose-reading is a natural implication; a C-chain like *(9)*, which, strictly speaking, must be read as stating only a mere succession of events, is readily interpreted as a sequence in which a specific intention on John's part is present. In other words, C-chains are likely to be interpreted as a series of events in which the first action is goal-oriented, and hence the demarcation between this type of construction and the neighbouring final construction tends to be blurred. The semantic overlap between the two constructions has its parallel in the syntactic encoding of the two constructions which can be observed in a number of languages. For instance, in Mangarayi (Eades, 1979) we find that there is one single device for the syntactic encoding of temporally successive events; the syntactic construction type in question may have a consecutive or a final interpretation, depending on the context. Also, in Mandarin (Li and Thompson, 1978) the serial verb construction which we discussed above is subject to this type of indeterminacy. Hence, a sentence like

(10) MANDARIN:
      Ta hui   'jiā   kān qīnqi
      he return home see parents
      'He returned home and saw/to see his parents'

may have both a consecutive and final reading. Even in English, we come across a construction in which features of final and consecutive chaining are combined. We can note that a sentence like *(11)* has the superficial form of a final chain, but the semantic content does not so much imply a purpose as a close succession of events. A parallel situation can be attested for Dutch. In this language, final constructions are typically encoded in the form of an infinitive preceded by the conjunction *om te* 'in order to' (see *(12a)*), but there are cases in which this construction must receive an interpretation which is more temporally successive than final (see *(12b)*). Cp.:

(11) ENGLISH:
      John came home to find his apartment looted

(12) DUTCH:
a.   *Ik ga naar Maastricht om mijn ouders te bezoeken*
      I   go to   M.   for my   parents to visit
      'I'm going to Maastricht to visit my parents'

b.   *De Boerenpartij   groeide stormachtig, om even   snel*
      The Farmers' Party grew   stormily   for equally rapidly
      weer te verdwijnen
      again to disappear
      'The Farmers' Party underwent a stormy growth, but had an equally rapid downfall'

In view of this fluctuating distinction between final and consecutive chaining, I have committed myself to the following guide-line. For those languages in which a clear syntactic separation can be demonstrated between chains that have an exclusive consecutive interpretation and chains with an exclusive final interpretation, I have excluded all instances of the latter construction from my data base. Final chains have been admitted to the data base only for those languages in which no definite distinctions between both types of constructions could be made. Thus, for example, the Mandarin construction illustrated in *(10)* is counted as an instance of a consecutive construction, even though one might equally be justified in rating it as an instance of final chaining.

Final chaining is not the only example of a construction type which tends to intrude upon the semantic area covered by consecutive chains. Most languages have also a type of construction which we may call *consecutional*. Here, the occurrence of a former event is seen as the fulfilment of a condition by which the occurrence of a later event is made possible. A typical English example of a consecutional construction is the following sentence:

(13)   ENGLISH:
John worked day and night so as to pay off his debts

As was the case with final chains, consecutional chains have a number of semantic features in common with consecutive chains: both types of construction imply a successive ordering between events, and both imply a certain close relationship between these events. Parallel to what we found in the case of final chains, we can also note a semantic difference here, which can be stated in terms of truth value; to put it briefly, a consecutional chain does not assert that the second event actually happened, whereas a consecutive chain does. Despite this semantic difference, however, we find that, at least for some languages, the distinction between consecutional and consecutive chaining is not formally expressed; Kanuri, a language which I will discuss in some detail in section 7.2.3, may be a case in point. Given this situation, I have adopted the same strategy for consecutional chains as I employed in the case of final chaining. Chains which may receive a consecutional interpretation are admitted to the data base only in those cases where the language has systematically neutralized the semantic differentiation between consecutional and consecutive chaining.

Finally, we find cases where constructions are neutral as to their interpretation between consecutive and *causal* or *concessive* chaining. In Latin, the Ablative Absolute construction, of which sentence *(14)* is another example:

(14)   LATIN:
Urbe   destructā
city-ABL. SG. FEM. destroy-PCP. PERF. PASS. ABL. SG. FEM
gaudebimus
be happy-FUT. IND. 1PL
'When/because/although the city has been destroyed, we will rejoice'

is essentially neutral between consecutive, causal and concessive readings. Again, we will take note of causal and concessive chains only in as far as a language fails to differentiate them formally from temporally interpreted chains.

Concluding this discussion on the notion 'consecutive chain', we may state the following. We will take this notion to be defined by at least the following semantic characteristics:

(a) the construction must express a successive temporal ordering between events;
(b) the construction must imply an intimate coherence between the events involved; and
(c) the construction must assert the actual performance of all the events in the chain.

As we have seen, there is some degree of semantic and formal overlap between the notion of 'consecutive chaining' and various other construction types which express successive temporal ordering. For this reason, the definition of the notion of consecutive chaining is not wholly airtight. It may be said, however, that, as far as our typological purposes are concerned, the above definition turns out to be reasonably applicable. I shall note explicitly those cases where there is some doubt as to the correct identification of the formal expression of consecutive chaining, and arguments for the actual decisions made in such a case will be discussed.

4.3   The formal expression of consecutive chaining

In this section I will introduce a first typological distinction in the ways in which consecutive chains are cross-linguistically encoded. To simplify the discussion, I will confine my examples to C-chains in which the consecutive relation holds between just two events. In discussing such consecutive pairs, I will use the term *anterior predicate* for the predicate which describes the earlier event in the chain; the other predicate in the chain will be called the *posterior predicate*. In the typical case, the semantic ordering between anterior and posterior events is matched formally by a left-to-right ordering in the syntactic expression of consecutive chains; as experiments by Eve Clark (1973, 1975) have shown, complex sentences in which the leftmost clause in surface structure expresses the earlier action in a succession are considerably easier to process than sentences in which this matching has been thwarted. Hence, the term *anterior predicate* covers a joint semantic and syntactic content: it refers to the predicate which describes the earlier event, and which is therefore the leftmost predicate in the syntactic C-chain. In the same way, the term *posterior predicate* refers to the predicate which describes the later event in a temporal succession, and which is therefore typically encoded as the rightmost predicate in the syntactic expression of that succession.

4.3.1   Two basic strategies: balancing and deranking

The first typological result of a cross-linguistic investigation of consecutive constructions can be stated as follows. In order to express the situation in which two events occur in a fixed consecutive order, a language may resort to one of two basic strategies. On the one hand, it may choose to express those two events by means of two independent clauses (and typically, though not necessarily, it will connect these clauses by means of a connective particle). In this case, the important thing is that the two predicates which express the two relevant actions remain structurally *of the same rank*; that is, they are embedded at the same level of structure (see Dik, 1968: 30). Hence, if the total construction is not embedded, both predicates in the chain will have the finite form of a main predicate. If the predicates happen to have the same subject, coordinative reduction of one of the subjects may take place, but this will not result in a 'de-balanced' structural configuration: a coordinated verb remains a finite verb, even if it has lost its subject, and it remains equally ranked to the other verb in the chain.

Chaining constructions in which predicates remain of the same rank I will call *balanced constructions*, and languages which choose this encoding option I will call *balancing languages*. Examples of balanced C-chains are the following:

(15)   ENGLISH:
       John jumped out of his chair and grabbed a gun

(16)   GUARANI:
       Oi-ke   kaagwi pe ha   o -henu petei avu
       he-went forest   in and he-heard one   noise
       'He went into the forest and heard a noise'

Thus, the defining characteristic of balancing languages is that their syntactic chains are structurally *coordinations*. As a consequence, consecutive chains in balancing languages are subject to the Coordinate Structure Constraint formulated in Ross (1967), as can be seen from the ill-formedness of *(17)* and *(18)*:

(17)   ENGLISH:
       What did John jump out of his chair and grab(bed)?

(18)   GUARANI:
       Ma?e pa oi -ke   kaagwi pe ha   o -henu   ?
       what Q he-went forest in and he-heard

Rather than keeping the balance, however, a language may also choose to represent the two predicates in a C-chain by reducing one of these predicates in rank. In such a case, only one of the predicates in the chain retains its finite verb form, whereas the other predicate is represented as a subordinate, usually non-finite, verbal construct. Languages of this type I will call *deranking languages*, and its syntactic chains I will call *deranked constructions*. From a strictly syntactic point of view, one may say that deranking languages do not have any consecutive coordination at all, since their surface structures do not permit consecutive predicates in configurations which embed them on an equal level of structure. That there is indeed subordination involved in deranked chains can be shown from examples in Tamil, a language in which consecutive chains are obligatorily deranked. Thus, in Tamil we find the following construction (taken from Annamalai, 1970):

(19)   TAMIL:
       Avaru   kavide   erudiittu   naaval
       he-NOM poetry-ACC write-PERF. GER novel-ACC
       moripeyarttaaru
       translate-PAST. IND. 3SG
       'He wrote poetry and then translated a novel'

In (19), one of the predicates (viz. *moripeyarttaaru* 'he translated') is represented as a finite main verb in the Indicative Past, while the other predicate (viz. *erudiittu* 'having written') has the non-finite subordinate form of the Perfect Gerund. Now, it can be shown that such Tamil sentences cannot be regarded as structural coordinations. In particular, the Coordinate Structure Constraint no longer applies; as the well-formed example (20) illustrates, it is possible to relativize the complement of the finite verb in (19):

(20)   TAMIL:
       Avaru   kavide   erudiittu   moripeyartta
       he-NOM poetry-ACC write-PERF. GER translate-PCP. PAST
       naaval
       novel
       '*lit:* the novel which he wrote poetry and translated'

4.3.2   *Deranking versus clause-embedding*

Regarding the concept of deranking which we introduced in the previous section, it may be useful to add a few clarifying remarks. To eliminate a possible source of confusion, it should be stressed at this point that the notion of deranking will be defined here as applying exclusively to the predicates of sentences, and not to whole sentences or clauses. In other words, I will classify a language as a deranking language only if, in the codification of its temporal chains, it is *the form of the predicate* in one of the sentences itself which signals the subordination of that sentence. Languages may employ various formal means to achieve this subordinate marking of predicates. But whatever the exact procedure for deranking may be, the essential point is that, in order for a construction to be called deranked, it must be the predicate of one of the sentences itself which is marked as a form of non-equal rank to the main predicate in the chain.

The above definition of the concept of deranking is meant to create a sharp delineation between the deranking of predicates and another possibility of subordination, viz. *the embedding of whole clauses* in the syntactic encoding of a temporal chain. As I see it, in encoding a temporal chain a language may choose one of three structural options (and sometimes more than one of these options). First, the language may choose to encode temporal chains in the form of a coordination; in that case, the language will be called a balancing language. A second possibility is to downgrade the whole of one of the sentences in the chain, and to subordinate it to the other sentence, which will then become the main clause in the chaining construction. Usually, this second possibility of complete clause-embedding is effectuated by means of a subordinating conjunction. An English example of a C-chain in which this second option has been chosen is:

(21)   ENGLISH:
After John had left, I poured myself a well-deserved drink

In this construction, the anterior sentence in the C-chain (viz. *John left*) has been embedded as a whole in the form of a subordinate clause, marked by the subordinating conjunction *after*.

A typical characteristic of a case of clause-embedding is that it is not the predicate of the subordinate clause as such which has been marked for subordination; it is rather the whole anterior (or, as the case may be, posterior) sentence which has been marked as such. As a result, the predicate in a subordinate clause like the *after*-clause in *(21)* is a normal finite verb form, which is characterized by the same morphological devices as the main verb in the construction.[1]

Now, I will assume that balancing and clause-embedding are two variants of one and the same structural strategy. Both options share the feature that the clauses as such are kept intact in surface structure. One might say, equivalently, that under both options both of the clauses in the chain retain their full sentential characteristics, a fact which must be formally represented by the presence of two separate S-nodes in the surface P-markers of these constructions. In my opinion, the choice between a balanced coordination or the embedding of one of the clauses in a chain is not so much a matter of structural necessities as a result of the application of functional considerations. In certain contexts, there may be reasons for a functional (or, if one prefers that term, a pragmatic) backgrounding of one of the events in the chain.[2] If such a backgrounding occurs, the structural match of this procedure will be the embedding of one of the clauses in the chain, whereas in the absence of such a need for backgrounding a coordinate structure appears to be the most appropriate way to codify the chain. In this connection, we may point out that, apparently, the boundaries between coordination and clause-embedding are not very sharp anyway; for an elaboration of this point see Talmy (1978). At any rate, we will adopt the view here that consecutive (and, in general, temporal) chains which are encoded as cases of clause-embedding do not form a significant variant in our typology of chain formation. Hence, such cases will be lumped together with balanced constructions in the typology.

Opposed to balanced and clause-embedded constructions we find cases of what might be called 'real' deranking, that is, cases in which the predicate of one of the sentences in the chain has itself been marked for subordination. Thus, we will count as instances of deranking languages only those languages in which the verbal form of the subordinate clause in a temporal chain has undergone a specific formal change, so that this predicate is formally distinguished from finite main predicates. The construction in Tamil which we illustrated in sentence *(19)* is a case in point: in this construction, the predicate of the anterior clause in a C-chain receives a specifically marked morphological form, viz. the form of the non-finite Perfect Gerund. In some languages, deranking of a predicate leads to the reduction of one of the sentences in the chain to the status of a phrase instead of a clause; that is, sentences in which a predicate has been deranked are no longer dominated by a separate S-node. It should not be thought, however, that this complete loss of sentential status is a necessary defining condition on our notion of 'deranked structure'; other languages may choose less radical solutions in the representation of deranked clauses, so that at least some of the sentential properties are retained in the surface representation of such clauses. Once more, it should be emphasized that the defining character-istic of the notion of deranking which is used here consists of *the explicit subordinate marking on the predicate of a clause.*

At the risk of labouring the obvious, let me point out that, given our definition of deranking, English sentences like the ones in *(22)* will be rated as instances of deranked chains, since the predicate in one of their clauses is, by virtue of its participial form, specifically marked for subordination. On the other hand, the semantically equivalent sentence *(23)* is a case of clause-embedding and hence, in our view, essentially a balanced structure:

(22)   ENGLISH:
a.   *Having locked the door, John undressed*
b.   *After locking the door, John undressed*

(23)   ENGLISH:
     After John had locked the door, he undressed

Thus, one might say that, of two possible interpretations of the notion of deranking, I will choose the definition which defines the narrower set of structures. Clearly, if a language deranks its predicates (in the sense which we adopted above), that language will also necessarily downgrade its temporal clauses. The opposite, however, need not be the case. For instance, we find that in Guarani both coordinated structures and cases of embedded temporal clauses are possible, but that this language appears to lack the means to derank its predicates in temporal chains. For this reason, Guarani will be classified not as a deranking, but as a balancing language.

To be sure, it is not always easy to decide whether a particular case of a non-coordinated chaining construction is a case of 'real' predicate deranking, or rather a case of clause-embedding. To give but one example of a language in which this kind of indeterminacy occurs, let us consider the consecutive construction in Tibetan. From the description of this language given in Lalou (1950), we learn that the anterior clause in a Tibetan C-chain contains the element *-nas*, a particle which is also in use as the marker of the ablative case in nominals:

(24)   TIBETAN:
     Yul   -la bleb -nas   ri -la son
     village-to arrive-from hill-to went
     'He arrived at the village and went to the hills'

Now, the problem with which this Tibetan construction confronts us is this. From the surface form of this construction, it is very hard to judge whether the marker *-nas* functions as a marker on the predicate in the anterior clause, or as a subordinating conjunction which is used to subordinate the anterior clause as a whole. One might argue that the subordinative marker *-nas* is morphologically bound to the anterior predicate, and that therefore this construction can be rated as an instance of (consecutive) deranking. Unfortunately, however, such an argumentation lacks decisive force. In fact, one might just as well argue that *-nas* is a subordinating conjunction which is placed in clause-final position, and which is then attached to the last item in the clause, by the application of some morpho-phonological rule of attraction. Since Tibetan is a very strict verb-final language, it will normally be the predicate which is the last item in a clause, so that the attachment of *-nas* to the predicate is only to be expected; but this does not necessarily imply that the scope of the item *-nas* cannot include the anterior clause as a whole. We must conclude, then, that the attachment of *-nas* to the predicate in the anterior clause in itself does not allow us to rate this predicate as a deranked form.

Other arguments which, in other languages, can be adduced to force a decision between deranked or embedded status of a clause also fail to apply in Tibetan. For instance, one finds in many languages that deranked predicates lack a number of verbal categories which 'normal' finite main verbs have; in particular, it is common for deranked predicates to have lost the ability to agree with their subjects in person and/or number. This criterion, however, is of no help in the case of Tibetan, since in this language no predicate (not even a main predicate) ever shows any person/number agreement with its subject. In other words, the absence of agreement fails to distinguish between deranked and non-deranked predicates in Tibetan, and, accordingly, the fact that the predicate in the anterior clause in *(24)* does not show agreement with its subject is of no consequence here.

Luckily, however, we can trace a number of other characteristics which differentiate the predicate in anterior consecutive clauses from main predicates in Tibetan temporal chains. We can observe that, while predicates in Tibetan are never marked for subject agreement, they can be morphologically marked for tense; the verb for 'to drink', for example, has a Present form *a-thun*, a Future form *d-thun*, and a Perfect form *b-tun*. Now, one of the properties of the predicate in a Tibetan anterior clause like the one in *(24)* is that it can never be marked for tense; in this type of construction, predicates invariably appear in their root form, deriving their temporal interpretation from the tense marking on the following main predicate. From this we can conclude that, in Tibetan, predicates in anterior consecutive clauses are at least in some respect different from main clause predicates: they are defective in some of the categories of verbal flexion which this language allows. On these grounds, one may be justified in rating the anterior clause in (24) as an instance of 'real' deranking, rather than as an instance of 'mere' clause-embedding. As a result, one may classify Tibetan as a deranking language.

4.3.3 The morphology of deranked predicates

Discussions of cases such as the above example from Tibetan lead us to a second point which is connected with the notion of deranking, viz. the variety of ways in which deranked predicates are formally manifested in surface structure. As I stated earlier, the actual morphological outcome of the deranking procedure may diverge from one language to another. In Tibetan, a deranked predicate takes the form of a verbal root, which is marked further by the attachment of an adverbial case suffix. In Tamil, specific gerundial forms are used to derank consecutive predicates; while English can, among other things, represent a deranked consecutive predicate in the form of a Perfect Participle. These three formations by no means exhaust the options for the morphological encoding of deranking predicates; in part two we will come across a large variety of deranked forms, many of which are completely different from the ones we have met so far.

Now, in our typology of chaining constructions, the morphological form which a deranked predicate takes in a particular language will not be taken to constitute a categorizing factor. That is, I will not propose a division among deranked constructions on the basis of the differences in the morphological manifestation of deranked predicates. In my estimation, the factors which influence the choice of, say, a gerund or a participle as the representation of a deranked predicate in a given language do not play a part in the explanation of the typological variation of comparative constructions; and, as may be recalled, it is this explanation which the typology of chaining constructions is meant to foster. Hence, the actual forms which deranked predicates may assume will not be treated systematically in this essay; they will only be gone into for the purpose of illustration.

Nevertheless, it may be of some use to the reader if he has at least some general idea of the various ways in which deranking of predicates can be effectuated across languages. To give some global indication of this variation, we can note first that, in a considerable number of languages, deranking of a predicate is brought about by a *reduction* of the verbal morphology which is normally allowed to predicates. Above, we hinted at the fact that deranked predicates are often characterized by the loss of personal flexion. In other cases, such as Tibetan, we find that deranked predicates cannot take the normal tense affixes, while in still other languages deranked predicates appear to be severely restricted in the choice of mood and aspect marking. Moreover, it should not be thought that this reduction of verbal morphology can affect only one verbal category at a time; we find cases where deranked predicates have suffered a loss of both personal flexion and tense marking, of both tense marking and mood marking, and so on.

A second general strategy in the deranking of predicates (which may in fact be a more radical application of the reductionist strategy mentioned above) involves *a change of category status of the deranked predicate.* We often find cases in which the deranked predicate has lost some or all of its verbal characteristics, and has been turned into a nominal form (e.g., an infinitive or an action nominal), an adverbial form (for which the traditional term 'gerund' will be used here), or an adjectival form (e.g., a participle).

Thirdly, deranking may be effectuated by a strategy which is more or less the opposite of morphological reduction. In such a case, the deranked predicate is marked by *the addition of some specific marker,* or by the application of a special subordinate conjugational form, a so-called 'dependent mood'.

Lastly, we should remark that it is quite normal for a language to combine different strategies in the morphological codification of its deranked predicates. As the above example from Tibetan shows, the deranking of a predicate can be effectuated by a reduction in tense, while at the same time involving the addition of a specific (in this case, ablative) marker.

4.4 Aspects of consecutive deranking

In the preceding section, I stated that the cross-linguistic variation in the morphological outcome of the deranking procedure will not be regarded as a significant typological factor in this essay. From this, it should not be inferred that the category of deranked constructions will from now on be treated as an undivided whole. While consecutive constructions in balancing languages show a great deal of structural uniformity (in that, basically, they are all coordinate structures), consecutive constructions in deranking languages may differ from one another in at least two respects, which are connected with structural conditions that can be imposed on the deranking procedure. As I will argue later on, the typological variation which is brought about by these two structural factors is instrumental in the explanation of (at least a part of) the typological variation of comparatives. Hence, these two factors must be rated as typologically significant, given the explanatory purpose for which the typology of chaining constructions is set up. In the following sections, I will comment on these two factors, and discuss the interrelation which appears to exist between them.

4.4.1   Conditionality

If we take a look at the various languages in which deranking of one of the predicates in a consecutive chain is permitted, we note that, for a number of languages, the application of the deranking procedure appears to be restricted by specific structural conditions. In particular, we find that there are languages which can derank consecutive predicates only in cases where the two predicates in the C-chain have *identical subjects*; if different subjects are involved, the construction must remain balanced. Such a situation we encounter in Wolof (Rambaud, 1903). In this language, C-chains with identical subjects derank their posterior predicates into a subjunctive form, which is characterized by the presence of a specific particle *a* and special rules for the placement of pronouns. If the subjects in the C-chain are not identical, the only option is the use of a coordinate construction, which may be asyndetic, but can also contain the coordinative particle *te* 'and'. Cp.:

(25)   WOLOF:
a.   *Demal   a   o*
       go-IMP SUBJCT. PRT   call-SUBJCT   him
       'Go and call him'

b.   *Nyeu   on   na   te   wakh   on   na   ma   ko*
       come   PAST   IND. PRT   and   tell   PAST   IND. PRT   I   him
       'He came and I told (it to) him'

As far as I know, there is no traditional label for the set of constructions (and languages) in which this specific identity-condition on consecutive deranking holds. In what follows, I will refer to this group of constructions as *conditionally deranked* consecutive constructions, and the group of languages which exhibit this possibility will be termed *languages with conditional* (consecutive) *deranking*.

In opposition to those languages in which the deranking procedure is subject to a structural condition on subject-identity, we also find languages in which no such condition seems to obtain. That is, these languages may derank one of the predicates in a C-chain *regardless of whether the predicates in the chain have identical or non-identical subjects*. As a consequence, such languages can have consecutive constructions in which both the deranked predicate and the finite main predicate have their own overt subject. In keeping with traditional terminology, I will use the term *absolute construction* for a construction type in which a deranked predicate has its own overt subject; hence, languages in which such a structural possibility exists will be called instances of *absolute deranking languages*.

An example of a language in which absolute consecutive deranking is clearly possible is Tamil. Judging from sentence *(26)*, it appears that, in this language, the deranked consecutive predicate (i.e., the gerundial form *kuduttu* 'having given') and the fiinite main predicate (*poonan* 'went') may have their own separate subject (viz. *naan* 'I' and *avan* 'he', respectively). Cp.:

(26) TAMIL:

Naan panan   kuduttu   avan   sinimaa-vukku
I-NOM money-ACC give-GER. PERF he-NOM movie -to
poonan
go-PAST. IND. 3SG
'I gave (him) money and he went to a movie'

Another example of this absolute deranking of C-chains can be found in Maasai. In this language, deranking takes place by putting the posterior predicate in a C-chain in the so-called Dependent Mood, a subordinate verbal form which is characterized by the prefix *n-* and the absence of tense marking. As sentence *(27b)* shows, identity of subjects is not required in this construction. Cp.:

(27) MAASAI:
a.   E -iput-a   emoti n -e -pik en-kima
     she-fill -PAST   pot   DEP -she-put on-fire
     'She filled the pot and put it on the fire'

b.   E -iput-a   emoti n -a-pik en-kima
     she-fill -PAST   pot   DEP -I-put on-fire
     'She filled the pot and I put it on the fire'

For the sake of clarity, it should be noted explicitly that our notion of absolute deranking is defined here so as to include the possibility of conditional deranking. That is, languages which permit the deranking of predicates under non-identity of subjects will always allow deranking to take place in cases of subject-identity, but the converse does not hold.

Alternatively, we may state as a universal fact of natural language that there are no languages in which deranking under non-identity of subjects is possible while at the same time deranking under identity of subjects is forbidden. Apparently, conditional deranking is, somehow, easier to execute than deranking under non-identity of subjects. Hence, given the plausible principle that one can perform a difficult task only if one has mastered all the easier ones, it is only to be expected that the possibility of absolute (i.e., non-identity) deranking will necessarily imply the ability to achieve deranking under identity of subjects.

With respect to the concepts of conditional and absolute deranking which are developed here, two additional remarks need to be made. First, we should comment on cases of uniformity and differentiation in the procedures for these two types of deranking. As we stated above, languages which allow for absolute deranking may derank their consecutive predicates both in cases of identity and in cases of non-identity of subjects. Now, in the above examples from Tamil (see sentences *(19)* and *(26)*) and Maasai (see sentences *(27a/b)*) we can observe a parallelism in the deranking procedure, in that the deranking of a predicate in a C-chain is always effectuated by the same morpho-syntactic mechanism, regardless of whether there is identity or non-identity of subjects in the chain. For example, the Dependent Mood in Maasai can be used both in deranked chains with identical subjects (see *(27a)*) and for deranked predicates which have a subject that is different from the subject of the main predicate (see *(27b)*). It should not be inferred, however, that such a uniformity of the deranking procedure is mandatory for languages with absolute deranking. We can also find cases of absolute deranking languages in which deranked predicates receive morpho-syntactically different forms, depending on whether there is identity or non-identity of subjects in the chain. A case in point is Latin. As can be seen from the sentences *(4a/b)* and *(14)*, absolute deranking in Latin C-chains requires the use of the Ablative Absolute construction. However, in Latin C-chains with identical subjects the Ablative Absolute is not employed; in this case, the anterior predicate receives the form of a participle which agrees in case, gender and number with the subject of the main predicate. Cp.:

(28)   *LATIN:*
   Pompeius victus   *necatus est*
   P.-NOM   defeat-PCP. PERF. PASS. -NOM. SG. MASC   killed   is
   'Having been defeated, Pompeius was killed'

Another case of this differentiation between the procedures for absolute and conditional deranking can be documented in Burushaski (Lorimer,

1935). In this language, we find that a C-chain with identical subjects requires the deranking of the anterior predicate into a Past Participle (see *(29a)*). However, when the subjects in the chain are not identical, the anterior predicate must be turned into a verbal noun, which is then put into the ablative case (see *(29b)*). Cp.:

(29)   BURUSHASKI:
a.   *Dinin*   *dogaru-su -mi*
      come-PCP. PAST asked -her-3SG. MASC
      'He came and made inquiries about her'

b.   *Xurts   lang   manum-tsum   mumie*
      dust-NOM   away move-VN-ABL mother-his-NOM
      yet -su -man
      saw-him-3SG. FEM
      'The dust moved away and his mother saw him'

As a second remark, it should be pointed out that matters are actually somewhat more complicated than a simple bipartition into conditional and absolute deranking suggests. For some languages (e.g., Latin and Mangarayi), we find that conditional deranking is not only possible if the subjects of the two predicates in the chain are identical; in addition, the procedure for conditional deranking can also be applied if the subject of the deranked predicate is identical to *some other, non-subject, NP in the other clause of the chain*. Thus, in addition to a case of 'real' conditional deranking like *(30a)*, in which there is subject-identity for both predicates in the C-chain, Latin also allows constructions like *(30b)*; in this latter construction, a predicate has been deranked conditionally on the basis of the fact that its subject is identical to the *indirect object* of the other clause. Cp.:

(30)   LATIN:
a.   *Pompeius victus*   *Caesari   naves*
      P.-NOM   defeat-PCP. PERF. PASS. NOM C.-DAT ships-ACC
      reddidit
      give back-PERF. IND. 3SG
      'After Pompeius had been defeated, he gave back the ships to Caesar'

b.   *Caesar   Pompeio victo*   *naves*
      C.-NOM P.-DAT   defeat-PCP. PERF. PASS. DAT ships-ACC
      reddidit
      give back-PERF. IND. 3SG
      'After Pompeius had been defeated, Caesar gave the ships back to him'

It must be said, however, that this possibility of conditional deranking under identity with a non-subject is rather marginal in natural languages. As far as I know, no language permits this type of non-subject identity on conditional deranking while at the same time forbidding conditional deranking under subject-identity. On the other hand, there are numerous languages which permit conditional deranking *only if* the identity relation holds between two subjects.

It must be noted that we will consider cases of deranking like the Latin sentence *(30b)* as a (marginal) instance of conditional deranking, and not as an instance of absolute deranking. The reason for this is that, in sentences like *(30b)*, there is at least some condition of identity involved, even if this identity does not hold between two subjects. On the other hand, in cases of absolute deranking no condition of identity holds between any constituents of the two clauses in the chain.

4.4.2   Directionality

In addition to the typological variation brought about by the presence or absence of subject-identity conditions, there is a second structural factor which leads to a typological subcategorization of deranked consecutive constructions. This factor concerns *the direction of the deranking procedure*. That is, we can divide deranked C-chains into two typologically significant classes, on the basis of whether it is the anterior predicate or the posterior predicate which is affected by the deranking procedure. In what follows, I will refer to these two options as *anterior (consecutive) deranking* and *posterior (consecutive) deranking*, respectively.

Now, it can be observed that, in the choice between anterior and posterior consecutive deranking, *basic word order* seems to play a determining role. In particular, it appears to be the rule that *deranking languages with SOV word order derank all anterior predicates in a consecutive chain*; that is, they derank all predicates in a C-chain except the last one. Thus, the unmarked case for a C-chain in a deranking SOV-language is a construction in which only the last predicate in the chain retains its finite form, while all preceding predicates receive the form of a participle, a gerund or some other specifically marked morphological complex. The preference of deranking SOV-languages for anterior consecutive deranking is illustrated in the examples from Latin, Tamil and Burushaski quoted above, and in the following sentence from Korean:

(31) KOREAN:
Pulle   il   sigjera
call-PERF. GER work force-IMP
'Call him and force him to work'

In deranking SVO-languages and VSO-languages, the opposite directionality seems to be the rule. In deranking languages with these basic word orders, the unmarked case is that only the first predicate in a consecutive chain retains its finite status, while all following predicates are deranked into root forms, infinitives, verbal nouns or specific conjugational forms. Clear examples of SVO-languages which have posterior consecutive deranking are Igbo, where deranked consecutive predicates receive a special Narrative Form (see *(2)*), and Wolof, where posterior consecutive predicates are marked by the particle *a* and the Subjunctive Mood (see *(25a)*). A third example of the preference of deranking SVO-languages for posterior consecutive deranking is the following sentence from Bari (Spagnolo, 1933). In this language, deranked posterior predicates in C-chains appear in the form of the so-called Narrative Imperative, a verbal formation which 'happens to resemble the Imperative, beginning each phrase usually with the copula *á*' (Spagnolo, 1933: 13). Cp.:

(32) BARI:
Nan a   -tu mede á   nan rené . . .
I   IND. PAST-go home PRT I   sweep-IMP
'I went home and swept (the house) and . . .'

In VSO-languages, the process of consecutive deranking is a bit more elusive. Part of the difficulty is that, quite often, VSO-languages lack many or all categories of verbal flexion, so that the distinction between finite and deranked verbal forms tends to be blurred from the outset. Nevertheless, in those VSO-languages in which deranked consecutive forms can be established, we note a clear preference for the deranking of posterior predicates. Above, we mentioned the case of Maasai (see *(27a/b)*), a VSO-language in which posterior predicates get marked for 'Dependent Mood'. Another example of this preference for posterior deranking is Jacaltec (Craig, 1977), where we find that the posterior predicate in a C-chain must be marked by the subordinating suffix *-ni*. Cp.:

(33) JACALTEC:
Speba ix te   pulta sah -ni   ix te wentana
closed she the door opened-PRT she the window
'She closed the door and opened the window'

In summary, then, we can formulate the following two universal statements on the directionality of consecutive deranking:

(34) a. *If an SOV-language deranks its C-chains, it will derank anterior predicates.*
     b. *If SVO-languages or VSO-languages derank their C-chains, they will derank posterior predicates.*

It is only fair to point out here that these two statements must be taken as tendencies rather than laws: they formulate the unmarked cases of directionality. Thus, for instance, statement *(34a)* implies that it is normal for a deranking SOV-language to prefer anterior deranking of consecutive predicates, but this preference should not be conceived of as a law which permits no deviation. In our sample, we come across at least one counterexample to statement *(34a)*; Kanuri is a deranking SOV-language which nonetheless prefers posterior deranking in C-chains.[3] With statement *(34b)*, counterexamples are even more numerous. Finnish, English, Dutch and French are all cases of SVO-languages which have at least marginal possibilities for deranking, and these languages all prefer anterior deranking procedures.[4] Similar remarks can be made for Classical Arabic and Biblical Hebrew; these two VSO-languages have a marginal possibility to derank C-chains, and the procedure which they prefer is the deranking of the anterior instead of the posterior predicate. However, despite these counterexamples, I hold that we are justified in saying that the conclusions in *(34)*, if taken as tendencies, can be shown to be fairly well established. I trust that the general empirical validity of these two tendencies will become more apparent in the chapters of part two, where individual instances of consecutive deranking will be presented.

Apart from the question of the empirical validity of the statements in *(34)*, it is also natural to ask whether there is a principled explanation for the state of affairs which they describe. Of course, one might very well argue that the explanation of these correlations between deranking types and word order types is really beyond the scope of our investigation. It will be recalled that the motivation for the establishment of a typology of chaining constructions lies in the assumption that such a typology may prove to be useful as a determinant of the typology of comparatives. From this perspective, the fact that this 'second' typology turns out to be correlated with word order preferences may be rated as an interesting, but essentially concomitant phenomenon. Although I agree that such a position is certainly defendable, I would nonetheless like to offer some speculations on the reasons behind the word order preferences of certain types of deranking. To the extent in which these speculations are plausible, support is given to our claim that the word order preferences of certain comparative types, which we formulated in section 3.2, are not accidental, but can be accounted for automatically once we assume that comparative-type choice is determined by the possibilities of chaining-type choice.

As I see it, the correlations between word order and deranking type which are laid down in *(34)* can be accounted for on the basis of the following general principle:

The Forward Principle of Deranking:
If a language deranks its consecutive chains, deranking will affect the *posterior* predicate, unless there is some special reason to reverse this direction.

Thus, this principle claims that the directionality of deranking which is opted for by SVO-languages and VSO-languages is the unmarked case of directionality. Behind this principle we may postulate a general functional or perceptual strategy, according to which the decoding of a deranked predicate is easier when it is encountered after the main predicate in the chain has been decoded. In this case, the structural position and function of the deranked predicate has already been defined by the main predicate, whereas, if this order is reversed, the structural decoding of the deranked predicate has to be suspended until the main predicate has been perceived. That the Forward Principle of Deranking is not applicable to SOV-languages can be attributed to the fact that in these languages it is mandatory to have a finite main verb in sentence-final position. If SOV-languages were to follow the Forward Principle, finite predicates would never be able to turn up in their obligatory position, and hence there is no other choice for these languages than to reverse the direction of the deranking procedure. For languages with SVO or VSO order, there is no obligation to place finite predicates in sentence-final position, which is why they can follow the Forward Principle and have posterior consecutive deranking.

4.4.3 The interrelation of conditionality and directionality

In the two preceding sections, we have noted that the cases of deranked consecutive constructions can be subcategorized along either one of the following two parameters:

(a) *Conditionality:* a deranked C-chain may be either a case of *conditional* deranking or a case of *absolute* deranking.
(b) *Directionality:* a deranked C-chain may be either a case of *anterior* deranking or a case of *posterior* deranking.

Now, if it were the case that these two parameters were completely independent, the categorization of deranked C-chains would obviously lead to four subtypes. As it turns out, however, one of these logically possible subtypes does not occur in reality, due to the fact that there seems to exist an interdependency of the two parameters in question. To be specific, there is no counterexample in my sample to the following universal claim:

(35)   *If a language has anterior deranking* (and is therefore typically SOV; see section 4.4.2), *it has absolute deranking.*

Thus, the sample does not provide us with one single instance of a language in which anterior consecutive predicates can be deranked only if there is identity of subjects between the clauses in the chain. In other words, at least one logically possible subtype of consecutive deranking (viz. a chain with *conditional anterior deranking*) does not appear to exist. Again, the discussions in part two will clearly demonstrate that *(35)* is a hard empirical fact.

With respect to cases of *posterior* deranking of consecutive predicates, we can observe that the two logically possible variants are indeed represented in the data. That is, of the languages which prefer posterior deranking in C-chains some can be shown to have only conditional deranking, while others permit the wider option of absolute deranking. It turns out, however, that the choice for absolute or conditional deranking is not wholly unpredictable in this case; the options on this point appear to be firmly tied up with the basic word order of the languages in question. For the languages in my sample, the following two statements are nearly without exceptions:

(36)   a.   *If a language has posterior consecutive deranking and its word order is SVO, then it has conditional deranking.*
       b.   *If a language has posterior consecutive deranking and its word order is VSO, then it has absolute deranking.*

With regard to these two universals, I must refer once more to the data in part two, especially those in chapter 7 and chapter 8. It will become clear there that the statements in *(36)* represent valid generalizations, to which only incidental counterexamples can be found in the sample.

The statements in *(34)*, *(35)* and *(36)* can be brought together in the following universal tendencies, which state the correlations between word-order type and type of consecutive deranking:

(37) a. *Languages with absolute consecutive deranking have either SOV or VSO word order.*
   b. *Languages with absolute anterior consecutive deranking typically have SOV word order.*
   c. *Languages with absolute posterior consecutive deranking typically have VSO word order.*
   d. *Languages which permit only conditional deranking of C-chains have posterior deranking and typically prefer SVO word order.*

Again, while the empirical validity of these statements is beyond dispute, it is justifiable to ask for an explanation of the correlations laid down in *(37)*. I do not have the pretension that I can offer a conclusive answer on this point, but I would like to advance the following considerations. In deranking languages with SOV or VSO word order, the consecutive predicate which undergoes deranking is perceived by the hearer (and, presumably, also encoded by the speaker) *before the second subject in the chain is perceived.* Thus, in a deranking SOV-language, which has C-chains of the following general form:

$$S_1 \quad O \quad V_1 \quad - \quad S_2 \quad O \quad V_2$$

the anterior predicate (V_1) must be deranked; as can be seen, this predicate is ordered in the chain prior to the second subject (S_2). A similar situation obtains in deranking VSO-languages. Again, the predicate which undergoes deranking (i.e., the posterior predicate V_2) is ordered before the second subject S_2. Cp.:

$$V_1 \quad S_1 \quad O \quad - \quad V_2 \quad S_2 \quad O$$

In contrast to this situation in SOV-languages and VSO-languages, deranking SVO-languages have C-chains in which the deranked predicate (viz. the posterior predicate V_2) *follows the second subject S_2.* Cp.:

$$S_1 \quad V_1 \quad O \quad - \quad S_2 \quad V_2 \quad O$$

In view of this contrast, the following conclusion suggests itself. In deranking SOV-languages and VSO-languages, deranking of predicates is perceived before identity or non-identity of subjects in a chain is established, while in deranking SVO-languages identity conditions on the subjects in the chain are known at the time that the deranked predicate is perceived. From this, one might venture the hypothesis that deranking languages with SOV or VSO order must have the freedom to derank their consecutive predicates under any conditions, whereas deranking SVO-languages can limit themselves to the 'easier' procedure of conditional deranking. It goes without saying, however, that this explanation of the facts in *(37)* is rather a tentative one, and that much psycholinguistic research into the process of deranking will be needed before we can tell whether there is any plausibility to an analysis of this kind.

4.4.4   Subtypes of consecutive deranking

If we accept the validity of the universals presented in section 4.4.3, we are in a position to reduce the subcategorization of deranked consecutive constructions to a typology which contains *three basic subtypes.* These three typological options form clusters of properties which are connected with conditionality, directionality and basic word order, and can be defined as follows:

(a) consecutive chains with *absolute deranking of the anterior predicate.* Typically, languages with this option have *SOV word order.*

(b) consecutive chains with *absolute deranking of the posterior predicate.* Typically, languages with this option have *VSO word order.*

(c) consecutive chains with *conditional deranking of the posterior predicate.* Typically, languages with this option have *SVO word order.*

4.5   The formal expression of simultaneous chaining

In the preceding sections of this chapter our main concern has been with the way in which the semantic concept of consecutive chaining is codified in the syntactic surface structures of natural languages. I will now make a few remarks on the codification of the other variant of temporal chaining, viz. *simultaneous chaining.* Our discussion of this subtype of temporal chaining can be relatively brief, since a number of notions which are necessary in the description of the various types of simultaneous chains have been dealt with extensively during our survey of the subtypes of consecutive chains.

As far as the semantic, language-independent definition of the notion of 'simultaneous chaining' is concerned, matters are relatively straightforward. We can define a simultaneous chain (or *S-chain*) crosslinguistically as that construction type which expresses a situation in which *two events happen at the same point in time,* or a situation in which *two states obtain at the same point in time.* Included in this definition are also situations in which *two events or states overlap in time*. Thus, in the typical case S-chains correspond in meaning to those English adverbial clauses which are introduced by the conjunctions *(at the time) when or while*. A somewhat special case of simultaneous chains is formed by those chains in which the two events or states are set off against each other in a relation of *adversativity*. Roughly speaking, in this case the two events or states are said to happen c.q. obtain at the same time despite expectations to the contrary. A typical codification of such an adversative chain in English is a coordinated structure in which two sentences are linked by the connective *but*.

The syntactic encoding of simultaneous chaining parallels the encoding of consecutive chaining in a number of important respects. For one thing, just like C-chains, S-chains may be expressed either by a *balanced* or by a *deranked* structural configuration. That is to say, in some languages the simultaneous chain has the shape of a syntactic coordination between clauses or sentences c.q. the shape of a main clause with an embedded temporal clause, whereas in other languages one of the two predicates in the S-chain is morphologically marked for subordination. An example of a language in which S-chains have to be balanced is Pala:

(38) PALA:
  Da   enum ra tamat ma da   so   ra hansik
  one-will eat the big   and one-will plant the small
  'The big (yams) will be eaten and the small ones will be planted'

Tibetan, on the other hand, is a language in which simultaneous chains are obligatorily deranked, in the manner shown by example *(39)*:

(39) TIBETAN:
  Lam nan-pa -yin-las rta   agrul-ma -thub
  road bad-one-be -PRT horse walk -not-able
  'The road was bad and the horses could not walk'

A second parallelism between the codification of simultaneous and consecutive chains lies in the fact that deranked structures of both types of temporal chaining are subject to *the same kind of conditionality*. In the same manner as we observed for deranked C-chains, deranked S-chains can be subdivided into structures in which *absolute deranking* is possible (that is, in which the deranking procedure operates independently of the identity or non-identity of the subjects in the chain), and structures in which only *conditional deranking* is possible (that is, deranking under identity of subjects). An example of absolute simultaneous deranking is provided by the above sentence from Tibetan (see *(39)*). Conditional simultaneous deranking seems to be the rule in Igbo; the deranked simultaneous construction in this language, which we illustrated in example *(1)*, is only allowed in cases in which there is subject-identity between the predicates in the chain (see Welmers, 1973).

With respect to *directionality*, the other condition on the deranking procedure in consecutive chains, there is, however, a fundamental difference between the two types of temporal chaining. In consecutive chains, the propositions which express the events involved are temporally ordered. As we saw, this temporal ordering has its formal–syntactic counterpart in the left-to-right ordering of predicates (or sentences) in the consecutive structure, to the effect that the predicate or sentence which describes the earlier event in the temporal succession is ordered structurally as the leftmost predicate or sentence in the chain. We noted in section 4.4.2 that this (temporal and structural) ordering of consecutive predicates plays an important role in the procedure of consecutive deranking: it may either be the temporally anterior (and structurally leftmost) predicate or the temporally posterior (and structurally rightmost) predicate which is affected by the deranking procedure. As we have shown, the choice between these two alternatives is at least in part influenced by the basic word order which the language in question has.

Now, in the case of simultaneous action there is of course no successive temporal ordering between the two events in the chain: both of these events are supposed to take place at the same point in time. This essential lack or neutrality of temporal ordering in a simultaneous chain is mirrored in semantics by the fact that, in chains with a simultaneous reading, both possible orderings of the two event-expressing propositions are expressions of one and the same state of affairs. In simultaneous chains, the choice for one of the possible orderings in a given situation is not made on semantic grounds (as is the case in consecutive chains), but is presumably influenced by considerations of a pragmatic or functional nature. Thus, the English sentences in *(40)*, when taken in their natural simultaneous interpretation, are semantically equivalent. In contrast to this, the sentences in *(41)*, which are naturally interpreted as consecutive chains, are not semantically equivalent, since they do not satisfy the same truth conditions:

(40)   ENGLISH:
a.   *John wore a cap and sported sneakers*
b.   *John sported sneakers and wore a cap*

(41)   ENGLISH:
a.   *Gary bought a gun and rode into town*
b.   *Gary rode into town and bought a gun*

A structural counterpart of this essentially unordered nature of simultaneous chaining is the fact that, in languages which derank their S-chains, both of the event-expressing predicates in the structure may be candidates for deranking. For instance, in English, a language which optionally deranks its simultaneous predicates, the two sentences in *(43)* are both possible deranked variants of the balanced simultaneous structure *(42)*:

(42)   ENGLISH:
           John stood on the corner and smoked a cigarette

(43)   ENGLISH:
a.   *Standing on the corner, John smoked a cigarette*
b.   *Smoking a cigarette, John stood on the corner*

Now, from a structural point of view, simultaneous chains are of course entities which are deployed in time; therefore, they have a linear order, just like any other linguistic entity. Hence, it will always be possible to mark predicates as leftmost or rightmost, even in S-chains. Some languages which derank their S-chains may have a preference for the deranking of a leftmost or a rightmost predicate in such chains. Tibetan, for example, obligatorily deranks leftmost predicates in simultaneous constructions (see *(39)*); this preference can be attributed to the fact that Tibetan, a strict SOV-language, always requires a finite main verb in sentence-final position. Despite these structurally motivated preferences for direction, however, the essential point remains that, even in Tibetan, there would be no change in truth value if one were to invert the clauses in *(39)* linearly and in terms of deranking. In other words, the terms 'anterior' and 'posterior' have no application in the description of simultaneous chaining constructions.

As a consequence of this feature of simultaneous chaining, we can note that, unlike consecutive deranking, simultaneous deranking does not seem to be subject to conditions which are connected with basic word order. If a language deranks its S-chains, word order does not come into play, and therefore no subcategorization of simultaneous deranking types can be made on this point. In other words, while deranked consecutive structures can be subcategorized into structures with anterior deranking and posterior deranking, simultaneous deranking does not have directional subtypes, and can only be pitted as a whole against the alternative of simultaneous balancing. As a result, we can summarize the structural types of simultaneous chains in the following three categories:

(a) cases of *simultaneous balancing*
(b) cases of *conditional simultaneous deranking*
(c) cases of *absolute simultaneous deranking*.

4.6   Summary: syntactic types in temporal chaining

In the preceding sections of this chapter, it has been my aim to present a typology of the ways in which the semantic or cognitive notion of temporal chaining is syntactically encoded in natural languages. Our major results can be summarized as follows.

First, the semantic concept of temporal chaining appears to cover two subtypes, viz. simultaneous action and consecutive action. For at least a number of languages, these two subtypes are structurally represented by different surface constructions; in other languages the semantic distinction between these subtypes has been formally neutralized in a total or partial manner.

Secondly, for both of these semantic subtypes a primary split in their possibilities of syntactic codification involves the distinction between the structural options of balancing and deranking.

Thirdly, within the category of deranked chaining constructions, both consecutive and simultaneous chains can be subcategorized as instances of either conditional or absolute deranking.

Fourthly, in the case of deranked consecutive constructions, the split between conditional and absolute deranking interacts with the distinction between anterior and posterior deranking; this latter distinction correlates with the basic word order of the languages at issue. The interaction of the two distinctions produces a three-way division within the category of deranked consecutive chaining constructions.

In sum, the typology of the syntactic variation in the codification of temporal chaining consists of the following seven types:

A.1   consecutive balancing
A.2.1   consecutive conditional (posterior) deranking (typically SVO)
A.2.2   absolute (consecutive) anterior deranking   (typically SOV)
A.2.3   absolute (consecutive) posterior deranking   (typically VSO)
B.1   simultaneous balancing
B.2.1   conditional simultaneous deranking
B.2.2   absolute simultaneous deranking

4.7   Language types in temporal chaining

In the previous section, we have summarized the syntactic forms in which natural languages may encode the semantic concepts of simultaneous and consecutive action. This typology of chaining constructions can now be used as the basis of *a typology of languages in the expression of temporal chaining*. That is, we will now investigate the ways in which languages make their choice from this list of possible encodings, and, as a result, we will establish a classification of the languages in the sample on the basis of their options in the formalization of consecutive and simultaneous action.

I assume it will be obvious that any natural language will have to have the possibility to codify both simultaneous and consecutive action, and that, therefore, any language must make a choice from both the possible types of simultaneous chains and the possible types of consecutive chains listed in section 4.6. Now, given that there are four possible ways to codify consecutive action and three possible ways to codify simultaneous action, it follows that a typology of language classes in chaining formation will theoretically consist of 12 different categories of languages. In reality, however, this number of language types turns out to be rigorously restricted, due to the operation of a general principle which regulates the selection of consecutive and simultaneous chaining types for a given language. This principle can be formulated as follows:

The Principle of Parallel Chaining:
In its codification of temporal chaining, a language will select parallel options for consecutive and simultaneous chains.

It is, of course, natural to conceive of this principle as a kind of economy principle operating in the systems of natural languages; basically, the principle is a manifestation of the general tendency in rule systems not to complicate procedures beyond what is strictly necessary, and thus to employ similar procedures for similar tasks. As we noted in section 4.1, in some languages the Principle of Parallel Chaining has led to the 'radical' consequence of neutralization. In these languages, the options which are selected for the encoding of consecutive and simultaneous action are not just parallel, they are identical.

The Principle of Parallel Chaining can be seen to operate both in the balancing–deranking distinction in chain formation and in the absolute–conditional distinction in deranked temporal chains. To start with the first distinction, we can note that a language which balances its C-chains will tend to choose the balancing option for its S-chains, and vice versa. Conversely, if a language deranks its C-chains, it will, as a rule, also derank its S-chains, and vice versa. In my sample, there are only very few counterexamples to this general tendency. One conspicuous case in which this parallelism is absent is Nuer, a Nilotic VSO-language, which balances its simultaneous chains, but has the possibility of absolute deranking for its consecutive predicates. The same situation holds for

Maasai, another Nilotic VSO-language. Opposed to this, two Australian languages (viz. Gumbainggir and Mangarayi) and the two Polynesian languages in the sample (Maori and Samoan) have the possibility to derank predicates in simultaneous chains, but, as far as I know, they lack a deranking option for consecutive chains. However, the general tendency in my sample is clearly that languages will employ the same basic strategy in both the formalization of simultaneous action and the formalization of consecutive action.

The structural parallelism between consecutive and simultaneous encoding can also be observed in the kind of conditionality under which the two types of chaining constructions can be deranked in a language, given that they can be deranked at all. In general, it appears to be the case that, if a language has absolute consecutive deranking, it will also have absolute simultaneous deranking, and vice versa; as the examples above clearly demonstrate, Tibetan is a case in point here. Conversely, if a language has only the option of conditional consecutive deranking, the same type of restriction tends to be imposed on the deranking of simultaneous constructions, and vice versa; Igbo (see sentences *(1)* and *(2)*) is a language in which this situation obtains. A possible counter-example here is Quechua, a language which seems to have absolute consecutive deranking, but only conditional simultaneous deranking (see chapter 10). However, we can state with some confidence that the structural parallelism between the types of C-chains and S-chains which a deranking language selects is confirmed by the large majority of the relevant languages in the sample.

If we accept the general validity of the Principle of Parallel Chaining, we are in a position to limit the set of language types in chaining formation to the following *three categories*:

(a) *Balancing languages.* These languages have both balanced simul-taneous constructions and balanced consecutive constructions; that is, in these languages the form of S-chains and C-chains is that of a coordination. Since, typically, coordination is a uniform procedure, it will be expected that neutralization of consecutive and simultaneous chaining will be very common in the languages of this type; disambiguization of the chaining construction will typically be effectuated by the optional use of temporal adverbs with either a definite consecutive meaning ('and then', 'and thereafter') or a definite simultaneous meaning ('and also', 'and at the same time'). Furthermore, it will be expected that the languages in this class *do not have a preference for a particular type of basic word order*, since the choice for a coordinated chaining construction is not in any way dependent on the type of word order which a language happens to have.

(b) *Conditionally deranking languages.* The languages of this type have S-chains and C-chains in which one of the predicates is deranked under identity of subjects; as we have seen in section 4.4.3, it is the posterior predicate which is deranked in C-chains of this type. Since conditional deranking of C-chains is typically a property of deranking SVO-languages, it will be expected that languages of this class will have, as a rule, *SVO word order.* Neutralization of simultaneous and consecutive action is certainly possible in languages of this type, as is shown by the case of Mandarin, but it is not mandatory. There are also languages of this type, such as Igbo, in which there is morphological difference in the encoding of the two types of temporal chaining.

(c) *Absolutely deranking languages.* The languages of this type can have S-chains and C-chains in which one of the predicates is deranked even if there is non-identity of the subjects in the chain. As we noted in section 4.4.2 and 4.4.3, the languages of this type can be divided into two subtypes, on the basis of the directionality of the deranking procedure in their C-chains. Thus we have:

(1) languages with absolute simultaneous deranking and absolute *anterior* consecutive deranking. These languages will, as a rule, have *SOV as their basic word order.*

(2) languages with absolute simultaneous deranking and absolute *posterior* consecutive deranking. These languages will typically have *VSO as their basic word order.*

Regarding the phenomenon of neutralization, it can be observed that complete neutralization is very uncommon for languages of this type; Amharic (see *(4)*) is an exceptional case in this class. In most cases, there is either no neutralization at all, or only partial neutralization between simultaneous and consecutive action, in that the same morphological predicative form is marked by different subordinating particles (Tibetan), or the same subordinating particle is used to mark predicative forms which are marked differently for tense (Latin).

This, then, sums up our classification of the languages in the sample on the basis of their options in the selection of syntactic chaining types. However, before we can conclude this chapter, I must call attention to a factor which tends to weaken the strictness of this classification. From the discussions so far, the reader may have got the impression that a language, in codifying its C-chains and S-chains, must be either balancing or deranking, and that in cases where both options are available the choice is governed by specific considerations of conditionality on the deranking procedure (as in the case of Wolof; see *(25a/b)*). If this were indeed the case, the typology would be pleasantly neat and strictly defined; but, unfortunately, reality is a bit more complex than this. We can also find cases in which a language appears to be able to vary freely between the options of balancing and deranking. The codification of consecutive chains in English may serve as an illustration here.

In English, consecutive chains may be balanced; that this is so is made evident by examples like *(15)*, repeated here as *(44)*. On the other hand, this language has also at least a limited (and perhaps stylistically marked) possibility to derank its C-chains. A sentence like *(45)* shows that English has anterior consecutive deranking. That the choice between consecutive balancing and consecutive deranking in English is not (or not completely) determined by conditions on the identity or non-identity of subjects can be seen from the (at least marginal) acceptability of a case of absolute consecutive deranking like *(46b)*:

(44) ENGLISH:
John jumped out of his chair and grabbed a gun

(45) ENGLISH:
Having jumped out of his chair, John grabbed a gun

(46) ENGLISH:
a. *John's wife left him and he took to drinking*
b. *His wife having left him, John took to drinking*

Moreover, English also seems to have a limited possibility of posterior consecutive deranking, which (English being an SVO-language) is restricted to cases in which there is identity of subjects. Predicative chains of the type *go and V* or *try and V* are clearly not genuine coordinations, since they do not form islands. Cp.:

(47) ENGLISH:
a. *Let's go and see a fortune teller*
b. *Let's try and clean up this mess before mother comes home*

(48) ENGLISH:
a. *Who did you go and see?*
b. *What did you try and clean up?*

Yet another English construction which might be viewed as a case of posterior consecutive deranking is the *to*-construction mentioned in section 4.2. In a sentence like *(49)*, the *to*-infinitive does not have a purpose-reading, but rather the reading of a posterior predicate in a consecutive chain:

(49) ENGLISH:
John came home to find his family murdered by terrorists

In view of such a situation, it seems to be more adequate to say that a language like English *can* be balancing or deranking, rather than to say that it *is* balancing or deranking. I will use the terms *optional balancing* and *optional deranking* to describe such a state of affairs. On the other hand, there are also languages in which only one of the basic strategies for codifying consecutive and simultaneous chaining seems to be allowed. For example, Tibetan is a language in which no balancing of chaining constructions occurs, whereas Guarani is a language which does not permit any form of deranked predicates. In what follows, I will refer to these latter types of languages as *strictly deranking* and *strictly balancing*, respectively.

5

Comparative Type and Chaining Type

5.1 Introduction

In the preceding chapters, I have presented two cross-linguistic typologies, viz. the typology of comparative constructions (chapter 2) and the typology of chaining constructions (chapter 4). In this chapter, I want to put forward the claim that there is a correlation between these two typologies. To be specific, I want to claim that the second typology, which states the attested variation among languages in the formal representation of temporal chaining, must be conceived of as the basic upon which the attested extension of categories in the typology of comparatives can be predicted. Below, I will present a set of implicational universals in which this claimed correlation is made explicit and specific. These universals will be referred to as *chaining-based universals* of comparative-type choice, as opposed to the word-order-based universals which we discussed in chapter 3.

Throughout the following discussion, it should be kept in mind that the formulation of the set of chaining-based universals serves a twofold scientific purpose. On the level of cross-linguistic description, this set of universals is intended as a statement of a number of correlations between categories from two independently constructed linguistic typologies. Thus, to the extent that these claimed correlations can be validated by the data, the set of chaining-based universals can be said to constitute a *descriptive* research result in a specific area of Universal Grammar.

Beyond this purely descriptive function, however, the ultimate aim of the set of chaining-based universals is of an *explanatory* nature. I intend this set of universals to be a formulation of the hypothesis that the typological parameter of temporal chaining must be looked upon as the *determinant* of the typology of comparatives, in the sense of the definition of this term which was given in section 1.2. My universals thus embody the claim that all the possible variations in the typology of chaining constructions have their exact match in the typology of comparatives. In other words, we claim that the options which languages have in the codification of comparison are restricted by the possible options of languages in the codification of temporal chaining: the fact that the typology of comparatives contains the attested (and no other) categories is taken to be a consequence of the fact that the typology of chaining constructions allows only the attested (and no other) typological variants. In this way, the typology of chaining constructions serves as the basis upon which the non-randomness of variation in the typology of comparatives can be accounted for.

As a result, the claims which are contained in the set of chaining-based universals may be viewed as an operationalization of the idea that, in natural languages, comparative constructions must not be looked upon as an 'elementary', 'basic', or 'autonomous' construction type. Instead, our universals are the embodiment of the assumption that the encoding of the concept of comparison in natural language systems is 'parasitic' upon the encoding of the concept of temporal chaining, which, accordingly, is seen as a more elementary or deeper-lying concept. In order to express this relation of dependency between the linguistic codifications of comparison and temporal chaining, we will say that, in natural languages, the linguistic codification of comparison is claimed to be *modelled upon* or *borrowed from* the ways in which the concept of temporal chaining can be encoded in natural language systems.

I would like to point out here that, if the above modelling-hypothesis can be shown to be validated by the cross-linguistic data, our research results may have consequences for cognitive theory, semantic theory and formal linguistic theory alike. From a cognitive point of view, our hypothesis leads to the contention that the mental operation by which two objects are compared may not be an independent, 'primitive' operation; at least as far as its codification into language is concerned, the mental act of comparison must be seen as a conceptual extension of the mental operation by which two events are ordered with respect to their occurrence in time. This claim that, in a sense, *comparison is a cognitive metaphor of temporal chaining* may be of interest to both semanticists and cognitive psychologists. In formal linguistic theory, acceptance of our modelling-hypothesis may lead to the conclusion that, in universal grammatical theory, we do not need construction-specific syntactic rules to generate comparative constructions. These constructions will be derived automatically by rules which are independently needed for the syntactic derivation of chaining constructions.

5.2   The set of chaining-based universals

Taking the modelling of comparison on temporal chaining as a starting point, I will now proceed to formulate a set of implicational universals in which this modelling is made more explicit for the various types of comparative constructions mentioned in chapter 2. As I noted in section 2.2.2, a first split in the typology of comparatives concerns the distinction between comparatives in which the standard NP has *derived case* and comparatives in which the standard NP is put into a *fixed case*. Now, our claim is that the distribution of these two options over the languages in the sample can be predicted from the way in which these languages can be categorized with respect to the first major formal distinction in the expression of chaining constructions, viz. the distinction between *balancing* and *deranking* languages. To be specific, the first universal which I propose reads as follows:

UNIVERSAL 1A: *If a language has a derived-case comparative, then*
                that language is balancing.
UNIVERSAL 1B: *If a language has a fixed-case comparative, then that*
                language is deranking.

By statements of this kind, we claim explicitly that the chaining-type of a language acts as a determining factor in the choice of a particular type of comparative construction for that language, and that therefore this comparative construction can be seen as being modelled upon the type of chaining-construction which that language has selected.

For both of the implicational universals given above further refinements can be formulated. First, let us consider Universal 1B. As we saw in section 2.2.3, the class of fixed-case comparatives permits a further subcategorization into, on the one hand, the class of *Exceed Comparatives* (in which the standard NP has the fixed form of a direct object) and, on the other hand, the class of *adverbial comparatives*. Our claim is that this distinction in comparative types is matched by the distinction between *conditionally* and *absolutely deranked chaining* in the following way:

UNIVERSAL 2A: *If a language has an Exceed Comparative, then that*
                language has conditional deranking.
UNIVERSAL 2B: *If a language has an adverbial comparative, then that*
                language has absolute deranking.

Thus, Universal 2A states that Exceed Comparatives are modelled on cases of chaining constructions which are deranked only if the two subjects in the chain are identical. (As we will see in chapter 8, the majority of the languages with an Exceed Comparative choose to model their comparative on the simultaneous variant of the conditionally deranked chains; we do find, however, occasional instances of languages in which the consecutive construction has served as the model for the Exceed Comparative.) To put it differently, Universal 2A claims that if a language is not a conditionally deranking language, it cannot have an Exceed Comparative. The matching between adverbial comparatives and absolutely deranked chains in Universal 2B may be paraphrased in a similar fashion.

As far as Universal 2A is concerned, no further refinement is needed; with this statement we have accounted for the occurrence of one of the terminal categories in the typology of comparatives. Universal 2B is in need of further specification, due to the fact that adverbial comparatives can be subcategorized into three distinct subtypes. The claim made in this study is that the tripartite division of adverbial comparatives into the Separative, the Allative and the Locative Comparative must be seen as a consequence of the fact that absolutely deranked chains also allow for three distinct subtypes. We will argue for the validity of the following three implicational universals:

UNIVERSAL 3A: *If a language has a Separative Comparative, then it must have an absolutely deranked anterior consecutive construction.*

UNIVERSAL 3B: *If a language has an Allative Comparative, then it must have an absolutely deranked posterior consecutive construction.*

UNIVERSAL 3C: *If a language has a Locative Comparative, then it must have an absolutely deranked simultaneous construction.*

Again, we might give an alternative formulation of these universals in terms of the notion of modelling. We might say that languages with a Separative or an Allative Comparative appear to model their comparatives on the respective ways in which they codify their C-chains, whereas languages with a Locative Comparative appear to prefer a modelling on the simultaneous variant of their absolutely deranked chaining constructions.

With the statement of Universal 2 and Universal 3, the four types of fixed-case comparatives have all been accounted for, in that they have all been matched to different variants of deranked chaining. To conclude this section, we must make a few comments on the other major type of comparative constructions, viz. derived-case comparatives. According to

Universal 1, the claim is that such languages model their comparatives on the balanced chaining construction which they possess. Now, as we have seen in section 2.2.5, one typical subcategory of derived-case comparatives is the Conjoined Comparative. For this class, the following claim will be maintained in this study:

UNIVERSAL 4: *If a language has a Conjoined Comparative, it must have a balanced simultaneous chaining construction.*

Thus, we claim that languages with a Conjoined Comparative borrow their formal encoding of this comparative from the balanced S-chain which they have; or, conversely, we claim that if a language does not permit balanced S-chains, it can never have a Conjoined Comparative.

While the claim with regard to the Conjoined Comparative is fairly straightforward, no such determinate statement can be made for the residual cases of derived-case comparatives, the so-called Particle Comparative. In chapter 9, I will demonstrate that all the languages in my sample which have a Particle Comparative are predominantly balancing, so that they confirm Universal 1A. However, it can also be shown that some instances of particle comparatives are modelled upon a simultaneous chain, whereas other particle comparatives borrow their formal expression from the balanced consecutive chain in the languages in question. In other words, while all conjoined comparatives are extensions of simultaneous chaining, particle comparatives can be modelled on either of the two semantic variants of temporal chaining. This, of course, leads to the question of why it should be the case that, of the languages which take simultaneous balanced chaining as their model, some should come up with a Conjoined Comparative, while others prefer the form of a Particle Comparative. This matter will be taken up in chapter 9, and will be elaborated further in chapter 15, where the distribution of languages over the various classes of comparative constructions will be discussed from an over-all perspective.

5.3   Further remarks on the universals

In the preceding section, I have formulated a set of chaining-based universals for the choice of comparative type. Taken as a whole, these universals are meant to be an expression of the claim that the comparative construction in a given language is derivative of one of the temporal chaining constructions which that language permits. Obviously, these universals are at present nothing more than hypotheses, which should be validated by confronting them with the actual linguistic data of the languages in the sample. In the chapters which constitute part two of this study, I will examine each of the proposed universals in turn. First I will concentrate on the primary languages for each comparative type, present the regular cases briefly, and comment on apparent counterexamples. In the last chapter of part two, I will turn to those cases in which languages appear to have more than one option for choosing a particular type of comparative. I will argue that these 'double' cases too are to be explained on the basis of the universal tendencies stated above.

Before we undertake a full-scale testing of the proposed universals, a few preliminary remarks may be useful. First, an important thing to note is that, in these universals, basic word order is no longer indicated as a direct determinant of the choice of comparative type. Within the framework which we adopt here, basic word order is now assumed to play only a limited and concomitant role in the choice of some of the comparative types, namely, the fixed-case comparative constructions. In the case of these four comparative types, basic word order comes into play in as far as it is connected with the subtypes of deranked chains which a deranking language may have; the general rules regarding this connection have been formulated in the statements *(4.34)* and *(4.37)*. Thus, in our opinion, a statement such as

(1)   *Languages with a Separative Comparative generally prefer SOV word order* (see section 2.3.2).

must be replaced by the following syllogism:

(2) *a.* UNIVERSAL 3A: *Languages with a Separative Comparative are languages with absolute anterior consecutive deranking.*
  b. *Languages with absolute anterior consecutive deranking typically prefer SOV word order* (see section 4.4.4).
  c. *Therefore: languages with a Separative Comparative typically prefer SOV word order.*

It must be stressed again here that it is always chaining type, rather than word-order type, which we claim to be the decisive factor in the possibilities of comparative-type choice. Hence, if a language has a Separative Comparative, we will expect that language to have the option of an absolutely deranked anterior C-chain, even if that language should have no SOV-order, thereby constituting a deviation of the unmarked case for languages with chaining constructions of this particular type.

Concerning the Locative Comparative, we have observed in section 2.3.3 that languages in this class appear to have a preference for either SOV-order or for VSO-order. At the present point in the discussion, we are able to account for these preferences, by pointing out that, as a rule, absolutely deranking languages are either SOV-languages or VSO-languages. Now, in the case of the absolute deranking of consecutive chains these two word-order options are formally kept apart, by virtue of the fact that they are in correlation with opposite directions in which the deranking procedure takes place. However, in the case where the absolute deranking procedure affects predicates in simultaneous chains, no such factors of directionality obtain; as a result, we find absolute deranking of simultaneous predicates attested for both SOV-languages and VSO-languages. Now, if we assume the validity of Universal 3C, which claims that the possibility of having an absolutely deranked simultaneous chain is a prerequisite for the choice of a Locative Comparative, the observed fact that languages with a Locative Comparative are either SOV-languages or VSO-languages is immediately accounted for.

Finally, we have concluded in section 2.3.5 and section 2.4 that generalizations cannot be made about basic word order in languages with a Conjoined Comparative or with a Particle Comparative. This fact can be explained by assuming the correctness of Universal 1B, which claims that languages with a derived-case comparative model their comparatives on a balanced temporal chain. As we saw in section 4.7, the procedure of (simultaneous and consecutive) balancing is not influenced by basic word order in any way.

As a second preliminary remark, we must comment briefly on *the notion of counterexample* which we will adopt in the following chapters. Throughout the present chapter, we claimed repeatedly that the options with respect to the codification of temporal chaining in a given language serve as the basis upon which the choice of a certain comparative type can be predicted for that language. It is, however, extremely important to realize that we will take the occurrence of a certain chaining type as *only a necessary, and not a sufficient, condition* on the choice of a certain comparative type in a language. Thus, taking Universal 3A as an example, we predict that any language which has a Separative Comparative should have the option of an absolutely deranked anterior C-chain, but the reverse implication need not hold. Given this interpretation of the content of our universals, we can now state explicitly what will and what will not count as a counterexample to our universals.

Again, let us take Universal 3A as an example. In this universal, the occurrence of a Separative Comparative in a language is made dependent on the occurrence of an absolutely deranked anterior C-chain in that language. Now, from the way in which this universal is formulated, it is obvious that languages which have both a Separative Comparative and an absolutely deranked anterior C-chain conform to the prediction made by Universal 3A, and thus provide for corroboration of that universal. It is equally obvious that languages with a Separative Comparative but no possibility to form absolutely deranked anterior C-chains are direct counterexamples to the claim contained in Universal 3A. Now, suppose we were to find a language which has an absolutely deranked anterior C-chain but no Separative Comparative. In my conception of the content of Universal 3A, such a language would not constitute a counterexample to this universal. There are two reasons for taking this point of view. First, our universals claim that, apparently, both simultaneous and consecutive chaining may be factors in the choice of comparative type. Hence, a language which has an absolutely deranked anterior *consecutive* chain need not necessarily choose a Separative Comparative; instead, it may also choose to model its comparative on its codification of *simultaneous* chaining, and, as a result, it may come up with, say, a Locative Comparative (by Universal 3C). Secondly, we have seen in section 4.7 that languages may have double options in the formalization of their chaining constructions: some languages may both balance and derank their simultaneous and consecutive chains. Therefore, even if a language selects its comparative on the basis of its consecutive chaining, it may still be the case that having an absolutely deranked anterior C-chain is not enough reason to choose a Separative Comparative. If the language has the additional possibility of balancing its C-chains, it might choose this balanced consecutive chain as its model for the codification of its comparative, and, as a result, it might come up with, say, a Particle Comparative (see section 5.2).

To sum up, we must conclude that our chaining-based universals are *uni-lateral*; the choice of a particular comparative type in a language is claimed to be *constrained* by the possibilities of temporal chaining in that language, but it is *not uniquely determined* by any one of its options in the codification of temporal chaining.

Part Two

Testing the Set of Chaining-based Universals

6

The Separative Comparative

6.1 Introduction

In the chapters which constitute part two of this study, the set of universals which I have formulated in chapter 5 will be confronted with the actual data of the languages in my sample. The present chapter will be devoted to an examination of Universal 3A, which I repeat here for convenience:

UNIVERSAL 3A: *If a language has a Separate Comparative, then it must have an absolutely deranked anterior consecutive construction.*

Thus, what we have to do now is to check for each language with a Separative Comparative whether or not this language can be shown to have a C-chain in which the anterior predicate can be deranked under non-identity of subjects. As we saw in section 2.3.1, the Separative Comparative is the largest class in the typology of comparative; no less than 32 languages in the sample select this type of comparative as their primary option. The unmarked word order for this type turns out to be SOV; there are, however, four exceptions to this tendency to be observed in the sample.

Below, I will present a discussion of each individual language in this class. For reasons which will become clear shortly, I have found it useful to organize this discussion into four separate sections. We can state beforehand that it will turn out that Universal 3A is confirmed for a large majority of the languages which have a primary Separative Comparative. No more than two languages present serious difficulties; these counter-examples will be commented upon in section 6.5.

6.2 Direct corroboration from SOV-languages

Of the 28 SOV-languages in the sample with a Separative Comparative as their primary choice, we find that there are 14 which corroborate Universal 3A in a strikingly straightforward way. In these languages, the correlation between the Separative Comparative and their consecutive chain is brought out by *an overt parallelism in surface structure*; they form their deranked anterior consecutive predicates by means of a separative marker on verbal stems or verbal nouns, so that a direct formal relation between the two constructions at issue can be demonstrated. We must note in passing that the languages involved here all seem to be instances of strictly deranking languages: structural coordination of predicates or sentences does not seem to be possible here.

A first example of the overt parallelism between the codifications of comparison and consecutive action is Tibetan. The form of consecutive deranking which can be observed in this language has been discussed extensively in section 4.3.2. Briefly, we can say that Tibetan obligatorily deranks its anterior predicates in C-chains, by suffixing the element *-nas* to the 'bare' (which, in this case, means 'tense-less') verb stem. That this deranking procedure allows for absolute constructions is proven by the occurrence of the following sentence:

(1a)   TIBETAN:
     Nam langs-nas   athon-te-son
     night rise -from outside-go
     'After night had fallen (he) went out'

Now, it turns out that the marker *-nas* on the deranked anterior predicate is also in use as the separative marker 'from' on nominals, including the standard NP in the Tibetan comparative. Cp.:

(1b)   TIBETAN:
     Rta -nas   khyi chun -ba yin
     horse-from dog small-one is
     'A dog is smaller than a horse'

A completely parallel situation can be encountered in Vayu, the other Himalayan language in my sample. Here, too, obligatory deranking of anterior consecutive predicates takes place, in that the bare verb stem (which has no person, tense or marker of indicative mood) has a suffix which also marks separative phrases and standard NPs in comparatives. Absolute use of deranked predicates is common. Cp.:

(2)   *VAYU:*
a.   Go *wathim-khen cho -mi*
      I   him   -from small-IND
      'I am smaller than him'

b.   *Upo   met'-khen tawo-khata-ha chhing-ngak yang-ngak ma*
      father die -from son -PL   -AG much   little   not
      papa-ha ling-me -m
      do   -by get -3PL-IND
      'After the father has died, the sons equally inherit him'

In Mundari, the separative marker *-ete* 'from' also functions as a suffix on deranked anterior consecutive predicates. These predicates are obligatorily marked for person, so that absolute use is certainly a possibility. Deranked predicates, cannot, however, be marked for tense, whereas main predicates can. Cp.:

(3)   *MUNDARI:*
a.   *Sadom-ete   hati   mananga-i*
      horse -from elephant big   -3SG
      'The elephant is bigger than the horse'

b.   *Sena-ing -ete   hiju -a -i*
      go   -1SG-from come-FUT-3SG
      'After I have gone, he will come'

The consecutive construction in Burushaski has been introduced in section 4.4.1. We noted there that this language formally differentiates between cases of absolute and conditional anterior deranking of consecutive predicates. The absolute consecutive construction requires that the anterior predicate be turned into a verbal noun, which must then be marked by the separative item *-tsum.* This same suffix is attached to the standard NP in the Burushaski comparative. Cp.:

(4)   *BURUSHASKI:*
a.   *Un -tsum je kam apa*
      you-from I less not be-PRES. 1SG
      'I am not inferior to you'

b.   *Xurts lang manum-tsum mumie   yet-su -man*
      dust away moving-from mother-his see-him-3SG
      'After the dust had moved away, his mother saw him'

The situation in Lamutic is in many ways comparable to that in Burushaski. Again, this is a language which has strict deranking of C-chains; and, again, this is a language which has a formally different encoding for cases of absolute and conditional consecutive deranking. In both cases, the anterior predicate takes the shape of a non-finite form, the so-called Aorist Participle. In the absolute construction, this deranked form must be followed by the marker -*k*, a general separative suffix meaning 'from', which also marks standard NPs. The subject of the absolutely used anterior predicate in the Lamutic C-chain is represented by means of the non-reflexive possessive suffixes, which follow the separative marker -*k*.[1] Cp.:

(5) LAMUTIC:
a. *Anna Marja-du-k nosecce*
    A.   M.   -from is-young
    'Anna is younger than Marja'

b. *Bazikar em -re   -k   -en hurrit*
    day-NOM come-AOR. PCP.-from-its go-PAST. 1PL
    'When morning had broken, we went on our journey'

Bedauye, a Cushitic language of the Lower Branch, has a so-called Temporal Form, which indicates anterior action in a consecutive chain. The form consists of the suffix -*ka*, which is attached to the so-called Relative Perfect, a subordinate tense form which is marked for person, and which is most frequently encountered in relative clauses. The marker -*ka* turns out to be the general separative marker 'from', which also appears as a suffix on the standard NP in Bedauye comparatives:

(6) BEDAUYE:
a. *Hammad-i   o -gaw -i-ka Abdalla-y   u -gau*
    H.   -GEN the-house-from A.   -GEN the-house
    hanyis
    beautiful
    'Abdalla's house is more beautiful than Hammad's house'

b. *Wu-or efray-e   -ka   hadda ihe*
    the -boy born-REI. PERF. 3SG -from lion   seize-PAST. 3SG
    'After the boy had been born, the lion seized him'

In Andoke, the standard NP in comparatives is formed by the suffix -*aha*, which must be glossed as 'since' or 'from the point of view of' (Landaburu, 1979: 162–3). This particle also appears as a suffix on the anterior predicate in C-chains; in this case, the anterior predicate has been nominalized by the suffix -*i*, and its subject must be represented by possessive infixes. Cp.:[2]

(7)   ANDOKE:
a.   *Yado yo'hê b -aya sebe-ê yado ya -aha*
      this man   he-is strong this this-from
      'This man is stronger than that man'

b.   *Eka -se   s   -e -te -i   -aha be ka -siko-i*
      river-this down-its-dry-NOUN-from IND 1PL-fish -ASS
      'The river has fallen and we have fished'

The deranking of anterior predicates by means of a nominalizing
strategy is also the procedure chosen in Jurak. Apart from the nominalization suffix -*an*, a deranked anterior predicate is also obligatorily
marked for subject, regardless of whether this subject is identical or non-
identical to the subject of the main verb. Given that the deranked
predicate is a nominalization, it is not surprising that this subject
marking takes the form of possessive affixes. Finally, a deranked anterior
predicate in a Jurak C-chain requires the presence of the marker
-*had/kohod*. This is a separative case suffix which may appear with all
nominals, including the standard NP in comparatives. Cp.:

(8)   JURAK:
a.   *Ty   wuenu-kohod pircea*
      reindeer   dog -from   big
      'A reindeer is bigger than a dog'

b.   *Ma -kan-ta taewma-had -an   -ta haewtita jasoko*
      tent-to -his arrive -from-NOUN-his rib   pieces-ACC
      ngani ma -ta sid -in-ta mojoida
      again tent-his two-to-its keep throwing-them-3SG
      'After he arrived home, he threw the pieces of rib to both sides of
      his tent'

The Australian language Aranda is, in the words of Strehlow (1944:
207), 'a language of participles; and most English clauses in which a
finite verb is introduced by a conjunction would be rendered into Aranda
by turning this finite verb into a participle and omitting the conjunction.'
The participle which represents anterior predicates in C-chains is called
the Preterite Participle. This is a form which consists of the verbal stem,
followed by the past tense marker -*ka* and the subordinating suffix -*la*. If
this participial form is used absolutely, the whole complex receives yet
another suffix, viz. the element -*nga*. An example may illustrate this
rather complicated formation:

(9a)   ARANDA:
  Era pitji -ka -la -nga arbunintjara argan-era -ka
  he come-PAST-SUBORD-PRT others   glad -they-PAST
  'After he had come, the others were glad'

Now, it turns out that the absolutive marker *-nga* can also be employed as a separative suffix on nominals, including standard NPs in comparatives; if the suffix is attached to pronouns, it has the form *-kanga*. Thus, we see that there is an overt structural parallelism between the expressions of comparison and consecutive chaining in Aranda:

(9b)   ARANDA:
  Jinga etna-kanga mara-lkura nama
  I   they-from good-PRT be-PRES
  'I am better than them'

Carib is a strictly deranking language, which has a considerable number of so-called gerunds at its disposal. These are verbal forms, which do not occur as main predicates, but represent dependent verbal constructions; they are not marked for mood, but may have marking for tense, and can be accompanied by possessive prefixes which indicate person and number. Since Carib is an ergative language, the person marking on the gerund indicates the subject if the verb is intransitive, and the direct object if the verb is transitive. Deranking of anterior predicates in C-chains takes place by means of the Perfect Gerund. This form is characterized by the suffix *-xpo*, an alternant of the separative marker *-kopo*, which is used to encode the standard NP in Carib comparatives. Absolute use of the Perfect Gerund is documented by a sentence like *(10b)*. Cp.:

(10) CARIB:
a. *Kuliali a -kuliali kopo apoto-me mang*
  canoe your-canoe from big -one is
  'My canoe is bigger than your canoe'

b. *Wewe e -karama -xpo kinixsang*
  wood its-being sold-from go away-PAST
  'After the wood had been sold, he went off'

Next, let us consider the situation in two other Southern American languages, viz. Quechua and Aymara. In both of these (possibly related) languages, the primary comparative construction is of the separative type, as is shown by the following examples:

(11) QUECHUA:
Kam noka-manta sintsin
you I -from strong
'You are stronger than me'

(12) AYMARA:
Napi huma-ta   hucampi amauta
I   you -from more   prudent
'I am more prudent than you'

The Separative Comparative in Quechua has its overt parallel in the way in which anterior predicates in C-chains are encoded. Such predicates are obligatorily deranked into a form which consists of the verbal stem followed by the perfective suffix *-ska*. This form, which von Tschudi (1884: 223) calls the 'Perfect Infinitive', is essentially nominal, as can be seen from the fact that subjects are marked by possessive suffixes. If the form is used as the expression of anterior consecutive action, it optionally receives the separative suffix *-manta* 'from'. Absolute use of the form is a definite possibility. Cp.:

(13) QUECHUA:
a. *L'amka-ska   -y -manta mikhusah*
    work -PERF. INF.-my -from   eat-FUT. 1SG
    'After I have worked, I will eat'

b. *Wahya-ska   -yki tsay-lam hamurkany*
    call -PERF. INF. -your that-on come-PERF. 1SG
    'After you called, I came'

In Aymara, very much the same situation obtains. Again, anterior predicates in C-chains are encoded in a specific nominalized form, which is called the Perfect Participle (de Torres Rubio, 1966: 57), and which is marked for subject by possessive suffixes. In the anterior consecutive chain, the form receives the separative suffix *-ta* 'from'. Cp.:

(14) AYMARA:
Mancata-ha -ta . . .
eating -my -from
'After I have/had eaten . . .'

Finally, we must discuss two languages in which the parallelism between the encoding of comparison and consecutive action is a bit more obscure. First, let us look at the situation in Turkish. This language has a Separative Comparative; standard NPs are marked by the suffix *-den* 'from', which has the forms *-dan* and *-ten* as its alternants:

(15) TURKISH:
> Sen gül -den   güzel   -sin
> you rose-from beautiful-be-2SG
> 'You are more beautiful than a rose'

Now, if we consider the ways in which Turkish represents the predicates in chaining constructions, we find that this language has a predilection for the use of 'gerunds' (Lewis, 1967: 177) or 'subordinate predicates' (Swift, 1963: 162). These gerunds are adverbial formations, which have the by now familiar shape of a bare verb stem with suffixes. Absolute use of such forms is possible, as can be derived from the following statement in Swift (1963: 162):

> The absence of a topic within the subordinate clause results, in most cases, in the performer denoted by the verb of the subordinate clause being constructed as the same as the performer of the action of the ensuing clause. . . . This type of construction is true of all types of subordinate clauses where there do not occur post-predicate suffixes on the predicate. . . . In others of the examples, however, there is a clearly stated topic in the subordinate clause: *Kapi . . . ac,ilinca* 'upon the door being opened' and the like.[3]

Concerning the encoding of anterior predicates in C-chains, Turkish has a number of different possibilities, which represent different shades of consecutive meaning. The gerund in *-inca* denotes that 'the action or state of this subordinate clause is/was/will be immediately prior to that of the ensuing predicate but not necessarily related to it' (Swift, 1963: 161). In addition, Turkish has also a gerund with the suffix *-erek/-arak*, which denotes that 'the state or action denoted by this verb is/was/will be prior to and in some sense prerequisite to that of the ensuing predication' (Swift, 1963: 164). It seems to me that it is this latter gerund which is particularly relevant to our discussion, given the fact that this gerundial form may optionally be accompanied by the separative marker *-dan*: 'This form also occurs with the relational suffix *-dan* . . . without appreciable change of denotation. This variation seems to be largely stylistic' (Swift, 1963: 165). Sentence *(16)* illustrates the use of the separative marker on deranked anterior predicates in Turkish C-chains. It is only fair, however, to point out that the other author on Turkish syntax which I have consulted has a different opinion on the use of the gerund in *-erek-ten*: 'The provincial *-erek-ten* denotes only activity contemporaneous with, never prior to, the main verb' (Lewis, 1967: 177n.).

(16)   TURKISH:
       Evé   gid-erek-ten   mantosunu   aldi
       home go -GER-from   overcoat-her get-PAST. 3SG
       'She went home and got her overcoat'

Lastly, we must discuss the consecutive construction in Manchu. From the point of view of overt parallelism between comparison and consecutive action, this language might be qualified as a 'near miss'. Manchu has a Separative Comparative, in which the standard NP is marked by the case suffix -*ci* 'from':

(17)   MANCHU:
       Morin indaho-ci   amba
       horse dog   -from big
       'The horse is bigger than the dog'

Predicates in chaining constructions are deranked into the form of so-called converbs. These are adverbial formations, which are characterized by the attachment of suffixes to the tense-less verbal stem. Anterior predicates in C-chains receive the form of the Preterite Converb, which is marked by the suffix -*fi*. An example of the absolute use of this converb is sentence *(18)*, quoted from Adam (1873: 53):

(18)   MANCHU:
       Temujin holha be   ucara-fi   juwe niyehe
       T.   thief ACC meet -PAST. GER two ducks
       deye-me   jimbi
       fly   -PRES. PCP come-PAST. IND
       'After Temujin had met the thief, two ducks came flying over'

Now, the interesting point is that Manchu has another converbal form, which is marked by the separative suffix -*ci*. The primary function of this converb is the representation of conditional clauses, which is why it is called the Gerundium Conditionale by Haenisch (1961: 55). However, this author remarks that this converb is, in certain contexts, 'also used temporally' (my translation). Cp.:

(19)   MANCHU:
       Yamun de tuci -fi   tuwa-ci
       hall   in go out-PAST. GER see -COND. GER
       'When/as he, having gone into the hall, saw . . .'

6.3   Indirect corroboration from SOV-languages

In the previous section, we presented those languages in the sample which exhibit an overt surface parallelism between their Separative Comparative and their expression of consecutive action; as such, these languages can be said to provide 'direct' corroboration of Universal 3A. Other languages with a Separative Comparative do not show this overt parallelism. However, it can be shown that almost all of these languages have an absolutely deranked anterior consecutive chain, so that they can be rated as at least indirect corroborations of the relevant universal. In this section, I will confine myself to languages which have SOV as their basic word-order, the unmarked case for languages with a Separative Comparative.

Starting with Bilin, a Cushitic language, we note the existence of so-called Subordinate Tense forms. These are verbal forms which are marked for person and tense, but the verbal morphology employed differs from that of predicates in main clauses. Anterior predicates in C-chains receive the form of the Perfectum Subordinatum (Reinisch, 1882: 57). It is perfectly possible to use this type of subordinate predicate in an absolute construction. Cp.:

(20)   BILIN:
a.   *Ni ku -lid   bahar gin*
     he you-from big   be-3SG. IND
     'He is bigger than you'

b.   *Inta dan   insausu qualdi-noe*
     your brother chained see   -PERF. SUBORD. 2SG
     inta labbaka egirgir yiraikum
     your heart   pity   say-FUT. IND. 3SG
     'When you have seen your brother in chains, your heart will take pity on him'

In Laz, a Caucasian language of the South-West group, we come across the rather exceptional situation that finite verbal forms may show nominal declension. Dirr (1928: 113) remarks: 'In Laz there exists a possibility to express in one and the same word the relation to time, to person and to place simultaneously. In other words, verbal forms, even the finite ones, can be declined' (my translation). Anterior predicates in C-chains have the form of the finite Aorist, which is marked by the genitive case suffix -*i* and followed by the postposition *kule* 'behind'. Since these deranked forms are explicitly and obligatorily marked for person, it will be obvious that they can be used in absolute constructions. Cp.:

(21)   LAZ:
a.   Ham   bozo   da -skimi-se   msk'ua   on
       this   girl   my-sister-from   pretty   is
       'This girl is prettier than my sister'

b.   Gec'e-b   -ilc'ked-i   -s   kule
       down-1SG-look   -AOR-GEN   behind
       'After I had looked downwards'

Amharic uses so-called gerundial forms to represent one of the clauses in consecutive (and simultaneous)[4] chains. These forms exhibit a specific vocalization of the verb stem and a special set of person markers. Gerundial forms occupy a subordinate position in propositions; having no tense of their own, they derive their temporal interpretation from the tense marking of the main predicate. The subject of a gerundial form can be identical to that of the main verb, but absolute use is definitely possible. Cp.:

(22)   AMHARIC:
a.   Zaf-u   ke   -byet   -u   yebelt'-al
       tree-the   from-house-the   big   -be-IND. 3SG
       'The tree is taller than the house'

b.   Talast   sastwo   tamallasna
       enemy-NOM   flee-GER. 3SG   return-PERF. IND. 1PL
       'After the enemy had fled, we returned'

With respect to the formal encoding of chaining in Tajik, Rastorgueva (1963: 100) remarks: 'If there are several verbs in a sentence that are related to a single subject and not dependent on each other, then all of them, except for the very last, are usually in the gerund form, thus making together with their supplementary and explanatory words the so-called gerundial phrases . . . . The past gerund here indicates an action which precedes that expressed by the finite verb.' As to the conditionality of this deranking procedure, the author states explicitly that 'there is quite wide-spread in Tajik a so-called absolute construction, i.e., the kind of situation when a finite verb and a gerund, within the limits of a single sentence, each have their own separate subject' (Rastorgueva, 1963: 101). Cp.:

(23) TAJIK:
a. Ruy-ash az   barf kham   safed ast
    face-her from snow and/too white is
    'Her face is whiter than snow'

b. Bacha rui gilem nichasta   piramard kitob
    boy   on carpet sit-PERF. GER old man book
    mekhond
    read-PAST. 3SG
    'After the boy had sat on the carpet, the old man read a book (to
    him)'

Gerundial forms as representations of anterior predicates in C-chains
can also be encountered in Hindi, where such forms are marked by the
attachment of the suffix -*kar*/-*ke* to the bare (i.e., tense-less and person-
less) verb stem. Absolute use of such forms is possible; McGregor (1977:
39) observes that 'the subject implied in an absolute form is generally the
same as that of the main verb in its sentence, but not invariably.' Cp.:

(24) HINDI:
a. Ap us -se   bare haim
    you him-from big be-PRES. 2SG
    'You are bigger than him'

b. Vahim baith-kar   bat   -em   homgi
    there sit   -PERF. GER matter-PL. FEM be-FUT. 3PL. FEM
    'We will sit there and have a conversation'

The situation in Kashmiri is very similar to that in Hindi, its Indo-
Aryan relative in my sample. In Kashmiri, too, anterior predicates in C-
chains are deranked by means of the attachment of a subordinating suffix
to the bare verbal stem. Absolute use of these forms is permitted. Cp.:

(25) KASHMIRI:
a. Yi   kani nishin trakur chu
    this-INAN stone from hard   is
    'This is harder than stone'

b. Nalama -ti   rat -ith   tamis mithi ditsön
    embrace-with seize-PERF. GER to-him kisses were-given-by-him
    'He embraced him and kissed him'

The attachment of subordinating suffixes to bare verb stems is a
deranking procedure which appears to be rather popular among the
languages of this class. This strategy in the encoding of anterior consecutive
predicates is also followed in Japanese, Burmese, Korean, Khalka,

Eskimo, Tupi and Piro. As the examples given will show, all these languages permit absolute use of their deranked anterior predicates in C-chains.

The Separative Comparative in Japanese is matched by the so-called Gerundive (Kuno, 1973: 195) or Continuative (Kuno, 1978: 121–2) Form, which consists of the bare verb stem with the suffix -*te*. The semantics of this form are rather intricate (see Kuno, 1973: 196–9), but there is no doubt that it is a subordinate form (ibid.: 200–9) and that its basic meaning is that it 'represents a temporal or logical sequence (i.e., "and then, and therefore") . . . It implies that S1 has taken place before S2 does' (Kuno, 1978: 122). Cp.:

(26) JAPANESE:
a.   *Nihon-go wa   doits-go yori   muzukashi*
      Japanese TOP German from difficult
      'Japanese is more difficult than German'

b.   *Bukka ga   agat-te   minna ga   komatte iru*
      prices TOP rise -GER all   TOP suffering are
      'Prices have risen and all are suffering'

In Burmese, deranking of anterior predicates in C-chains is effectuated by suffixing the subordinating particle -*pi* 'after' to verbal stems:

(27) BURMESE:
a.   *Thu-hte? pein   -te*
      him -over be thin-NONFUT
      'She is thinner than him'

b.   *Sei   pye   -pi   ein   pyan -thwa-te*
      mind be destroyed-GER. PERF home return-go   -NONFUT
      'He got fed up and went home'

In Korean, we note again the existence of so-called Converbs, that is, 'verbal formations which, through their ending and meaning lead us to understand that the sentence is not finished but . . . the main verb is following. In the European languages the two verbs are united by the normal conjunctions, but the Korean language, which has no conjunctions, possesses, like all Altaic languages, many special formations for connecting one action with another' (Ramstedt, 1968: 87). For our purpose, the most relevant of these converbs is the Converbum Perfecti, which is formed from verbal stems by means of the suffix -*el*-*sje*. 'It would be possible to call this form converbum anterioris. It gives the action of the first verb as in time preceding that of the following verb' (ibid.: 89). Unfortunately, all the examples of this converb given by Ramstedt are instances of non-absolute use; one of these examples is:

(28) KOREAN:
Phenzir-il s   -sje   najera
letter-ACC write-CONV. PERF send-IMP
'Write the letter and send it'

We may note, however, that absolute use of the Converb Perfecti can be documented in constructions where this converb is modified by adverbial particles, which give the converb a concessive meaning. An example of this case is sentence *(29)*; as Ramstedt (ibid.: 89) explicitly remarks, the converb in *-sje* is used here 'to stress the difference in time':

(29) KOREAN:
Mawe -sje   do   mekesso
be bitter-CONV. PERF even eat-FUT
'Although it is better, I will eat it'

Also, it can be observed that other converbal formations may certainly appear in absolute constructions (ibid.: 95 and 103):

(30) KOREAN:
Muri kiphi-na   kenne kagesso
water deep -CONV. CONCESS we   go over-FUT
'Although the water is deep, we will cross it'

(31) KOREAN:
Pab -il meget-ca   sarami wata
food-ACC eat   -CONV. MOMENT man   come-PAST
'Just as I had eaten, a man arrived'

Given these facts, I think it is safe to assume that the Converb Perfecti, which represents deranked anterior predicates in Korean C-chains, may also have an absolute use. Parallel with his consecutive construction we find a Separative Comparative, in which the standard NP is marked by the postposition *-ese/-eso*. As Pultr (1960: 224) suggests, this separative marker may actually be a composition of the two suffixes *-e* and *-sje* which form anterior converbs. Cp.:

(32) KOREAN:
Na-eso   to kheda
I   -from he big-PRES
'He is bigger than me'

Converbs, of the kind discussed above, are also a common feature of the codification of chaining in Khalka. Street (1963: 219) mentions a considerable number of such adverbialized forms, which are all formed from verb stems by the suffigation of 'converbial particles'. For our purpose, it looks as if the converb in *-j* is the most relevant, since it refers, among other things, to 'an action that precedes another in time, but is somehow related to it' (Street, 1963: 221). Absolute use of this converb is quite common. Cp.:

(33) *KHALKA:*
Uur cai -j   gjegjee orloo
day dawn-CONV light   appear-PERF. IND. 3SG
'Day has dawned and light has appeared'

The possibility of absolutely deranked anterior predicates in C-chains is matched by the occurrence of a Separative Comparative in Khalka:

(34) *KHALKA:*
Jamc cham-aas   targan
J.   you -from fat-PRES. 3SG
'Jamc is fatter than you'

In the gerundial or converbial constructions presented above, the deranked predicate did not change its category status; although being deranked, it retained its full verbal characteristics, such as the possibility to take subjects and direct objects. In other languages, the deranking of a predicate stem by means of suffigation leads to a loss of verbal character. Specifically, it turns out that, in some cases, the deranking procedure results in a nominalization of the predicate; this nominal character is brought to light by the fact that such deranked predicates take possessive affixes or genitives to mark their subjects.

One case of this nominalization is Eskimo. This language has Sub-ordinate Forms, marked by specific suffixes after the verbal stem. The suffix for the Past Subordinate Form, which is used to encode anterior action in C-chains, is *-nga/mma*. To this suffix, personal suffixes are obligatorily attached; it can be observed that these personal markers are related to the possessive suffixes on nominals (Thalbitzer, 1911: 1045). By the use of these person markers, absolute construction of the Past Subordinate Form is made possible. Cp.:

(35) *ESKIMO:*
Angu-ssa   -tik   qalat-tari   -nga   -ta
catch-PCP. PASS.-REFL. POSS boil -through-PAST. SUBORD.-3PL
natsern-mut poonutaq ili -ssu   -aat
floor -DAT dish   put-FUT. IND.-3PL. TRANS
'After the things they have caught have been boiled, they will put them on the floor in a dish'

(36) Una apum-it   qaqo -R-ne   -R- u   -wo   - q
      this snow-from white NOUN   exist PRES. IND 3SG
      'This is whiter than snow'

In Tupi, anterior predicates in C-chains are deranked by means of the postposition -rire 'after' on verbal stems, which cannot have tense marking in this case. The nominal character of the predicate in this construction is illustrated by the fact that its subject must be marked by possessive prefixes. Cp.:

(37) TUPI:
a.   Xe-catu ete   nde-cui
      I -good really you-from
      'I am better than you'

b.   O -co-rire   xe-eu
      his-go-after I -cry
      'After he had gone, I cried'

A decidedly nominal strategy for anterior consecutive deranking is also followed in Piro (Matteson, 1965: 174). In this language, the entire anterior clause is nominalized by means of the suffix -nu, which usually forms abstract nominals (e.g., yotsiha-nu 'dazzling brightness' from yotsiha 'to dazzle'). Cp.:

(37) PIRO:
a.   Kositsine-ru   pnute   tsru
      K.   -GEN beyond big
      'He is greater than Kositsine'

b.   R -heta-ko -klu -nu   yohima-xitxa-ka
      he-see -PASS-PAST-ABSTR. NOUN hide-command-PASS
      'He was seen and was told to hide'

6.4   Corroboration from non-SOV-languages

Among the languages with a Separative Comparative which confirm Universal 3A, three languages merit some special attention. These languages constitute direct evidence for our claim (made in section 5.3) that it is not basic word order, but in fact chaining type which is the predicting factor in the determination of comparative-type choice.

As a first example, let us consider the case of Cœur d'Alene. This Salishan language has basic VOS word order,[5] but the standard NP in its comparative is marked by the preposition täl 'from'. Cp.:

(38)   CŒUR D'ALENE:
    Tcin-tsäc-alq^w   täl   kuwä
    1SG -tall -PRES from you
    'I am taller than you'

Now, it can be observed that Cœur d'Alene has at least a marginal possibility to derank anterior predicates in C-chains. In this case, the anterior predicate is nominalized by means of the suffix *-äs*, and must be preceded by the nominal articles *xwä* or *lä*; these articles mark definiteness on NPs and may be glossed as 'the' or 'this'. An example of the construction in question is (39). From this sentence, it can be deduced that there need not be identity of subjects in the chain, so that we can take this sentence as an instance of absolute deranking. Perhaps a more clear example of the absolute use of this deranked anterior C-chain is sentence (41). This is an example from Kalispel (Vogt, 1940: 70), a language which is very closely related to Cœur d'Alene. Cp.:

(39)   CŒUR D'ALENE:
    Lä   xälp   -äs   at'sqää
    ART become light-PCP he-go out-PAST
    'When it had become light, he went out'

(40)   KALISPEL:
    Cink^utunt   tel   anui
    I-big   from you
    'I am bigger than you'

(41)   KALISPEL:
    Lu -wist   -es   se'i cu
    ART-finish-3PL-PCP then say-PAST. 3SG
    'After they had finished, then he said . . .'

Thus, we may conclude that Cœur d'Alene (and Kalispel) are cases of (indirect) corroboration of Universal 3A, despite the fact that they constitute a deviation of the unmarked word order for their class.

Similar observations can be made with regard to Classical Arabic and Biblical Hebrew,[6] although for these languages the facts are a little bit more problematic. There can be no doubt that the comparative in these two Semitic VSO-languages is of the separative type. The standard NP in both constructions is marked by the preposition *min*, which is also used freely as a spatial marker with the meaning 'from':

(42)   CLASSICAL ARABIC:
    Laysat al -nisa   'adcafa min al -rijali
    not   the-women weaker from the-men
    'Women are not weaker than men'

(43) BIBLICAL HEBREW:
Hakam 'ettēh mid – dāni'ēl
wise   you   from D.
'You are wiser than Daniel' (Ezechiel, 28,3)

Now, from the literature on these languages (see, e.g., Nasr (1967) and Yushmanov (1961) for Classical Arabic and Brockelmann (1956) for Biblical Hebrew) it turns out that the normal way of expressing consecutive action in these languages is the use of a balanced construction with a connective particle. Cp.:

(44) CLASSICAL ARABIC:
Qama   fa   kataba
stand up-PAST. 3SG and write-PAST. 3SG
'He stood up and wrote'

(45) BIBLICAL HEBREW:
Halak   Dāvid waj-jidros'
go-PAST. 3SG. MASC D.   and-search PAST. 3SG. MASC
'et   has's'ar
the-ACC   officer
'David went and looked for the officer'

Given this state of affairs, one might conclude that both Classical Arabic and Biblical Hebrew are counterexamples to Universal 3A; they have a Separative Comparative, but their C-chains are balanced. I think, however, that these two apparent counterexamples can be explained away. If we look a little closer at the options for consecutive chaining in these languages, we find that they have also a limited possibility of deranking their consecutive predicates. In Classical Arabic, it is possible to turn anterior VPs into verbal nouns, the subject of which comes to be constructed as a genitive (c.q. possessive) form. The anterior clause is further marked by a nominal preposition, usually *ba'da* 'after', but we also find cases in which the preposition *min* 'from' is used with the meaning of our subordinating conjunction *since*. An example is:

(46) CLASSICAL ARABIC:
Ba'da duhuli -ni   al -bayta   kataba
after entering-my the-house-ACC write-PAST. 3SG
'After I had entered the house, he wrote'

In Biblical Hebrew, a very similar situation holds. Here too we find that anterior clauses in C-chains can be constructed as prepositional phrases, in which the anterior predicate has the form of the so-called 'infinitivus constructus'. This is a nominalized form, the subject of which must be indicated by a genitive NP or a possessive suffix. Clearly Biblical Hebrew permits absolute use of anterior predicates which are deranked in this way. An example is:

> (47)   *BIBLICAL HEBREW:*
> *Min mosa'   dābār   s'alu'îm   s'ib'āh*
> from go out-INF word ... weeks   seven
> 'From the moment that the word went out ... (it has been) seven weeks' (Daniel 9,25)

It must be admitted that the procedure of deranking which is described above is rather untypical, or at least stylistically marked, for both languages; there is a strong preference for coordinated structures, and instances of absolute consecutive deranking are fairly rare. They are, however, real structural possibilities for these languages, and the fact that such constructions exist at all may be sufficient reason to cancel both Classical Arabic and Biblical Hebrew as genuine counterexamples to Universal 3A. Moreover, we can note that absolutely deranked structures of the type illustrated in *(46)* and *(47)* provide for direct corroboration of the universal at issue; the preposition *min*, which marks the standard NP in comparatives, is also employed to mark the nominalized anterior predicate in the deranked C-chains of both languages.

6.5   Counterexamples

Turning now to the counterexamples to Universal 3A, we must note two cases which are problematic to a more or less serious degree. My sample contains two languages which clearly have a Separative Comparative, but which do not seem to be able to form C-chains in which the anterior predicate has been deranked in an absolute construction.

A first possible counterexample is Nama, a Khoin-language with basic SOV word order. From the grammatical descriptions which I have been able to find (Schils, 1891; Meinhof, 1909) it can be deduced that Nama has both a Locative Comparative and a Separative Comparative. In this latter case, the standard NP is marked by the postposition *cha* 'from' (see Schils, 1891: 55):

> (48)   *NAMA:*
> *Ne khoi -b   gye tita cha   a geisa*
> this person-MASC. PRT I   from is strong
> 'This man is stronger than me'

Now, if we look at the way in which chaining is formally expressed in Nama, we find that the language has a number of participial forms at its disposal. Of special relevance to the present discussion is the Preterite

Participle, a verbal formation which consists of the (tenseless) verb stem to which the suffix *-tsí* has been attached.[7] This Preterite Participle is used to express anterior action:

(49) NAMA:
    Znou-toa -tsi   tita gye hai   -be damai gye
    strike-ready-PCP. PAST I   PRT Damra-ACC chase PRT
    'I struck the Damra and chased him away'

(50) NAMA:
    Mu-bi -tsi   -ta gye gye gowa -u
    see -him-PCP. PAST-I   PRT PRT speak-PAST
    'I saw him and addressed him'

From these examples it becomes clear that Nama has the possibility to express anterior predicates in C-chains by means of deranked forms. However, the problem with these examples is that they are all instances of non-absolute constructions; in all the examples which I have been able to trace the subject of the Preterite Participle is identical to that of the following main predicate. From what I have been able to find out about the syntax of Nama, it is not clear whether this language actually forbids absolutely deranked C-chains; it may be that the non-occurrence of such constructions is simply a matter of insufficient data. But however this may be, given the present state of knowledge about Nama syntax the honest thing to do is to rate this language as a counterexample to Universal 3A, at least as far as the conditionality of its consecutive construction is concerned.

The second, and perhaps most damaging, counterexample to Universal 3A is Guarani, an SVO-language spoken in Paraguay. Both grammars which I have consulted (Guasch, 1956; Gregores and Suárez, 1967) agree that this language has a Separative Comparative. The standard NP in the comparative is marked by the postposition *-gwi* or *-hegwi*, an item which also occurs freely as the spatial marker 'from'. Cp.:

(51) GUARANI.
a. *Se Paragwai gwi*
    I P.   from
    'I am from Asunción'

b. *Se se-tuvisa-ve ne hegwi*
    I I -big -PRT you from
    'I am bigger than you'

Now, it seems that, in the encoding of chaining, Guarani favours a strict balancing approach. Deranked predicative forms do not seem to be possible in this language; Guasch (1956: 141) states explicitly that 'Guarani . . . has neither an infiinitive nor a gerund, nor a supinum with its own grammatical forms.' Instead, we find coordinated structures of the type exemplified in *(52)*:

(52) GUARANI:
      Oi-ke   kaagwi pe ha   o -henu petei avu
      he -went   forest in and he-heard one   noise
      'He went into the forest and heard a noise'

Also, Guarani has the possibility to subordinate whole clauses by means of (clause-final) subordinating conjunctions. However, since in such constructions the predicate of the subordinated clause is not itself marked for subordination, we are not permitted to rate this structural option as a case of deranking (see section 4.3.2). An example of a case of clause-embedding in Guarani is:

(53) GUARANI:
      A-karú rire   a-pitu?ú
      I -eat   after I-rest
      'After eating I rest'

All in all, we are forced to conclude that Guarani has a Separative Comparative but not an absolutely deranked anterior consecutive construction, and that this language is therefore a genuine counterexample to Universal 3A.

I have not been able to find a completely convincing way to neutralize this counterexample. Perhaps a little hope for Universal 3A can be derived from a remark by Guasch (1956: 142), who states that, in the embedded clauses of Guarani, the clause-final conjunctions such as *rire* 'after' tend to form an intonational unity with the predicate which directly precedes them. It might be possible to regard this phenomenon as a very early (or, as the case may be, a very late) stage of predicate deranking in Guarani. In this connection, we may also point to the situation in Tupi, a language which is commonly assumed to be related to Guarani. As we saw in sentence *(37b)*, the item *rire* 'after' is in use as the marker of deranked anterior predicates in the C-chains of Tupi. The difference between Tupi and Guarani seems to be that, in Tupi, the anterior predicate marked by *rire* is a clear case of deranking, and that the anterior predicate in Guarani C-chains like *(53)*, despite its being marked by the same element *rire*, must be considered to be essentially a non-deranked finite form. The fact that Tupi has made a radical choice for predicate deranking while Guarani appears to hesitate on this point may very well be connected with the difference in word order between the two languages. Tupi is a strict SOV-language; in languages of this type, the predicate in an embedded clause always immediately precedes clause-final subordinating conjunctions. Guarani, on the other hand, has basic SVO word order, and hence the predicate in an embedded clause and the clause-final conjunction of that clause are not necessarily neighbouring elements. Now, if we assume that one of the ways in which deranking of predicates in natural languages takes place involves the (intonational and/or morphological) incorporation of a subordinating clause-marker into a predicate, and if we assume further that this incorporation is easier for languages in which the embedded predicate and the clause-marker must always occur in direct sequence, we may have a framework in which the observed difference between Tupi and Guarani might be explained. Guarani might be looked upon as a language in which deranking of predicates has reached (c.q. has been reduced to) the stage of intonational incorporation of clause markers, but in which this incorporation is hindered by the fact that the embedded predicate and the clause-marker are not contiguous items in all constructions. However, although this solution does not sound entirely implausible, it must be admitted that it is highly speculative as it stands, and that, therefore, it seems best to conclude that Guarani remains a problematic case for Universal 3A.

6.6   Conclusion

In this chapter, we have examined the validity of Universal 3A, by testing this universal against the facts of the languages in our sample with a primary Separative Comparative. We have found that Universal 3A is confirmed by 30 of the 32 languages involved. Moreover, we have noticed that there is a direct surface parallelism between comparative construction and consecutive construction for 17 languages in this class. Lastly, we have seen that the facts adduced in this chapter confirm the claim that it is chaining type rather than basic word-order type which must be seen as the determinant of comparative-type choice.

7

The Allative and the
Locative Comparative

7.1 Introduction

Having examined the languages with a primary Separative Comparative, we now turn to the other two classes of adverbial comparatives. From the lists of languages presented in chapter 2, we learn that both of these types are relatively infrequent, at least in as far as primary options are concerned; they number 7 and 12 languages, respectively. Given the rather small size of the classes, it is convenient to deal with them in a single chapter.

Apart from practical considerations, there is also a more principled motivation for a joint discussion of Allative and Locative Comparatives. As we will see below, the phenomenon of partial indeterminacy, which I commented upon in section 2.2.5, is not uncommon when the Locative and the Allative Comparative are involved. Three of the languages which I have listed provisionally under the heading of the Locative Comparative actually exhibit a certain degree of neutralization in the spatial distinction between locative and allative relations, so that the typological status of these languages is, to a certain extent, indeterminate. We will discuss these indeterminate cases in a separate section at the end of this chapter.

7.2 The Allative Comparative

In this section, we will examine the empirical validity of Universal 3B, which has been formulated in section 5.2 in the following manner:

UNIVERSAL 3B: *If a language has an Allative Comparative, it must have an absolutely deranked posterior consecutive construction.*

Thus, we will have to check for each language with a primary Allative Comparative whether or not this language can be shown to have C-chains in which the posterior predicate can be deranked under non-identity of subjects. The languages with a primary Allative Comparative form a set of seven members. The unmarked word order for this set is VSO.[1] Kanuri, an SOV-language, is the only deviation of this tendency in the sample.

7.2.1   Direct confirmation of Universal 3B

Within the set of languages with a primary Allative Comparative, we find two languages which may be seen as 'direct' confirmation of Universal 3B. In these languages, we can observe an overt parallelism in the way in which comparison and consecutive chaining are formally expressed in surface structure. Unfortunately, however, for both of these languages the data are of a relatively low quality. In particular, there is uncertainty as to whether absolute use of the consecutive construction is permitted in these languages.

The first language which we will discuss in this context is Siuslawan. This Kushan language has a large freedom of word order, but a certain preference for verb-initial constructions can be established.[2] The standard NP in the comparative of Siuslawan has the so-called 'objective form', which is characterized by the presence of the suffix *-tc/-na*. It can be observed that the suffix *-tc* is also the normal marker of allative motion. Cp.:

(1)   SIUSLAWAN:
a.   *Liu'wa"x   qiutcilmä -tc*
      come-PAST. 3DUAL   old woman-PRT
      'The two of them came to an old woman'

b.   *Sea his   na -tc*
      he   good   me-PRT
      'He is better than me'

As Frachtenberg (1922: 555) remarks, the suffix *-tc/-na* has a further use as an adverbializing marker on verbal stems. By the use of this particle, posterior predicates in C-chains can be deranked. The construction appears to be of a limited distribution, and is subject to certain specific conditions: 'When added to verbal stems, *-tc* is almost invariably followed by the verb *xint-* to go, to start and *hiq!-* to start, to begin' (ibid.). Examples of this deranked construction are the following:

(2)   SIUSLAWAN:
a.   Ul kapi   -tc xintit ants tci
     and being low-to went that water
     'And the water began to get low'

b.   Ul qatcent yexa"-tc ansitc tcmani
     and he-went see -to that   cousin-his
     'And he went to see his cousin'

It must be conceded that Siuslawan does not present a very strong case in favour of the correctness of Universal 3B. For one thing, the deranked consecutive construction does not seem to be generally applicable. A second reservation to be made is that we have not been able to find examples of absolute use of the deranked consecutive construction, nor any indication that such absolute use is actually permitted. On the credit side, examples like those in (2) can be used as a demonstration that Siuslawan uses a deranked predicative form as a model for the encoding of its comparative.

A comparable situation can be encountered in Tarascan, an isolated VSO-language spoken in Southern Mexico. In this language, adjectival stems must have the suffix -pe if they are used predicatively. Furthermore, comparison is marked in the adjectival predicate by the so-called 'disjunctive' suffix -ku; with non-adjectival predicates, this suffix signals the presence of an indirect object. The standard NP in comparatives and the indirect object in non-comparative constructions are marked by the case suffix -ni. Thus, we get the parallelism in (3a/b), which shows that Tarascan has an Allative Comparative:

(3)   TARASCAN:
a.   Xi u -ku -aa -ka -ni   ima-ni
     I do-DISJ-FUT-IND-1SG him-DAT
     'I will do it for/to him'

b.   Xi as -pe -ku -s -ka -ni   ima-ni
     I good-PRED-DISJ-PRES-IND-1SG him-DAT
     'I am better than him'

Now, we can observe that the allative marker -ni also shows up as the suffix on deranked consecutive predicates. In this function, the suffix is placed immediately after the verbal stem of the posterior predicate, thereby creating the so-called Participial Mood (Foster, 1969: 56). The anterior predicate, which is a finite form, usually has the infix -s-pi, which 'marks a non-continous action, begun in the past, which is contingent on the performance of another action or condition' (Foster, 1969: 55). An example of this construction is:

(4) TARASCAN:
     Xura-spi   -ti   ese-ni
     come-PERF. PAST.-3SG see-DAT
     'He came and saw'

It must be remarked here that the construction illustrated in *(4)* has a definite consecutive interpretation, and not a final reading. In order to express purpose, Tarascan uses the Spanish loanword *para* 'to, for' in front of the participial form marked by *-ni*. Cp.:

(5) TARASCAN:
     Xura-ska   -ti   para ese-ni
     come-PRES. IND.-3SG *for*   see-DAT
     'He comes to see'

As was the case with Siuslawan, a problem with the data of Tarascan is that we lack the information as to the possibility of an absolute use of the deranked C-chain. In this connection, we may point out that at least one example can be attested in which the participial form in a purpose construction has its own independent subject. The example in question is the following phrase:

(6) TARASCAN:
     Tire-kwa para-ksi   tire-ni
     food   for -they eat -DAT
     'Food for them to eat'

However, it remains unclear whether this possibility of absolute use of the Tarascan *-ni*-form can be carried over to the consecutive use of this form, and whether or not such an absolute use is a generally applicable option in the constructions at issue.

7.2.2   *Indirect confirmation of Universal 3B*

Three other languages in the class under discussion lack overt surface parallelism, but can nevertheless be shown to have both an Allative Comparative and an absolutely deranked posterior C-chain. In this way, these languages constitute (indirect) evidence for the correctness of the claim which is laid down in Universal 3B.

First, let us consider the case of Maasai. In section 4.4.1 we have already noted the existence of the so-called 'Dependent Tense' in Maasai, a form which is employed to represent posterior predicates in C-chains.

The Dependent Tense is a form of predicate deranking, characterized by the prefix *n-* and the absence of any tense marking. Since predicates in the Dependent Tense are obligatorily marked for person, absolute use of this form is obviously permitted. Cp.:

(7) *MAASAI:*
a. *Sapuk ol -kondi to l -kibulekeny*
    is-big the-deer to the-waterbuck
    'The deer is bigger than the waterbuck'

b. *E   -iput-a   emoti n -a -pik en-kima*
    3SG. FEM-fill -PAST pot   DEP-1SG-put on-fire
    'She filled the pot and I put it on the fire'

Nuer has a 'Narrative Mood', a verbal form which has the following features: 'The particle of the Narration is *cóo*. It is used for connecting successive particulars of an event or transaction' (Crazzolara, 1933: 136). The posterior predicate which follows the particle *cóo* has the form of a participle; it is not marked for tense. As example *(8b)* shows, deranked posterior predicates in Nuer may be independently marked for subject. Cp.:

(8) *NUER:*
a. *Diid ne gän ke ji*
    big am I to you
    'I am bigger than you'

b. *Cike   ngar , cô -re peean cô -re cioohde   tol*
    did-3PL play   PRT-he fall-PCP PRT-he break-PCP leg
    'They played, and he fell and broke his leg'

The third language which we must mention in this context is Jacaltec. In this language, NP-comparison is expressed by the preposition *sataj* 'before, in front of' as the marker of the standard NP:

(9) *JACALTEC:*
    Ka' icham hin s -sataj   naj Pel
    more old   I   him-before he P.
    'I am older than Pel'

Matched with this Allative Comparative we find in Jacaltec a special procedure for the deranking of posterior consecutive predicates, viz. the 'Sequential Aspect'. Craig (1977: 65) remarks: 'The sequential aspect is a special aspect used to coordinate sentences which express actions happening in a chronological order. . . . [It] is composed of the aspect word *cat* followed by an aspectless embedded verb.'[3] As example *(10)* demonstrates, absolute use of predicates with sequential aspect is definitely possible:

(10) JACALTEC:
Babel x   -cuwatx'e skoyehal cat sto yoxal
first COMPLET. 1PL-make   dough   PRT go   achiote
'First we make dough, then the achiote goes in'

With respect to the matching of comparison and consecutive chaining in Jacaltec, we can make some additional observations. As is stated by Craig (1977: 65), the sequential aspect construction can be used only if the sequence has Present or Future reference. If the consecutive chain is marked for Part or Pluperfect, a different type of consecutive expression must be used. This latter construction involves simple juxtaposition of predicates if the posterior verb is intransitive; if the posterior verb is transitive, it can have no aspect marking, but instead it is marked by the suffix -ni, an item which indicates 'a weak coordination and may be found linking long chains of transitive sentences in the context of a narrative' (Craig, 1977: 35). Examples of this second type of C-chain in Jacaltec are given in (11); as sentence (11b) shows, absolute use of this construction is possible. Cp.:

(11) JACALTEC:
a. Speba ix te pulta sah -ni   ix   te   wentana
    closed she the door open-PRT she the window
    'She closed the door and opened the window'

b. Xichecoj ix slah -ni   yunin   ix
    started   she finish-PRT her-child she
    'She started (it) and her child finished (it)'

Now, the interesting thing is that this second type of C-chain appears to be matched by the way in which Jacaltec encodes its *clausal comparatives*. If the comparative construction contains a 'standard clause' instead of a standard NP, the predicate of this clause must be an aspectless verb, which is marked by the suffix -ni if it is transitive (Craig, 1977: 40). The striking parallelism between the formation of clausal comparatives and a certain type of consecutive chaining in Jacaltec is brought out clearly by the following example:

(12 JACALTEC:
Ka   wohtaj naj sataj haca hach wohtaj-ni
more I-know him before how you I-know-PRT
'I know him better than I know you'

7.2.3   Possible counterexamples

In the set of languages with a primary Allative Comparative we come across two languages which are problematic to such a degree that they might be rated as counterexamples to Universal 3B. The first of these languages is Breton, the Allative Comparative of which is illustrated in sentence *(13)*:

(13)   BRETON:
  Jazo bras-ox   wid-on
  he   big -PRT for -me
  'He is bigger than me'

Now, in contrast to the prediction made by Universal 3B, it appears that Breton does not have a procedure to derank posterior predicates in C-chains. Instead the usual expression of consecutive action turns out to be a balanced construction, in which two finite verbal forms are connected by the coordinate particle *ag* 'and':

(14)   BRETON:
  Wel endyd   edoure   xu-war ag   efeze
  all   the-men till-PAST his-field and be-PAST. 3PL
  laked   en -avelew
  put-PCP. PAST. PASS   the-potatoes
  'Everybody ploughed his field and then the potatoes were planted'

Hence, we are forced to conclude that Breton constitutes a genuine counterexample to Universal 3B.

Perhaps the strength of this counterexample can be weakened somewhat if we are permitted to take diachronic data on Breton into account. It appears that in Middle Breton (and in the medieval forms of other Celtic languages) deranking of posterior predicates in C-chains was certainly possible. Thus, in his study of early Welsh, Strachan (1909: 79) writes: 'The verbal noun may carry on the construction of a finite verb.' The same observation is made by Lewis and Pedersen (1974: 316), who state: 'In W(elsh) the verbal noun can be used instead of a finite verb . . . continuing a finite verb construction.' These latter authors present examples from various Middle Celtic languages, in which the posterior predicate in a C-chain has been deranked into a non-finite verbal noun. Unfortunately, the one example which they give of this type of deranking procedure in Middle Breton has a simultaneous reading:

(15) MIDDLE BRETON:
En   dougenn   hac e   caret
him respect-I-PAST and him love-VERB. NOUN
'I respected him and loved him'

Given these facts of Middle Celtic, the hypothesis one might venture is this. In earlier forms of Celtic, there existed a possibility to derank the posterior predicate in a C-chain into a verbal noun. It is probable that this structural option was rather marginal even in earlier Celtic; in this connection, we may point to the fact that the posterior predicate, even though it has a deranked form, must be connected to its anterior clause by a coordinating conjunction. Hence, in later stages of Celtic this deranking procedure has been abandoned altogether in favour of the unmarked balancing procedure. Now, Breton is the only Celtic language in which the comparative construction has been modelled upon the earlier deranked consecutive construction, instead of on the more central balancing construction; in contrast to all other Celtic languages (which have a Particle Comparative), Breton has retained an Allative Comparative, despite the fact that the deranked construction on which this comparative is modelled has been lost. In short, one might assume that the comparative construction in Breton is more conservative than the consecutive construction, and that the Allative Comparative reflects an earlier stage in the development of the language, a time when the relation between consecutive type and comparative type could still be documented.[4]

Needless to say, the above sketch of an explanation for the facts in Breton is highly speculative. Moreover, we must point out that, even if this explanation were to be accepted, we are still faced with the fact that we lack the data to decide whether the deranking procedure in Early Breton permitted absolute use of the deranked posterior predicate. It is true that in some of the examples from other Middle Celtic languages the deranked posterior predicate can be seen to be accompanied by its own subject NP. Strachan (1909: 79) quotes the following example from Early Welsh:

(16) EARLY WELSH:
Ac a dywawt na wnaethpwyt   oe bleit ef   drwc
and he said   not it-had-been-done on behalf him evil
yn y byt   y Briaf , namyn rodi
in the world to B.   but   give-VERB. NOUN. PASS
Esonia idaw ef   o   achaws y dewret
E.   to   him for reason his valour
'And he said that on his part no evil in the world had been done to Priam, but that Hesione had been given to him for his valour'

However, I have not been able to trace examples of this kind for Middle Breton. For these reasons, we are obliged to admit that, in all probability, Breton remains a counterexample to the prediction made by Universal 3B.

The problem with which Kanuri (see Lukas, 1937) confronts Universal 3B is of an entirely different nature. There can be little doubt that this language has an Allative Comparative; the standard NP is marked by the case suffix *-ro*, an item which primarily indicates the goal of a movement and the indirect object. Cp.:

>   (17)   KANURI:
>   Ate-ma   tutu-ro   ngela   go
>   this-EMP   that-to   good   PRT
>   'This is better than that'

We find that this element *-ro* is also employed as a marker on subordinate predicates, which in this case must be deranked into the form of a verbal noun. The construction permits absolute use:

>   (18)   KANURI:
>   Leman   bannazai   avima   gapse   -nyi -ro
>   money   waste-PRES. 3PL   anything   be-left-VERB. NOUN-NEG-to
>   'They waste money so that nothing is left'

As can be seen from the translation of sentence *(18)*, the main problem with the situation in Kanuri is that the semantics of the construction which formally matches the Allative Comparative are not right. If we apply the criteria which were formulated in section 4.2, it cannot be maintained that this construction is a genuine case of consecutive action; from all the examples given in Lukas (1937) it becomes clear that it has a definite and unmistakable final reading. What is more, Kanuri turns out to have several deranked constructions which correspond to our definition of consecutive chaining in a completely straightforward way. First, the language has a Dependent Past, a finite verb form which is marked for subordination by a special infix. The form is used to represent anterior predicates in C-chains:

>   (19)   KANURI:
>   Mai Aji Makka-ro ci -gannya
>   king A. M.   -to go-DEP. PAST. 3SG
>   'After King Aji had gone to Mecca . . .'

A second verbal formation in Kanuri which may be relevant in this context is the so-called Conjunctive. Again, this is a finite form, marked by special personal suffixes, which is used to represent all predicates except the last one in C-chains:

(20)   KANURI:
       Kamu   nagadero   cize   kalgo   goze
       wife   quickly   rise-CONJ. 3SG vessel take-CONJ. 3SG
       tuljin
       wash-PAST. IND. 3SG
       'The wife stood up at once, took the vessel, and washed it'

Thus, the problem which Kanuri poses is this. Kanuri is an SOV-language which has the possibility to derank anterior predicates in C-chains under non-identity of subjects. Now, given that this language chooses to model its comparative on its C-chaining, the normal thing for this language would be to have a Separative Comparative. Instead, this language is deviant in that it does not select its consecutive construction, but rather the semantically adjacent purpose-construction as the model of its comparative.

In my opinion, the estimation of the status of the Kanuri comparative with regard to Universal 3B depends on the rigorousness with which one wants to apply the criteria for consecutive constructions that were laid down in section 4.2. In Kanuri, there is no indeterminacy between final and consecutive constructions; the distinction between the formal codifications of these two semantically cognate constructions is perfectly clear. Therefore, if one wants to stick to the literal interpretation of the content of Universal 3B, one must conclude that the Kanuri comparative is not matched by an absolutely deranked posterior C-chain and that, therefore, Kanuri is a genuine counterexample to this universal. However, if one is willing to allow that, occasionally, a language may expand the notion of consecutive action to include purpose-constructions, Kanuri ceases to be a counterexample; on the contrary, the language then becomes a direct confirmation of Universal 3B, in that it shows a straightforward surface parallelism between its comparative and its 'consecutive' construction. My personal opinion on this matter is that not much harm is done to the over-all claim contained in our set of universals if the second alternative is opted for. The number of languages which turn out to model their comparative on their purpose-construction is negligible; apart from Kanuri, we find this situation in only two other cases, viz. the primary comparative in Fulani (see section 8.3) and the secondary comparative in Mangarayi (see section 10.4).

7.3   The Locative Comparative

The last type of adverbial comparative constructions which we must discuss is the Locative Comparative. For this class, the relevant universal is Universal 3C, which has been formulated in section 5.2 in the following way:

> UNIVERSAL 3C: *If a language has a Locative Comparative, then it must have an absolutely deranked simultaneous construction.*

Hence, in order to confirm the correctness of Universal 3C, we should be able to demonstrate that languages with a Locative Comparative have the possibility to derank one of the predicates in an S-chain under non-identity of subjects.

The languages with a primary Locative Comparative form a set of 11 members; in addition, a considerable number of languages select this comparative-type as their secondary option. The preferred word order for languages in this class is either SOV or VSO; a sketch of an explanation for this fact has been presented in section 5.3.

Within the class of languages listed under the heading of the Locative Comparative, three languages are indeterminate as to their classification as either a Locative or an Allative Comparative. For the moment, I will leave these cases aside, and concentrate on the nine languages which can be shown unambiguously to have a Locative Comparative as their primary option.

7.3.1   *Direct confirmation of Universal 3C*

Of the nine languages under discussion, three show the by now familiar phenomenon of overt surface parallelism between the formal expressions of comparison and temporal chaining. Hence, these languages constitute direct evidence for the correctness of the claims which are contained in our set of chaining-based universals.

Within the class under discussion, the first example of overt surface parallelism is Chuckchee. In this language, predicates in subordinate clauses are represented as nominalizations, which are then marked for grammatical function by means of case suffixes. The locative suffix *-ik/-ok/-tik*, which marks the standard NP in Chuckchee comparatives, is also the marker for simultaneity on predicates:

(21)   CHUCKCHEE:

a.   *Gamga-qla'ul-ik   qetvu -ci   -ium*
     all   -men -on strong-more-1SG
     'I am stronger than all men'

b.   *Ge -rine -lin   puker-in   -ok*
     PAST-fly up-3SG   arrive-3SG-on
     'When he arrived, the other one flew up'

In Naga, the standard NP in comparatives is marked by the suffix *-ki*, which has the locative meaning 'on'. Again, we find that this marker is also in use as a marker of deranked simultaneous predicates; it is attached to verbal stems, which in this case can no longer take tense particles. It must be noted that the suffix *-ki* on deranked predicates is used only in cases where there is absolute simultaneous deranking; if the S-chain is non-absolute, the deranked predicate must take the suffix *-di*. Examples are:

(22)   NAGA:

a.   *Themma hau lu   ki vi   -we*
     man   this that on good-is
     'This man is better than that man'

b.   *A de   kepu -ki themma lu   a   vu-we*
     I   words speak-on man   that me struck
     'As I spoke these words, that man struck me'

c.   *Po de   pu-di   ta-te*
     he words speaking went
     'Speaking these words, he went away'

The third example of a language in which the Locative Comparative is formally parallel to the encoding of S-chains is Ubykh, a Caucasian language of the North-West group. Like all languages in its family, Ubykh possesses a very rich system of deranked predicative forms, which can also be used absolutely. In particular, Ubykh offers the possibility to form 'participes-gérundifs' (Dumezil, 1933: 223). These are verbal forms which are marked for person, but which receive nominal case inflexion. The locative case suffix *-n* marks simultaneous action when it is attached to such a deranked verbal form.[5] Cp.:

(23)   UBYKH:

a.   *Yi -gune wo -gune-n   ca   -qasaqa-j*
     this-tree that-tree -on more-big   -3SG
     'This tree is taller than that tree'

b.   A -c'ä   -ga a -leli -n   e -bie   -qa
the-house-in   she-be in-on   he-her see-PAST
'She being in the house, he saw her'

7.3.2   *Indirect confirmation of Universal 3C*

The six remaining languages in our sample for which a primary Locative
Comparative can be unequivocally attested do not show direct surface
parallelism, but they clearly have the possibility to derank S-chains under
non-identity of subjects. Thus, as far as the languages are concerned
which have a clear instance of a Locative Comparative as their primary
choice, Universal 3C has no counterexample in our sample.

Miwok has a subordinate mode, the present tense of which is
employed to express simultaneous action. Freeland (1951: 82) notes:
'These subordinate tense forms are treated quite differently according to
whether or not their subject is the same as that of the main verb.' In the
case of identity of subjects, the subordinate mode has no pronominal
affix to indicate its subject: 'the reference to the main verb is simply
understood' (ibid.: 83), and the subordinate form is characterized by the
suffix -*ʔpak* on the verbal stem. In case the subjects are non-identical, no
special subordinating suffix occurs, but the subordinate forms must be
marked for subject by means of possessive pronouns: 'these forms are
really a subjective absolute construction, comparable to the ablative
absolute in Latin' (ibid.: 50). Cp.:

(24)   MIWOK:
a.   Oŝ'akci-ʔ   tunic'kci -ʔ   manik nangakci-y
girl   -NOM small one-NOM more   boy   -on
'The girl is smaller than the boy'

b.   Hinaka -ʔpak   -ton   mili-na -k
cook-PRES-SUBORD -you-DAT. PL sing-PAST-1SG
'While cooking for you, I sang'

c.   ʔiwaʔ   -mok siyici   mutos
eat-PRES -your watch-PRES-I-you
'While you are eating, I am watching you'

Salinan deranks simultaneous predicates by means of the subordinating prefix *le*; in this construction, the deranked predicate no longer takes
tense marking. Simultaneous predicates which are deranked in this
fashion may freely occur under absolute conditions. Cp.:

(25) SALINAN:
a.   *Ragas-mo in   luwa ti hek*
      surely-you more   man on-me
      'You are certainly more of a man than me'

b.   *Le   yax   tum-te -ma   komaiyu   hek tum-Xolon*
      SUBORD-come to -my-house leave-PAST I   to -X.
      'When he came to my house, I had left for Xolon'

Mandinka matches its Locative Comparative by the fact that predicates in S-chains can be deranked freely into absolutely used participial forms:

(26) MANDINKA:
a.   *A ka gya ni ma*
      he is big me on
      'He is bigger than me'

b.   *A tara-to   kongo -la sangyi berahali*
      he go -PCP. PRES country-to rain   fell hard
      'As he went to the country, it was pouring with rain'

A situation which is completely parallel to the case of Mandinka can be noted for Tamazight, the Berber language in our sample. In Tamazight comparatives, the standard NP is marked by the preposition *fell/foul*, which is generally translated by French grammarians as *sur* 'upon' (see, for instance, Hanoteau (1896: 52)). Cp.:

(27) TAMAZIGHT:
      Enta ihengrin foull i
      he   is-tall   upon me
      'He is taller than me'

This comparative construction is matched by the use of so-called Participles in Tamazight. These are verbal forms which are marked for person and for tense (viz. Past, Present and Future), but which are also marked for subordination by special suffixes; the Present Participle is formed by attaching the suffix *-n* (Masc.) or *-t* (Fem.) to the third person singular of the Present Indicative. The most conspicuous use of these participles can be found in relative clauses and (direct and indirect) WH-questions; in these clause types, the predicate must have the form of a participle if the antecedent (c.q. the WH-word) is the subject of the clause. This deranking of a finite main verb into a subordinate participial form takes place despite the fact that relative clauses and WH-questions must be introduced by independent (relative or interrogative) pronouns. Cp.:

(28)   TAMAZIGHT:
a.   Ales oua   ittaten
       man this-DEM/who-REL   eat-PCP. PRES. MASC
       'The man who eats'

b.   Ma   ittaten
       who-Q eat-PRES. PCP. MASC
       'Who eats?'

Apart from this non-absolute use, we can also find ample evidence for the absolute participial construction. Hanoteau (1896: 33) presents a number of examples of simultaneous structures in which one of the predicates has a participial form, while the other is an indicative main verb. Thus, Tamazight has deranked S-chains, in which, moreover, deranking can be absolute:

(29)   TAMAZIGHT:
       Tamet' tarer' telabasset
       woman this   be plain-PCP. PRES. FEM
       ta   nnek   tehousi
       that of-you be pretty-PRES. IND. 3SG. FEM
       'This woman is plain (but) your (woman) is pretty'

The next language which we will have to discuss in the present context is Navaho. For this language, a clear assessment of the facts is hampered by the lack of sufficiently reliable data. Pinnow (1964: 66) states explicitly that Navaho has a comparative construction of the form illustrated in *(30)*; applying the criteria which we adopted in chapter 2, we must rate this construction as an instance of the Locative Comparative. Cp.:

(30)   NAVAHO:
       Bi -laah   'ansneez
       him-above big-PRES. 1SG
       'I am bigger than him'

Unfortunately, however, Pinnow does not indicate the source of this example. The only full grammatical description of Navaho that I know of (Haile, 1926; see also Haile, 1941) does not mention Pinnow's construction at all. While discussing the expression of comparison in Navaho, Haile (1926: 61) remarks that this language employs a method of 'itemizing, or pointing out, for instance, this is short, that not long enough, this rough, that smooth, etc.' A plausible conclusion to be drawn from this passage would be that Navaho apparently has a Conjoined

Comparative, but, again, no clear examples are available on this point.

With respect to the codification of temporal chaining in Navaho, the facts are more straightforward. Haile (1926: 99) notes that 'perhaps the most common form of particip'ializing is offered by adding the suffix -*go* to any tense form'. If this suffix is added to a predicate which is marked for present tense, the verbal construct can be used as a predicate in an S-chain; since the verbal form retains the possibility of having its own subject, we can conclude that such predicates can be used absolutely. An example is:

(31)   NAVAHO:
       Naholtxa -go
       rain-PRES -ADV
       'When/while it rains'

One might question here whether the verbal form exemplified in the above sentence is a real case of deranking, since it does not seem to be reduced in personal and temporal morphology. I think that this objection can be refuted by pointing out that the suffix -*go* which marks this Navaho predicate is an item which has a very general subordinating function in the language. Haile (1926: 70–1) states that 'we may well consider the suffix -*go* as indicative of the Navaho adverb, regardless of its being found after a noun, pronoun, postposition, numeral, adverb or verb. Its modifying relation to the predicate is unmistakable, as their position, even when there are several adverbs of this calibre, is always before the predicate.' Thus, the suffix -*go* not only adverbializes predicates; it is also employed to mark a subordinated form of adjectives (cp. *nizuni* 'nice' vs. *nizuni-go* 'nicely'), of nouns (cp. *dine* 'man' vs. *dine-go* 'as a man'), and of other parts of speech. Given these facts, I think we are justified in rating constructions like (31) as instances of absolutely deranked S-chains. Taken in conjunction with Pinnow's example (30), these constructions thus provide for (indirect) confirmation of the correctness of Universal 3B.

Finally, we must discuss the case of Tamil. This Dravidian language has a large variety of comparatives, the selection of which may be influenced at least partially by sociolinguistic considerations (see Asher, 1982: 88). That Tamil has a Locative Comparative is documented by the following sentence (taken from Beythan, 1943: 135):

(32)   TAMIL:
a.   *At -il -um ittu cinnatu*
       that-on-PRT this big
       'This is bigger than that'

This Locative Comparative is matched by a deranked simultaneous construction in which the deranked predicate has the form of the Infinitive on *-a*. Absolute use of this Infinitive is common:

(32) TAMIL:
b.   Avan var -a   kanteen
      he   come-INF see-PAST. 1SG
      'While he was coming, I saw (him)'

Interestingly, this deranked simultaneous construction also functions as the model of another comparative construction in Tamil. In this comparative, the standard NP is marked for accusative case (i.e., it has the form of a direct object) and it is followed by the marking element *vita*. Cp.:

(32) TAMIL:
c.   Enka viitte   vita avaru viittu   pericaa irukkutu
      our house-ACC PRT his   house-NOM big   be-PRES. 3SG
      'His house is bigger than our house'

The important question with respect to this construction is, of course, what the category status of the element *vita* may be. All authors on Tamil syntax whom I have consulted agree that this element is not a spatial postposition. Asher (1982: 88) refers to the element *vita* as a postposition, but does not qualify this solution. Other authors (in particular, Arden (1942: 111) and Beythan (1943: 135) analyse the item *vita* as the old Infinitive of the verb *vittu* 'to leave, to leave behind'. If this analysis is followed, the modelling of the *vita*-comparative on the deranked simultaneous construction becomes evident: the literal meaning of sentence (32c) will then be something like 'His house, leaving behind our house, is big.' It will be noted that this *vita*-comparative is closely related to an Exceed Comparative, both in its meaning and in its structural manifestation.

7.4   Indeterminate cases

The phenomenon of partial neutralization of spatial marking is relatively frequent in the case of the marking of locative versus allative relations. My sample contains three cases in which the classification of a comparative construction as either a Locative or an Allative Comparative is affected by this kind of indeterminacy. In section 2.3.3, I classified these languages as members of the category of Locative Comparatives. In the discussion which follows, I will adduce some justification for this decision. It must be kept in mind, however, that classification of indeterminate cases such as these will, by its very nature, always be arbitrary to some extent.

First, let us discuss the situation in Mapuche. As we already noted in section 2.2.5, the standard NP in Mapuche comparatives is marked by the postposition *meu*, which has a very general locational meaning; it may indicate position, but it is also employed as the marker of indirect objects. Cp.:

(33)   MAPUCHE:
a.   *Karlos doi   fucha-i   Francesko meu*
      K.   more tall -3SG F.   on/to
      'Karlos is taller than Francesko'

b.   *Tani welelchi manshun Antonio meu*
      his sold-PCP ox   A.   to
      'The ox which he sold to Antonio'

c.   *Ruka ni rani   meu*
      house its middle in
      'In the middle of the house'

Thus, on the face of it, the comparative in Mapuche must be rated as an indeterminate case between the Locative and the Allative Comparative.

The reason why I have ultimately classified Mapuche as a language with a Locative Comparative lies in the fact that this comparative has its overt structural parallel in the way in which Mapuche encodes its S-chains. Mapuche deranks its simultaneous predicates by putting them into the infinitive form, which consists of the bare verb stem and the nominal suffix *-n*. That these infinitives are nominals is brought out by the fact that subjects of deranked simultaneous predicates must have the form of a genitive phrase or a possessive pronoun. Now, the point is that, in the expression of simultaneous action, the deranked predicate must be followed by the postposition *meu*:

(34)   MAPUCHE:
      Ni amu-n   meu inche kai amu-a -n
      his go -INF on I   too go -FUT-1SG
      'When he goes, I will go too'

Given this situation, we can conclude that, if we take Mapuche to have a Locative Comparative, this language forms a direct and straightforward confirmation of Universal 3C. In other words, the decision to classify Mapuche as a language with a Locative Comparative enables us to describe this language as an instance of a regularity which has been attested independently for at least eight other languages in the sample. If we choose the opposite solution of categorizing Mapuche as a case of the Allative Comparative, we must conclude that this language is a counter-example to Universal 3B, since no possibility of posterior deranking in C-chains can be documented in Mapuche. Faced with these alternatives, I think it is methodologically justifiable to opt for the solution which enables us to treat Mapuche as an instance of a regularity. Hence, I have finally decided to classify the Mapuche comparative as a case of the Locative Comparative.

A similar line of reasoning can be followed in defence of the decision to classify Cebuano as a language with a Locative Comparative. In Cebuano, the standard NP in comparatives is put into the Goal-case, which is marked by the prepositions *sa* (for definite NPs) or *ug* (for indefinite NPs), or by specific case-affixes (for pronouns). The grammatical function of an item in the Goal-case depends on the voice of the verb in the setence; in active sentences, the Goal-case marks the patient or recipient of the action, while in passive sentences the case can be used to indicate the indirect object, the location of an action, or the direction of a movement. Examples in which the indeterminacy of the Cebuano Goal-case is illustrated are the following:

(35)   CEBUANO:
a.   *Muqinum   ku ug   tubaq*
      want-drink I   GOAL   palm toddy
      'I want to drink palm toddy'

b.   *Muqadtu ku sa   Banawa*
      go-PRES   I   GOAL B.
      'I am going to Banawa'

c.   *Dihaq   ku sa   Banawa*
      be-present I GOAL   B.
      'I am in Banawa'

Examples of the comparative construction in Cebuano are:

(36)   CEBUANO:
a.   *Taqas siya   nimu*
      tall   he-NOM   you-GOAL
      'He is taller than you'

b.   *Maqayu bir ug   tubig*
      good   beer GOAL   water
      'Beer is better than water'

Now, as was the case in Mapuche, we can note that in Cebuano, too, the comparative construction has a direct surface match in one of the simultaneous action constructions of this language. The deranked predicate in this S-chain has the so-called Abstract Form (see Wolff, 1967, I, 346–8), that is, a verbal stem with the prefix *pag-/pagka-/inig-*. The form is a nominalization, which requires genitive case for its subject; from this, it follows that absolute use of such nominalized predicates is permitted. Now, when such Abstract Forms are used as the deranked predicate in S-chains, they may optionally be marked by the presence of the Goal-marker *sa*; cp.:

(37) CEBUANO:
      (Sa) pag -qabut nilau sa   Urmuk,
      GOAL ABSTR-arrive their GOAL U.
      waq na   dihaq   si   papa   nila
      not   anymore be-present the-NOM father their
      'When they arrived at Urmuk, their father was no longer there'

Thus, we can observe a direct parallelism between the expressions of comparison and simultaneous chaining in Cebuano. Accordingly, we arrive at a classification of this language as a member of the Locative Comparative class, using the same argumentation which we have followed in the case of Mapuche.[6]

Finally, we must consider the rather complicated state of affairs in Tubu. In the comparative of this Saharan language, the standard NP is marked by the postposition *du*, an item which has a very general locational meaning, and which may be glossed as 'in', 'on', 'at', 'to' or 'with', depending on the context. Thus, we may conclude that the Tubu comparative is indeterminate as to its classification as an Allative or a Locative Comparative. An example of the construction is:

(38) TUBU:
      Sa -umma gere   du   madu
      his-eye   blood LOC red
      'His eye is redder than blood'

If we look at the ways in which temporal chaining is formalized in Tubu, we find that the locational marker *du* is also employed as a marker of adverbial temporal clauses. In this case, the item functions as a postpositional marker to a clause in which the predicate has retained its normal finite form. Examples of the construction are:

(39) TUBU:
a.   *Arko cidi   du   zapten*
      goat cry-PAST. 3SG LOC return-PAST. 3SG
      'The goat returned weeping'

b.   *Nce   du   tere*
be-PRES. 2SG   LOC   come-FUT. 1SG
'While you are there, I will come'

It is unclear whether the construction type illustrated in *(39a/b)* is a case of predicate-deranking, or rather a case of clause-embedding. Lukas (1953: 175) calls the item *du* in this function a 'postposition', contrasting it to items like *ago* 'when' and *nano* 'so that', which are clause-initial and are taken to be 'subordinating conjunctions'. Lukas writes: '[Postpositions] have as their essential task to expand sentences. The Tubu language thus achieves with their help what we achieve by means of subordinate clauses. Hence, these postpositions replace subordinating conjunctions, which are almost completely absent' (my translation). From this quotation, one might deduce that clauses which are marked by 'postpositional' clause-final elements like *du* must be conceived of as NPs, whereas clauses introduced by clause-initial conjunctions have the structural status of sentences. Thus, a case might be made for the deranked status of the predicate in the clause marked by *du*; one might rate it as a case in which a whole clause is nominalized. However, one might also rightfully argue that, since there is certainly no trace of deranking on the predicate itself, the construction is actually a case of clause-embedding and hence of no relevance as a confirmation of Universal 3C.

It must be added that, whatever status one wants to assign to the complement of *du* in *(39a/b)*, the indeterminacy of the typological status of the Tubu comparative will not be dissolved by it in any case. As it turns out, constructions with clause-final *du* can have a simultaneous reading, but the construction also allows freely for a purpose-interpretation. Moreover, if the verb in the clause is in the negative form, the clause must be translated as a 'before'-clause, thus indicating the posterior event in a consecutive chain. Cp.:

(40)   TUBU:
a.   *Turku ga   nusu   du   re*
jackal ACC he-kill LOC   he-came
'He came to kill the jackal'

b.   *Cubbunde   du   adema   fadege*
he-stab-NEG LOC   woman   said
'Before he stabbed her, the woman said . . .'

In other words, even if we view the *du*-construction as a case of predicate-deranking which serves as a model for the comparative construction in Tubu, we will still be at a loss to decide whether this comparative should be classified as an Allative or as a Locative Comparative.

In this context, it is useful to point out that, in addition to the *du*-construction, there is also a case of genuine, unambiguous simultaneous deranking in Tubu. This is represented by the First Temporal Form (Lukas, 1953: 95), which is formed from the (tense-less, but person-marked) Aorist Indicative by means of the suffix *-go/-wo*. Cp.:

> *(41)* TUBU:
> Yir   nun   -go   yari   terege
> come-IMP say-you-TEMP I-run I-come
> 'When you say "come", I come in a hurry'

Given the existence of such a form, we are allowed to consider Tubu as at least indirect confirmation of Universal 3C. There remains, however, one rather puzzling fact. If we look at the functions which are performed by the simultaneous suffix *-go*, we find that this element is also employed as an allative marker on nominals (Lukas, 1953: 161). Thus, it seems that the simultaneous action construction in Tubu has been modelled on an allative spatial relation; this is of course highly untypical. The allative codification of S-chains in Tubu has not led to a comparative in which the standard NP is marked by *-go*; instead, the language has chosen to employ the indeterminate marker *du*, which is employed as a postposition of clauses which can be interpreted as simultaneous, final or posterior consecutive chains. All in all, we can conclude that the situation in Tubu is rather muddled, and that the distinction between locative and allative relations has been neutralized by this language in highly unorthodox ways. However, as I stated above, I do not think that the indeterminacies which can be observed in Tubu should lead to the consequence that this language should be regarded as a counterexample to the set of chaining-based universals of comparative-type choice.

7.5   Conclusion

In this chapter, we have tested the validity of Universal 3B and Universal 3C against the data from the languages in the sample. Of the 19 relevant languages, we have found that 15 confirm the prediction made by either Universal 3B or Universal 3C. Moreover, at least five of these languages can be shown to exhibit a direct surface parallelism between their comparative and the relevant chaining construction. In three cases, an indeterminacy of the typological status of the comparative construction must be attested. We have argued that it is best to consider these constructions as instances of the Locative Comparative and that, as such, they confirm the prediction made by Universal 3C.

The four languages which are problematic to a certain extent are all languages which have an Allative Comparative. For two of these languages (Siuslawan and Tarascan), the problem is that no absolute use of their posterior deranking procedure could be documented; it is possible (though, of course, not certain) that this problem can be cancelled once we have more detailed data on these languages at our disposal. In Breton, the problem is that the Allative Comparative is not matched by a deranked C-chain, at least not in the present stage of the development of the language. Finally, Kanuri presents the rare case of a comparative which has not been modelled on a strict chaining construction, but rather on the semantically related final construction.

8

The Exceed Comparative

8.1 Introduction

In the two previous chapters, we have examined the various subtypes of the class of adverbial comparatives. Now, we must turn to the other class of comparatives in which the standard NP has fixed case, viz. the Exceed Comparative. From the listing in section 2.3.4 it can be seen that the Exceed Comparative is among the largest classes of comparative constructions in our sample; 20 languages select this type of comparative as their primary option. Also, it is clear that the option for an Exceed Comparative is firmly tied up with SVO word order, at least as far as the primary instances of this category are concerned.

In the set of chaining-based universals, the universal which is relevant to the Exceed Comparative is Universal 2A:

UNIVERSAL 2A: *If a language has an Exceed Comparative, then it may have only conditional deranking.*

Thus, what we have to do in this chapter is to demonstrate that the languages which have an Exceed Comparative are languages which may derank their predicates in temporal chains, but only if the condition is met that the subjects of the predicates in the chain are identical. It will become clear below that it is usually the (conditionally deranked) simultaneous construction which serves as the model for the comparative in these languages; cases in which the Exceed Comparative can be shown to be modelled on the (conditionally deranked) consecutive construction are very rare. It must be added, however, that the semantic distinction between simultaneous and consecutive action has been formally neutralized in a considerable number of the languages at issue, so that in these cases the identification of the modelling chaining construction is necessarily indeterminate.

As we observed in section 2.3.4, the Exceed Comparative can be attested in three formally distinct variants. It is my opinion that this formal diversification is not caused by factors which are specific to the typology of comparative constructions; in other words, I assume that the differences in the surface structure of Exceed Comparatives are not significant for our typological purpose, and that they are the result of variation with respect to properties that are independent of the choice of a particular comparative-type. Some suggestions as to the nature of these independent properties will be presented in the final section of this chapter. In the meanwhile, I will maintain the tripartite division of Exceed Comparatives, but it must be understood that my main reason for doing so is to serve the clarity of the exposition.

8.2   The Exceed-1 Comparative: serialization

One highly typical and easily identifiable variant of the Exceed Comparative is the construction in which the exceed-verb and the comparative predicate are parts of a so-called 'serial verb string'. Before I present the data of those languages in which such an Exceed-1 Comparative can be attested, it may be useful to make some clarifying remarks on this phenomenon of verbal serialization. In particular, I will comment upon the conditionality and the semantic function of constructions in which verbs are serialized.

In the words of Hyman (1975: 136), the term *serialization* 'generally refers to verbs which occur in sequence, but which are not overtly marked for coordination or subordination with respect to each other'. In other words, in a serialization verbs are simply strung one after the other, thus forming a 'serial verb string' or 'Reihensatz' (Dempwolff, 1939: 67).[1] The phenomenon of serialization is widely spread among the languages of West Africa, in particular the Kwa group (see George, 1975), but it also occurs in Mandarin Chinese (see Li and Thompson, 1973a/b), in Vietnamese, Thai and Cambodian, and in a number of pidgins and creolizations (for example Sranan; see Voorhoeve, 1962). Examples of constructions in which such a serial verb string occurs are:

(1)   CAMBODIAN:
    Ta   yok dong-pakka seese sombotr
    old-man take pen   write letter
    'The old man took a pen and wrote a letter'

(2)   YORUBA:
    Mo fi   ade   ge idi
    I   took machete cut wood
    'I took a machete and cut wood/I cut wood with a machete'

(3) SRANAN:
A tjary a buku kon gi mi
he carry the book come give me
'He has brought me the book'

Whether such serial verb constructions have their diachronic origin in coordinate structures is open to dispute; there seems to be some evidence that they have (see Hyman, 1971; Awolobuyi, 1973; Li and Thompson, 1973a/b). But whatever position one takes with respect to diachronic origin, there can be little doubt that, from a synchronic point of view, serial verb constructions can no longer be treated as symmetric structures. In other words, in synchronic syntax serial verb constructions must be interpreted as structures in which the verbs in the string are not (or no longer) of equal structural rank: it must be assumed that all the non-first verbs are deranked with respect to the verb that occupies the initial position in the string. That this must be the case can be shown from Sranan; in this language, NP-complements can be extracted from a serial verb string, which proves that such strings are not subject to the Coordinate Structure Constraint:

(4) SRANAN:
a. *Yu go teki tyari a batra na abrasey*
you go take carry the bottle to other-side
'You brought the bottle over to the other side'

b. *San yu go teki tyari na abrasey ?*
what you go take carry to other-side
'What did you bring over to the other side?'

A similar phenomenon can be observed in Mandarin Chinese. In this language, NP-complements of a serial verb can be placed in topic position (see Mullie, 1947):

(5) MANDARIN:
a. *Wo tsjeng i kin zjow laî*
I weigh one pound meat come
'I will buy one pound of meat'

b. *I kin zjow , wo tsjeng laî*
one pound meat I weigh come
'One pound of meat I will buy'

Other arguments in favour of a deranking analysis of serial verb constructions stem from the fact that, in a serial string, it is only the first verb which stays marked for normal verbal morphology. As Givón

(1975: 84) remarks, 'one of the first things that may happen to erstwhile serial verbs . . . is loss of ability to take normal verb affixes, such as modalities, subject agreement or object pronouns. This process is obviously gradual, so that a verb may lose its ability to take some affixes but not all at the same time.' Furthermore, Givón calls attention to the fact that, in many languages, non-first verbs in a serial string tend to be syntactically reanalysed as prepositions or conjunctions. (Again, this is a gradual process so that a serial verb, even when reanalysed, may retain a number of syntactical verbal traits. For one thing, it may remain at the original serial verb position, even if this position is not the one which is normally occupied by prepositions or conjunctions.) All these facts lead to the conclusion that serial verb constructions are not a case of syntactic coordination, at least not as far as synchronic syntax is concerned; despite the absence of overt subordinate marking, they are instances of temporal chains in which non-first predicates have been deranked.

With respect to the *conditionality* of this type of deranked chaining construction, authors generally agree that the formation of a serial verb string requires the identity of subjects. Such, for example, is the opinion of Welmers (1973: 367), who writes: 'Serialization . . . seems to involve actions that can be associated with each other only if they are performed by the same subject.' It is true that we come across occasional instances of serialization in which the string appears to have been truncated, to the effect that a certain NP within the string functions at the same time as the direct object of the verb which precedes it and as the subject of the verb which follows it. An example of such a case is offered by the following sentence from Sranan,[2] in which the NP *a batra* 'the bottle' can be seen to perform this double function:

(6)   SRANAN:
      A trowé   a   batra go na abrasey
      he throw the bottle go to other-side
      'He threw the bottle to the other side'

Similar cases are attested for Mandarin Chinese by Li and Thompson (1973a). On the whole, however, it must be said that cases such as these occupy a marginal position within the domain of serialization and that, in the overwhelming majority of cases, Welmers' observation turns out to be confirmed by the facts. Hence we may conclude that, from a structural point of view, serial verb constructions are instances of conditionally deranked chaining constructions.

As for the *semantic function* of a serial verb string, it can be observed that such constructions are essentially indeterminate. This semantic vagueness is illustrated clearly for Mandarin Chinese by Li and Thompson

(1978), who note that serialization in this language may be interpreted as indicating parallel events, consecutive events, simultaneous events, purpose-constructions or result-constructions. Li and Thompson (1978: 241) state explicitly: 'What is evident . . . is that the serial verb construction is used to encode a number of different relationships between predicates in Mandarin. These predicate relationships are structurally distinct in most other languages because of the presence of grammatical markers.' In short, serial verb strings are formal neutralizations of the semantic distinction between simultaneous action, consecutive action and several other semantic relations, in much the same way as balanced coordinations are typically neutral in this respect (see section 4.1).[3] Just as is generally the case with balanced structures, the appropriate interpretation of a serial verb construction must be inferred on the basis of such factors as pragmatic and contextual knowledge, knowledge of the meaning of the particular lexical items in the string, and clues which derive from aspect marking of the first verb in the series.

To sum up, we can say that a serial verb construction is a type of conditionally deranked temporal chain, in which the distinction between simultaneous and consecutive action has been neutralized. Now, if we turn to the 20 languages in the sample which make up the primary instances of the Exceed Comparative, we find that ten of them have the possibility to form a serial verb construction. In these languages, a straightforward parallel between chaining construction and comparative formation can be established. As the examples presented below will demonstrate, the comparative in these languages *is a special case of the general serial verb construction*; to be exact, it is a serial verb string which contains a gradable predicate and an exceed-verb as its members. Obviously, these ten languages provide strong and direct support for the claim which is contained in Universal 2A. Examples include:

(7) CAMBODIAN:
a. *Ta   yok dong-pakka seese sombotr*
   old-man take pen   write letter
   'The old man took a pen and wrote a letter'

b. *Bony-sreuy khngom crieng pirueh cireng nih*
   elder-sister my   sing   good   exceed this
   'My elder sister sings better than this'

(8) DAGOMBA:
a. *Nana   san -la   o -suli n -dum nira*
   scorpion take-HAB his-tail PREF-sting people
   'The scorpion stings people with its tail'

b.   *O -make dpeoo   n   -gare   -ma*
     he-has   strength PREF-surpass-me
     'He is stronger than me'

(9)   DUALA:
a.   *A mala nongo diwendi*
     he go   fetch knife
     'He went and fetched a knife'

b.   *Nin ndabo e kolo buka   nine*
     this house it big   exceed that
     'This house is bigger than that'

(10) GBEYA:
a.   *Wa kay wa   a´ nu*
     they take them put ground
     'They take them and put them on the ground'

b.   *Ngma mo   gan ó ngay gán   nzapa na*
     some thing NEG is strong surpass God   NEG
     'There is nothing stronger than God'

(11) JABEM:
a.   *Ngapale ke-tang ke-ko   andu*
     boy   he-cries he-remain house
     'The boy is crying in the house'

b.   *Tamoc kapoeng ke-lelec   ae su*
     father is-big   he-exceed me ready
     'My father is taller than me'

(12) MANDARIN:
a.   *Wo na   hwo-penn wai-peul kiu*
     I   carry stove   outside go
     'I carry the stove outside'

b.   *Wo na p'i   ma   pi   ni   na p'i   ma   kwai*
     I   this CLASS horse exceed you this CLASS horse is-big
     'My horse is bigger than your horse'

(13) NGUNA:
a.   *Ku po   mari a paki nia*
     you PERF do   it go-to him
     'You have done it to him'

b.   *Namauriana e parua liu   navinaga*
      life   it great   exceed food
      'Life is more than food:
      man does not live by bread alone'

(14) THAI:
a.   *Phom jang moong araj   maj-hen*
      I   still look-at thing not-see
      'I still can't see anything'

b.   *Khaw jaj kwaa   phom*
      he   big exceed me
      'He is bigger than me'

(15) VIETNAMESE:
a.   *Ong khong co   dem vo-con qua   Ben-Phap*
      he   NEG   PERF take family go-over France
      'He has not brought his family over to France'

b.   *Vang qui   hon   bac*
      gold valuable exceed silver
      'Gold is worth more than silver'

(16) YORUBA:
a.   *Mo fi   ade   ge igi*
      I   took machete cut wood
      'I took the machete and cut wood'

b.   *Ile mi kere ju   tiwon*
      house my small exceed theirs
      'My house is smaller than theirs'

Regarding these examples, we must make a few additional remarks. First, it will be noted that in a serial Exceed Comparative of this type it can be either the exceed-verb or the comparative predicate which is the deranked (i.e., non-first) predicate in the construction. This essential lack of ordering becomes understandable once we realize that such serial verb constructions allow for a definite simultaneous interpretation, and that, generally, S-chains imply no directionality (see section 4.5). Secondly, the above examples show that the usual form of a deranked verb in a serial verb string is that of a bare verbal stem, which lacks all morphological marking for tense, mood, aspect or person. Only two cases are exceptional in this respect. In Jabem, we note that the deranked verb has retained its person marking (see *(11a/b)*). Nevertheless, the construction must be considered to be a case of predicate deranking. Dempwolff (1939: 81) explicitly states that there is a grammatical contrast between a 'Reihensatz' like *(11a)* and a construction which involves several independent sentences. Consequently, Dempwolff deals with cases like *(11a)* in his section on the simplex sentence in Jabem. Conjunction with the connective element *ma* 'and', which is illustrated in

(17) *JABEM:*
      Ganggom ke-som bingmakic , ma ngpapale se -omac
      G.   he-told jokes   and children they-laughed
      'Ganggom told jokes, and the children laughed'

expresses 'reine zeitliche Folge', that is, a succession of events without the implication of a total event (Dempwolff, 1939: 83). In conjunctions with *ma*, change of subjects is possible; a 'Reihensatz', on the other hand, can only be constructed under identity of subjects in the string.

In Dagomba (see *(8a/b)*), non-first verbs in a serial verb string have no subject pronoun, but the conjugational prefix *-n*. In contrast to first verbs in a string, non-first verbs cannot be marked for tense (Fisch, 1912: 33–4). Hence, in this language too we can consider the serial verb construction as a case of predicate deranking.

As a last remark, we must point out that one of the languages with an Exceed-1 Comparative has also the possibility to form another variant of the Exceed Comparative. Hence, this language, Duala, will show up once more in the course of the discussion in the next section.

8.3 Other types of the Exceed Comparative

In contrast to languages with a 'pure', non-overtly marked serial verb construction, other SVO-languages may choose to derank their predicates in a more overt way. A widely used procedure for this type of deranking involves putting the predicate into some nominalized (infinitival) or participialized (adjectival) form. In languages in which this 'overt' deranking procedure is chosen, there is usually a formal distinction between the encoding of simultaneous and consecutive action. In other words, if a deranking SVO-language does not have a serial verb string, then neutralization of mode of chaining is generally abandoned. An illustration of this point is formed by the two chaining constructions in Igbo, which we discussed in section 4.1. As we will see below, Igbo lacks the possibility to form a serial verb string of the type illustrated in the previous section.

In the 11 instances of the Exceed Comparative which we will deal with in this section, it is either the exceed-verb or the comparative predicate which is the main predicate in the construction, while the remaining predicate is overtly marked for subordination. For ease of reference, I will use the term 'Exceed-2 Comparative' for cases where the comparative predicate has been subordinated, and the term 'Exceed-3 Comparative' for the opposite case.

For a large majority of languages which have one of these types of Exceed Comparatives, a direct parallelism between the surface form of the comparative and the form of one of the chaining constructions (usually, the S-chain) can be established. A first case in point is Igbo. As we saw in section 4.1, simultaneous predicates in Igbo are deranked into abstract verbal nouns, which are formed from verbal stems by means of the prefix *à/-è-*; application of this deranking procedure requires identity of subjects. This formation of S-chains has a straightforward match in the Igbo comparative, in which the comparative predicate is put into the form of an adverbially used abstract noun. Cp.:

(18) IGBO:
a. *Ha no n'oce nà èri   nri*
    they sat down PRT eating food
    'They sat down eating'

b. *Ge ka   m   ike*
    you exceed me strength
    'You are stronger than me'

A similar case of surface parallelism can be documented in Margi. In the Exceed-2 Comparative of this language, the comparative predicate has the form of an abstract nominal; it is constructed here as the complement of the preposition *de* 'with', and thus functions syntactically as part of an adverbial phrase. This same adverbial construction is used to derank predicates in S-chains; in this case, the preposition *de* has an infinitive (which, in this language, is a nominalized form) as its complement. This type of simultaneous deranking can be applied only if there is identity of subjects in the chain. Cp.:

(19) MARGI:
a. *Nanda ga sha de   wiwi*
    they SUBJ came with run-INF
    'They came running'

b. *Naja ga   mdia -da de dzegam-kur*
    he   SUBJ exceed-me with tall   -ABSTR. NOUN
    'He is taller than me'

The situation in Banda is practically identical to that in Margi. Again, we find that the comparative predicate is nominalized into an abstract noun, and that it forms a part of an adverbial phrase as the complement of the preposition *de*. Here, too, the comparative is matched exactly by the formation of S-chains; predicates in such chains are deranked under subject-identity into infinitives, which must, in this construction, be preceded by the preposition *de*. Cp.:

(20) BANDA:
a.   Anda ne mo dere   ne ze de   ayan
      house of me exceeds of you with bigness
      'My house is bigger than your house'

b.   Se sete gute   de   ke mbi iti   ni
      he was returning with INF sing song his
      'He returned, singing a song'

In Bari, we find a case of the Exceed-3 Comparative; the comparative predicate is the main verb in the construction, while the verb *tongun* 'to exceed' is deranked into an infinitive, by reduplication of the first syllable of the stem. It turns out that such infinitives can also be used as participles (Spagnolo, 1933: 232), that is, they may represent deranked predicates in S-chains under identity of subjects:

(21) BARI:
a.   A   kirut lopeng kwekwindye ngwayik ko   mugun
      and then he   showed   the-boys with body
      nanyit , mö-mökin
      his-own. INF-try
      'And then he showed it to the boys with his own body, trying
      (the exercises)'

b.   Körsuk a lokong to -tongun Jökö
      K.   is wise   INF-exceed J.
      'Körsuk is wiser than Jökö'

The formation of the comparative in Yagan is essentially parallel to Bari. Yagan, too, has an Exceed-3 Comparative; in this case, the exceed-verb *manaan* has been marked by the suffix *-a*, an element which turns out to be the regular marker for Present Participles. Unfortunately, no full sentences in which such a Present Participle is used are available. Cp.:

(22) YAGAN:
a.   Kik'i-keia manaan-a   ulpaki
      him -ACC exceed -PCP. PRES sinner
      'more sinful than him'

b.   *Kuru-a*
     love -PCP. PRES
     'loving'

c.   *Uei   -wöschtagu-a*
     adultery-do   -PCP. PRES
     'committing adultery'

Wolof is one of the rare cases where the Exceed Comparative has a direct surface parallel in a consecutive action construction. In this language, there exists a Consecutive Form, which is used to represent posterior predicates in C-chains. Formally, such a deranked predicate consists of a verb in the (subordinate) Subjunctive Mood, preceded by the marker *à*; identity of subjects is obligatory in this construction. Exactly the same construction is used to express NP-comparison. Cp.:

(23) WOLOF:
a.   *Dem na   ma à   o   ko*
      go   IND I   SER. MARK call-SUBJUNCT him
      'I went and called him'

b.   *Sa   yai   gen   na à   bakh*
      your mother exceed IND SER. MARK is-good-SUBJUNCT
      sa   bai
      your father
      'Your mother is better than your father'

Next, let us take a look at the three Bantu languages in the sample. As might be expected, these languages employ basically the same procedure in the formation of their comparatives. In particular, they represent the subordinate predicate in their respective Exceed Comparatives in the form of a noun, which is marked by a prefix as a member of the nominal class of abstract nouns and infinitives.

Starting with Swahili, we can note that the primary comparative in this language is an Exceed-3 Comparative, in which the exceed-verb *-shinda* has been nominalized by means of the infinitival prefix *ku-*:

(24) SWAHILI:
      Mti huu ni mrefu ku -shinda ule
      tree this is big   INF-exceed that
      'This tree is taller than that'

The use of an infinitive in the Swahili comparative is matched by the fact that such forms may also be used to represent one of the predicates in an

S-chain if there is identity of subjects. In this case, the two simultaneous predicates are joined together by the connective particle *na*, an item which can only be followed by nominals and which is best regarded as the equivalent of the English preposition *with*. Loogman (1965: 376) writes, 'When two coordinated verbs are joined together by *na*, the second form is always an infinitive. Between two personal [i.e., non-finite] verb-forms the coordinating *na* cannot be used.' Brauner and Bantu (1964:146) state explicitly that the construction in which *na* is followed by an Infinitive is limited to simultaneous action, and that identity of subjects is obligatory. An example of the construction at issue is:

(25) SWAHILI:
      Tuliendela   safari   na   ku -ona   njaa
      we PAST-continue-it journey PRT   INF-be hungry   very
      'We continued our journey and were very hungry'

Another comparative construction in Swahili which appears to have been modelled on the *ku*-infinitive is the following (Ashton, 1947: 201):

(26) SWAHILI:
      Nyumba nyake nzuri sana ku-liko nyumba yangu
      house his   it-is good PRT   house my
      'His house is better than my house'

In this construction, the standard NP is marked by the particle *kuliko*. In its etymology, this item is the infinitive of a verbal stem *-liko* 'to be at, to be present'; in other words, the construction in (26) has as its literal meaning: 'His house is big, while there is my house'. Given this analysis, one might propose that this particular comparative is an indeterminate case, somewhat similar to the comparative in Telugu (see section 2.5). The *kuliko*-comparative in Swahili is a construction which is modelled on the conditionally deranked simultaneous chain in that language, but, untypically, this modelling has, in this case, not led to the selection of an exceed-verb.

Essentially the same situation as in Swahili can be encountered in Duala, the only difference being that Duala has (in addition to its serial Exceed Comparative; see section 8.2) an Exceed-2 Comparative instead of an Exceed-3 Comparative. In its Exceed-2 Comparative, Duala encodes the comparative predicate in the form of an abstract verbal noun in adverbial function. This abstract noun is characterized by the class prefix *di-/j-*, an element which also derives infinitives from verbal stems, cp.:

(27) DUALA:
Mbo e buki   ngoa jangwa
dog it exceed pig   being-smart
'A dog is smarter than a pig'

The chaining construction which matches this Exceed Comparative is completely parallel to the Swahili construction illustrated in *(25)*. Again, we find that, in an S-chain with identical subjects, one of the predicates must be deranked into an infinitival form, which is preceded by the preposition *nà* 'with'. Cp.:

(28) DUALA:
Di sibi   nà   jondea
we climbed PRT descend-ABSTR. NOUN
'We climbed and descended'

In Kirundi, the last Bantu language in the sample, both an Exceed-2 Comparative and an Exceed-3 Comparative are possible. In the former construction, the comparative predicate is encoded in the form of an (adverbially used) abstract noun in case the predicate is an adjective; if the comparative predicate happens to be a verb, it has the surface form of the infinitive, marked by the nominal class prefix *ku-*. In this latter case, the infinitive may optionally be preceded by the preposition *mu* 'in':

(29) KIRUNDI:
A -rusha   abaandi (mu) ku -kora
he-exceed others   in   INF-work
'He works harder than others'

In the Exceed-3 Comparative, the exceed-verb *-ruta* has the form of the infinitive marked in *ku-*; cp.:

(30) KIRUNDI:
Uyo ni mukuru ku -ruta   urya
this is big   INF-exceed that
'This is bigger than that'

It can be demonstrated that these variants of the Exceed Comparative are matched directly by the simultaneous action construction in Kirundi. In this construction, one of the simultaneous predicates is conditionally deranked into an infinitive; again, this infinitive may optionally be preceded by the preposition *mu*. Cp.:

(31) KIRUNDI:
Ndarushe   mu ku -kora
tire-PERF. 1SG in   INF-work
'I have tired myself while working'

It should be added here that the form of the Exceed-3 Comparative illustrated in *(30)* appears to be employed only when the comparative predicate is encoded as an adjective. If the comparative predicate has the form of a verb, the following type of construction is preferred:

(32)   KIRUNDI:
    A -karwaana a -ka -rusha   ibiindi
    he-fight-PAST he-PRT-exceed others
    'He fought better than the others'

This latter construction is paralleled directly by the Narrative Form, a type of consecutive chain which occurs in various Bantu languages. In this construction, posterior predicates are marked for subordination by the narrative infix *-ka-*. The Narrative Form presupposes identity of subjects in the chain. Cp.:

(33)   KIRUNDI:
    A -kiruka   a -ka   -gwa
    he-run-PAST he-NARR-fall
    'He ran away and fell'

Summing up the cases of the Exceed Comparative discussed so far, we can state that they all show direct surface parallelism with a conditionally deranked chaining construction; typically, it is the S-chain which has been selected for this modelling function. Thus, we can conclude that, for a large majority of languages with a primary Exceed Comparative, Universal 2A is corroborated in the strongest possible way. Now, the last two languages with which we must deal in this chapter are less straightforward, in that the modelling of their Exceed Comparative on their chaining formation seems to be tenuous, to say the least. The languages in question are Hausa and Fulani, both West African languages; the speakers of these languages are in close contact, especially in Northern Nigeria, but the languages are presumably not genetically related.

First, let us present the relevant facts of Hausa. All consulted sources which offer information on the Hausa comparative (Marré, 1901; Mischlich, 1911; Taylor, 1949; Abraham, 1941; Smirnova, 1982) state that Hausa has a construction of the type which we have called the Exceed-2 Comparative. In this construction, the verb *fi* 'to exceed' is the main predicate, while the comparative predicate is morphologically encoded in a nominal form. In some cases, we find that this nominal form is actually a verbal noun, which has been derived from verbal stems by means of one of several nominalizing suffixes. In other cases, the comparative predicate is codified as an abstract noun, which denotes a quality ('strength', 'badness', 'tallness', or the like). Such abstract nouns are non-derived, primary lexical stems; from a formal point of view, one might say that 'adjectives' are in fact nouns in Hausa, or, alternatively, that in this language there is no distinct class of adjectives at all. An example of a Hausa comparative which contains such an abstract noun is the following:

(34) *HAUSA:*
        Daki -n-nan ya-fi   daki -n-tshan girma
        house this it -exceed house that   bigness
        'This house is bigger than that house'

It should be added here that one author (viz. Marré, 1901: 47) states that the nominal comparative predicate in a Hausa comparative may be optionally preceded by the preposition *da* 'with':

(35) *HAUSA:*
        Marokachi ya-fis   -shi da   muganta
        beggar   it -exceed-him with craziness
        'The beggar is crazier than him'

Now, if we look at the expressions for temporal chaining in Hausa, we find that an asyndetic coordination is the preferred procedure. It seems that C-chains can never be deranked in Hausa; the normal way to express consecutive action seems to involve the formation of a paratactic string of finite verbs. A typical example is:

(36) *HAUSA:*
        Dila   ya janye   nama, ya tafi waje   , ya tshanye
        jackal he took-away meat   he went outside   he ate
        'The jackal took away the meat, went outside and ate it'

With simultaneous chains, too, a balanced construction seems to be the rule. An example is *(37)*, taken from Smirnova (1982: 41):

(37) *HAUSA:*
        Ya-fi   su   yawa   , (kuma) ya-fi   su
        it -exceed them abundance   also   it -exceed them
        amfani
        use
        'It is more abundant, and also more useful than they are'

However, in the case of simultaneous chaining Hausa turns out to have a secondary option, which involves the use of present participles. These participles are derived from verbal nouns by the prefix *mai-*. Etymologically, this prefix seems to be a contraction of the preposition *ma* 'to' and the personal pronoun *ya/i* 'he'. Hence, its original meaning must be thought of as something like 'the one to whom is . . .' or 'the one who has . . .' (Abraham, 1941: 28); thus, the participle *mai-zuwa* 'coming' would mean literally 'the one to whom an event of coming is'. Given this analysis of the prefix *mai-*, it will not be surprising that this prefix can also be used to derive possessor nouns from concrete nouns (cp. *mai-doki* 'horse owner' from *doki* 'horse'), and that it can even derive attributive modifiers from abstract nouns. In other words, the encoding of adjectival notions in Hausa is diametrically opposed to that in English. Whereas in English the attributive adjective *good* may be derived into the abstract noun *goodness*, in Hausa the primary abstract noun *kyau* 'goodness' is the basis upon which the attributive modifier *mai-kyau* 'good' can be formed.

The use of *mai*-participles in the representation of one of the predicates in a Hausa S-chain turns out to be restricted by conditions of subject-identity. The following example, taken from Mischlich (1911: 19) is an illustration of this point:

(38)   HAUSA:
       Matshe mai-azumi ta -na   zamne tshan
       woman   PCP-fast   she-is   sitting there
       'The woman is sitting there fasting'

From this we may conclude that the Exceed Comparative in Hausa is indirectly matched by at least a secondary possibility in this language to form conditionally deranked simultaneous chains.

Given the facts of Hausa presented above, the reader may well wonder why I consider this language to be problematic at all. It is true that Hausa is only an indirect confirmation of Universal 2A, whereas all other languages in this class show direct surface parallelism. But, one might argue, the fact that a language does not show overt surface parallelism has not kept us from rating, say, Bilin as a confirmation of Universal 3A. In short, one might ask why indirect confirmation in the case of Universal 2A should be any worse than indirect confirmation for other universals.

Nevertheless, I still think that the situation in Hausa gives rise to some problems. These problems are not of a mere correlational nature; on that score, the facts in Hausa are not in conflict with the prediction made by Universal 2A. To me, the main problem with this language is that the facts seem to be at odds with the background assumption which forms the basis of the set of chaining-based universals. As we stated in chapter 5, the main claim in this study is that temporal chaining must be seen as the conceptual model of comparison, and that hence the encoding of the comparative construction is parasitic on the encoding of (one of) the chaining constructions in a given language. Now, with all other cases of the Exceed Comparative this modelling relation has been shown to be completely straightforward. Indeed, for these languages one might go as far as to say that the comparative construction *is* a temporal chain, instead of being merely modelled upon it. In Hausa, however, the relation between the relevant temporal chain and the Exceed Comparative is unclear. Thus, we do not find that present participles of the type presented in *(38)* can appear as the expression of the comparative predicate; a sentence like *(39)* – which, if it occurred, would constitute a case of direct surface parallelism – is ungrammatical:

(39) HAUSA:
     Daki -n-nan mai-girma   ya-fi   daki -n-tshan
     house   this PCP-bigness it -exceed house   that
     'This house is bigger than that house'

In short, one cannot suppress the feeling that a simultaneous chain like *(38)*, conditionally deranked though it may be, is not really the model upon which the formalization of the Hausa comparative is based.

This uneasy feeling about the data in Hausa is strengthened further by the fact that, in this language, we can identify another syntactic pattern which, unlike temporal chaining, does seem to provide a direct parallel to the Exceed Comparative. In the formation of adverbial manner-phrases, abstract nouns are commonly used in Hausa. In this case, they must be preceded by the preposition *da* 'with', an element which – as we saw in *(35)* – may also optionally precede the abstract noun on the Exceed Comparative. An example of this formation of manner adverbials in Hausa is:

(40) HAUSA:
     Audu ya zo   da   zaufi
     A.   he come-PAST with rapidity
     'Audu came quickly'

Given the obvious parallel between a sentence like *(40)* and the Exceed Comparative, one might conclude that the Hausa comparative is not so much a special case of temporal chaining as, rather, a special instance of adverbial modification. This conclusion runs counter to the general modelling-assumption which forms the background of our chaining-based universals. Evidently, all our troubles with Hausa would be over if it could be demonstrated that, in natural languages, the encoding of manner adverbials also takes some form of temporal chaining as its model. While there is evidence that such an assumption is not completely without grounds,[4] it will be understood that a systematic exploration of this latter modelling-assumption is way beyond the scope of the present study.

Turning now to the situation in Fulani, we find that it is similar to that in Hausa in a number of significant respects. Fulani, too, has – in addition to its Mixed Comparative; see section 2.5 – an Exceed-2 Comparative, and again we find that the comparative predicate in this construction has received a nominal form. Since in Fulani, as opposed to Hausa, predicates which denote qualities are morphologically encoded as verbs, Fulani shows no variation in the form of the nominal in the comparative construction. In all cases, we find that the Infinitive is used, a nominal form derived from verbal stems by suffixes such as *-ugo, -de* or *-ki*. Leith–Ross (1922: 57) notes that this infinitive in the comparative can optionally be preceded by the preposition *i* 'with'. Examples of the Exceed Comparative in Fulani include:

(41)   FULANI:
a.   *Samba buri   Amadu mawn-de*
      S.   exceed A.   big   -INF
      'Samba is taller than Amadu'

b.   *Zainabu buri   Faidima i   wod   -ugo*
      Z.   exceed F.   with beautiful-INF
      'Zaina is prettier than Faidima'

Similarities between Hausa and Fulani can also be observed in the possibilities for the expression of temporal chaining. Like Hausa, Fulani appears to be predominantly balancing for both S-chains and C-chains:

(42)   FULANI:
a.   *'O mayi 'o achi bingel*
      he died he left   son
      'He died leaving a son'

b.   *'O famti fandu woru 'o tawi   dinaruje   'o fudatti*
      he split gourd one   he found gold-coin he repeated
      'He split one gourd, found a gold-coin and began again'

Also on a par with Hausa, Fulani has a secondary possibility to form participles. These are essentially adjectival forms, which agree in gender and number with the noun which they modify. The formation of these participles is rather complex (see Gaden, 1909: 20). We will confine ourselves here to the formation of the Present Participle, which, in case it functions as a modifier of a singular noun with personal gender, is derived from the Present or Aorist Tense by means of the suffix *-do/-ido*. Thus, from a finite form like *'o lami* 'he rules' the Present Participle *lami-*

do 'ruler, ruling' can be formed; other examples of Present Participles are *kallu-do* 'bad' (from *halli* 'it is bad') and *peni-do* 'killer, killing' from the verb form *fen* '(he) kills'.

To sum up, Fulani is essentially the same case as Hausa, and hence it confronts us with the same problem. The occurrence of Present Participles of the type illustrated above guarantees that an (admittedly not straight-forward) correlation between the Exceed Comparative and a conditionally deranked S-chain can be established in Fulani; in this sense, Fulani is not a counterexample to Universal 2A. However, infinitives like the ones employed in the Fulani Exceed Comparative are never used as the representation of deranked simultaneous or consecutive predicates, and, conversely, the Present Participles which offer a secondary possibility of conditional simultaneous deranking never appear as the form of the comparative predicate. As a consequence, the general modelling-assumption behind our universals is brought into jeopardy by the Fulani facts.

In Fulani, like in Hausa, we can observe a direct surface parallel between the formation of the Exceed Comparative and the encoding of manner adverbials. Infinitives like those which appear in the Exceed Comparative are freely used in manner-adverbial modification, preceded by the preposition *i* 'with':

(43) FULANI:
      Mi windi i   hakkilo
      I   wrote with care
      'I wrote carefully'

A second possibility for a direct parallel to the Exceed Comparative in Fulani is offered by the encoding of purpose-constructions. It appears that, in such a final sequence, the posterior predicate can be conditionally deranked into an infinitive (Leith–Ross, 1922: 52; Taylor, 1921: 49). Cp.:

(44) FULANI:
      Mi yehi hotj -ugo ledde
      I   went fetch-INF wood
      'I went to fetch wood'

Thus, Fulani could be rated as a direct confirmation of Universal 2A if we are willing to accept that, just for this once, an Exceed Comparative has been modelled on a purpose-construction instead of on a temporal chain. Under this assumption, Fulani would be an exceptional case of the same type as Kanuri (see section 7.2.3), a language which is, incidentally, areally related to Fulani. But it goes without saying that this solution for the

Fulani problem is open to dispute, and that it cannot be denied that this language represents a recalcitrant case, if not for Universal 2A, then for our set of chaining-based universals.

8.4 Factors in the surface variation of the Exceed Comparative

In the introduction to this chapter I claimed that the tripartite variation among the formal manifestations of the Exceed Comparative does not constitute a typologically significant fact, and that the occurrence of this variation must be attributed to the operation of independent structural parameters. At this point in the exposition, I would like to elaborate on this suggestion, by pointing out one structural property with which the variation in Exceed Comparatives seems to be correlated. This factor involves the way in which *predicative adjectives* are represented in the languages that are relevant here.

If we look at the predicative adjective-construction (i.e., the construction which is the equivalent of the English expression *John is tall*) in the languages which have an Exceed Comparative, we find a striking opposition between two subgroups. In one group, predicative adjectives are treated on a par with 'normal' verbs (albeit that 'adjectival' verbs are commonly restricted to one single tense or mood form). In other words, in these languages we can note a categorial overlap (and sometimes even identity) between the encoding of adjectival concepts (i.e., properties) and verbal concepts (typically, events or states). Some examples of languages which are *verby* (see Ross, 1972) with respect to the categorization of adjectives are:

(45) YORUBA:

a. Mo lo
     I   go-PRES. IND
     'I go'

b. Mo tobi
     I   big-PRES. IND
     'I am big'

c. Onisowo ni   mi
     merchant COP I
     'I am a merchant'

(46) MANDARIN:

a. Wo k'iu
     I   go-PRES. IND
     'I go'

b. *Wo kwai*
    I   big-PRES. IND
    'I am big'

c. *Wo shih tsai -tsjoe*
    I   COP rich-man
    'I am a rich man'

In other languages, the opposite affiliation has taken place. Here, predicative adjectives are *nouny*; they are taken to belong to the same category as nouns, and appear in the same predicative constructions as nouns do, opposed to verbs. Examples of nouny Exceed-languages are:

(47) MARGI:
a. *Naja a   -wi*
    he PRES-run
    'He runs'

b. *Naja ngu dzegam*
    he   COP tall
    'He is tall'

c. *Naja ngu zameng*
    he   COP brother-your
    'He is your brother'

(48) SWAHILI:
a. *A -li -kwenda*
    3SG-PAST-go
    'He/she went'

b. *Mti ni mrefu*
    tree COP tall
    'The tree is tall'

c. *Mtoto huyu ni mwivi*
    boy this COP thief
    'This boy is a thief'

In Hausa, we find that there are no (or almost no; see Abraham, 1941: 49) such elements as adjectives at all. Here, the assignment of a property to an individual (that is, the semantic function which is performed by our adjectives) is syntactically encoded by means of a complex which has the form of a prepositional phrase, consisting of the instrumental/comitative marker *da* 'with', and an abstract noun which denotes the intended property. Cp.:

(49)   HAUSA:
       Ya-na   da   karfi
       he -PROG   with   strength
       'He is strong'

I will view such 'prepositional' cases as a special instance of the nouny construction of predicative adjectives.

I have no explanation to offer for this distinction between nouny and verby languages; that is, I do not know what makes a language choose either of these alternatives. I am of the opinion, however, that such an explanation would lie beyond the scope of this inquiry in any case. Since the distinction between nouny and verby adjective-categorization is not limited to languages with an Exceed Comparative, it is safe to assume that the principles underlying this distinction are largely independent of the principles which govern the choice of a particular type of comparative. What is important here is that, apparently, the choice between the variants of the Exceed Comparative is correlated with the nouny or verby character of a language. Moreover, this correlation turns out to hold as a bi-directional implication. If we look at the 20 Exceed-languages in the sample, we find that the following implications obtain:

(50)   a. *If a language has an Exceed-1* (i.e., a serial) *Comparative, it is verby. If an Exceed-language is verby, it has an Exceed-1 Comparative.*

       b. *If a language has an Exceed-2 Comparative or an Exceed-3 Comparative, it is nouny. If an Exceed-language is nouny, it has either an Exceed-2 or an Exceed-3 Comparative.*

A few languages may illustrate this remarkable parallelism. Examples of languages with an Exceed-1 Comparative and verby adjectives are:

(51)   YORUBA:
a.   *Mo tobi*
       I   big-PRES
       'I am big'

b.   *Mo tobi   ju   u*
       I   big-PRES exceed him
       'I am bigger than him'

(52)   MANDARIN:
a.   *Wo kwai*
       I   big-PRES
       'I am big'

b. Wo *pi*   *ni*   *kwai*
   I   exceed you   big
   'I am bigger than you'

On the other hand, languages with an Exceed-2 Comparative (like Igbo) or an Exceed-3 Comparative (like Swahili) are typically nouny:

(53) IGBO:
a.   *Ibu   di*   *alo*
     load is-describable-as heaviness
     'The load is heavy'

b.   *Ibu   á   ka   ibu   aho alo*
     load this exceed load that heaviness
     'This load is heavier than that load'

(54) SWAHILI:
a.   *Mti   ni   mrefu*
     tree COP   big
     'The tree is tall'

b.   *Mti   huu ni   mrefu ku -shinda ule*
     tree this COP   big   INF-exceed that
     'This tree is taller than that one'

In this context, a particularly telling case is presented by Duala. This language has both an Exceed-1 and an Exceed-2 Comparative. This fact can be correlated with the fact that in Duala some adjectival notions are encoded as verbs, whereas others are encoded as nouns:

(55) DUALA:
a.   *Bono bo kolo*
     boat it big-PRES
     'The boat is big'

b.   *Bono bo kolo   buka   ndabo*
     boat it big-PRES exceed house
     'The boat is bigger than the house'

(56) DUALA:
a.   *Modi e   bwala*
     M.   COP-PRES. 3SG   lazy/laziness
     'Modi is lazy'

b.   *Modi a   buki   Edimo bwala*
     M.   he exceed E.   laziness
     'Modi is lazier than Edimo'

Thus, we can conclude that the choice for one of the variants of the Exceed Comparative can be shown to be correlated with a parameter that is not unique for languages with an Exceed Comparative. To avoid misunderstandings, let me point out that the statements in *(50)* are not intended as an explanation for the surface variation in Exceed Comparatives. These statements are purely descriptive observations, which register the existence of a particular cluster of properties in languages of a specific type. Eventually, such observations will have to be integrated in a broader explanatory framework. For the moment, let it suffice to say that the variation in the forms of the Exceed Comparative is, in all probability, caused by factors which are independent of the typology of comparative constructions as such.

8.5   Conclusion

In this chapter we have tested Universal 2A against the facts of the 20 languages in the sample which have a primary Exceed Comparative. We have found that 18 of these languages confirm Universal 2A in the strongest possible way, by showing a direct parallel between their comparatives and one of their chaining constructions. Of the two problematic cases, Hausa and Fulani, the latter is a case in which the comparative has not been modelled on a temporal chain in the strict sense, but on the semantically cognate purpose-construction.

9

Derived-case Comparatives

9.1 Introduction

Now that, in the foregoing chapters, the primary instances of the various subtypes of fixed-case comparatives have been examined, it remains for us to do the same for the other major type of comparative constructions, viz. the derived-case comparatives. Within the set of chaining-based universals, the relevant universal for derived-case comparatives is Universal 1A, which reads as follows:

> UNIVERSAL 1A: If a language has a derived-case comparative, it must be balancing.

Thus, the first thing which we will have to do in this chapter is to show that the languages with a primary derived-case comparative are languages in which temporal chains are (predominantly or obligatorily) expressed in the form of coordinations. For one subtype of derived-case comparatives, viz. the Conjoined Comparative, this demonstration can be very straightforward. We can even be a bit more specific about this class, and show that the following implication is valid:

> UNIVERSAL 4: If a language has a Conjoined Comparative, it must have a balanced simultaneous construction.

For the remaining instances of derived-case comparatives, the so-called Particle Comparatives, the correlation between the comparative and coordinated chaining constructions is much more obscure; a discussion of these cases will be given in section 9.3 and section 9.4.

9.2 The Conjoined Comparative

The 20 languages in the sample which make up the primary instances of the Conjoined Comparative all provide for straightforward corroboration of Universal 1A and Universal 4. This, of course, is hardly surprising; indeed, the existence of languages with a Conjoined Comparative has been one of the primary reasons for setting up the set of chaining-based universals in the first place. Since the languages in this class have a comparative construction which has the surface form of a balanced S-chain, a statement to the effect that such balanced simultaneous structures are possible in these languages becomes almost trivial. Therefore, I trust that the data presented below will need no further comment:

(1) ABIPON:
a. *Negetink chik naâ , oagan nihirenak la   naâ*
    dog   not   bad yet   tiger   already bad
    'A tiger is more ferocious than a dog'

b. *Eneha klatum-keen evenek,   oagan netachkaik*
    he   maybe   beautiful yet   bashful
    'He is beautiful, but nevertheless bashful'

(2) CAYAPO:
a. *Gan ga   prik , bubanne ba i pri*
    you you big   but   I   I small
    'You are bigger than me'

b. *Ga ja   , nium no*
    you stand   he   lie-down
    'You are standing, and he is lying down'

(3) DAKOTA:
a. *Mastingcala king waste, tka singthela   king sice*
    rabbit   the   good   but rattle-snake the   bad
    'The rabbit is better than the rattle-snake'

b. *'Iyaye -waci , tka oyuspapi*
    want-go-3SG   but catch-3SG. ACC.-3PL
    'He wanted to flee, but they caught him'

(4) EKAGI:
a. *Akia oaa   ko ibo ko beu , ania ko ibo*
    your house it big it not   my   it big
    'My house is bigger than your house'

b. *Ino jooni-gai   , ino   animaki-gai*
    some stand-PRES. 3PL , some sit   -PRES. 3PL
    'Some are standing and some are sitting'

(5) GUMBAINGGIR:
a. *Njammi djammei jungu , nigar darui*
woman very bad man good
'The man is better than the woman'

b. *Gudgu nigar nayinggi dulungmi*
over-there man sit-PRES smile-PRES
'The man is sitting there smiling'

(6) HIXKARYANA:
a. *Kaw-ohra naha Waraka , kaw naha Kaywerye*
tall -not he-is W. tall he-is K.
'Kaywerye is taller than Waraka'

b. *Hohtyakon hati , nenahyakon hati*
she-was-picking-it they-say she-was-eating-it they-say
'They say that she was picking it and eating it'

(7) KOBON:
a. *U kub u pro*
that big this small
'This is bigger than that'

b. *Pi hagub ajang al -ei -a*
child pandanus-fruit pith shoot-DUR-REM. PAST. 3SG
nap au asik mid-ei -a
his-father there sit be -DUR-REM. PAST. 3SG
'The child threw down the piths of the pandanus-fruit, and his
father was sitting there (i.e., at his father who was sitting there)'

(8) MANGARAYI:
a. *Ngaya nga-balayi , nangi na -jijga*
I 1SG-big you 2SG-small
'I am bigger than you'

b. *Na-wuwa balan na-wunggu daymingan*
this-side non-sacred that-side sacred
'This side is not sacred, that side is sacred'

(9) MAORI:
a. *He waka pakari tenei , he waka ou*
INDEF. ART canoe old this-one INDEF. ART canoe new
tena
that-one
'This canoe is older than that canoe'

b. *E   anani taku , e   apara tone*
    PRES orange mine   PRES apple hers
    'I have some oranges, she has some apples'

(10) MENOMINI:
a. *Apeqsek tata'hkesew , nenah teh kan*
    more   he-is-strong I   and not
    'He is stronger than me'

b. *Nekanet wekewam , eneq teh weh-amehneh*
    rot-PERF house   thus and topple-PRES
    'The house has rotted, and therefore it is toppling'

(11) MISKITO:
a. *Yan kau tukta , man almuk*
    I   more young he old
    'I am younger than him'

b. *Man disa   , man yamni sna*
    he drink-PRES. 3SG   he good be-PRES. 3SG
    'He drinks and is merry'

(12) MIXTEC:
a. *Luu caa nuu   yaha, nasuu nuu   ndijnu*
    good very people this not   people Tlaxiaco
    'This people is better than the Tlaxiaco people'

b. *Chunaa yo   pasaje yo te   quihin yo*
    pay   ADHORT. 1PL passage our and go   ADHORT. 1PL
    'Let us pay our passage and go there'

(13) MONUMBO:
a. *Tsek angam, ek put*
    you tall   I short
    'You are taller than me'

b. *Korumbe mbo-wen , pangarang mbo-wen*
    children 3PL -die   adults   3PL -die
    'Both children and adults may die'

(14) MOTU:
a. *Ina na namo herea, una na dia namo*
    this is good more that is not good
    'This is better than that'

b. *E gwauheni-gu , e kwadi-gu*
   he scold   -me he beat -me
   'He scolded me and thrashed me'

(15) CLASSICAL NAHUATL:
a. *In   Petoloh cualli , zan oc-cencah cualli in   Xuan*
   ART P.   good   but more   good ART X.
   'John is better than Peter'

b. *Ni-cocoxqui , zan ti -qualli*
   I -sick   but you-good
   'I am sick, but you are well'

(16) PALA:
a. *A hansik   kanin , a   tamat   kanin*
   the small-one this   the big-one that
   'This one is smaller than that one'

b. *Da   enum ra tamat   ma da   so*
   one-will eat the big-ones and one-will plant
   ra hansik
   the small-ones
   'The big ones (i.e., yams) will be eaten and the small ones will be
   planted'

(17) SAMOAN:
a. *Ua loa   lenei va'a , ua puupuu lena*
   is long this boat   is short   that
   'This boat is longer than that boat'

b. *Ua lelei isi   tama , ua leaga isi   tama*
   is good some boys   is bad   some boys
   'Some boys are good, some boys are bad'

(18) SHIPIBO:
a. *Nato aibo   hakun   , wuitsa kiskaribi*
   this woman beautiful   others not-be-so
   'This woman is more beautiful than others'

b. *E ra kai   sobo -n , xuni sobo -wuowuon yakati*
   I am going house-in   man house-near   sit
   'I went into the house, but the man remained sitting near it'

(19) SIKA:
a. *Dzarang tica gahar , dzarang rei   kesik*
   horse   that big   horse   this small
   'That horse is bigger than this horse'

b.   *Cilu caung cenang nei   manu ,*
       trap my   catch PERF chicken
       cilu aung cenang nei   buro
       trap your catch PERF falcon
       'My trap has caught a chicken, and yours has caught a falcon'

(20)   YAVAPAI:
a.   *Kmtu   -v   -c   mine: rav -a   kmtuq^{w}ath-c   ke*
       watermelon-DEM-SUBJ tasty   very-TNS , cantelope -SUBJ not
       mine: rav -a   om-i
       tasty   very-TNS not-TNS
       'Watermelons are tastier than cantelopes'

b.   *Kithiye-v   -c   pa   -qeyat-i   , pa -kelkyoci-c*
       doctor -DEM-SUBJ person-much-PRES   person-police -SUBJ
       pe   msay -e
       and mean-PRES
       'Doctors are rich and policemen are mean'

With respect to the comparative construction in this last language, Yavapai, Kendall (1976: 146) remarks: 'Such implicit or explicit comparatives are obviously not derived by transformational operations. They are straightforward strings of sentences, loosely conjoined or not conjoined at all.' Somewhat further, the author states as her opinion that 'the derivation of Yavapai "comparatives" is neither problematic nor particularly interesting. Given that they are formally equivalent to other assertions, they may be accounted for in the PS-rules for non-complex declarative sentences' (ibid.: 147).

Given the general framework of the present study, it will be evident that I disagree with Kendall's contention that Conjoined Comparatives like the one in Yavapai are 'not particularly interesting'. On the contrary, I claim that the occurrence of such comparatives is primary evidence in favour of our hypothesis that, in natural languages, the formal expression of comparison is modelled on the codification of temporal chaining. This point aside, however, Kendall's remarks are right on target.

9.3   Particle Comparatives

Although Particle Comparatives form a residual category which, in all probability, is not homogeneous, they share at least the feature that they are instances of derived-case comparatives. Therefore, the universal which is relevant to them is Universal 1A; we should be able to demonstrate that languages with a Particle Comparative formalize their chaining constructions preferably as coordinated structures.

The examination of the 18 cases of primary Particle Comparatives in the sample can be structured on the basis of the fact that, in many constructions, the comparative particle can be identified as an item which performs yet other functions in the language. Thus, for example, we find in a number of cases that the comparative particle is also in use as *the marking element in some type of coordinate construction*. Most of the examples that are relevant in this context have already been presented in section 3.3, so that a brief summary may suffice here.

First, the sample contains one example of a Particle Comparative in which a straightforward parallel between the comparative and the expression of *and*-coordination can be established. In Javanese, the particle *karo* marks the standard NP in comparatives, but is also employed as a conjunction or adverb which marks (simultaneous and consecutive) chains (see sentences *(3.4a/b)*).

Secondly, there are languages in the sample which employ a comparative particle which is also used as an adverbial element in a balanced consecutive chain. Such is the case in Toba Batak, where the comparative particle *asa* can be identified as a temporal adverb with the meaning 'then', 'and after that' (see examples *(3.5a/b)*).

In Standard Dutch, we note that the item *dan*, which introduces standard NPs and standard clauses in comparatives, is at least homonymous, if not historically identical, to the temporal adverb *dan* 'then', which introduces the second member of a paratactic, and balanced, temporal chain (see examples *(3.6a/b)*).

Several authors on the diachronic syntax of English (Mätzner, 1880; Skeat, 1901; Small, 1923; Curme, 1931) claim that the English comparative particle *than* is historically identical to the adverbial item *then*, which marks consecutive succession of balanced predicates or clauses. However, the identification of English *than* with *then* is not undisputed; for an alternative analysis see, for instance, Joly (1967). We will say more about the properties of the comparative construction of English in the next section. For the moment, we will confine ourselves to the observation that, whatever the status and origin of the particle *than* may be, English is certainly a confirmation of Universal 1A, since temporal chains are preferably balanced in this language.

Finally, in section 2.5 we discussed the status of the element *nöria* in the comparative of Goajiro. We argued there that this item must be looked upon as an adverb (meaning 'thereafter') rather than as a separative marker on the standard NP. If this analysis is accepted, then

Goajiro is a language with a Particle Comparative. This is matched by the fact that C-chains in Goajiro are balanced:

(21)   GOAJIRO:
    Na -sanai   teria-ka , na -leehai
    they-took-it mat -the   they-brought-it
    'They took away his mat and brought it with them'

A *third* group of Particle Comparatives is formed by constructions in which the comparative particle is represented by an item which has also the function of marking adversative relation between coordinated sentences or clauses. This is probably[1] the case in the primary comparative construction in Basque, where the comparative particle *baino/bainan* functions as the adversative conjunction 'but' (see examples *(3.8a/b)*). The same observations as for Basque can be made in the case of Ilocano with regard to the status of the comparative particle *ngem* (see sentences *(3.9a/b)*). In this connection, we should also recall that the element *but* is sometimes used as a replacement of comparative *than* in earlier English and in several modern English dialects (see sentences *(3.10)* and *(3.11)*).

As a *fourth* type of Particle Comparative, we must call attention to the comparative construction in Scottish Gaelic, where standard NPs and standard clauses are marked by the particle *na* (see sentence *(3.16a)*). This particle *na* functioned in all Middle Celtic dialects as the marker for negative coordination 'nor' (see Lewis and Pedersen, 1974: 187), and continues to do so in a number of Modern Celtic languages. Thus, apparently, Scottish Gaelic has modelled its comparative on balanced chains which have a negative-conjunctive interpretation. This situation is matched by Scottish English, in which the element *nor* is used as the particle of comparison (see sentences *(3.14a/b)*). Positive temporal chains (both simultaneous and consecutive) are expressed in Modern Scottish Gaelic by means of balanced constructions with the connective particle *agus* 'and'. This particle also functions as the marker of the comparative of equality. Cp.:

(22)   SCOTTISH GAELIC:
    Is beag agus mi
    is small PRT me
    'He is as small as me'

In connection with this type of Particle Comparative, we should also repeat that a comparative particle with the original meaning 'nor' is also present in (one of the variants of) the Particle Comparative in Latvian (see sentences *(3.18a/b)*).

A *fifth* variant of the Particle Comparative is represented in the

sample by Classical Greek. This language employs a comparative particle
ē, which is identical to the item which connects balanced disjunctive
clauses or phrases (see sentences *(3.12a/b)*). It should be noted that
positive, non-disjunctive temporal chains in Classical Greek are balanced
(though not obligatorily so; see section 10.5). Both in S-chains and
C-chains the conjunction *kai* 'and' can be used:

(23)   CLASSICAL GREEK:
      Hoi polemioi   *etoxeusan*   *kai*   *Kleomenos*
      the   enemies-NOM   shoot-AOR. 3PL   and   K.-NOM
      etoxeuthē
      shoot-AOR. PASS. 3SG
      'The enemies shot (their arrows) and Kleomenos was hit'

Furthermore, it should be recalled that a comparative particle with the
original meaning 'or' can also be encountered in East- and Westflemish
(see examples *(3.13a/b)*), in Gothic, and in several other languages (see
section 3.3).

In the above five groups of Particle Comparatives, the connection with
coordinated structures is fairly direct; all comparative particles discussed so far are coordinate markers of some sort. In other cases of Particle
Comparatives, this connection is less transparent; there are even cases
where the particle employed is unique for the comparative construction,
and where the etymology of the item offers no decisive indication of its
categorial status.

In a *sixth* group of Particle Comparatives, we find that the particle is
also in use as *an element with the meaning 'like' or 'as'*. In all of these
cases, this element does not govern a fixed-case NP, so that it cannot be
classified as a preposition.

A very straightforward example of a 'like'-comparative can be ob-
served in Sranan. In the primary comparative of this language, standard
NPs are preceded by the element *leki*, which has its direct origin in the
English conjunction *like*:

(24)   SRANAN:
      Hugo can lon moro betre leki Rudi
      H.   can   run   more   better   PRT   R.
      'Hugo can run better than Rudi'

In its representation of temporal chaining, Sranan has the ability to form
serial verb strings; this possibility is matched directly by the older,
secondary, Exceed Comparative (see section 10.3). The primary Particle
Comparative of Sranan is matched by the fact that balanced temporal
chaining is the predominant option:

(25)   SRANAN:
    Mi bigi , da   yu   pikin
    I   big   and you small
    'I am big and you are small'

A second language in the sample in which the comparative particle is an item with the meaning 'like' is Malagasy. According to Ferrand (1903: 165), the element *noho*, which appears as the comparative particle, must be translated as Fr. 'comme':

(26)   MALAGASY:
    Lehibe noho ny   zana-ny Rabe
    tall   PRT   the son -his R.
    'Rabe is taller than his son'

The Particle Comparative in Malagasy has its match in the predominantly balancing formalization of temporal sequencing. In cases of sentential coordination, the connective item *ary* 'and' is used, while the conjunction *sy* 'conjoins only phrases, never sentences' (Keenan, 1978: 320). Cp.:

(27)   MALAGASY:
a.   Misotro taoka   Rabe ary mihinam-bary Rabe
        drink   alcohol R.   and eat   -rice   R.
        'Rabe is drinking alcohol and Rabe is eating rice'

b.   Misotro taoka   sy   mihinam-bary Rabe
        drink   alcohol and eat   -rice   R.
        'Rabe is drinking alcohol and eating rice'

In Modern Hungarian, the normal particle in comparatives is the element *mint/amint*, which is also in use as the marker of the comparison of equality 'like'. Etymologically, the element *mint/amint* is probably an obsolete case form of the neuter interrogative/relative pronoun *ami* 'what'. Cp.:

(28)   HUNGARIAN:
a.   Istvan magasa-bb mint Peter
        I.   bigger   PRT P.
        'Istvan is bigger than Peter'

b.   Fenylik vala mint a   villam
        sparks were like the lightning
        'The sparks were like lightning'

According to Simonyi (1907: 427–8), the use of the element *mint* as a marker of comparison of inequality is a relatively recent development. In earlier stages of Hungarian, combinations of the element *mint* 'like' with the negative item *sem* were preferred in this function. The use of these complex forms has gradually been abandoned in favour of the simplex equality-marker, but a form like *mintsem* is still widely used in inequality-comparatives which contain a standard clause:

(29)   HUNGARIAN:
       Kevese-bb hite   vagyon   mintsem az ordög-nek
       less   faith   is-to-him like/than the devil -at
       'He has less faith than the devil has'

The situation in Hungarian is, in some respects, similar to that in Latin. As we saw in section 2.1, the primary comparative in Latin employs the particle *quam* in front of standard NPs and standard clauses. As far as I have been able to find out, the etymology of the particle *quam* is still unclear. The prevailing opinion (see Walde and Hoffmann, 1954: 213) seems to be that this element must be identified as the Accusative Feminine Singular of the relative/interrogative stem **quo-*; in this way, *quam* should be taken to belong to the same class of adverbial formations as the items *tam* 'so, so much' (derived from the demonstrative stem **to-*), *nam* 'for, because, thus' (derived from the demonstrative stem **no-*), and *iam* 'already' (from a pronominal stem **io-*). If this etymology of Latin *quam* is accepted, the element has an origin which is similar to that of Hungarian *mint* (see above). Another similarity with Hungarian is the fact that Latin *quam* has also a limited possibility to mark equality, in the combination *tam . . . quam* 'as much . . . as'. Cp.:

(30)   LATIN:
a.   Cicero est eloquentior   quam Cato
       C.   is   more-eloquent PRT   C.
       'Cicero is more eloquent than Cato'

b.   Est tam dives quam frater
       is   PRT rich   PRT   brother
       'He is as rich as his brother'

While the combination *tam . . . quam* is commonly used to express equality in Latin, identity or difference usually require the presence of the particles *ac* or *atque* (see sentence *(31a)*). The elements *ac* and *atque* occur freely as coordinators of balanced constructions, as sentence *(31b)* will show. Now, the interesting thing is that we can find Latin sentences in which the equality-construction (with *tam-quam*) and the similarity-construction (with *ac/atque*) appear to have been contaminated (Ernout and Meillet, 1979: 551). That is, next to the regular instance of the similarity-construction in *(31b)*, we also find sentences in which the particles *ac/atque* have been replaced by the item *quam*. Cp.:

(31) LATIN:
a. *Illi   sunt alio   ingenio   atque tu*
    they-NOM are different-DAT character-DAT PRT you-NOM
    'They are of a different character than you' (Plautus, Eudolus,
    1134).

b. *Senatus   ac populus   ei   genti   iratus erat*
    senate-NOM and people-NOM this-DAT tribe-DAT angry was
    'The senate and the people were mad at this tribe'

c. *An eandem   Romanis   in bello   virtutem*
    Q same-FEM. SG. ACC Romans-DAT in war-ABL virtue-ACC
    quam in pace   lasciviam   adesse
    PRT   in peace-ABL indiscipline-ACC be present-INF
    creditis
    believe-PRES. 2PL
    'Or do you believe that the Romans have the same virtue in war
    as the indiscipline which they have during peace-time?' (Tacitus,
    Agricola, 32.1).

We can conclude, then, that the comparative particle *quam* in Latin, like
the particle *mint* in Hungarian, is probably an adverbial element derived
from an interrogative/relative stem, and that it can also be used as a
marker of quality and similarity. In this latter option, the element *quam*
is a variant of elements which, in their origin, are clearly connective
markers of balanced structures.

A further example of a language in which the comparative particle is
an item with the meaning 'like' may be Albanian, but in this language the
facts are far from clear. All the authors whom I have consulted on the
structure of Albanian (Weigand, 1913; Lambertz, 1959; Camaj, 1969;
Hetzer, 1978; Kacori, 1979) state that the primary comparative employs
the particle *se* in front of standard NPs and standard clauses. As far as I
am aware, the etymology of this item is unknown. Cp.:

(32) ALBANIAN:
    Hekuri asht ma   i   rande   se   guri
    the-iron is   more the heavy-one PRT the-stone
    'Iron is heavier than stone'

If we look for further uses of the item *se*, we find that it is some kind of
all-purpose subordinating item, comparable in its function to English
that or French *que*. Thus, it is used to mark direct object clauses like the
one in *(33)*, and it can also be found as a part of other subordinating
conjunctions:

(33) ALBANIAN:
 Tha   se   vjen
 say-PAST. 3SG that come-PRES. 3SG
 'He said that he will come'

According to most authors, the comparison of equality is indicated in Albanian by the element *si* 'like'. The following example is taken from Weigand (1913: 49):

(34) ALBANIAN:
 Asht i   kukj   si   molla
 is   the red-one like apple
 'It is as red as an apple'

Whether there is a relation, or even identity, between this latter item *si* and the comparative particle *se* remains unclear. Some authors make a clear distinction between the two items, while others seem to imply an identity between them, by pointing out that both elements can also be used in instrumental adverbial function, with the meaning of 'how'.[2]

As a last case of a 'like'-comparative, we can adduce one of the variants of the Particle Comparative in Latvian. In addition to the 'nor'-comparative mentioned above, standard NPs in Latvian comparatives can also be introduced by the element *ka* 'like', which may be a fossilized locative adverb (see Endzelin, 1922: 467).

To conclude this section, let us consider the Particle Comparatives in Russian, Finnish and French, which may be viewed as a *seventh* group. Above, we noted the cases of Latin and Hungarian, where a comparative particle is employed that has its etymological origin in *an oblique case form of the relative/interrogative pronoun*. Now, in Russian, Finnish and French we find the same situation, the only difference with Latin and Hungarian being that the comparative particles in the former three languages do not occur as items with the meaning 'like'.

The Russian comparative particle *cem* is generally considered to have been developed from the instrumental case of the neuter form of the relative/interrogative pronoun *cto* 'who, what'. It may be added that the Russian instrumental case also covers essive functions, and must often be translated as 'as X, like (an) X'. An example of the Russian Particle Comparative is:

(35) RUSSIAN:
 On umnjee   cem ja
 he clever-er PRT I
 'He is more clever than me'

Modern French has a primary Particle Comparative in which the standard NP or clause is preceded by the item *que*. From a synchronic point of view, this particle is homonymous with the general subordination marker *que* 'that'; historically, however, we have a case of syncretism here. While the subordinating marker *que* has its origin in the Vulgar Latin subordinator *quod* (i.e., the Accusative Neuter of the interrogative/relative pronoun stem **qu-*), the comparative particle *que* is originally the Ablative Neuter of this same pronominal stem, viz. *quo*. As the Ablative case disappeared in Old French, both forms coincided into *quod*, and hence they turned up as *que* in Modern French. We may conclude, then, that the original meaning of the French comparative particle has been something along the lines of 'by which'. An example of the Particle Comparative in Modern French is:

(36)   FRENCH:
   Angélique est plus   charmante   que Marie
   A.   is   more charming-FEM PRT M.
   'Angélique is more charming than Marie'

In the primary Particle Comparative in Finnish, the standard NP or standard clause is marked by the particle *kuin*. Etymologically, this item is presumably some fossilized locative case of the interrogative/relative pronominal stem *ku-* (cp. also *ku-n* 'when', *ku-nves* 'until', *ku-ka* 'who?'). That the particle *kuin* is not a spatial marker is clearly brought out by the fact that the standard NP which it precedes is not in a fixed case, but derives its grammatical function from that of the comparee NP. Cp.:

(37)   FINNISH:
   Hän on pite-mpi kuin sina
   he is big -PRT PRT you
   'He is bigger than you'

Hungarian, Latin, Albanian, Russian, French and Finnish are all languages which have a limited (and, in general, stylistically marked) possibility of deranking their temporal chains under absolute conditions; we will see in the next chapter that this possibility of deranking is matched by the secondary comparatives of these languages. However, the unmarked way to express simultaneous and consecutive action in these languages is to construct VPs or sentences as a balanced configuration, in which the members are typically connected by a conjunction. Examples include:

(38)　HUNGARIAN:
　　　Janos egy almatt vett　　　*és*　*Vili öt evett*
　　　J.　　one apple　bought　and　V.　it　ate
　　　'Janos bought an apple and Vili ate it'

(39)　LATIN:
　　　Caesar venit　　　*et*　*vicit*
　　　C.　　come-PERF. 3SG　and　conquer-PERF. 3SG
　　　'Caesar came and conquered'

(40)　ALBANIAN:
　　　Ai degjoi fishkëllimën　　*e*　*lokomotives*
　　　he　heard　whistle-the-ACC　of　locomotive-the
　　　e　*pa*　*trenin*
　　　and　saw　train-the-ACC
　　　'He heard the whistle of the locomotive and saw the train'

(41)　RUSSIAN:
　　　On wysmorkaltsja i　　　*torzjestwenno ulybnultsja*
　　　he　blew-nose　　and　triumphantly　smiled
　　　'He blew his nose and smiled triumphantly'

(42)　FRENCH:
　　　Jean se levait et　　*s'en allait*
　　　J.　self lifted and　went-away
　　　'Jean stood up and left'

(43)　FINNISH:
　　　Syo-i　*-mme ja*　*men-i*　*-mme elokuvi-in*
　　　eat -PAST-1PL　and　go -PAST-1PL　cinema-to
　　　'We ate and went to the cinema'

Summarizing this section, we may conclude that Universal 1A is confirmed for all 18 languages in the sample which have some kind of primary Particle Comparative. Thus, the real problem with Particle Comparatives is not so much a matter of description; it is rather a question of explanation. In contrast to what can be observed for Conjoined Comparatives, the modelling function of coordinated chains is far from self-evident in a number of instances of the Particle Comparative. Indeed, it looks as if the correlation between coordinated chains and Particle Comparatives, real though it may be, is nothing more than accidental for a number of relevant languages. Moreover, given that coordinated chains are already employed as the model for Conjoined Comparatives, one may well ask why Particle Comparatives should exist at all.

The peculiar phenomenon of Particle Comparatives will be discussed further in chapter 15 within the general context of an explanation of comparative-type choice. In order to explore some basic concepts which may play a role in such an explanation for Particle Comparatives, I will conclude this chapter with a more detailed discussion of the facts in two specific Particle Comparatives, viz. the primary comparatives in Dutch and English.

9.4   The comparative construction in Dutch and English

In the preceding section, we established that Dutch and English are both languages with a Particle Comparative; their comparative particles are *dan* and *than*, respectively. Since these two languages are both predominantly balancing in their formalization of temporal chaining, they can be considered confirmations of Universal 1A. In this section, I want to discuss the comparatives in these languages in some detail. I hope it will become clear that the correlation between the occurrence of a Particle Comparative and the possibility of coordinated chaining in these languages is not a merely accidental fact, but that it can, at least given some specific assumptions, be explained on the basis of the modelling-hypothesis which forms the explanatory background of our investigation. Furthermore, I hope that this discussion will shed some more light on the peculiar status of Particle Comparatives in general. From the facts in Dutch and English, and from the contrasts which can be observed between them, I think some insights can be gained which can be put to use in chapter 15 within a more general explanatory context.

Even if we limit ourselves to publications which were written within the theoretical framework of transformational-generative grammar, the literature on the comparative in English and other European languages is considerable. Apart from the role which the study of comparatives has played in general theoretical debate, the construction itself has been subjected to linguistic analysis from various points of view, giving rise to questions such as the correct phrase structure analysis and transformational derivation of the construction (Lees, 1961; Pilch, 1965; Doherty and Schwartz, 1967; Bresnan, 1971, 1973; Klooster, 1972, 1979; Seuren, 1973; Hendrick, 1978), the exact nature of the rule system needed to derive elliptical comparatives (Bresnan, 1975; Kuno, 1981), the negative polarity which can be observed in comparative clauses (Joly, 1967; Seuren, 1973; Mittwoch, 1974; Napoli and Nespor, 1976; Cantrall, 1977; Seuren, 1984) and the syntacto-semantic analysis of degree words (Klooster, 1976, 1978, 1979; Seuren, 1978).

Differently tuned approaches to the comparative problem are found in present-day 'formal semantics', in particular in studies by Cresswell (1976), Hellan (1981), Hoeksema (1983), Klein (1980) and von Stechow (1984). These studies have in common a general predilection for 'surface semantics', i.e., the view that no separate level of semantic representation is required for a semantic calculus to work upon. It is an explicit aim, in this form of semantics, to circumvent all obstacles, traditional or newly discovered, to surface semantics by the application of new formal techniques. Without denying relevance to such work in other contexts, we must decide that in the context of the present study the relevance of this work is, at least at this moment, not apparent.

This is mainly due to the fact that the psychological relevance of work in formal semantics is either low or not apparent, as is widely recognized. The present work, on the contrary, is clearly oriented towards criteria of psychological relevance (see part three), as is most work in universalist linguistics. Moreover, the surface semantics view adopted in current formal semantics excludes accounts of grammatical structures in terms of historical reanalysis from originally transparent constructions. Now, as will be made clear in section 9.4.3, our analysis of Particle Comparatives is based on the theory, proposed by authors such as Givón (1979), that historical development of grammatical structures often involves a process of 'grammaticalization', by which a semantically transparent construction 'jells' into a new and separate derived grammatical construction which is then no longer transparent. Since for formal semantics *all* constructions are by definition semantically transparent, provided a powerful enough formal apparatus is applied to sentences, there is no room in formal semantics for a theory involving grammatical reanalysis through time. Yet, the evidence for such processes is impressive. We shall, as a general rule, leave the formal semantic treatments of comparatives undiscussed.

Thus limiting ourselves to the framework of the present study, we must conclude that not all research results obtained or claimed in those linguistic approaches that fall within our scope are of equal relevance. To name but one topic, it must be recalled that the approach adopted in this study is essentially model-neutral, at least as regards the models that fit into our framework. Hence discussions centring around the question of the exact formal nature of the (transformational or PS) rule system needed for the derivation of various types of comparative constructions are largely outside our domain of interest. We shall discuss the comparatives of English and Dutch with a specific problem in mind: our aim here is to argue that, despite superficial indications to the contrary, the Particle Comparatives in these languages can be shown to be modelled on balanced chaining constructions, albeit that this modelling has come to be obscured by the operation of interfering processes.

Given this aim, the empirical issue which is of specific interest to us concerns *the grammatical status of the English and Dutch comparative clause* (i.e., the clause following *dan/than*). In particular, it is of relevance for us to know whether this clause must be thought of as *a subordinate clause or a main clause*; if the latter alternative can be made plausible, the conclusion must follow that the comparative in Dutch and English consists of *two main clauses*, which would suggest an analysis of this construction in terms of coordination. Related to this issue of the status of the comparative clause is the matter of *the categorial status of the comparative particle*; given our general demarcation of the problem, it is relevant for us to determine whether the items *dan* and *than* must be conceived of as *prepositions c.q. subordinating conjunctions*, or rather as *temporal adverbs which mark balanced chaining constructions*.

In what follows, I will first deal with some structural properties of the Dutch Particle Comparative. Following that, I will contrast the Dutch data with the facts of the English comparative. As it will turn out, the comparatives in the two languages have a significant number of features in common, but they can also be shown to differ in some interesting respects.

9.4.1   The grammatical status of the Dutch comparative clause

Apart from cases of NP-comparison like the one in *(44)*, the particle *dan* in Dutch can be followed by a large variety of other structural units, such as full clauses (see *(45a)*), adjective phrases (see *(45b)*), prepositional phrases (see *(45c)*), verb phrases (see *(45d)*), and strings which do not form single constituents (see *(45e)* and *(45f)*):

(44)   DUTCH:
    Ik ben ouder dan mijn neef
    I am older than my cousin
    'I am older than my cousin'

(45)   DUTCH:
a.   *Vliegen is goedkoper dan U denkt*
       flying is cheaper than you think

b.   *Hij is eerder dom dan slecht*
       he is rather stupid than malicious

c.   *Onze ploeg speelt beter dan in het vorige seizoen*
       our team plays better than in the last season

d. *Joggen is gevaarlijker   dan wordt verondersteld*
   Jogging is more dangerous than is   assumed

e. *Ik besteed meer geld   aan boeken dan Jan aan eten*
   I   spend more money on books   than J. on food
   'I spend more money on books than Jan does on food'

f. *Beter één vogel in de hand dan tien in de lucht*
   better one bird in the hand than ten in the sky
   'A bird in the hand is worth two in the bush'

Now, with respect to comparative constructions like those in *(45)*, it is generally assumed in the literature that they must be accounted for by the application of some procedure of *ellipsis*, which relates them to structures with 'full' comparative clauses. The position on these 'incomplete' comparative clauses (which can be encountered not only in Dutch, but also in other languages with a Particle Comparative) is summed up succinctly by Hankamer (1973: 182), who, in his discussion of the Particle Comparatives in Latin and Classical Greek, writes:

the conjunctions of comparison [i.e., Latin *quam* and Greek ē] may be followed by all kinds of constituents, and even by non-constituents. This 'clause-junk' can be accounted for only as the remains of underlying full clauses which have undergone ellipsis. Any other account would fail to capture the generalization that the junk in comparative expressions is always possible left-overs from a full clause, and never, say, two verbs in succession, or three NPs in the genitive case.

Since the facts of the 'incomplete comparatives' in Latin and Classical Greek are completely parallel to the facts in Dutch, we will take Hankamer's analysis to apply also to the sentences in *(45)*, and we will therefore assume that all these sentences have an underlying representation in which the comparative particle *dan* is followed by a full, non-elliptical clause.

It should be added here that it is a moot point whether this elliptical analysis of the sentences in *(45)* can also be extended to cases of NP-comparison in Dutch. Hankamer (1973) argues that, at least in English, NP-comparison has structural properties which are different from those of clause-comparison. This leads him to the conclusion that, in English, NP-comparatives are non-elliptical, and that therefore there must be assumed to exist two items *than* in English, one element being a preposition which takes NPs as its complement, while the other is a clause-initial particle. I will present the main points of Hankamer's argumentation in section 9.4.2, and demonstrate there that the structural differences between NP-comparison and clause-comparison in English are largely absent in Dutch. For the moment, however, I will not deal with cases of NP-comparison in Dutch; I will concentrate on comparatives such as those in *(45)*, that is, cases of Dutch comparatives for which the clausal status of the string following *dan* is undisputed.

Now, given that, in sentences like those in *(45)*, the comparative particle is followed by a clause, the main question which will concern us here is whether this comparative clause must be conceived of as a *subordinate* (adverbial) *clause* or as a *main clause*. Under the first alternative, the element *dan* is seen as a subordinating conjunction, which is of essentially the same type as other elements which introduce Dutch adverbial clauses, such as *voor* 'before', *sinds* 'since' and *terwijl* 'while'. If we accept the second alternative, we are forced to conclude that the Dutch comparative contains two main clauses. A plausible way to account for this would be to assume that, at least in some stage in the derivation, the comparative in Dutch has (or had) the form of a coordination, and that the comparative particle *dan* is, at least in its origin, identical to the temporal adverb *dan* which marks balanced temporal chains in Dutch.

In what follows, I will argue that both positions on the structural status of the Dutch comparative clause have their strong points. Given the dilemma created by this, I will offer an analysis of the Dutch comparative in which the notion of 'syntactization', as developed in Givón (1979), plays a crucial role.

Perhaps the most telling argument in favour of a subordinate status of the Dutch comparative clause stems from facts with respect to the word order in this clause. In Dutch, as in German, there is difference in word order between main clauses and subordinate clauses; while main clauses are basically SVO, subordinate clauses have obligatory verb-final order:

(46)   DUTCH:
a.   Ik zag hem voor   hij mij zag
     I   saw him before he me saw
     'I saw him before he saw me'
b. * Ik zag hem voor hij zag mij

Now, it is clear that the word order in Dutch comparative clauses is verb-final:

(47)   DUTCH:
a.   Ik zag hem eerder dan hij mij zag
     I   saw him earlier than he me saw
     'I saw him earlier than he saw me'
b. * Ik zag hem eerder dan hij zag mij

Obviously, the complete word-order parallelism between sentences *(46a)* and *(47a)* is a strong argument for the subordinate analysis of Dutch comparative clauses.

A second argument which militates strongly in favour of this analysis can be derived from the fact that, in Dutch adverbial clauses, the clause-initial conjunction can often be optionally followed by the general subordinating conjunction *dat* 'that'. Although, at least in some cases (for instance, in adverbial clauses introduced by *terwijl* or *sinds*), the use of the additional element *dat* is considered somewhat substandard, sentences like the *b*-examples below are frequently encountered in colloquial Dutch:

(48) DUTCH:
a. Ik heb hem opgebeld voor   hij naar Afrika vertrok
    I   have him phoned   before he to   Africa departed
    'I phoned him before he left for Africa'
b. Ik heb hem opgebeld voordat hij naar Afrika vertrok

(49) DUTCH:
a. Sinds we in België   wonen , voel ik me   gelukkig
    Since we in Belgium live   feel I   myself happy
    'Ever since we've lived in Belgium, I feel happy'
b. ? Sinds dat we in België wonen, voel ik me gelukkig

(50) DUTCH:
a. Terwijl hij dat zei, lachte   hij afkeurend
    as   he   that said laughed he   disapprovingly
    'As he said that, he laughed disapprovingly'
b.?? Terwijl dat hij dat zei, lachte hij afkeurend

Now, the optional occurrence of the complementizer *dat* in adverbial clauses is paralleled completely by the optional appearance of this element in Dutch comparative clauses:

(51) DUTCH:
a. Hij praat meer dan goed voor hem is
    he   talks more than good for   is
    'He talks more than is good for him: he talks too much for his own good'
b. ? Hij praat meer dan dat goed voor hem is

What is more, the same feeling of non-standardness which is generated by the use of *dat* in some adverbial clauses can be observed among Dutch speakers with respect to the use of *dat* in comparatives.

Thus, on the face of it, it looks as if matters are fairly straightforward. The above observations point unequivocally to an analysis of the Dutch comparative clause as an instance of adverbial complementation, in which the element *dan* functions as a complementizer. I think it is useless to deny the validity of these observations. However, below I would like to point out a number of facts which appear to be at odds with a subordinate analysis; these data suggest that, at least in some derivational stage, the Dutch comparative clause must be considered to have main-clause status.

First, it can be observed that Dutch comparative clauses are restricted in the positions which they can occupy in a sentence. In general, adverbial clauses (and other adverbial elements) in Dutch can occupy at least three different positions in a main sentence: they can be sentence-initial, or sentence-final, or in a position immediately following the finite verb. The examples in *(52)* illustrate this relative freedom for Dutch adverbial clauses:

(52)   DUTCH:
a.   *Hij is erg   veranderd sinds hij hoogleraar is*
          he is a lot changed   since he professor   is
          'He has changed a great deal since he became a professor'
b.   *Hij is, sinds hij hoogleraar is, erg veranderd*
c.   *Sinds hij hoogleraar is, is hij erg veranderd*

Now, in contrast to this, comparative clauses introduced by *dan* are allowed neither in sentence-initial nor in post-verbal position.[3] Their only distributional option is the sentence-final position, i.e., the position in which we would expect them to show up if we were to assign to them the status of coordinate clauses:

(53)   DUTCH:
a.   *Hij is meer veranderd dan je   zou   denken*
          he is more changed   than you might think
          'He has changed more than you might think'
b.   * *Hij is dan je zou denken meer veranderd*
c.   * *Dan je zou denken is hij meer veranderd*

Secondly, main-clause status for Dutch comparative clauses can be argued from the behaviour of certain sentential adverbials. Dutch has a class of sentential modifiers, such as *eerlyk gezegd* 'to be honest' and *naar ik vrees* 'I fear', which can occur only in main clauses and in clauses for which a main-clause status has been argued, such as unrestricted relative clauses:

(54)   DUTCH:
a.   *Hij is , eerlijk   gezegd , nogal saai*
          he is   honestly said   rather dull
          'To be honest, he is rather dull'

b.   *Onze burgemeester, die , eerlijk gezegd, nogal saai is*
     our   mayor   who honestly said   rather dull is
     'Our mayor, who, to be honest, is rather dull'

c. * *Het is een feit dat hij, eerlijk gezegd, nogal saai is*
     it   is a   fact that he   honestly said   rather dull is

As can be expected, these modifiers cannot be permitted in adverbial clauses introduced by *voor* or *sinds*:

(55) DUTCH:
a.   *Hij liep   weg   voor   ik een antwoord had*
     he walked away before I   an   answer   had
     'He walked away before I could think of an answer'
b. * *Hij liep weg voor ik, eerlijk gezegd, een antwoord had*

In contrast to this, comparative clauses in which such modifiers occur do not give rise to unacceptability:

(56) DUTCH:
     Hij beweert meer dan hij, eerlijk   gezegd, kan bewijzen
     he claims   more than he honestly said   can prove
     '*lit*. He claims more than, to be honest, he can prove'

As a third point, let us consider the operation of a specific deletion rule in Dutch. Just like English, Dutch has a rule of Gapping, which deletes a finite verb in a coordinated sentence, given the identity of that verb with the verb of the preceding sentence:

(57) DUTCH:
a.   *Jan spaart postzegels en   ik spaar   munten*
     J.   collects stamps   and I   collect coins
     'Jan collects stamps and I collect coins'
b.   *Jan spaart postzegels en ik munten*

It is generally assumed that Gapping is defined only for coordinate structures.[4] Hence, it is not surprising that verbs in adverbial clauses cannot be deleted by this rule:

(58) DUTCH:
a.   *Ik zag hem voor   hij mij zag*
     I   saw him before he me saw
     'I saw him before he saw me'
b. * *Ik zag hem voor hij mij*

However, we can observe that Gapping (or some rule which has essentially the same output as Gapping, and operates under the same structural conditions) is applicable to comparative clauses in Dutch:

(59)   DUTCH:
a.   *Ik koop meer boeken dan Jan platen koopt*
        I   buy   more books   than J.   records buys
        'I buy more books than Jan buys records'
b.   *Ik koop meer boeken dan Jan platen*

Given the grammaticality of *(59b)* as opposed to the ill-formedness of *(58b)*, one may argue that Dutch comparative clauses should be viewed as having the essential properties of coordinate clauses; it is only under this assumption that a generalized formulation of Gapping in Dutch can be kept intact.

In summary, we can conclude that the facts in Dutch are contradictory as far as the grammatical status of the comparative clause is concerned. In other words, it seems that the Dutch comparative clause is a 'hybrid' construction, which may be the object of 'multiple analyses', in the sense of Hankamer (1977). Now, in order to get out of the dilemma which is created by these conflicting data, I propose the following analysis. I assume that the Dutch comparative has its origin in a coordinated structure, which is modelled on a balanced temporal chain; there is no conjunction in the chain, but temporal chaining is indicated by the occurrence of the temporal adverb *dan* in the second sentence. Furthermore, I assume that the second sentence in this chain has undergone, in the course of the development of Dutch, a process of *syntactization*. The concept of syntactization has been developed by Givón (1979), who defines this term as referring to a diachronic process by which 'loose, paratactic, "pragmatic" discourse structures develop – over time – into tight, "grammaticalized" syntactic structures' (Givón, 1979: 208). Evidence for the operation of such a process stems from a large diversity of grammatical phenomena, such as the relation between topicalization and passivization, the relation between topicalization and relative-clause formation, the rise of complex genitive constructions, the development of inflectional verbal morphology, and the formation of cleft-constructions and WH-questions (see Givón, 1979: 206–33). Of particular interest to the present discussion is the claim made by Givón (1979: 213–15) that various cases of verb-phrase subordination (such as the infinitival complements of verbs which impose Equi-conditions, and the serial verb constructions in Niger–Congo languages and Mandarin) must be explained on the basis of a process of 'condensation', which gradually transforms a loose, conjoined pattern into a tighter, subordinate pattern. It is this kind of process which I assume has been at work in the development of the Dutch comparative; from a paratactic pattern, modelled on a temporal chain, a construction has been developed which has definite subordinate traits. It is probable that this process has been helped along by the fact that the adverbial marker *dan* in paratactic Dutch coordinations is preferably clause-initial:

(60) DUTCH:
a.   *Eerst is het licht rood , dan is het groen*
      first is the light red   then is it green
      'First the light is red, then it is green'
b.   *Het licht is eerst rood, dan is het groen*
c. * *Eerst is het licht rood, het is dan groen*
d. * *Het licht is eerst rood, het is dan groen*

Since the adverbial marker *dan* in paratactic coordinations has, as it were, been 'frozen' into clause-initial position, a reanalysis of this item as a complementizer does not meet with structural impediments, as complementizers, too, are always clause-initial in Dutch. It must be added that, in Dutch at least, the assumed process of syntactization does not seem to have yet reached its final stage. The Dutch comparative clause, while having certain defining surface characteristics of subordinate clauses, still retains several properties which are reminiscent of its erstwhile coordinate status.

By assuming a process of syntactization in the formation of Dutch comparative clauses, we have created a framework in which the observed contradictions in the data on this construction can, at least in principle, be accounted for. It may be added here that the wish to reconcile these apparent contradictions is not the sole motivation for the postulation of a syntactization process; this process is supported by some further observations on the Dutch comparative, which are of a lexical and a synchronic syntactic nature.

First, we have stated that the comparative particle *dan* is at least homonymous with the temporal adverb *dan*, and that one might venture the hypothesis that these elements are in fact historically identical. In the (admittedly, very scanty) literature on the etymology of the Dutch comparative particle, I have found no indication that such an identification should be rejected. In this connection, I may also point out that in High German the particle *denn*, which has its origin in a phonological variant of the temporal adverb *dann* 'then', has also a limited function as a comparative particle. The normal particle in High German comparatives is *als*:

(61) HIGH GERMAN:
     Er ist dummer   als   ich
     he is more stupid than I
     'He is more stupid than me'

However, if a comparative construction in High German threatens to receive a surface form in which two occurrences of the item *als* would succeed each other (a situation which may arise as a result of the fact that the item *als* is also used as the equative or essive marker 'as', 'like'), then the comparative particle will be replaced by the item *denn*:[5]

(62)   HIGH GERMAN:
a. * *Er spielt besser als Torwart   als   als Mittelstürmer*
        he plays better as goal-keeper than as centre-forward

b.   *Er spielt besser als Torwart denn als Mittelstürmer*
       'He plays better as a goal-keeper than as a centre-forward'

Evidently, an etymological identification of the comparative particle *dan* with the temporal adverb *dan* will provide for direct support for our claim that the Dutch comparative has its origin in a modelling on a temporal chain in which the temporal adverb *dan* occurs.

Another piece of support for the proposed process of syntactization can be derived from the parallelism which can be observed to exist between the output of Coordination Ellipsis and Comparative Ellipsis. Above, we saw that Dutch comparative clauses can undergo a reduction process which has the same effect as the application of Gapping in coordinate structures; this fact distinguishes comparative clauses from 'real' adverbial subordinate clauses. In addition to Gapping, other types of Coordination Ellipsis have their parallel in elliptical comparative clauses in Dutch. As is shown by the pairs of sentences in (63), Subject-Verb-Deletion is permitted both in comparative clauses and in co-ordinations in Dutch. In contrast, the pairs in (64) and (65) demonstrate that Subject-Object-Deletion and Forward Object-Deletion are forbidden for both construction types:

(63)   DUTCH:
a.   *Ik koop boeken en   ik koop platen*
       I buy books and I buy records
       'I buy books and I buy records'
b.   *Ik koop boeken en platen* (Subject-Verb-Deletion)

c.   *Ik koop eerder boeken dan (dat) ik platen   koop*
       I buy rather books than that I records buy
       'I buy books more readily than I buy records'
d.   *Ik koop eerder boeken dan platen* (Subject-Verb-Deletion)

(64) DUTCH:

a. *Ik koop boeken en   ik lees   boeken*
   I   buy   books   and I   read   books
   'I buy books and I read books'

b. * *Ik koop boeken en lees* (Subject-Object-Deletion)

c. *Ik koop eerder boeken dan (dat) ik boeken lees*

d. * *Ik koop eerder boeken dan lees* (Subject-Object-Deletion)

(65) DUTCH:

a. *Ik koop boeken en   Jan leent   boeken*
   I   buy   books   and J.   borrows   books
   'I buy books and Jan borrows books'

b. * *Ik koop boeken en Jan leent* (Forward Object-Deletion)

c. *Ik koop eerder boeken dan (dat) Jan boeken leent*

d. * *Ik koop eerder boeken dan Jan leent* (Forward Object-Deletion)

Given these facts, we can conclude that there is some evidence which suggests that Hankamer's (1979: 386) claim that, for English, 'the Comparative Reduction Rule is formally similar to the rule of Co-ordinate Deletion' can also be applied to describe the situation in Dutch.

It must be added immediately, however, that, besides the above cases of parallelism, there are also cases of ellipsis in which the matching of comparative clauses and coordinate structures in Dutch appears to break down. The pairs of sentences in (66) show that deletion of identical subjects is possible in coordinations, but not in comparative clauses. On the other hand, deletion of identical VPs (see (67)) is readily permitted in comparative clauses, whereas this operation in coordinate structures leads to results which are only marginally acceptable: the only way to make (67b) well formed is to provide it with heavy contrastive stress on *ik* and *Jan*. Cp.:

(66) DUTCH:

a. *Ik lees   boeken en   ik draai   platen*
   I   read   books   and I   play   records
   'I read books and I play records'

b. *Ik lees boeken en draai platen* (Subject-Deletion)

c. *Ik lees eerder boeken dan (dat) ik platen draai*

d. * *Ik lees eerder boeken dan platen draai* (Subject-Deletion)

(67)   DUTCH:
a.   Ik koop boeken en   Jan koopt boeken
  I buy   books and J.   buys books
  'I buy books and Jan buys books'
b. *? Ik koop boeken en Jan (VP-Deletion)

c.   Ik koop eerder boeken dan (dat) Jan boeken koopt
d.   Ik koop eerder boeken dan Jan (VP-Deletion)

Now, in my opinion these apparent differentiations in the respective outputs of Coordination Deletion and Comparative Ellipsis can be neutralized completely, if we are willing to assume that it is not the normal *and*-coordination, but rather paratactic *dan*-chaining on which the comparative construction in Dutch has been modelled. Sentences *(68a/b)* demonstrate that balanced paratactic *dan*-chains, unlike co-ordinations with *and*, do not permit deletion of identical subjects either. If there is identity of subjects in a *dan*-chain, Dutch has no other choice than to pronominalize the second subject. Since sentence *(66d)* shows that the same condition holds for comparative clauses, a parallel between *dan*-chains and comparatives can be established on this point:

(68)   DUTCH:
a.   Eerst lees ik boeken , dan draai ik platen
  'First I read books, then I play records'
b. * Eerst lees ik boeken, dan draai platen (Subject-Deletion)

Secondly, it can be noted that VP-Deletion is much more normal in paratactic *dan*-chains than in *and*-coordinations (see sentences *(67b)* and *(69b)*, respectively). Again, since VP-Deletion is freely permitted in comparative clauses (see sentence *(67d)*), the parallelism between *dan*-chains and comparative clauses in Dutch will be evident:

(69)   DUTCH:
a.   Eerst lees ik het boek, dan leest Jan het boek
  'First I read the book, then Jan reads the book'
b.   Eerst lees ik het boek, dan Jan (VP-Deletion)

Finally, it can be observed that, in those cases of ellipsis where *and*-coordinations match comparative clauses, paratactic *dan*-chains do so, too. Thus, *dan*-chains permit Gapping and Subject-Verb-Deletion, while disallowing Subject-Object-Deletion and Forward Object-Deletion. Cp.:

(70)   DUTCH:
a.   *Eerst koop ik een boek, dan koopt Jan een plaat*
   'First I buy a book, then Jan buys a record'
b.   *Eerst koop ik een boek, dan Jan een plaat* (Gapping)

(71)   DUTCH:
a.   *Eerst koop ik boeken, dan koop ik platen*
   'First I buy books, then I buy records'
b.   *Eerst koop ik boeken, dan platen* (Subject-Verb-Deletion)

(72)   DUTCH:
a.   *Eerst koop ik het boek , dan lees ik het boek*
   'First I buy the book, then I read the book'
b. * *Eerst koop ik het boek, dan lees* (Subject-Object-Deletion)

(73)   DUTCH:
a.   *Eerst koop ik het boek, dan leent Jan het boek*
   'First I buy the book, then Jan borrows the book'
b. * *Eerst koop ik het boek, dan leent Jan* (Forward Object-Deletion)

We can conclude that there is complete agreement between *dan*-chains and comparative clauses in Dutch with regard to the possibilities of ellipsis. Evidently, this agreement provides strong evidence in favour of the claim that the comparative construction in Dutch is modelled upon a balanced, paratactic *dan*-chain.

9.4.2   *Contrasts between English and Dutch*

In the previous section I presented an array of seemingly conflicting facts about the Dutch comparative and, following that, I offered an analysis in which these conflicts can be reconciled. Briefly speaking, I have argued that the Dutch comparative should be conceived of as a construction which has its origin in a modelling on a balanced *dan*-chain, but which has undergone a process of syntactization by which the original co-ordinate status has gradually faded to yield a subordinate construction. This process of syntactization can be elucidated somewhat further by looking at the Particle Comparative in English, contrasting the English *than*-comparative with the corresponding construction in Dutch.

First of all, then, we can note that English, too, offers some indication of an erstwhile coordinate status of its comparative clause. Most importantly, elliptical rules of the kind illustrated for Dutch can also be found in English. Hankamer (1979) and Kuno (1981) provide examples in which the parallel between Coordination Ellipsis (or Coordination Reduction, as Hankamer calls it) and the reduction of comparative clauses is demonstrated:

(74) ENGLISH:
a.   *Jack is cunning and Jack is brave → Jack is cunning and brave*
b.   *John likes soccer and Bill likes soccer → John likes soccer, and Bill, too*
c.   *John has lived in New York and John has lived in LA → John has lived in New York and in LA*
d.   *John gave a dime to Susan and John gave a nickel to Sandy → John gave a dime to Susan and a nickel to Sandy*

(75) ENGLISH:
a.   *Jack is more cunning than he is brave → Jack is more cunning than brave*
b.   *John likes soccer more than Bill likes soccer → John likes soccer more than Bill*
c.   *John would rather live in New York than he would live in LA → John would rather live in New York than in LA*
d.   *I would rather give a dime to Susan than I would give a nickel to Sandy → I would rather give a dime to Susan than a nickel to Sandy*

As we have noted above, Hankamer (1979: 386) arrives at the conclusion that the rule which reduces comparative clauses is formally similar to the rule of Coordination Deletion. In both cases, we have a rule which is downward bounded, i.e., it cannot reach into embedded clauses:

(76) ENGLISH:
a.   *Jack is cunning and Mary thinks he is brave*
b. * *Jack is cunning and Mary thinks brave*

(77) ENGLISH:
a.   *Jack is more cunning than Mary thinks he is brave*
b. * *Jack is more cunning than Mary thinks brave*

Furthermore, both the reduction of comparative clauses and the reduction of coordinations are subject to the condition that the deleted constituents are identical with corresponding constituents in an identical structure. In Hankamer's terminology, these reductions are instances of 'blanket rules', that is, deletion rules in which the identity condition 'cannot be formulated with reference to any particular constituent, since *any* constituent . . . can be deleted under identity with a "corresponding" constituent in the matrix' (Hankamer, 1979: 385). As such, the reduction of comparative and coordinate structures is opposed to other types of deletion rules, which can delete elements only if the identity with some particular constituent in the matrix is specified. From the fact that the reduction procedures for comparatives and coordinations turn out to be so closely similar, one may derive an argument in favour of (at least some degree of) coordinate status for the English *than*-clause.

It must, however, also be noted that the coordinate status of comparative clauses is considerably more obscure in English than in Dutch. Thus, we can observe that a number of coordinative traits of the Dutch comparative cannot be attested in English. For one thing, English does not allow the application of Gapping in comparative clauses. The following facts are taken from Hankamer (1979: 383), who judges *(78c)* to be ungrammatical, although he adds that 'some people, in fact, find [it] not too bad':

(78) ENGLISH:
a. *John writes more radical pamphlets than Harry writes scatological letters*
b. *John writes more radical pamphlets than Harry does scatological letters*
c. * *John writes more radical pamphlets than Harry $\emptyset$ scatological letters*

Furthermore, sentence adverbials like *to be honest* or *I fear* yield awkward, if not unacceptable results when they are inserted into English comparative clauses:

(79) ENGLISH:
a. * *Jack is more cunning than he is, I fear, brave*
b. * *Jack is smarter than, to be honest, he looks*

These facts suggest that the process of syntactization, which leads ultimately to the transformation of a coordinate clause into a subordinate structure, has gone farther in English than in Dutch. One might say that, with respect to the syntactization of the comparative clause, English is the more 'radical' of the two. This radicalness of English in comparison to Dutch can, I think, be illustrated clearly by contrasting the properties of NP-comparatives in both languages.

There are a number of considerations which militate against the position that the Dutch comparative particle *dan*, when followed by a single NP, has the categorial status of a *preposition*. First, unlike 'real' prepositions in Dutch, which invariably govern accusative case, the particle *dan* does not require a fixed case form of its following NP. In other words, the NP-comparative in Dutch is a derived-case comparative:

(80)   DUTCH:
a.   *Ik   vertrouw   jou   meer dan hij*
       I-NOM trust   you-ACC more than he-NOM
       'I trust you more than he (trusts you)'

b.   *Ik   vertrouw   jou   meer dan hem*
       I-NOM trust   you-ACC more than him-ACC
       'I trust you more than (I trust) him'

It must be added, though, that there is a tendency in Dutch to use the accusative case for NP-complements of comparative *dan* regardless of the grammatical function of that NP. Although it is still considered poor style in written Dutch, colloquial Dutch gradually develops into a situation in which a sentence like *(81a)* is considered normal usage, in addition to the 'more correct' sentence *(81b)*:

(81)   DUTCH:
a.   *Hij is een betere schaker   dan mij*
       he is a   better chess-player than me-ACC
       'He is a better chess-player than me'

b.   *Hij is een betere schaker   dan ik*
       he is a   better chess-player than I-NOM
       'He is a better chess-player than I (am)'

Given the framework adopted here, we may say that, in Dutch, the process of syntactization in the formation of comparatives gradually leads to a situation in which the originally reduced coordinate clause *dan* + *NP* comes to be reanalysed as an adverbial phrase, in which *dan* acts as a preposition. Now, it can be observed that this process has started to apply earlier in English than in Dutch. As Visser (1963: 249) notes, instances of accusative case for underlying subjects in English comparative clauses can be attested from the first half of the sixteenth century onwards. The process has developed into a situation in which a sentence like *(82a)* is rated as good usage, while the variant *(82b)* is considered to be stilted and old-fashioned:[6]

(82)   ENGLISH:
a.   *You're stronger than me*
b.   *You're stronger than I*

The difference in the extent to which English *than* and Dutch *dan* have been syntacticized into prepositions in NP-comparatives can also be shown from the difference in the application of movement rules. As Hankamer (1973: 18) states, there is an increasing possibility in at least some English dialects to apply WH-Movement to standard NPs in comparatives; in sentences where this rule has applied, the particle *than* is treated as a stranded preposition, on a par with cases of 'real' preposition stranding like the one in *(83b)*:

(83) ENGLISH:
a. *Who is he bigger than?*
b. *Who is he looking at?*

In contrast, application of WH-Movement to standard NPs is completely forbidden in Dutch. While Dutch normally allows preposition stranding (see *(84a)*), a sentence like *(84b)* is absolutely ill-formed, even in colloquial and non-standard speech:

(84) DUTCH:
a. *waar kijkt hij naar?*
     where looks he at/to
     'What is he looking at?'
b. * *Waar is hij groter dan?*

To sum up, I think that the above comparison of Dutch and English comparatives demonstrates that syntactization must be seen as a gradual process, which allows for intermediate stages; apparently, the process has progressed further in English than in Dutch. In the present situation in English, it is not unjustified to claim that there are, in fact, two *thans* in English, one a preposition and the other a subordinating particle (see Hankamer, 1973). In English, there is an increasing tendency to treat the string *than + NP* as a prepositional phrase, and, as a result, the relation between NP-comparison and other comparatives becomes gradually weaker. In Dutch, too, we can observe some first signs of this increasing independence of NP-comparison; one may very well expect that, in a not too distant future, it can be argued that there are two *dan's* in Dutch. For the moment, however, the Dutch comparative still hangs together as a homogeneous construction type.

9.4.3 *Further comments on the process of syntactization*

If we accept the syntactization analysis for the comparatives in Dutch and English, it does not seem to be implausible to extend this analysis to all other types of Particle Comparatives. A number of features of the Dutch and English comparatives which argue for this analysis can also be attested for other instances of the Particle Comparative; in particular, all Particle Comparatives have in common that the standard NP in NP-comparatives has derived case instead of fixed case. Moreover, we have noted that, in a considerable number of Particle Comparatives, the relation with an erstwhile coordinate structure has been retained directly in synchronic surface structure; in such languages, the particle in the comparative construction is historically identical to some conjunctive marker. For these reasons, I will adopt the working hypothesis that some process of syntactization is at the basis of the development of Particle Comparatives in general.

To this, however, it should be added immediately that I do not claim that the coordinate structure which gets syntacticized into a Particle Comparative has exactly the same form for all the languages at issue. That is, while I claim that all Particle Comparatives are the result of a gradual downgrading of a coordinate clause into a subordinate clause, I do not intend this to imply that this coordinate 'input'-structure is formally invariant across the relevant languages. As we will see shortly (and more fully in chapter 12), this coordinate input-structure must be considered to allow *a range of formally distinct (though semantically equivalent) variants*. As a consequence of this variation in the input-structure of syntactization, it follows that the process of downgrading will not necessarily always involve the same mechanisms. It is an unfortunate fact that the intermediate stages in the syntactization of comparative clauses can be documented only for a few languages, and even in those cases our knowledge is far from complete. Hence, any statement about the actual mechanisms of syntactization will, of necessity, contain a large amount of vagueness and speculation. Nevertheless, we can give at least some general comments on the nature of the syntactization process which have a reasonable degree of plausibility.

First, it appears that a necessary condition for the start of any syntactization of a comparative clause lies in the ability of the language to reduce clauses by means of elliptical rules. In other words, if a structural configuration is to be syntacticized into a subordinate clause, the language will have to possess the means to reduce this clause. For some languages with a Particle Comparative, this process of Coordination Reduction appears to be not only a necessary, but also a sufficient prerequisite for the formation of the comparative construction. In languages like Basque, Javanese, Toba Batak and Ilocano, we find a situation in which the comparative clause has the form of a reduced coordinate clause which has gradually come to be reanalysed, to a greater or lesser extent, as a subordinate structural unit. For languages of this type, it seems plausible to assume an 'input'-structure which consists of *the mere coordination of two positive clauses*.

In other languages, however, the form of the input-structure seems to be more complex, and hence the syntactization of the comparative clause seems to involve more than just ellipsis. In some languages with a Particle Comparative, there are grounds to assume the presence of *an underlying negative element* in the coordinate input-structure of their comparative clauses. The fact that such an underlying negation tends to crop up in comparatives must presumably be accounted for in terms of the semantics of comparison; I will say more about this in section 12.3. For the moment, I will restrict myself to the consequences which the presence of an underlying negation has for the process of syntactization of comparative constructions.

For some languages at issue here, syntactization of the comparative clause appears to involve the *morphological incorporation* of the underlying negative element into the comparative particle. Clear and straightforward examples are Gaelic, Scottish English, Latvian, and perhaps also Classical Greek;[7] in these languages, the comparative particle itself has the morphological form of a negative conjunction. In addition to these cases, we can also find indications for the presence of an underlying negation in a number of languages where the comparative particle does not (or not overtly) show incorporation of a negative element. Thus, in French the negative particle *ne* shows up obligatorily in a comparative clause if that clause contains a finite verb:

(85) FRENCH:
    Il est plus grand que vous ne pensez
    he is more tall than you NEG think
    'He is taller than you think'

A similar phenomenon can be observed in Italian (see Seuren, 1973: 535). In formal Italian style, clausal comparatives are introduced by the particle *che*, which (just like its French counterpart *que*) has its etymological origin in Latin *quo* 'by which'. Use of *che* in comparatives requires the presence of the negative item *non* in the comparative clause, and the verb in the clause has to be in the Subjunctive Mood (cp. (86a)). An alternative formation of Italian comparative clauses involves the use of the complex comparative particle *di quello che*. In this case, the verb in the clause is in the Indicative Mood, and the negative item *non* is no longer present. Cp.:

(86) ITALIAN:
a.   *Gianni è più grande che non pensassi*
    G. is more tall than NEG think-PAST. SUBJUNCT. 1SG
    'Gianni is taller than I thought'

b. * *Gianni è più grande di quello che non pensassi*
c.   *Gianni è più grande di quello che pensavo*
    G. is more tall than think-PAST. IND. 1SG
    'Gianni is taller than I thought'

The intimate relationship of the comparative construction with negation in at least some of the languages with a Particle Comparative is also supported by a number of observations from English and Dutch. As is noted by Seuren (1973, 1984), comparative clauses in these languages may contain so-called negative-polarity items, i.e., lexical items or idioms which typically may occur only in constructions in which a negative element is present. Cp.:

(87)   ENGLISH:
a.   *I would never have thought that John was an impostor*
b.   * *I would ever have thought that John was an impostor*
c.   *John is a bigger liar than I ever would have thought*

(88)   DUTCH:
a.   *Ik kan die   mensen niet luchten*
        I   can those people NEG put up with
        'I can't put up with those people'
b.   * *Ik kan die mensen luchten*

c.   *Ik heb er   al   meer mensen gezien*
        I   have there already more people   seen
        dan ik kan luchten
        than I can put up with
        'I have seen already more people there than I can put up with'

Opposed to this, so-called positive-polarity items (i.e., lexical items or idioms that cannot occur with negation) are excluded from English and Dutch comparative clauses:

(89)   ENGLISH:
a.   *You have already eaten too much*
b.   * *I haven't already eaten too much*
c.   * *He has got more support than you already have*

(90)   DUTCH:
a.   *Hij is verdomd vervelend*
        he is damned   boring
        'He is damned boring'
b.   * *Hij is niet   verdomd vervelend*

c.   * *Hij is vaker   onderhoudend dan verdomd*
        he is more often   entertaining   than damned
        vervelend
        boring

Further syntactic arguments for the presence of a negation in English comparative clauses are advanced in Mittwoch (1974) and Napoli and Nespor (1976). Finally, we may add here that, for some authors at least (see Joly, 1967: 17), the English particle *than* has developed from *thonne*, that is, a combination of the instrumental case of the neuter demonstrative article *thaet* and the negative item *ne* 'not'. If this etymology is accepted, English *than* may be counted as another example of the incorporation of a negative element into the comparative particle.

Apart from Coordination Ellipsis, and (for at least some of the languages at issue) the incorporation c.q. retainment of underlying negative items, syntactization of comparative clauses sometimes seems to involve a process which shares essential features with *relativization*. Straightforward evidence for such a process is presented by those languages in which the comparative particle is historically an adverbial case form of the relative/interrogative pronoun; examples are Russian, Italian, French, Finnish, and probably also Latin and Hungarian. We may add that, for English, it has been argued repeatedly in the literature that the particle *than* is, in its etymology, closely related to a demonstrative/relative stem, it being either an oblique case form of this stem (Campbell, 1959) or a combination of such a case form with the negative element *ne* (Joly, 1967).

In addition to these etymological data, there are also several structural arguments which point to a close similarity of Relative Clause Formation and Comparative Formation in English. Observations to this effect are presented in Bresnan (1971, 1973). One of the most telling arguments in favour of this analysis is the fact that, in some non-standard varieties of English, this relativization even shows up overtly in surface structure, giving rise to constructions like

(91)   ENGLISH:
       John is a lot smarter than what you'd think (he is)

On the basis of the data given in Bresnan (1973) and of observations like *(91)*, Hankamer (1979) proposes an analysis of English comparative formation in which the comparative clause contains a constituent which is marked for relativization. Application of Relative Clause Formation (which implies the fronting of the relativized constituent in the comparative clause) results in non-standard forms like *(91)*; in standard English, the relative element *what* is obligatorily deleted. A syntactic analysis of English comparative clauses which is roughly comparable to Hankamer's account is put forward in Kuno (1981). According to this author, the quantified constituent in the underlying comparative clause undergoes promotion by a rule of X-Quantifier Raising, leaving behind a clause which can then be reduced further by some elliptical rule. All in all, it thus seems plausible to conclude that, for English at least, the formation of comparatives involves a set of formal procedures which is essentially similar to the rule system needed in the formation of relative clauses. As I see it, this conclusion holds independently of the specific formulation one chooses for the rule system at issue.

If we accept the above conclusion, we must ask ourselves what the form of the 'input structure' for the Particle Comparative in English should be assumed to be. As an approximation of a solution to this problem, I will adopt the analysis of the English comparative which is proposed by Seuren in several publications. In this proposal, English comparatives are analysed in terms of an underlying structure which crucially involves *existential quantification over extents*. Thus, a comparative like *Jim is taller than Joe* is analysed as

$$(92) \qquad \exists_{e:extent} \qquad (\textit{Jim is tall to } e \wedge \sim (\textit{Joe is tall to } e))$$

or, to rephrase this analysis in a non-logical form: 'There is an extent e such that Jim is tall to e and Joe is not tall to e.' There are several independently motivated arguments for the correctness of an analysis of this type. Apart from the fact that the analysis accounts for the underlying negation which must be assumed to be present in English comparative clauses (see above), the quantification over extents which is embodied in this proposal provides a framework for the description of the phenomenon of positive and negative connotations of English gradable adjectives (see Seuren, 1973: 535–7), and enables us to account for the occurrence of adverbial measure-phrases in comparative clauses (Seuren, 1984). Furthermore, it can be shown that this analysis is able to deal with the ambiguity in a sentence like

(93)   ENGLISH:
       Planes are safer now than they were 30 years ago

in a straightforward fashion (Seuren, 1973: 528–9; Seuren, 1984).

From the point of view of the present study, the main attractiveness of Seuren's proposal lies in the fact that it is able to reconcile two seemingly contradictory requirements on the 'input structure' for the English Particle Comparative. On the one hand, we have argued that the input-structure for all Particle Comparatives should be viewed as basically a coordinated structure; this requirement is met by the presence of the *and*-conjunction in *(92)*. On the other hand, we have also concluded that the formation of the English comparative involves some procedure of relativization. Structure *(92)* offers a possibility for the application of this procedure, in that it specifies an existentially quantified antecedent for a constituent of the comparative clause; this constituent (viz. the extent-phrase *e*) becomes thereby eligible for relativization.

9.5 Conclusion

In this chapter, we have examined the validity of Universal 1A and Universal 4 against the facts of the languages in the sample which have a primary derived-case comparative. As could be expected, languages with a primary Conjoined Comparative confirm these two universals in a straightforward fashion. Regarding the more problematic class of Particle Comparatives, we have put forward the hypothesis that their occurrence must be understood on the basis of a diachronic process of syntactization. We have assumed that Particle Comparatives are initially modelled on balanced temporal chains; under this assumption, the fact that languages with a primary Particle Comparative are all confirmations of Universal 1A can be immediately accounted for. Furthermore, we have claimed that the coordinate status of the comparative clause in these languages is gradually undermined by the operation of a downgrading process. As a result, the comparative construction loses its semantic transparency to a greater or lesser extent. The comparative in these languages may thus eventually be reanalysed as a new, independent construction type. Alternatively, the comparative construction may come to be fitted into the mould of a construction type that already exists in the language. This is what we claim is happening in English, where NP-comparison is gradually allying itself to the already available prepositional phrase construction.

In order for the downgrading process to start, a minimal requirement seems to be that the language be able to apply elliptical rules to its coordinate structures. For some languages, this appears to be also a sufficient requirement for the formation of a Particle Comparative. Hence, for these languages a coordinate input-structure consisting of two positive sentences seems to be the appropriate hypothesis. In other languages, however, the coordinate input-structure must be thought of as being more complex. Some of the languages at issue seem to have a negative sentence in their input-sentence; this may (but does not have to) lead to the incorporation of the negative element into the comparative particle. Still other languages must be assumed to have a coordinate input-structure with quantification over extents; in these languages, signs of relativization (typically manifested in the form of the comparative particle) can be traced. Finally, there are some languages (viz. English, French, Italian, and possibly also Dutch) in which both an underlying negation and an underlying existential quantification must be assumed for the coordinate input-structure of the comparative construction.

10

An Examination of Secondary Choices

10.1 Introduction

In the preceding sections of part two, the set of chaining-based universals formulated in chapter 5 has been tested against the primary comparative type options of the languages in the sample. Now, it is my claim not only that this set of universals should be considered to state predictions for primary comparatives, but that it should also be able to predict correctly the occurrence of secondary options for a given language. Therefore, this final chapter of part two will be devoted to a testing of the relevant universals against the secondary choice of comparative type. As has been noted in the tables in chapter 2, the sample contains no less than 34 cases of secondary comparative-type choice; for some languages, there is even more than one secondary option available. In general, however, it will turn out that the discussion of the cases at issue can be mercifully brief.

Another matter connected with the phenomenon of secondary comparative choice is the question of whether there are any regularities in the combinations of primary and secondary comparative types in natural languages. That is, one might ask whether or not the choice of a secondary comparative in a language may be completely independent of the choice of the primary comparative made in that language. I will pursue this question further in chapter 15. For the moment, however, our sole attention will be with the secondary options themselves, and with the extent to which they can be shown to be confirmations of the set of chaining-based universals.

10.2 Secondary derived-case comparatives

I will start the examination of secondary comparative-type choices by looking at those languages which have a secondary derived-case comparative, that is, a Conjoined Comparative or some variant of a Particle

Comparative. Following Universal 1A and Universal 4, we should be able to demonstrate that, for these languages, the secondary comparative is matched by the possibility of having balanced temporal chaining constructions.

The sample contains six languages with a Conjoined Comparative as their secondary choice. To start with, let us consider the case of Banda, a language which has an Exceed Comparative as its primary option (see section 8.3). As a secondary option, this language possesses a Conjoined Comparative of the polar variety. Rather trivially, this option is matched by a balanced simultaneous construction:

(1)   BANDA:
a.   Anda   ne   mo   gere   nini,   e   ne   ze   gere
     house of me   big   not   it of you   big
     'Your house is bigger than my house'

b.   Mo   owe   ani   ,   ane ani   ta   oboe roe
     you chase them   and they say not   thing
     'You have chased them, and they haven't said anything'

In section 7.7 I argued that the best way to deal with the primary comparative in Mapuche is to classify it as a Locative Comparative. In addition, Mapuche also permits the use of a Conjoined Comparative of the polar kind. Naturally, this secondary option is matched by the occurrence of a balanced S-chain:

(2)   MAPUCHE:
a.   Karlos   doi   kimi   ,   Francisko   doi   kim -la -i
     K.   more know-3SG   F.   more know-not-3SG
     'Karlos knows more than Francisko'

b.   Manuel   aku-la -i   ,   Francisko   kafei   aku-la -i
     M.   go -not-3SG ,   F.   too   go -not-3SG
     'Manuel does not go, and neither does Francisko'

Nuer is a language with a primary Allative Comparative; as we noted in section 7.2.2, this Allative Comparative is matched by the so-called Narrative Mood in Nuer, which is employed to derank posterior predicates in C-chains. However, it appears that this deranking procedure is available to Nuer only for cases of consecutive chaining; in simultaneous chains a balanced construction appears to be required. Thus, Nuer is one of the very few languages in the sample which do not show a structural parallelism in the encoding of the two semantic subtypes of temporal chaining. Parallel to the balanced S-chain of Nuer we find a Conjoined Comparative of the antonymous kind:

(3) NUER:

a. Diid ne jin , kwiy ne gän
   big be·you   small be I
   'You are bigger than me'

b. Loke   je , ke cë nhok
   reject-PRES. 3PL him   but not accept-FUT. 3SG
   'They reject him, but he will not accept it'

Ilocano, a VSO-language with a primary Particle Comparative, is reported in Lopez (1928) to have the additional option of a Conjoined Comparative:

(4) ILOCANO:
    Nasayaat   ni Dolores , sumangka-sayaat pay
    pretty-one SUBJ D.   more   -pretty even
    ni Enkarnasion
    SUBJ E.
    'Enkarnasion is prettier than Dolores'

Since the Particle Comparative in Ilocano can be directly connected with a balanced simultaneous construction, in that this comparative employs the item *ngem* 'but' as a particle (see section 9.3), the matching of the secondary Conjoined Comparative with the relevant chaining construction is trivial.

In section 8.3 we showed that the primary Exceed Comparative in Swahili has a direct parallel in the simultaneous action construction, which, in the unmarked case, is an instance of conditional deranking. However, Swahili has also a secondary comparative, namely, a Conjoined Comparative of the antonymous subtype. It turns out that this secondary option is modelled upon a marked subtype of simultaneous balancing in Swahili. As Loogman (1965: 375) reports, the normal deranking procedure for S-chains in Swahili cannot be applied if the chain has the semantic content of an opposition. In such a case of adversative chaining, the structure appears to be obligatorily balanced; the two members of the structure can be juxtaposed without any connective element. Parallel to this coordinated type of simultaneous chaining we find the secondary comparative of Swahili:

(5) SWAHILI:
a. Joogoo wa Ali hodari , yule wa Juma dhaifu
   rooster of A. strong   that of J.   weak
   'Ali's rooster is stronger than Juma's rooster'

b. *Ni-me -leta   machungwa , u -me -leta   ndizi*
    I -PERF-bring oranges   you-PERF-bring bananas
    'I have brought oranges, you have brought bananas'

Exactly the same situation as that in Swahili can be attested for
Kirundi. This Bantu-language, which has a primary Exceed Comparative, has its secondary Conjoined Comparative matched by a balanced S-
chain:

(6) KIRUNDI:
a. *Uyo ni mukungu , urya ni mworo*
    this is rich   that is poor
    'This one is richer than that one'

b. *Nti-hiica umwaami , hiica abasavyi*
    not-kill king   kill   courtesans
    'It's not the king who is murderous, it's the courtesans'

In addition to the six languages with a secondary Conjoined Comparative, the sample contains two languages which select some other type of
derived-case comparative as their secondary option. One of these
languages, viz. Bari, has already been introduced in section 3.4. As we
saw in sentence *(37a)*, the Particle Comparative in Bari involves the
element *na gwon* if the standard constituent is a clause. We can add here
that the item *gwon* (which is possibly some fossilized form of the verb 'to
be') is deleted when the standard constituent is an NP. Cp.:

(7) BARI:
a. *Nan kita   bya   na gwon do   yeyeju*
    I   work more   PRT   you think
    'I work more than you think'

b. *Monye a lo'but bya   na   tore lonyit*
    father is good more PRT son his
    'The father is better than his son'

The particle *na/na gwon* has a number of other functions in the syntax of
Bari. For one thing, *na gwon* can be used as the adversative conjunction
'but' (Spagnolo, 1933: 266). Also, *na* or *na gwon* may be used as the
equivalent of our temporal conjunction 'while'; in this case, the temporal
clause is marked at its end by a repetition of the particle *na* (Spagnolo,
1933: 257). Finally, we find cases of clauses marked by *na ... na* in
which a consecutive interpretation seems to be implied (Spagnolo, 1933:
256). Relevant examples are:

(8)   BARI:
a.   *Sörömundi   kata , na gwon kala 'bayin*
      ground-nuts exist   PRT   teeth not-exist
      'We have ground-nuts, but no appetite'

b.   *Na gwon ki jöjön na , ngutu gwogwolong kadi*
      PRT   it rain PRT   people be-at   house
      'While it rains, the people stay inside the house'

c.   *Na Komandan aje jam kulya sine na ,*
      PRT commander was say words these PRT
      á   ngutu akujönö   parik
      and/then people become-afraid very much
      'After the Commander had said these words, the people grew
      much afraid'

Given these examples, I think it is safe to conclude that the secondary
Particle Comparative in Bari has a direct surface parallel in the balancing
procedure which the language employs to encode its various forms of
temporal chaining.

As a last case in this category, we must draw attention to the secondary
comparative in Classical Nahuatl. In section 9.2 we saw that the primary
option for this language is a Conjoined Comparative. In addition to this,
Andrews (1975: 350ff.) lists a comparative of the type illustrated in

(9)   CLASSICAL NAHUATL:
      Nehhuātl oc-achi   ni-tlamatini, in ahmō iuhqúi tehhuātl
      I   a bit more I -learned   PRT   you
      'I am a bit more learned than you'

As we can see, the standard NP in this construction is preceded by a series
of items. In this item string, the element *ahmo* is obligatory; this element
is the general negative element 'not'. In the comparative construction at
hand, the negation *ahmo* is commonly preceded by the item *in*, an
element which functions as a general adjunctor and is, among other
things, the equivalent of our definite articles and relative pronouns.
Furthermore, the negative item in this construction may optionally be
followed by the element *iuh/iuhqui*; in its origin, this element is a verb
with the meaning 'to be so, to be thus'. The whole of the item string
preceding the standard NP is glossed by Andrews (ibid.) as 'while not
thus, i.e., than'. Given this translation, and given the etymological origin
of the items involved, it seems appropriate to rate this secondary
comparative as a type of Particle Comparative; to be exact, we might see
it as a Particle Comparative in which both the procedures of relativization

and negative incorporation have been effectuated (see section 9.4.3). Since Nahuatl has a Conjoined Comparative as its primary option, it will come as no surprise that the secondary Particle Comparative, too, can be matched by a balanced chaining construction. As a matter of fact, Classical Nahuatl appears to be a language which is predominantly, if not strictly, balancing. A further example of a coordinated structure in this language is:

(10)   CLASSICAL NAHUATL:
　　　O -motlalih , ihuan   ō -tlacuah
　　　he-sat down   moreover he-ate
　　　'He sat down and ate'

10.3   Secondary Exceed Comparatives

Next, we turn to the six languages in the sample which select an Exceed Comparative as their secondary option. Of these languages, Universal 2A predicts that they should have either a conditionally deranked S-chain, or a conditionally deranked C-chain, or both. As it turns out, all six languages at issue can be shown to fulfil this requirement; in some cases, however, we will come across specific problems which deserve some further comment.

Relatively straightforward cases in this class are Sranan and Sika. In Sranan, an English-based creolization, the modern comparative is a Particle Comparative which employs the particle *leki* 'like' (see section 9.3). This construction has replaced the older Exceed Comparative, which was modelled on the serialization construction that formed a part of the African substratum of Sranan. As sentence *(11b)* shows, serialization is still a living syntactic option in modern Sranan:

(11)   SRANAN:
a.　　A koni pasa   mi
　　　he smart surpass me
　　　'He is smarter than me'

b.　　A tyari a   buku kon gi   mi
　　　he carry the book come give me
　　　'He has brought me the book'

Sika is a language with a primary Conjoined Comparative. This primary option is matched by the fact that a balancing procedure is largely favoured in the encoding of both simultaneous and consecutive chains in Sika. However, it appears that a form of serialization is permitted for a limited number of cases; the language has a number of verbal forms which are constructed as the posterior element in a serial-verb-string, and which gradually adopt the function of prepositions:

(12)   SIKA:

a.   Nimu tutur nora guru
      he   talk   have teacher
      'He talks about the teacher'

b.   Cau ou   wheli micu ceca
      I   search give you food
      'I will search food for you'

From these examples, it will be clear that this construction can be used only if the subjects of the predicates involved are identical; moreover, these examples show that the serial construction in Sika covers instances of both simultaneous and consecutive chaining. As we have seen in section 8.2, these are general characteristics of serial verb strings. The serialization construction in Sika is directly matched by the secondary comparative for this language:

(13)   SIKA:
      Au gahar toi   wucé   aung
      you big   excel brother your
      'You are bigger than your brother'

Maasai presents a rather exceptional case, in that it is the sole language in the sample which combines a secondary Exceed Comparative with a primary Allative Comparative. Thus, given that our set of chaining-based universals is valid, Maasai must be one of the very few languages in the sample in which the procedural parallelism in the formation of S-chains and C-chains has broken down; while the primary comparative is matched by the absolutely deranked consecutive construction which is possible in Maasai (viz. the Dependent Tense; see section 7.2.2), the secondary Maasai comparative is modelled on a simultaneous construction of the conditionally deranked type.

The simultaneous construction which is relevant here appears to be limited in use. Tucker and Mpaayi (1955: 198) observe that Maasai has a class of so-called 'temporal verbs' like *a-itoki* 'to do afterwards', *a-siooki* 'to do soon' and *a-yooki* 'to do in the morning', which are the semantic equivalents of our temporal adverbs. These verbs are obligatorily followed by another verbal form, which refers to the action performed at the time stipulated by the temporal verb. This second verb has the form of an infinitive, but it agrees in number with the subject of the preceding temporal verb, having the prefix *a-* (Singular) or *aa-* (Plural):

(14) MAASAI:

a.   E -yooki   a   -tur
      3SG-do in the morning INF. SG-dig
      'He will dig it in the morning'

b.   I-yooki   -ki aa   -tur
      2-do in the morning-PL INF. PL-dig
      'You (PL) will dig it in the morning'

The fact that there is number agreement between the two verbal forms suggests that the infinitives in *(14)* are not cases of direct-object complementation, but rather a deranked form of a simultaneous predicate. There are two facts of Maasai syntax which further strengthen this suggestion. First, it appears to be the case that, in Maasai, infinitives are never used to represent subject-clauses or object-clauses; if such clauses have a non-finite form, the language employs a type of verbal noun, which is characterized by the suffix *-ata/-oto*. Formally, such formations are to be classified as feminine nouns; their logical subjects and objects take the genitive case. Cp.:

(15) MAASAI:
      Sidai en   -kirrit-ata enye oo   kishu
      is-good the-FEM. SG-herding his of-the-MASC. PL cattle
      '*lit*. His herding of the cattle is good: it is good that he herds cattle'

As a second point, we must note that the infinitives in *(14)* cannot be considered as cases of action nominals in the Singular or Plural. That is, it is not adequate to gloss the sentences in *(14)* as 'He will do (a) digging' or 'They will do diggings', since the elements *a-* and *aa-* are not in use as nominal number markers in Maasai. Given these facts, it seems best to conclude that the infinitives in *(14)* represent a case of serialization, in which the posterior predicates have lost some, but not all, of their verbal morphology. If this analysis of the constructions in *(14)* is correct, Maasai is a regular instance of Universal 2A; the secondary Exceed Comparative in Maasai, which matches the serialized construction in *(14)*, has the following form:

(16) MAASAI:
      Sapuk ol -kondi a   -lang ol -kibulekeny
      is-big the-deer INF. SG-excel the-waterbuck
      'The deer is bigger than the waterbuck'

In summary, we can state that Maasai can have both an Allative Comparative and an Exceed Comparative by virtue of the fact that this language, untypically, deranks its C-chains like a VSO-language and its S-chains in the typical manner of an SVO-language. This particular double option for Maasai may be connected with the fact that this language, while having basic VSO-order, has subject prefixes on verbs, so that in cases of pronominal subjects the order of elements is SVO. Cp.:

(17) MAASAI:

a.   E -tur   ol -tungani en -kurma
     he-hoes the-man   the-field
     'The man hoes the field'

b.   E -tur   en -kurma
     he-hoes the-field
     'He hoes the field'

Next, we must consider the case of Quechua and Aymara, two languages which are possibly genetically related. As we saw in section 6.2, these languages have a primary Separative Comparative which is modelled directly on the absolute consecutive construction; in early Quechua, this consecutive construction employs a separative marker on the Perfect Infinitive, a form which consists of a bare verbal stem with the suffix *-ska*. Now, the simultaneous counterpart of this Perfect Infinitive in early Quechua is the Present Infinitive, a bare verbal stem with the suffix *-spa*; etymologically, the suffix *-spa* can be identified as the nominal genitive case suffix, so that the form is commonly referred to as the Genitive Infinitive (see von Tschudi, 1884: 449). Regarding the semantic function of this infinitival form, von Tschundi (ibid.) remarks that it has 'allzeitige Kraft', i.e., it derives its temporal reference from the temporal marking on the main predicate, and indicates simultaneity or concessivity. Based on this procedure of simultaneous deranking is the Genitive Comparative in early Quechua, in which the standard NP has been put into the genitive case:

(18) QUECHUA:
     Kam noka-pa   sintsi
     you   me -GEN strong
     'You are stronger than me'

Now, the interesting structural property of the Present Infinitive is that, somehow, this form has lost the ability to appear under absolute conditions. That is, in present-day Quechua the Present Infinitive can be used only in S-chains if the subjects in the chain are identical; if the subjects are not identical, Quechua has to use the Subjunctive, a finite subordinate form. Cp.:

(19)   QUECHUA:

a.   *Muna-spa -m   manan utsa   -tsi -nki*
     want -GEN-PRT not   achieve-FUT-2SG
     'You want it, but you will not achieve it'

b.   *Muna-pti   -yki -pas manam hamusah   -tsu*
     want -SUBJUNCT-2SG-even not   come-FUT. 1SG-NEG
     'You want it, but I won't come'

Given the fact that the Present Infinitive can nowadays be used only
under identity of subjects, the set of chaining-based universals predicts
that a modelling of comparative formation on the Present Infinitive must
lead to the selection of an Exceed Comparative in modern-day Quechua
(following Universal 2A). This prediction is borne out by the facts; von
Tschudi (1884: 389) notes the occurrence of the following Quechua
comparative, in which either the comparative predicate or the exceed-
verb has been deranked into the form of the Present Infinitive:

(20)   QUECHUA:

a.   *Tsaski-y   tsaski-yki -ta   puri-spa yali   -n*
     boat -my boat -your-ACC go -GEN exceed-3SG
     '*lit.* My boat exceeds your boat while going'

b.   *Tsaski-y   tsaski-yki -ta   yali   -spa puri-n*
     boat -my boat -your-ACC exceed-GEN go -3SG
     '*lit.* My boat goes while exceeding your boat: my boat is faster
     than your boat'

In this context, we may add some facts of Imbabura Quechua, which are
presented in Cole (1981: 93). This northern, Ecuadorian dialect has an
Exceed Comparative, in which the verb *yali* 'to exceed' is constructed as
a free relative clause, marked by the suffix *-j*. Cp.:

(21)   IMBABURA QUECHUA:

a.   *Marya riku-j   runa*
     M.   see -PCP. PRES man
     'the man whom Maria sees'

b.   *Tumas-ka   Marya-ta   yali   -j   ali*
     T.   -TOP M.   -ACC exceed-PCP. PRES good
     trabaja-n
     work -3SG
     'Thomas works better than Maria'

The participial form in *-j* can only be used in Imbabura Quechua if its
subject is identical to that of the main predicate. In addition, Imbabura

Quechua has also a form which can be used for absolute simultaneous deranking. This form has the suffix *-shpa*, that is, the same suffix which in other dialects of present-day Quechua can only be used for conditional simultaneous deranking (see *(19a/b)*). From this, we can conclude that Imbabura Quechua, although it has a form for absolute deranking, has come to model its comparative construction on the conditional simultaneous form. Within the framework that is adopted in this study, such a move should normally lead to the emergence of an Exceed Comparative in a language. Imbabura Quechua, as well as other dialects of Quechua, can be seen as a corroboration of this prediction, and hence they provide strong evidence for the correctness of the general modelling-hypothesis on which our set of chaining-based universals is founded.

The situation in Aymara is completely parallel to the one encountered in Quechua. Again, we find that the secondary comparative contains an exceed-verb which has the form of a present participle, and that the participial forms involved can be employed only under identity of subjects:

(22) AYMARA:
a. Napi *huma*   *llalli*   *-sina*   *saratha*
    I   you-ACC exceed-PCP. PRES go-PRES. 1SG
    'I walk faster than you'

b. *Cusisi* *-sina*   *saratha*
    be merry-PCP. PRES   go-PRES. 1SG
    'I go while being merry'

To conclude this section, we must comment upon the secondary comparative in Tamazight. In section 7.3.2 we argued that the primary comparative in this Berber language should be classified as an instance of the Locative Comparative. In addition to this, several authors (e.g. Hanoteau, 1896: 52) mention a secondary comparative which is of the Exceed-type. Cp.:

(23) TAMAZIGHT:
    Akal *in* *immek'keren i* *-oufi*   *akal*   *ennek*
    country my 3SG-big-PRES 3SG-exceed country your
    'My country is bigger than your country'

Now, if we look at the various ways in which temporal chaining is expressed in Tamazight, it seems fairly certain that the secondary Exceed Comparative has been modelled on the so-called Narrative Form, which is used to derank posterior predicates in C-chains. The existence of such a consecutive deranking possibility is observed by various authors on Berber syntax. Destaing (1920: 120) writes: 'In a discourse, in a story, a definite past which is placed in initial position is always expressed by a Perfect; the following verbs which are in the definite past are generally expressed by the Imperfect' (my translation). In Laoust (1918: 187–8) we find the following observation: 'When the first verb of a sentence or a story is in the preterite, the verbs of the following propositions are put into the Aorist and express a past' (my translation). In a similar vein, Johnson (1966: 135) remarks: 'In narratives, verb-phrases non-initial in a series following a verb-phrase in the perfect tense are often in the narrative aorist: 1) the verb-phrase has the unmarked form, as in the imperfect, but the IPF [i.e., the imperfect tense] prefix does not occur; 2) the movable affixes [which indicate person, number and gender] are postverbal, as in the perfect tense.' Examples of this type of consecutive construction, which, given its morphological characteristics, may be rated as an instance of deranking, are the sentences in *(24)*. The correspondence of this chaining construction with the secondary Exceed Comparative in *(23)* will be obvious:

(24)   TAMAZIGHT:
a.   *Inkr   ugellid , i -asi   ssif -ek*
     3SG-stand up-PERF king   , 3SG-take sword-his,
     i -ddu där tuaya   i -nna-yas
     3SG-go to negress , 3SG-say -her
     'The king stood up, took his sword, walked up to the negress, and said to her . . .'

b.   *Tamgart   da -t   -gan ar-ammas n -iid   ,*
     the-woman HAB-3SG. FEM-sleep to-middle of-night,
     t   -nker zik , t   -sag lqendil , the   -azzem
     3SG. FEM-rise early, 3SG. FEM-light the-lamp, 3SG. FEM-dress
     'A woman usually sleeps until midnight, rises early, lights the lamp, gets dressed . . .'

Thus, we may conclude that the secondary comparative in Tamazight has its direct surface parallel in a consecutive construction in which deranking of posterior predicates takes place. This conclusion, however, leads to a specific problem, which has to do with the conditionality of the C-chain involved. It must be noted that the Narrative Form in Tamazight is not limited to chains with subject-identity; in other words, the Narrative Form is not a case of conditional deranking. To be sure, the normal situation in the expression of narratives is that the topic is kept constant throughout successive events, but there is no syntactic restriction which prevents a deviation from this unmarked case; it is possible, at least in principle, to introduce a new topic in the narrative, so that absolute use of the Narrative Form is a definite, albeit rather uncommon, option. Hence, if we assume that the Narrative Form functions as the model of the secondary comparative in Tamazight, our set of chaining-based universals (and especially Universal 3B) would lead us to expect an Allative Comparative as a secondary option in Tamazight rather than the Exceed Comparative, which presupposes conditional deranking procedures. Now, there are indeed some indications that an Allative Comparative is a marginal possibility in at least some Berber dialects; Laoust (1918: 279) points out that the preposition *s* 'to' is sometimes employed to mark standard NPs in comparatives. On the whole, however, it seems that the Allative Comparative in Berber has given way to an Exceed Comparative of the type which we illustrated in *(23)*.

For the moment, I am unable to present a satisfactory solution to this particular problem with the secondary comparative in Tamazight. One possible way out might be to argue that, since the Narrative Form in Tamazight typically occurs in contexts where the subjects in the chain refer to the same individual, conditional C-chains are the norm in this language, so that an Exceed Comparative would be the obvious option. Alternatively, one might invoke the concept of syntactic borrowing. It is certainly true that the African languages with which Tamazight is in contact all select an Exceed Comparative as their primary option. Whatever solution one adopts, it can be added that the unclear situation regarding the secondary comparative in Tamazight is matched by the indeterminacy of basic word order in that language; while some authors (e.g., Hanoteau, 1896) mention basic SVO order for Tamazight, other grammarians (e.g., Johnson, 1966) list this language as basically VSO.

10.4   Secondary Locative and Allative Comparatives

In this section, we will occupy ourselves with an examination of those languages which have a Locative or an Allative Comparative as their secondary option. As will be recalled, Universal 3C predicts that languages with a Locative Comparative can be shown to have absolutely deranked S-chains; Universal 3B predicts that the occurrence of an Allative Comparative can be matched by the occurrence of C-chains in which the posterior predicate is deranked under absolute conditions.

One of the languages which we have listed in section 2.3.2 as having a secondary Allative Comparative can be shown to have yet another secondary option of comparative-type choice: Tamil combines its secondary Allative Comparative with a secondary Separative Comparative. The same goes for one of the languages with a secondary Locative Comparative; this language, viz. Basque, can be shown to have an additional Separative Comparative. I have preferred not to split up the discussion of these two languages over two separate sections, and hence I will deal with them in the next section, where secondary Separative Comparatives are presented in detail.

This, then, leaves us with nine cases of secondary comparative-type choice to be discussed in this section. For one of these cases, viz. Nama, I must concede right away that its secondary Locative Comparative will be a counterexample to Universal 3C, in exactly the same way in which its primary Separative Comparative is a problematic case for Universal 3A. As we saw in section 6.5, the problem with the Separative Comparative in Nama is that the deranked C-chain which is supposed to match it cannot be shown unequivocally to permit absolute use. We find a parallel situation with respect to the deranked predicate in S-chains in Nama. As example *(25)* demonstrates, Nama has the possibility to express predicates in S-chains by means of Present Participles, verbal formations consisting of the bare verbal stem, to which the suffixes *-se, -xnoni* or *-ta* are attached:

(25) NAMA:
  Ara-se   *gye tgaba*   *gye ha*
  cry -PCP. PRES PRT servant PRT come
  'The servant came in crying'

In all the examples which I have been able to find, Present Participles are constructed under subject-identity with the main predicate. At the present stage of my knowledge of Nama, I am unable to decide whether this situation is due to a lack of data or to a genuine structural restriction on the occurrence of participles in this language. If the latter is the case, then we must decide that the Locative Comparative in Nama, of which sentence *(26)* is an example, forms a contradiction to Universal 3C, at least as far as the conditionality of the S-chains in this language is concerned:

(26) NAMA:
  Gob neb gye noub ga-ei a xnou-acha
  boy this PRT that on   is smart
  'This boy is smarter than that boy'

The other eight languages which are relevant to the discussion in this section can all be shown to corroborate Universal 3B or Universal 3C, in either a direct or an indirect way. To start with Hungarian, Tompa

(1968) mentions a secondary comparative in which the standard NP is marked for Adessive case ('at', 'by') by means of the case suffix -*nel*/-*nal*. This Locative option is matched by the fact that Hungarian has the possibility to derank simultaneous chains; one of the predicates in a Hungarian S-chain may optionally be represented by the Present Participle in -*val*/-*ve*, which at least marginally allows for absolute use:

(27)   HUNGARIAN:
a.   A   konyha   villagos-abb   a   pince-nel
       the   kitchen   bright   -PRT   the   cellar-ADESS
       'The kitchen is brighter than the cellar'

b.   Igy   allvan   a   dolog ,   elmentünk
       thus   standing   the   matter   go away-PERF. 1PL
       'Matters being thus, we went off'

Like all Baltic languages, Latvian deranks its predicates into verbal adjectives; if simultaneity is implied, the language employs a set of forms known as Present Participles. If the construction has identity of subjects, the deranked simultaneous predicate has the form of the Present Participle in -*dams*, which agrees in case, number and gender with its antecedent in the main clause. In contrast, non-identity of subjects in an S-chain requires the use of the Absolute Dative construction. In this construction, the deranked simultaneous predicate has the form of a stem which is marked by the suffix -*nt*; in modern Latvian, the usual ending of the predicate in this construction is -*uot*. As Endzelin (1922: 721) remarks, it is probable that this absolute verbal form is a fossilization of an old dative case of the Present Participle.[1] The subject of the deranked simultaneous predicate has retained its dative case marking even in modern dialects. An example of the Absolute Dative is given in sentence *(28a)*; the construction is matched by the secondary Locative Comparative in Latvian. Cp.:

(28)   LATVIAN:
a.   Man   sienu   veduot   ,   uznaca   lietus
       I-DAT   hay-ACC   enter-PCP ,   come down-PAST   rain
       'As I was bringing in the hay, it started raining'

b.   Anna   smukaka   aiz   Trinas
       A.   prettier-FEM   on   T.-GEN
       'Anna is prettier than Trina'

In Dakota, and the closely related Assiniboine, the primary option for the comparative is the use of 'two contrasting clauses, one with a positive, the other with a negative verb or adverb' (Buechel, 1939: 96);

an example of this Conjoined Comparative has been presented in section 9.2. In addition, Dakota has also a comparative of the adverbial kind. In this case, the standard NP is marked by the postpositional elements *isam, isangb* or *iwangkab,* which probably originate from adverbial forms of verbs that have lost the ability to occur independently; the form *isam,* for example, must be seen as the adverbial form of the obsolete verb *sang-pa* 'to surpass', to which the instrumental prefix *í-* 'against, in reference to, by means of' has been attached (Boas and Deloria, 1941: 143).[2] In present-day Dakota, these elements function as locative postpositions, meaning 'on', 'on top of' or 'above'. In Assiniboine (see Levin, 1964), we find that the standard NP in the secondary comparative is marked by the postposition *aka* 'on'. Thus, it seems plausible to classify the secondary comparative in these languages as instances of the Locative Comparative. Cp.:

(29)   DAKOTA:
    Hoksila king atku -ku isam hangska
    boy   the   father-his on   tall
    'The boy is taller than his father'

(30)   ASSINIBOINE:
    Ne mi -aka haska
    he   me-on   tall
    'He is taller than me'

The occurrence of a Locative Comparative in Dakota is matched indirectly by the fact that, in this language, predicates in S-chains may be adverbialized by means of the suffixes *-ya, -yela, -ha, -kel* or *-l,* which are attached to the bare verb stem (Boas and Deloria, 1941: 137). These forms have the definite possibility to appear in absolute use. Cp.:

(31)   DAKOTA:
a.   *T'i-ile hceha-l*   *Mato el'*   *i*
    house burn -PCP. PRES   Bear   there   arrived
    'While the house was on fire, Bear arrived there'

b.   *Yu -spa-ye -ya egnaka*
    CAUS-wet-PAST-PCP he put it away
    'He put it away, it having been wetted'

Mandinka has a Locative Comparative as its primary choice (see section 7.3.2). The secondary Allative Comparative in this language has its indirect parallel in the Injunctive Form, which 'marks . . . that the accomplishment of the action or the acquisition of the state is subordinated to the accomplishment of another action or the acquisition of another state' (Labouret, 1934: 202; my translation). This verbal form, which absolutely deranks posterior predicates in C-chains, is characterized by the introductory particle *ka* and the absence of tense marking. Cp.:

(32) MANDINKA:
a.   A ka gya ni -ye
      he is big me-to
      'He is bigger than me'

b.   A wuli-ra   ka a fo
      he rise -PAST PRT it say
      'He stood up and said it'

The next language which must be discussed in this context is Gumbainggir, an Australian language. This language has a Conjoined Comparative as its primary choice; however, Smythe (1948: 52) remarks that a Locative Comparative is also an option in Gumbainggir:

(33) GUMBAINGGIR:
       Jarang nigar barwai-ga   nanju-mbala
       this   man   big   -PRT me   -on
       'This man is bigger than me'

It follows, then, that we should be able to locate cases of absolute simultaneous deranking in Gumbainggir, if this language is to be a regular instance of Universal 3C on its secondary option. I think that it can be argued that such constructions do indeed exist in Gumbainggir, but the relevant data are rather unclear and merit some specific discussion.

Both sources which I have consulted (Smythe, 1948; Eades, 1979) state explicitly that the normal, unmarked form for S-chains in Gumbainggir consists of a paratactic, balanced construction of finite predicates. This fact is, of course, matched directly by the occurrence of a Conjoined Comparative as the primary option in this language. In addition, however, Gumbainggir has also a construction which is employed for the general subordination of predicates and clauses; this construction is called the 'Relative Clause' by Smythe (1948: 72), but, as we shall see, its domain of application covers more than just the equivalent of our relative clauses. Formally, the Relative Clause is characterized by the presence of the suffix *-ndi/-andi*, which is identified by Smythe (ibid.) as the possessive suffix. Semantically, the construction has a very general subordinative interpretation; it functions as the equivalent of our relative clauses, conditional clauses and causal clauses alike. Cp.:

(34)   GUMBAINGGIR:

a.   Buwar   jarang dulungmi-ng   niga-da -ndi bijamba-ng
        baby-SUBJ this   smile   -PAST man-LOC-PRT eat   -PAST
        'The baby smiled at the man who was eating'

b.   Ngaja   wali-w   bijagaja -ndi bijamba-w
        1SG-SUBJ die -FUT not-PCP -PRT eat   -FUT
        'I will die if/because I don't eat'

c.   Nginda   nagari-w -andi gidu -da gulunay-gu barway
        2SG-SUBJ play -FUT-PRT sand-LOC rain   -FUT big-SUBJ
        'If you play in the sand, there will be big storms'

In addition, Smythe (ibid.) presents an example in which this construction has a definite simultaneous interpretation:

(35)   GUMBAINGGIR:
        Guram -gundi ngari gawari-ng   bilagara-ng -andi
        poor man-GEN leg   break -PAST run   -PAST-PRT
        'The poor fellow broke his leg while running'

Thus, it looks as if the Relative Clause in Gumbainggir must be viewed as an abstract, syntactically homogeneous clause type, in which different semantic nuances have come to be neutralized. This syntactic uniformity of the Gumbainggir Relative Clause, which is defended explicitly in Smythe (1948: 70–5) but questioned by Eades (1979: 327), can be supported by data from other Australian languages, in which a similar type of clause can be attested. Hale (1976) argues that the relative adjoined clause in Australian languages must be seen as a multifunctional formal construction, which has a looser, more paratactic relation to the main clause than is usually found in subordinate structures in natural languages. The analysis proposed by Hale is adopted by Merlan (1982) in her description of the 'generalized subordinate clause' in Mangarayi (p.12), a construction which has roughly the same distribution as the Relative Clause in Gumbainggir. One of Merlan's examples is the following sentence (p.15):

(36)   MANGARAYI:
        Wurg-ga   -ni   wanggij jang?
        hide -3SG/3SG-AUX-PAST. CONT   child-ABS die
        wa   -Ø -ma -n
        SUBORD-3SG-AUX -PAST. PERF
        'He hid the child who'd died'

Of this sentence, Merlan remarks: 'There is no absolute criterion which distinguishes the given translation from an adsentential interpretation "He hid the child when he died".' Whether a generalized subordinate clause in Mangarayi can (or should be) interpreted as a relative clause, as a temporal clause, or as both, appears to depend on the interplay of a variety of formal and contextual factors (see Merlan, 1982: 15–18). All in all, we can conclude that 'in Mangarayi we find a single formal subordinate clause which is variably understood as adnominal or ad-sentential modifier' (ibid.: 13).[3]

Given these facts of Gumbainggir and other Australian languages, I think we can be justified in concluding that Gumbainggir has the possibility of forming deranked predicative constructions which may have the temporal interpretation of a simultaneous chain. Since, as the examples above have shown, the subordinatively marked predicate does not have to be in construction with the subject of the main predicate, it can also be concluded that simultaneous deranking in Gumbainggir can be absolute. Hence, the secondary comparative in this language turns out to be a confirmation of Universal 3C.

Speaking of Mangarayi, it should be noted that this language has apparently modelled its secondary comparative option not on its general-ized subordinate construction, but rather on a construction which deranks consecutively interpreted sequences. Merlan (1982: 10–11) mentions the fact that Mangarayi has a 'desiderative-intentional' con-struction. Predicates in this construction appear in a nominalized form, and are further marked by the suffix -*wu*, which is also in use as a case suffix to mark dative and genitive case in nouns. Direct objects of the nominalized verb are put into the genitive/dative case form. An example of this construction is:

(37) *MANGARAYI:*
    Na -bamar-wu   na   -juya -wu   Ø -ninga-n
    NOUN-steal   -DAT NOUN-meat-DAT 3SG-come-PAST
    'He came to steal the meat'

This 'absolute dative' (Merlan, ibid.) is '*usually* semantically purposive' (Merlan, 1982: 10; my italics). Again, one might deduce from this formulation that the construction at issue here has a certain amount of semantic indeterminacy, and that, therefore, it might be rated as a case of consecutive deranking, to which (as we saw in section 4.2) a purpose-reading is naturally attached. Alternatively, one might view Mangarayi as one of the rare cases of 'purpose-modelling' of comparatives, in the same way as Kanuri (see section 7.2.3). In any case, the 'desiderative-intentional' construction turns out to have its direct parallel in the secondary Allative Comparative of Mangarayi. Merlan (1982: 68) observes that Mangarayi has 'a less common (but nevertheless spontaneously produced) construction type', in which the standard NP is marked for dative/purposive case:

(38) MANGARAYI:
    Na-yaba na-balayi nganju
    brother big   1SG-DAT
    'My brother is bigger/older than me'

The last two languages in the sample with a Locative Comparative as their secondary option are Maori and Samoan. From the literature on various Polynesian languages it can be derived that they originally had Conjoined Comparatives, but that in recent times a Locative Comparative has been gaining ground. This Locative Comparative is typically marked by means of the multifunctional preposition *i/e* 'at' on the standard NP. Examples of this Polynesian Locative Comparative have been attested for Samoan (Marsack, 1975: 67), Marquesan (Dordillon, 1931: 12), Fijian (Milner, 1956: 34) and Maori (Rere, 1965: 16). Cp.:

(39) SAMOAN:
    Ua sili tele le mauga   i le fale
    PRES more high the mountain at the house
    'The mountain is higher than the house'

(40) MARQUESAN:
    Mea meitai Ionane i   Iakopo
    thing good I.   on I.
    'Ionane is better than Iakopo'

(41) FIJIAN:
    Sa levu na ka   oqo e na ka   oqori
    PRES big the thing this on the thing that
    'This is bigger than that'

(42) MAORI:
    Teia te rakau roa ake i   tena
    this the tree   big more on that
    'This tree is higher than that one'

Both Samoan and Maori can be shown to be unproblematic instances of Universal 3C. In these languages, like in all Polynesian languages, it is possible to derank simultaneous predicates by means of a nominalization. Thus, the predicate in the simultaneous clause is turned into a derived noun, and the tense-aspect-mood particle which is obligatory for finite verbal forms is replaced by a marker of specificity. In East Polynesian languages such as Maori, the nominalization rule also involves the attachment of some alternant of the nominalizing suffix *-anga* to the verb stem (see Chung, 1978: 298); in the Samoic-Outlier branch, of which Samoan is a member, the derived noun has the morphological form of the bare verbal stem. Nominalized predicates must be structurally rated as heads of NPs; their subjects are marked for genitive case by the particles *a* or *o*.

In Maori, deranked (i.e., nominalized) simultaneous predicates may be constructed either as a free NP, or as a prepositional phrase marked by the preposition *i* 'at'. In this latter case, direct surface parallelism between the secondary comparative and the deranked S-chain is achieved:

(43)   MAORI:
a.   Te tae -nga   o Hutu ki raro
       the arrive -NOUN of H.   to below
       'When Hutu arrived in the underworld . . .' (Chung, 1978: 300)

b.   I te are -nga   o ' tera tangata na   taatai ,
       at the walk-NOUN of this man   along beach
       kua site i   tetai pai
       PAST see ACC one   ship
       'While this man walked along the beach, he saw a ship'

In Samoan, simultaneous nominalizations are often preceded by the predicational particle *'o*. This particle has a number of different functions (see Marsack, 1975: 20–2), the most important of which appear to be the marking of nouns and pronouns 'standing by itself and not forming part of a sentence', or the marking of the subject when it precedes the verb. The deranked S-chain in Samoan is illustrated by sentence (44), which has been borrowed from Chung (1978: 306). Cp.:

(44)   SAMOAN:
       'O   le   sau a le   ta'avale a leoleo ,
       PRED the come of the car   of police
       'ou te   lē malamalama 'i ai
       I   UNSPEC not understand   to it
       'When the police car came, I wasn't aware of it'

10.5   Secondary Separative Comparatives

To conclude our examination of secondary options in comparative-type choice, we must consider the nine cases in our sample which have a secondary Separative Comparative. Following Universal 3A, these languages should have the possibility to form consecutive chains in which the anterior predicate is deranked under absolute conditions. As it turns out, all nine languages are clear confirmations of the universal at issue.

Starting with Tamil, we have remarked earlier that this language has an unusually large variety of comparatives at its disposal. In addition to the Locative Comparative and the *vita*-comparative discussed in section 7.3.2, several authors mention a secondary Separative Comparative and a secondary Allative Comparative for Tamil:

(45) TAMIL:
a. Ten -in -um initu enna
    honey-from-and what sweet
    'What is sweeter than honey?'

b. Ittu-ku atu nallatu
    this-DAT that good
    'This is better than that'

The secondary Separative Comparative in Tamil is matched by the occurrence of the so-called *Vinaiyeccam* (Beythan, 1943: 103), a gerundial form with the suffix *-ttu* attached to the verb stem. The form is the obligatory representation of anterior predicates in C-chains, and can be used freely under absolute conditions:

(46) TAMIL:
    Naan panam kudu-ttu   avan sinimaa-vukku
    I   money give -PERF. GER he   movie -to
    poonan
    go-PAST. 3SG
    'I gave him money and he went to a movie'

The Allative Comparative illustrated in *(45b)* is modelled directly on the purpose-construction which Tamil employs. In this construction, too, the predicate is deranked into a non-finite form. If there is identity of subjects between the main predicate and the predicate of the purpose-clause, this latter predicate has the form of the Infinitive in *-a*; in other words, in this case the purpose-construction has the same surface expression as the simultaneous action construction (see section 7.3.2). If, however, the subjects are non-identical, the predicate of the purpose-clause must be deranked into a verbal noun, which is then put into Dative case. It is this latter construction which provides the direct parallel with the secondary Allative Comparative in Tamil. Cp.:

(47) *TAMIL:*
a. *Engka ammaa-ve   paakka naan Cengkat-tukku pooreen*
     our   mother-ACC see-INF I   C.   -to   go-PRES.1SG
     'I am going to Chengam to see my mother'

b. *Avan   pustaka-m   vaang-kina   -tukku pana -m*
    he-NOM book   -ACC buy -PAST. NOUN-DAT   money-ACC
    kututteen
    give-PAST. 1SG
    'I gave him money so that he could buy a book'

The remaining eight languages with a secondary Separative Comparative are all European Particle-languages. For some of these languages, direct surface parallelism can be attested. A case in point is Basque; in addition to the Particle Comparative discussed in section 9.3, Lafitte (1944: 139–40) mentions two secondary (and somewhat archaic) Basque comparatives of the adverbial type. In one of these constructions, the standard NP is in the Mediative case, which is marked by the suffix *-z/-az*, and which normally indicates cause, manner, motive and temporal duration ('while, during'). Cp.:

(48) *BASQUE:*
      Gure jite   -az   goragoa
      our   nature-MED higher
      'superior to our nature'

This Mediative Comparative corresponds with the possibility of simultaneous deranking in Basque. Deranked predicates in S-chains have the form of the nominal Infinitive (with the suffix *-te*) or the Supinum (with the suffix *-i* or *-n*), which are then put into the Mediative case. For both forms, absolute use is permitted. If the deranked predicate has the form of the Infinitive, the subject is put either into the Genitive case (that is, the Infinitive is considered to be a noun) or into the Nominative c.q. Ergative case (that is, the Infinitive is taken to be a verb). The Supinum is a verbal form; its subject is always in the Nominative c.q. Ergative case. Cp.:

(49) *BASQUE:*
a. *Aita   ji -te -az   atsegin dut*
    father-NOM come-INF-MED happy   I-am
    'Now that my father is coming, I am happy'

b. *Aita -ren ji -te -az   atsegin dut*
    father-GEN come-INF-MED happy   I-am
    'Now that my father is coming, I am happy'

c.   *Hira   ji   -n -ez   atsegin dut*
he-NOM come-SUP-MED happy I-am
'Now that he is coming, I am happy'

In the other secondary comparative in Basque, the standard NP is put into the Elative case, marked by the suffix *-ik*. This Separative Comparative has its direct parallel in the way in which C-chains can be represented in Basque; anterior predicates are deranked into the form of the Supinum, which is then marked for Elative Case. The form clearly allows for absolute use, with subjects either in the Nominative or in the Ergative case. Cp.:

(50) BASQUE:
a.   *Nitar-ik   gorago-ko   norbait*
me   -ELAT higher -GEN someone
'someone who is superior to me'

b.   *Harek   erra-n -ik   badagiku*
he-ERG say -SUP-ELAT know-it-PRES. 1PL
'Now that he has said it, we know it'

As we saw in section 2.1, Latin has a secondary comparative in which the standard NP is put into the Ablative case; this is a case which indicates the agent of an action, and which is used furthermore in the complement of both locative and separative prepositions (cp. *ab urbe* 'from the town' and *in urbe* 'in the town'). Hence, there is a certain degree of indeterminacy in the classification of the secondary Ablative Comparative in Latin; we might rate it as an instance of the Separative Comparative, but there is also something to be said for a classification of this construction as a Locative Comparative:

(51) LATIN:
      Cato   Cicero-ne   eloquentior   est
      C.-NOM C.   -ABL   more eloquent is
      'Cato is more eloquent than Cicero'

The indeterminacy of the status of the Ablative Comparative is matched by the partial neutralization of the ways in which S-chains and C-chains are represented in Latin. As we saw in section 4.1, Latin deranks predicates in temporal chains by putting them into the form of participles; if the chain is simultaneous, the Present Participle is used, whereas in consecutive chains the anterior predicate gets the form of the Perfect Participle. In cases of absolute deranking, the participle and its subject are both put into the Ablative case, while the participle must agree with its subject in number and gender. Examples of absolutely deranked S-chains and C-chains in Latin are the following:

(52) LATIN:

a. *Servis*   *cantantibus*   *dominus*
slaves-ABL. MASC. PL   sing-PRES. PCP.-ABL. MASC. PL   master-NOM
bibit
drink-PRES. 3SG
'While the slaves sing, the master drinks'

b. *Caesar*   *Pompeio*   *victo*
C.-NOM   P.-ABL. MASC. SG   defeat-PCP. PERF. PASS-ABL. MASC. SG
Aegyptum adiit
A.-ACC   go to-PERF. IND. 3SG
'After Pompeius had been defeated, Caesar marched into Egypt'

It will be clear that the parallelism between the formalization of S-chains and C-chains in Latin is fairly far-reaching, in that it has led to near-neutralization; the only difference between the two types of chaining constructions lies in the tense marking of the participles involved. Given that the Ablative Absolute construction can be used for both S-chains and C-chains (depending on the tense of the participle employed), there is no telling whether the Ablative Comparative in Latin has taken the simultaneous construction or rather the consecutive construction as its model. Thus, we see that the near-neutralization in the formalization of chaining constructions has its counterpart in the indeterminacy of the classification of the Ablative Comparative in Latin.

A situation which is very similar to that in Latin can be encountered in Classical Greek. In this language, the secondary comparative was formed by putting the standard NP into the Genitive case, a form which had taken over the functions of the defunct ablative and locative cases. Again, we see that this indeterminacy is matched by a near-neutralization in the formalization of S-chains and C-chains; Classical Greek deranked the predicates in its temporal chains into participles, which under absolute conditions agreed in case, gender and number with its subject, which had to be in the Genitive case. Examples of the Genitive Comparative in Classical Greek, and of the Genitive Absolute construction for both S-chains and C-chains are the following:

(53) CLASSICAL GREEK:

a. *Filippos ēn sofōteros tōn*   *proterōn*
F.-NOM   was   more-wise   the-GEN. PL   earlier-GEN. PL
basileōn
king-GEN. PL
'Filippos was wiser than the kings before him'

b.   *Toutōn*   *legomenōn*
those-GEN. PL. NEUT   say-PCP. PRES. PASS.-GEN. PL. NEUT
anesthē
stand up-AOR. IND. 3SG
'While those things were being said, he stood up'

c.   *Tou*   *stratēgou*
the-GEN. MASC. SG   general-GEN. SG
keleusantos   *apechōrēsamen*
order-PCP. AOR. ACT.-GEN. SG. MASC   withdraw-AOR. IND. 1PL
'After the general had given the order, we withdrew'

A clear case of surface parallelism is also offered by Finnish, where the secondary comparative is characterized by a standard NP in the Partitive case. Anterior predicates in Finnish C-chains can be deranked into infinitival forms, which are then marked by the nominal partitive case suffix. Absolute use of such infinitives is common. Cp.:

(54)   FINNISH:
a.   *Nykinen professori on edellis -a   heiko-mpi*
current   professor is   former-PART weak -er
'The current professor is less strict than the former one'

b.   *Veljen palattu -a   työs -tä   menimme   elokuvi-in*
brother return-INF-PART work-from go-PAST. 1PL cinema -to
'Our brother came back from his work and we went to the cinema'

The last four languages in the sample which combine a primary Particle Comparative with a secondary Separative Comparative do not show direct surface parallelism on their secondary option, but they can be shown to have the possibility to derank anterior consecutive predicates under absolute conditions. Russian (see Pulkina and Zakhava–Nekrasova, 1974: 146) has a secondary comparative in which the standard NP is put into the Genitive case; as in Classical Greek, the Russian Genitive has taken over the functions of the defunct Ablative. Now, this secondary comparative option for Russian is matched by the existence of verbal nouns, i.e., non-finite verbal forms, which can be employed to represent the predicate in adverbial clauses. In the case of consecutive clauses, the verbal noun is preceded by the preposition *pósle* 'after', which governs Genitive case; for simultaneous chaining, verbal nouns are preceded by the preposition *s* 'with', which governs Instrumental case. Absolute use of verbal nouns is possible; subjects have the form of a Genitive NP or a possessive pronoun.[4] Cp.:

(55)   RUSSIAN:
a.   *Wolga dlinnée Dnepr-a*
     W.   longer D.   -GEN
     'The Wolga is longer than the Dniepr'

b.   *Pósle priezd   -a   egó*
     after come-NOUN-GEN his
     'After his coming: after he came'

c.   *S   priezd   -a   egó*
     with come-NOUN -GEN his
     'With his coming: the moment that he came'

The secondary Separative Comparative in Albanian, which is marked by the preposition *ka* 'from' on the standard NP (see Lambertz, 1959: 76), has its counterpart in chaining constructions by virtue of the existence of the Absolute Form, a non-finite verbal formation which replaces anterior predicates in consecutive chains. Formally this Absolute Form (see Camaj, 1969: 66–7) consists of the particle string *me nje te* followed by a participle.[5] Cp.:

(56)   ALBANIAN:
a.   *Kjo shtëpi është me i   nalte ka   ajo*
     this house is   more the big-one from that
     'This house is bigger than that one'

b.   *Me nje te ardhe   të   letres,*
        PRT   come-PCP the letter-GEN
     Agirmi i perjegji te jätit
     A.   answered the father-DAT
     'After the letter had arrived, Agirmi answered his father'

In Old French (see Valin, 1952: 9), the preposition *de* 'from, of' was in use as the marker of the standard NP in comparatives. Valin remarks: 'This use is still alive in Modern French in the alternation *plus que/plus de*.' The use of *de* instead of the normal comparative particle *que* is obligatory in Modern French comparatives which contain measure phrases, such as *(58a/b)*; the latter sentence is quoted from Bergmans (1982: 94). Cp.:

(57)   OLD FRENCH:
     Plus grant de   lui
     more tall from him
     'taller than him'

(58)   MODERN FRENCH:
a.   *Il   y   a   plus   d'   un   an*
       it   there has   more   from   one   year
       'It is more than a year ago'

b.   *Il   mesure   plus   d'   un   mètre soixante*
       he measure-PRES. 3SG more   from   one   metre sixty
       'He is taller than 1.60m'

The secondary Separative Comparative in French is matched by the fact
that the language has also a limited (and somewhat stylistically marked)
possibility to derank anterior predicates in C-chains, by means of the
absolute use of past participles. As Bergmans (1982: 105) remarks: 'The
class of these clauses is not limited to fixed expressions such as *ceci dit* or
tout compte fait'; he quotes an example from Henri Troyat's novel *Les
Désordres Secrets* (p.78), which I reproduce here as sentence (59):

(59)   FRENCH:
       La   paix   revenue   ,   tu   me   rejoindras   en   France
       the peace return-PCP. PERF you me join-FUT. 2SG in   F.
       'When peace has returned, you will join me in France'

To conclude this chapter, let us have a look at the secondary
comparative options for English. Joly (1967: 38) states: 'The pair *to/from*
has been and is still being used with an ordinary comparative.' The
examples given by Joly stem from Old English texts:

(60)   OLD ENGLISH:
a.   *Thou hast   maad him litil, a litil   lesse fro   aungelis*
       you have-2SG made him small a little less   from angels
       'You have made him small, a little less than angels'

b.   *Nys   none   of wymman beter borne to seint Johan*
       not-is no-one of women   better born   to saint John
       'Nobody is born of women better than St John'

Within the hypothetical framework adopted in this investigation, the
secondary *from*-comparative can be accounted for by pointing out that
English has a limited (and somewhat bookish) possibility of deranking
anterior predicates in consecutive chains by means of a participial form.
Absolute use of this construction is marginal, but can nevertheless be
attested in a number of instances:

(61)   ENGLISH:
a.   *This said, we must return to our main point*
b.   *All things considered, you'd better leave the country at once*

A plausible way to look at the *to*-comparative in Old English is to view the item *to* as the marker of the Old Germanic Dative case, which was the case of the standard NP in practically all Old Germanic languages (see Small, 1929: 19). This Old Germanic Dative case not only expressed allative spatial relations, but had also taken over the function of expressing locative relations. Following this line of reasoning, we may view the *to*-comparative in Old English as an instance of the Locative Comparative. If we adopt this position, the *to*-comparative is a regular case of Universal 3C, since absolute deranking of simultaneous chains is a definite possibility even in Modern English. Cp.:

(62) ENGLISH:
a.   *English being an SVO-language, it is not surprising that it has*
       Rightward Subject Deletion
c.   *John being the drunkard that he is, I pity his wife*

10.6   Conclusion

In this chapter, we have examined the validity of the set of chaining-based universals with respect to the cases of secondary comparative-type choice that have been attested in the sample. Of the 34 cases at issue, 30 can be shown to be unproblematic confirmations of the relevant universals. The most recalcitrant case of secondary comparative-type choice is represented by the secondary Exceed Comparative in Tamazight (see section 10.3). For the secondary Locative Comparative in Nama no conclusive affirmation of Universal 3C could be documented; thus, the problem with the secondary comparative in Nama is the same as that with which the primary Separative Comparative in that language confronts us (see section 6.5). Finally, there are two cases in the sample in which a secondary Allative Comparative appears to have its direct match in a purpose-construction. To the extent that one wishes to exclude this possibility of 'purpose-modelling' from the set of confirming data for our universals, these languages (viz. Tamil and Mangarayi) can be rated as counterexamples to Universal 3B on their secondary options.

Part Three

Towards an Explanation of Comparative-type Choice

11

Theoretical Background Assumptions

11.1 Introduction

In the foregoing chapters of this essay, we have first set up a typology of comparative constructions in natural languages (chapter 2). Following that, we have put forward the hypothesis that the options in this typology can be predicted on the basis of the types of temporal chaining constructions which are possible in natural languages (chapter 3). The proposed correlations between comparative types and chaining types have been laid down in a set of chaining-based universals of comparative-type choice (chapter 5). In the chapters of part two of this study these universals have been tested against the empirical facts of the languages in the sample.

Surveying the results of our investigation so far, I think we are justified in drawing the following conclusion. The examination of the various universals in the chapters of part two can be said to have led to an empirical confirmation of these universals; in view of the overwhelming majority of 'regular' cases, the few problematic cases for each of these universals may reasonably be rated as 'incidental'. Therefore, we can conclude that the claimed correlations between comparative-type choice and chaining-type choice are firmly established. Furthermore, we have been able to account for the attested correlation between word order types and some comparative types, by demonstrating that these word-order options are correlated with the particular chaining types which determine the comparative types in question.[1] This, then, constitutes the major *descriptive* result of our cross-linguistic inquiry.

However, as we stated explicitly in chapter 5, the set of chaining-based universals is not only intended as a purely descriptive statement of an observed correlation between two kinds of typological options in natural languages. In addition, this set of universals, taken as a whole, must be conceived of as the expression of the claim that, in natural language systems, the encoding of the concept of comparison is derivative of the encoding of the concept of temporal chaining. In other words, we claim that the correlations laid down in the universals are the way they are by virtue of the fact that comparatives are not an 'independent', 'autonomous' construction type; their syntactic expression has been *modelled* upon the way in which the 'deeper-lying' concept of temporal chaining has been formalized in language. In this way, the set of chaining-based universals lays claim to an *explanation* of the facts in the typology of comparative constructions.

With respect to this explanatory claim contained in our analysis, the first thing we must remark is that the view of temporal chaining as a more 'fundamental' concept than comparison is not implausible; it is certainly more plausible than the view that the modelling relation should be the other way around. The perception of temporal ordering between events is undoubtedly a very elementary psychological process, and the conceptualization of temporal relations (which, if localist grammarians are right, may in its turn be derivative of the conceptualization of spatial relations) is one of the prerequisites for such fundamental human faculties as memorizing and deductive reasoning. Moreover, the intuitive view that, of comparison and temporal chaining, the latter is the more basic concept has been affirmed by a number of psychological and psycholinguistic experiments, which we will touch upon in section 11.4. Thus, I think it can be argued with some confidence that our interpretation of the set of chaining-based universals in terms of a modelling of comparison on temporal chaining does not meet with serious difficulties, at least not in as far as the direction of modelling which is implied in this interpretation is concerned.

While our interpretation of the chaining-based universals in terms of a modelling relation does not seem to be implausible from a *conceptual* point of view, there are nonetheless a number of *empirical linguistic facts* which have not yet been explained within this framework. Concerning the explanation of the occurrence of the various types of comparatives, the reader will have noted that cases of Mixed Comparison, as well as the case of the Telugu comparative (see section 2.5) have not yet found their proper place within our set of universals. Moreover, the occurrence of the various sorts of Particle Comparatives remains a recalcitrant phenomenon. Despite the analysis of these cases in terms of the notion of syntactization (see chapter 9), there is one fascinating problem connected with Particle Comparatives which we have as yet hardly touched upon. This question can be put in the following way: given that languages which model their comparatives on balanced temporal chains can come up with a (semantically completely transparent) Conjoined Comparative, why should there be Particle Comparatives at all? Given the concept of syntactization, this question can be rephrased as follows: why do some languages syntacticize their balanced input-structures, while other languages prefer to keep them balanced?

Apart from the occurrence of various as yet unexplained comparative-types, there is also the curious phenomenon of 'double options' in comparative-type choice. In particular, it may be expected of our explanatory framework that it be able to account for the fact that some pairings of primary and secondary comparative types occur quite frequently, whereas other theoretically possible pairings seem to occur only incidentally or not at all.

In order to improve the explanatory value of our analysis on these points, I will develop in the following chapters *a new model for the prediction of comparative-type choice*. A fundamental characteristic of this new model is that it contains assumptions on both the cognitive-semantic and the syntactic representation of comparative constructions. Furthermore, it makes some specific claims about the interdependency between these two levels of representation. As for the syntactic encoding of comparatives, the new model incorporates the set of chaining-based universals proposed in chapter 5; that is, the new model, too, rests on the assumption that the encoding of comparatives in natural languages is modelled on the encoding options for temporal chaining. As will become clear, however, the new model transcends the original set of universals in that it does not take deranking to be the only relevant syntactic procedure in the formalization of temporal chaining. The new model will assume that, in addition to deranking, there is *a second grammatical procedure* which is relevant in the derivation of temporal chains (and hence, given the modelling hypothesis, in the derivation of compara-tives). This additional procedure, *identity deletion*, allows for a number of distinct options in its application, which can be shown to be paired off with the various typological options of deranking in a non-random way. As a result, we can formulate *a set of procedure-types with respect to chain formation*, in which a specific option of identity deletion is combined with a specific option in the deranking procedure. The new typology of chain formation which results from this will be examined for its value as a determinant of the typology of comparatives; it will turn out that this new typology has an explanatory power which exceeds that of our earlier set of universals, which were based solely on the typological options in the grammatical procedure of deranking.

The new model of comparative-type choice will be presented in detail in the following chapters. However, we must first make a short digression, in order to state a number of basic assumptions about some general conceptual matters in the theory of language. Although the framework within which our investigation is conducted is deliberately model-neutral, it is impossible to avoid at least a minimum of theoretical background assumptions about the general organization of the theory of language; without these, it would be impossible to formulate in an intelligible fashion a clarification of the universal properties of the comparative construction. However, thoughout the exposition which follows I have made efforts to frame my assumptions in terms of concepts which are by and large uncontroversial. None of the things I have to say on the theory of language in general will strike the reader as very original; the linguistic concepts employed here belong to the common stock-in-trade of post-war grammatical theory, while my views on certain psycholinguistic issues have been borrowed mainly from Fodor, Bever and Garrett (1974) and Fodor (1976).

11.2 Three levels of linguistic structure

My first assumption is that natural language is a mechanism which connects *thoughts* (i.e., mental representations) to *forms* (i.e., represent-ations which are ultimately expressed physically in sound), and that it is the task of the theory of language to provide a systematic description of the nature of this connection. Given this perspective, we can say that a complete description of the formal and contentive properties of a sentence in a given language will involve the statement of at least *two different levels of structure* for that sentence.

The first of these levels has, since Chomsky (1964), been commonly referred to as *(syntactic) surface structure*. Surface structure is the (theoretical reconstruction of the) structural form of the sentence as it is uttered by the speaker and perceived by the hearer; within the overall model of a linguistic theory, surface structure functions as the input for the rules of phonological interpretation. Surface structure provides both lexical information on sentences (in that it specifies the lexical items of which the sentence is composed) and structural information: it specifies the linear order of the lexical items in the sentence, and it furthermore describes the organization of constituent elements into larger structural units. A common way to represent surface structures graphically is the use of tree diagrams, in which both the linear order of constituent elements and the relative degree of structural cohesion which holds between them are depicted.

The second type of structure which is needed in a complete theory of language is at the very opposite of surface structure: it is the structure which represents the thought which the sentence is meant to convey, as conceived by the speaker and, if all goes well, interpreted by the hearer. This level of structure will be referred to as the *cognitive structure* of the sentence. I have gained the impression that there is no general agreement among psychologists about the exact nature of cognitive structures; I will follow the views put forward by Fodor (1976: 177ff.) on this point. Concerning the equally unresolved question of the graphical representation of a cognitive structure, I will adhere to the practice recently adopted by a number of authors, and represent the one cognitive structure which I need in this investigation in the form of a *topological* notation.

In short, we may say that a complete description of a sentence in a natural language involves a specification of the levels of surface structure and cognitive structure, and furthermore a statement of the relations between cognitive and surface structure which obtain in the sentences of that language. Now, in keeping with ancient tradition in the philosophy of language, I will make one further assumption about the organization of the theory of language. I assume that, between cognitive structure (which represents 'thought') and surface structure (which represents 'form') an *intermediate level of structure* must be postulated. This level represents the type of linguistic information traditionally referred to as *meaning*, and has been called 'deep structure', 'underlying structure', 'semantic representation' or 'logical form' in recent publications. In this study we prefer the term *underlying structure*, as it carries only a minimum of theoretical connotations. Underlying structure must be seen as the hinge between the formal and the cognitive aspects of linguistic structures; it is in itself a formal syntactic structure, but it functions also as the direct reflection of cognitive structures. Therefore, underlying structure can be viewed as the level at which thoughts are mapped onto language; it is a level which functions as the link between two all-important human faculties, viz. thinking and speaking.

Concerning the way in which an underlying structure must be represented in linguistic theory, I will make only a few very vague assumptions here. In accordance with prevailing opinions, I will take it that a type of enriched predicate calculus offers an approximation of underlying structure which is sufficiently adequate for our purposes. Hence, I will assume that the basic structural unit of organization in underlying structures is the proposition, an entity which consists minimally of a predicate and one or more arguments. Since such structures can be represented graphically in the form of hierarchical diagrams, one can agree with Chomsky (1980: 17), who states that logical form 'should have the form of a syntactic phrase-marker', and that its syntax 'involves quantifiers and variables in a familiar notation'. Essentially the same point of view has been defended in Lakoff (1972) and McCawley (1972).

Given the above assumptions, the organization of a theory of language can be represented schematically by the following model:

$$CS \longleftrightarrow US \longleftrightarrow SS$$

Thus, the task of a linguistic description minimally consists of the following:

(a) it must give an explicit statement of *the three levels of structure* for each sentence in every language;
(b) it must state the principles by which these three levels of structure are linked to each other. That is, it must state the *rules* by which cognitive structure (CS) is mapped onto underlying structure (US) and vice versa, and it must state the rules by which underlying structure is mapped onto surface structure (SS) and vice versa.

In what follows, I will call the first set of rules (which link CS to US) *strategies*, and I will refer to the rules which link US to SS as *(grammatical) procedures*. This latter term is meant to be neutral between concepts like 'transformation', 'projection rule', 'lexical rule' and 'interpretive rule' which have been advanced in recent linguistic literature. Apart from the assumptions which are contained in the above outline, the approach adopted here should be conceived of as theory-neutral. Thus, the model does not make any specific claims about the formal nature of strategies and procedures, nor is any chronology or directionality implied to obtain in the operation of the various rule types. Hence, a statement of the form 'Strategy A maps a CS onto a US of type X' should always be read as shorthand for the statement 'Strategy A maps a CS onto a US of type X, and vice versa'.

11.3 Further remarks on cognitive structure

With respect to the above sketch of the organization of a theory of language, one specific point deserves special comment. As will be noted, the model which I propose embodies the assumption that there is a distinction to be made between the levels of cognitive structure and underlying ('semantic', 'logical') structure. The primary motivation for this distinction stems from the consideration that these two levels seem to *differ as to their functional status*. Underlying structures are linguistic structures, that is, they are part of the language system *per se*. In opposition to this, cognitive structures are representations which are in themselves non-linguistic; they are not part of the system of natural language, but belong to the 'language of thought' (Fodor, 1976), and their existence is independent of whether or not they are mapped onto the language system. Thus, for instance, cognitive structures (that is, representations of thoughts) are also available to organisms which have no language at their disposal (see Fodor, 1976: 56–8 for an elaboration of this point), while, on the other hand, an organism may construct its cognitive structures on the basis of other than linguistic data, such as visual perception.

Apart from these general considerations, there are also some indications which seem to point to *a difference in formal nature* between these two levels of representation. Since the actual form of cognitive structures (and, for that matter, of underlying structures) is still very unclear, one should beware of making statements that are too definite, but it seems that at least one of the formal differences between these two levels involves *a difference in the order of the information* which they contain. As we observed above, underlying structures are generally taken to have the formal properties of syntactic phrase-markers. This implies, among other things, that the information contained in underlying structures has *a linear ordering*. In other words, underlying structures, like surface structures, are symbolic configurations *which are deployed in time*. Now, it is not at all clear that representations of thoughts have also an organization in which a linear-temporal ordering plays a role. There are indications that (at least some types of) cognitive structures are (at least to some extent) *pictorial* in nature. In the same manner as maps or blue-prints, cognitive structures may be 'images under description' (Fodor, 1976: 190–1) of the things they represent; they do not have to be an exact replica of the things they stand for, but they are picture-like in at least some respects (for instance, in representing the relations which hold between the basic units of the structure). Now, it can be maintained that such picture-like configurations are not deployed in time. That is, for representations of the type to which maps, blue-prints and cognitive structures belong, *no linear-temporal ordering of information is implied*. 'In principle, all the information is available simultaneously and can be read off in whatever order the observer chooses' (Fodor, 1976: 186). If this hypothesis about the nature of cognitive structures is accepted, we have a genuine formal difference between underlying structures and cognitive representations: the information contained in the former can be scanned in one order only,[2] whereas the information recovered from the latter is dependent on the scanning strategies of the observer.

11.4 Structural levels for comparative constructions

The model of the theory of language which has been outlined in the preceding sections may serve not only as a model for the structural description of sentences in a single natural language; it is equally possible to use it as a background for universalist typological research. In this latter function, the model can be viewed as a framework for the description of the process of universal linguistic encoding. That is, the model offers a scheme for an account of the ways in which a certain type of cognitive structure (which is taken to be the parameter of the typology) can be mapped onto the surface structures of various different languages. Thus, taking the subject of the present investigation as an example, we can say that the model presents a framework in which the mapping of the cognitive concept of comparison onto the surface structures of natural languages can be accounted for. Since the result of this mapping is not the same for all languages, our task is now to describe how the surface diversification in the encoding of the concept of comparison can be explained on the basis of the specific options which languages have in the selection of their strategies and grammatical procedures. In practice, this task boils down to the requirement that the following two specifications be made available:

(a) a specification of the universal options for the CS, the US and the SS of comparatives across natural languages;
(b) a specification of the options for strategies and grammatical procedures in the derivation of comparative constructions across natural languages.

In this chapter, we will confine ourselves to the first specification mentioned above, viz. the universal specification of the three levels of structure on which comparatives must be represented. Now, for the representation of comparatives on two of these levels (viz. the SS and the US) the preceding chapters of this book present some clear indications. Concerning the *surface representation* of comparatives across languages, the typology in chapter 2 has shown that a natural language typically selects one out of five basic options; furthermore, we have noted that some languages may select a 'mixed' comparative or some instance of a Particle Comparative. All in all, we may conclude that the range of universal options for the SS of comparatives (in other words, the range of possible outputs of the mapping of underlying structures of comparatives onto surface structures) can be established in a fairly straightforward and precise fashion.

With regard to the range of universal options for the representation of comparatives at the level of *underlying structure*, we can state the following. The foregoing chapters contain extensive argumentation for the claim that the US of a comparative construction in any natural language should be conceived of as having the form of a sequence of two propositions. To be exact, we have argued that comparatives are universally modelled on temporal chains; in terms of our theoretical model, we can rephrase this claim as implying that the US of a comparative construction has been 'borrowed' from the way in which temporal chains are represented at that level. In other words, we may conclude that the range of possible underlying structures for comparatives in natural languages (that is, the range of possible outputs of the strategies which map a cognitive representation of comparison onto the language system) is constrained by the requirement that *these underlying structures must all have the form of a temporal chain of propositions*. As we have seen, this modelling temporal chain has, in some cases, received a consecutive interpretation, while in other cases a simultaneous interpretation seems to be preferred.

With respect to the form which the *cognitive structure of comparisons* must be assumed to have, matters are considerably less clear. Since the nature of cognitive representations in general is still very much of a mystery, any proposal concerning the form of a cognitive representation for the mental act of comparison will necessarily be hypothetical and speculative to a high degree. Nevertheless, it can be observed that, in the linguistic literature on comparison, a certain tradition has developed on this point. Such diverse authors as Valin (1952), Joly (1967), Doherty (1970), Klooster (1976, 1979) and Seuren (1978) all represent the cognitive structure of comparison in the form of a *spatial configuration*. In this configuration, the parameter of the comparison (that is, the property with respect to which the comparison is made) is pictured as an axis, which is marked for positive–negative polarity. On this axis, the two objects which are to be compared are juxtaposed in such a way that the object which has the higher degree of the quality in question is placed farther to the positive side of the parameter. In this way, the positions of the two compared objects on the axis define extents, which represent the degree to which the compared objects possess the quality at issue, and which are juxtaposed to the effect that one of these extents envelops the other. Given this way of representation, the CS underlying a comparative construction like 'A is bigger than B' can be graphically pictured as the following diagram, in which it must be understood that the axis represents the gradable quality of being big:[3]

As noted, this way of representing the CS of comparison assumes that such a representation is basically *spatial in character*; relative degrees of intensity with respect to a certain quality are represented in terms of *relative distance on an axis*. It should be pointed out that there is independent motivation for taking such a point of view. First, it should be recalled that, in many languages, comparative constructions show a clear modelling on spatial relations; we have argued in section 3.2 that this modelling should be accounted for by assuming that comparison is, conceptually speaking, based upon spatial notions. In this context, it is also interesting to note that elements which characterize a certain degree of quality are often also employed as spatial items: an obvious example is the English adverbial expression *by far* or the German expression *mit Abstand* 'lit. with distance' (see Klooster, 1979: 198). Secondly, Bergmans (1982: 152) cites a number of psycholinguistic research results which support the claim that the CS of comparison should be represented in the form of spatial imagery. One of the fields from which evidence for this position can be derived is the study of aphasia. According to Erelt (1973: 139), 'it has been found out that damages in the occipital lobe of the brain that cause disturbances in spatial orientation and thus inhibit the understanding of sentences expressing spatial relations likewise cause disturbances in the understanding of comparative sentences (Luria, 1962; Bein, 1957).' Furthermore, there are introspective psycholinguistic data which suggest the proximity of comparative representations to spatial ones. Bergmans (1982) quotes Higgins and Huttenlocher (1971: 495–6), who note:

De Soto, London and Handel (1965) have pointed out that people tend to think about adjectival dimensions spatially, with the unmarked adjective (i.e., the positive member of the antonymous pair) frequently thought of as being at the top and the marked adjective at the bottom. Our Ss also report that they tend to think about 'more' and 'less' in terms of directional movement, with 'more' being a movement in an upward direction and 'less' a movement in a downward direction. Our Ss report that spatial imagery is intimately tied up with determining the order of items from comparative expressions.

Given this evidence, I think it is justifiable to adopt a spatial configuration like the one depicted above as the cognitive representation of comparisons, at least for as long as no other, more explicit and better-documented, alternative is available.

There is one point connected with our assumptions about the cognitive representation of comparison which deserves some further comment. In the above exposition, we tacitly assumed that this cognitive representation (like cognitive structures in general) is language-independent. That is, we take it that the cognitive structure representing the mental operation of comparison *is essentially the same for all speakers of all natural languages*. A consequence of this assumption is that the ultimate variation among languages in the encoding of the concept of comparison must be viewed as being caused by the choice of different options in the selection of the rules which map this universal cognitive structure onto the language system and, ultimately, onto surface structures. However, one may also defend an alternative view on the explanation of surface variation among languages. In particular, one may maintain that this variation is not a result of the choice of different options in the mapping operations, but that it stems from the fact that different groups of languages select different types of cognitive representations for the concept of comparison. In other words, the issue can be phrased as follows: given that two languages show a difference in surface form with respect to the codification of comparison, does this mean that they also differ in the cognitive structures of which these surface forms are a mapping? Or should we assume that there is one, universally valid, cognitive representation for the concept of comparison, and that surface variation is caused by divergence in the choice of strategies and/or grammatical procedures?

As far as I know, there is at present no empirical way to decide whether or not cognitive structures that represent a certain type of mental operation are alike for all speakers of human languages throughout the world. Therefore, this issue will have to be decided on a priori grounds. In this study, I have adopted the position that *the cognitive representation of comparison presented above is indeed valid for all languages*. The motivation for this decision rests on two kinds of considerations.

First, there is a general methodological consideration which, at least from the point of view of linguistics, leads to the assumption of universally valid cognitive structures. As we saw in chapter 1, the very feasibility of typological linguistics rests on the assumption that the parameter of a linguistic typology can, at least at some level of representation, be defined in language-independent terms. If we cannot be sure that such a language-independent definition for a given construction type is possible, we can never be certain that comparable items are brought together in a typology, and this would, in all probability, mean that

Typological Universal Grammar would cease to exist as a viable scientific enterprise. Furthermore, it must be repeated here that the aim of Typological Universal Grammar is to provide insights into the non-randomness of linguistic encoding. Now, if one were to maintain that the variation in linguistic coding is a mere reflection of variations in cognitive representations, the question of the non-randomness of linguistic coding can be reduced to the question of the non-randomness of cognitive representation. Such a reduction would have as its consequence that surface variation among languages would cease to be a matter of linguistic interest. Of course, it is absolutely conceivable that future research will show that a reduction of this kind is the sensible view to adopt. At present, however, I think that it cannot be expected of typological linguists that they give up a seemingly profitable problem area, at least not for as long as they are not forced to do so by irrefutable empirical evidence. In other words, given that there are no decisive arguments in favour of one of the two possible positions, the assumption that cognitive structures are universally valid is the more fruitful of the two, at least from the point of view of theoretical linguistics.

Apart from these methodological considerations (which ultimately boil down to a choice of tactics in the politics of scientific inquiry), we may adduce another argument for our position, which has to do with considerations of a general epistemical nature. If we assume that speakers of languages in which a certain concept has a different formal encoding also employ different cognitive representations for that concept (that is, if we assume that people who speak differently also think differently), we are inexorably committed to accept some version of linguistic relativism, in the sense of Whorf (1956). Now, as has been remarked repeatedly in the literature, linguistic relativism is a position which is very hard to falsify, if, indeed, it can be falsified at all. Nevertheless, there are a number of empirical data which seem to be at odds with at least the more radical versions of linguistic relativism. The fact that translations between languages are, to a large extent, successful, and the existence of language universals, are data which are difficult to explain within a relativist framework. For further discussion on this topic I refer to Fodor, Bever and Garrett (1974). For our present purposes, I will take it for granted that the consequence of linguistic relativism is a definite disadvantage for the position that cognitive representations which underlie a certain construction type are language-dependent.

11.5   Conclusion

The main points of this chapter can be summarized as follows. As is the case with any other construction type, the structural description of comparatives involves representations on three distinct levels. The *cognitive structure* underlying expressions of comparison can be visualized as a language-independent spatial configuration, in which the difference in degree of intensity is represented in terms of spatial distance between the two compared items. By the application of cognitive strategies this spatial configuration is to be mapped onto the language system; the output of this mapping is constrained by the requirement that any strategy must result in an *underlying structure* which has the form of a temporal chain of propositions. The underlying structures must further be mapped onto the *surface structures* of various languages by means of grammatical procedures. Again, the output of this mapping is constrained, in that the application of any grammatical procedure to an underlying structure of a comparative must result in the selection of one of the limited set of surface variants which have been attested in the typology of comparative constructions.

12

Cognitive Strategies in Comparative Formation

12.1 Introduction

In the previous chapter, we have established the minimal properties which must be attributed to the various levels of representation for comparative expressions. Following this, we must now turn to the question of the various rule types which are instrumental in the mapping of these structural representations onto one another. In this chapter, our concern will be with the nature of the *cognitive strategies* which are needed to achieve a mapping of the cognitive representation of comparison onto the underlying structures of comparatives. Again, the reader should be warned beforehand that much of what I have to say on this topic is highly speculative. For one thing, cognitive psychology itself does not seem to be very certain about the nature of cognitive mapping operations. On top of this, as a linguist I find myself here in the uncomfortable position of a trespasser on a domain in which I am not qualified. I can only hope that the exposition which follows will contain a certain degree of plausibility from a psychological point of view (I have, in fact, derived the gist of my ideas from psycholinguistic publications), and that it may encourage cognitive psychologists to have their say on these issues, too.

12.2 Basic features of cognitive strategies

As I see it, the task which cognitive strategies must accomplish is the transformation of a spatial cognitive structure into a linearly ordered linguistic structure. Thus, the mapping of the CS of comparison onto the US of a comparative involves a transition of a spatially modelled configuration onto a configuration which is modelled on a temporal chain: strategies 'read off' various bits of information from the CS and codify them in the form of (a sequence of) propositions.

As we noted above, spatially modelled configurations (such as pictures, maps, blue-prints and the like) have the property that the information which they contain is made available simultaneously. A consequence of this property is that the observer enjoys considerable freedom in dealing with such configurations: depending on the scanning strategy which he selects, he may read off whatever information he chooses in whatever order he chooses. In other words, since all information in the CS is presented to the observer 'in one piece', the observer has the freedom to decide for himself which feature of the CS is to serve as the primary focus of his scanning strategy. As an example, let us consider the case in which an observer is confronted with a picture of a red triangle (see Fodor, 1976: 187). In codifying the information which is contained in this spatially modelled configuration, the observer may choose to focus his scanning procedure on the colour of the picture, and hence he may come up with the proposition 'x is red' as a first mapping of information. However, there is nothing which prevents the observer from focusing his scanning strategy on another feature of the configuration, say, the form of the pictured object. If he chooses to do this, the first proposition which results from his mapping operation may be something like 'x is tri-angular'. The important point here is that nothing in the cognitive representation itself forces the observer to select a particular feature of that representation as his first focus of scanning; the decision to select a particular scanning strategy is completely up to the observer.

This being said, however, it must be added that it is quite plausible to assume that the decision for a particular scanning strategy in a given situation will be heavily influenced by considerations of 'salience'. That is, when confronted with a cognitive representation, the observer will naturally rate some features of that representation as more 'salient' (i.e., as more useful to his present purposes than other bits of information which are also objectively present in the configuration), and hence he will focus his scanning strategy on these salient features. In short, in mapping a CS onto a US a speaker/hearer may employ *various different strategies*, depending on his estimation of the importance of the various pieces of information which are contained in the cognitive representation.

Now, if we look at the CS of comparison which we have proposed in the foregoing chapter, we can observe that there are minimally three features of this configuration which are possible candidates for 'salience', and which may therefore be selected as the starting point of a cognitive mapping strategy. To be specific, we can see that the defining elements of which the CS of comparison consists are the following:

(a) *the axis*, which represents the spatial dimension along which gradience is demarcated;

(b) *the two compared items A and B*, which are juxtaposed on the axis to the effect that there is a distance between them;

(c) *the extents on the axis*, which represent the relative degrees of intensity which the two compared items possess.

In the next section, I will present three different mappings of the CS of comparison onto underlying structures. In other words, I will assume that the mapping of this CS onto the language system has at least three different outputs. The difference between these three mappings will be taken to be essentially a consequence of the selection of three different scanning strategies, based upon the selection of a different starting point for these scanning strategies in the CS. Whether these three strategies exhaust the possibilities of the ways in which the CS of comparison can be mapped onto the language system is a question which I cannot even begin to answer. For a discussion of this matter, we would have to have a much clearer view of the constraints which are to be imposed on the notion of 'possible scanning strategy'. Evidently, this is a problem area where cognitive psychologists will have to have their say first.

However, whatever their differences may be, there is at least one important respect in which all mapping strategies for comparative constructions must be alike. As we argued extensively in the foregoing chapters of this book, the codification of comparatives in natural languages must be conceived of as being modelled upon the codification of temporal chaining. From this, it follows that any strategy which the speaker/hearer may choose in scanning the CS of comparison must have the mapping result of a US which has the form of *a sequence of propositions with a temporal interpretation*. Given this requirement, there is one additional problem which we have to deal with: we must ask ourselves what the temporal interpretation of the resulting underlying structures of comparatives must be. To be specific, we need a criterion to decide whether a particular US-chain, mapped from the CS of comparison by a certain scanning strategy, is to receive the temporal interpretation of a simultaneous chain or that of a consecutive chain.

In order to be able to make a decision on this point, I will adopt the following line of reasoning. First, I will take it as a matter of principle that the actual left-to-right ordering of the propositions in a resulting US is a reflection of the actual order in which these propositions are read off from the CS by the relevant scanning strategy. In other words, I assume that the leftmost proposition in the US represents the piece of information which is read off first from the CS. Of course, this principle in itself does not enable us to tell whether a sequence of propositions in the US is to receive a consecutive or a simultaneous interpretation. Therefore, I will make a second a priori assumption: I will take it that the temporal interpretation of a US of comparatives is at least partially determined by the question of whether or not there is any logical necessity in the order in which the propositions are read off from the CS. To put the matter slightly differently: since the scanning operation is a physical procedure which is necessarily deployed in time, there will always be an actual order in which the various propositions are read off from the CS, but the factor which decides the temporal interpretation of the resulting sequence of propositions is whether or not this actual order of encoding is governed by considerations of logical necessity. A few examples may be helpful in clarifying the consequences of this particular assumption.

On the one hand, we have cases like the 'red triangle'-example introduced above. As we saw, in codifying the cognitive representation of a red triangle, the observer may focus his scanning strategy either on the colour of the represented object, or on the form of that object. If he selects the first alternative, he will first codify the proposition 'x is red', and only following that he will codify other pieces of information contained in the configuration (given, of course, that he is interested in codifying any further information at all). As a result, the US of a sentence in which this configuration is linguistically expressed will receive the form of the following sequence:

$$(x \text{ is red}) \quad \& \quad (x \text{ is triangular}) \quad \& \quad (\ldots)$$

If, however, the observer selects a scanning strategy which focuses primarily on the form of the represented object, the resulting US will have the form of a sequence like the following:

$$(x \text{ is triangular}) \quad \& \quad (x \text{ is red}) \quad \& \quad (\ldots)$$

The important thing to note about this example is that the two propositions 'x is red' and 'x is triangular' are read off independently from the CS at issue. That is, the CS itself imposes no necessary order on the procedure by which these two proposition are read off. The two propositions are, in other words, *logically unordered*, and the actual order in which they are encoded depends entirely on considerations of salience which the observer chooses to apply. Now, for underlying structures in which the constituent propositions are logically unordered, I take it that the natural way to interpret them temporally is to assign to them the status of a *simultaneous chain*. In other words, in such underlying structures the symbol '&' naturally receives the interpretation 'and also', 'and at the same time'.

In contrast to such 'red triangle'-cases, there are also cases of codification in which the CS does seem to impose a logical ordering on the various steps by which the constituting propositions of the US are read off. In such cases, the CS defines an orientation which the scanning procedure must follow once the starting point of the scanning is decided upon. Such cases are similar to the reading of a map or a street plan: if one wants to trace out a route from Central Square to Main Street, the information which the map offers must be read off by means of a series of successive steps, which cannot be completely interchanged at random. I will assume that sequences of propositions which result from the application of such an 'orientated' or 'ordered' scanning strategy will naturally lend themselves to a *consecutive* temporal interpretation. Hence, the natural interpretation of the connective '&' between the various propositions in such a US is that of 'and then', 'and after that'.

It will be observed that, in the formulation of the above principle, I have used the qualification 'natural' for some of the interpretive alternatives. This qualification is meant to indicate that the principle of temporal interpretation outlined above can only specify a *preferred* or *unmarked* interpretation for a given US, but that it does not impose one temporal interpretation on that US to the complete exclusion of the other. The reason for this relative indeterminacy lies in the fact that the mapping of a CS onto a US is, on the one hand, a procedure which may be influenced by considerations of logical consequence, but, on the other hand, also a physical event which is necessarily deployed in time. In other words, any mapping operation is a series of temporally successive sub-strategies, regardless of whether the actual order of these sub-strategies is governed by logical order or not. As a result of this 'double nature' of scanning strategies it may happen that a US in which the various propositions have no logical order is nevertheless interpreted as a consecutive chain, due to the fact that the leftmost proposition in the US has been codified first in the course of the actual mapping operation. Conversely, there is also a chance that underlying structures which are governed by logical order (that is, USs in which the logical ordering of propositions matches the actual order of codification) may nevertheless be interpreted temporally as S-chains, due to the fact that, even in cases of logical ordering of information, the information at issue is presented in the CS simultaneously, 'in one piece'. In short, we must conclude that the principle outlined above, which specifies the temporal interpretation of underlying structures for comparatives, constitutes a guide-line rather than a law.

12.3 Three cognitive strategies

After this exposition of background assumptions, we are now in a position to discuss the three strategies which I propose for the mapping of the CS of comparison onto underlying structures. These three strategies each take one of the salient features of the CS of comparison as their starting point. Furthermore, it is possible to subcategorize these three strategies, on the basis of the fact that, in two of them, the parameter of the comparison is explicitly associated with *both compared items*. In contrast, the third strategy specifies *only one of the compared items* as having the property which is indicated by the parameter of the comparison.

The first cognitive strategy in comparative formation may be called the *Independent Strategy*. In this mapping operation, it is the *axis* itself which is taken as the salient feature of the cognitive configuration. The two compared items A and B are not explicitly related to one another in this strategy, nor are the extents on the axis taken into consideration. Quite simply, in this strategy the two compared items A and B are associated with that side of the axis to which they are nearest; since the axis itself is a spatially defined entity, by way of such a polar association the existence of a distance between the two items on the axis (and, as a result, the existence of a difference in gradience between these items) can be inferred. There is, however, in this strategy no assertion of a direct matching of the items against each other; either item is located on the axis in a manner which is independent of the positioning of the other item.

The US which is derived as a result of the application of the Independent Strategy comes in two variants, due to the fact that the polarity of the axis can be encoded either in a pair of antonymous predicates, or in a negative–positive polarity with respect to one single predicate. In the literature we can find ample evidence for the thesis that these two codifications are functionally equivalent. To be specific, both linguistic and psycholinguistic observations lead to the conclusion that pairs of antonymous predicates must be considered to consist of a positive and a negative member. In other words, in a pair of antonymous predicates such as *big–small* one of the members (in this case, *small*) must be rated as 'logically negative' (see Higgins and Huttenlocher, 1971: 490). Support for this claim can be derived from the fact that different dictionaries consistently define the same member of the pair in terms of the negation of the other (ibid.). Internal linguistic evidence for the inherent negative–positive polarity in antonymous pairs is presented in Seuren (1978) and Klooster (1978). On the part of psycholinguistics, it has been shown that sentences which contain the positive member of an antonymous pair of predicates are easier to understand than sentences which contain the corresponding negative members (Sherman, 1969), and that deductive reasoning problems which are phrased in terms of positive members of antonymous pairs are solved significantly more quickly than problems in which the negative members of such pairs are employed (H. Clark, 1970).

Given these data, I think we can feel justified in postulating the following two equivalent outputs of the Independent Strategy:

US 1.1   (a BIG)   &   (b SMALL)
US 1.2   (a BIG)   &   (b not-BIG)

Thus, these two formulas must be viewed as my (very simplified and schematical) approximation of the US of a comparative which has been formed from the CS of comparison by the application of the Independent Strategy. In these underlying structures, the two compared items A and B are represented as two variables a and b, which function as the arguments of the two members of a negative–positive (c.q. an antonymous) pair of predicates; these predicates are the linguistic mappings of the positive and negative sides of the axis in the CS. Thus, in this strategy both compared items are explicitly associated with the parameter of the comparison.

As for the temporal interpretations of the two above formulas, it will be clear that the propositions of which these underlying structures consist are read off independently from the CS by this particular mapping operation. In other words, the Independent Strategy is not governed by considerations of logical ordering; the result of this mapping operation might equally well have led to underlying structures in which the order of the propositions has been reversed, as in

US 1.1   (b SMALL)   &   (a BIG)
US 1.2   (b not-BIG)   &   (a BIG)

Hence, it is plausible to assume that the natural way to interpret these underlying structures is to assign to them the status of a *simultaneous* temporal chain.

In the second mapping strategy, which I will call the *Ordered Strategy*, the salient feature of the CS is provided by the *extents* which are demarcated on the axis. As was the case with the Independent Strategy, the Ordered Strategy explicitly associates both compared items with the parameter of the comparison. However, the Ordered Strategy associates the compared items both with the positive side of the axis, so that they are represented in underlying structures as variables which are arguments of the same predicate.

The mapping of the CS of comparison onto the underlying structure consists here of the ordering of the two extents which the two compared items delineate on the axis. It should be noted here that, in this ordering, two orientations are possible. Thus, one may take the *positive* side of the axis as the starting point of the ordering, so that the larger extent is ordered before the smaller one. Alternatively, one may start from the *negative* side of the axis, thus ordering the smaller extent before the larger one. As a result, this strategy maps the CS of comparison onto two equivalent underlying structures, which are both codifications of the mental representation 'A is more X than B'. In *US-2.1* the negative side of the axis has been taken as the starting point of the scanning, whereas in *US-2.2* the positive side of the axis provides the orientation of the ordering:

US 2.1   (*b* BIG)   &   (*a* BIG)
US 2.2   (*a* BIG)   &   (*b* BIG)

Given the fact that an operation of successive ordering is essential in this mapping strategy, a *consecutive* interpretation of these underlying structures readily presents itself. Hence, the connective element '&' in these underlying structures will typically receive the interpretation 'and then', 'and following that'. A simultaneous interpretation of these underlying structures is not completely excluded, but it is clearly a secondary option under this strategy.

It will be observed that, in this strategy, the extents which are demarcated on the axis are themselves not qualified as to their size; the strategy consists of a scanning of the axis in either of the two possible directions, and imposes an ordering on the extents demarcated on that axis, in that the extent which is encountered first during the scanning is encoded in the first proposition in the resulting US. There is, however, also an alternative way in which the extents demarcated on the axis can be employed as the salient feature in the codification of the CS of comparison. In this latter strategy, the two extents are themselves qualified as to their extension on the axis. In the resulting US, we may represent these qualifications by means of different indices (say, x and y), letting it be understood that index x defines an extent on the axis which is larger than the extent defined by index y.[1] Hence, the difference in gradience between the two compared items can be inferred from the fact that the extents which these items delineate on the axis are marked by different indices. The US which results from this mapping operation will have roughly the form of the following formula:

US 2.3   (*a* BIG$_x$)   &   (*b* BIG$_y$)

In contrast to the mapping operation which produces *US-2.1* and *US-2.2*, the operation which produces *US-2.3* is not governed by considerations of logical ordering, due to the fact that both extents involved are qualified independently of each other. Hence, the mapping operation at issue might just as well have resulted in a US in which the order of the two propositions is reversed, as in

US 2.4   (*b* BIG$_y$)   &   (*a* BIG$_x$)

As a third alternative output of the mapping strategy under discussion, we may postulate the following formula:

US 2.5 $(a\,\mathrm{BIG_x})$ & $(b\,\mathrm{not\,BIG_x})$

In producing this latter US, the mapping strategy has made use of the fact that the smaller extent on the axis, demarcated by the position of the item B, is enveloped by the larger extent, which is demarcated by the position of the item A on the axis.

Given that the strategy which codifies the CS of comparison in terms of indexed extents is not governed by considerations of logical ordering, a *simultaneous* interpretation is the natural choice for the underlying structures which result from it. Again, however, we should stipulate that the assignment of a simultaneous interpretation to these USs should not be taken too absolutely, and that a consecutive interpretation is a real, if minor, possibility here.

Finally, we must discuss the third strategy by which the CS of comparison can be mapped onto a sequence of propositions. Under this mapping operation, which I will refer to as the *Relative Strategy*, it is not the axis, nor the extents on that axis, which are the salient features of the cognitive representation; it is rather *the two compared items A and B themselves, and the way in which they are spatially related*, which function as the focus of the mapping operation. Thus, the Relative Strategy relates the two compared items to each other in a straight-forward way, in that the spatial distance on the axis which exists between them is explicitly expressed in a separate proposition in the US. Hence, in the US which results from the application of the Relative Strategy, the axis (which represents the parameter of comparison) *is referred to only once*, whereas in the other strategies the axis is mentioned twice in the US. Furthermore, in this mapping strategy the comparee item A is usually the starting point or the 'topic'; it is only this item which is explicitly associated with the parameter of comparison (see *US-3.1*). Occasionally, it may be the standard item B which is selected as the topic, and which is therefore associated with the parameter (see *US-3.2*). As a result, the US which is produced by this mapping operation has the following schematical forms:

US 3.1 $(a\,\mathrm{BIG})$ & $(a\,\mathrm{BEYOND}\,b)$
US 3.2 $(b\,\mathrm{BIG})$ & $(a\,\mathrm{BEYOND}\,b)$

In this US, the two-place predicate BEYOND is meant to express the spatially defined relation between the compared items A and B on the axis of the comparison.

Given the fact that the two propositions in *US-3.1* and *US-3.2* can be read off independently from the CS of comparison, a *simultaneous* interpretation of this sequence of propositions is a natural decision. Hence, a possible variant of these USs are the following, reversed, sequences:

US 3.3   (*a* BEYOND *b*)   &   (*a* BIG)
US 3.4   (*a* BEYOND *b*)   &   (*b* BIG)

As was the case with other USs for which a simultaneous interpretation seems the most natural, a consecutive interpretation of the USs derived by the Relative Strategy is not totally impossible; but, given our principle of temporal interpretation outlined in section 12.2, we can predict that a consecutive interpretation of such structures will be fairly rare.

12.4   Conclusion

In this chapter we have presented three cognitive strategies for the codification of the CS of comparison into underlying structures, viz.

(a) the Independent Strategy, in which the compared items A and B are associated with the opposite sides of the axis of comparison;

(b) the Ordered Strategy, in which the compared items A and B are both associated with the positive side of the axis of comparison; and

(c) the Relative Strategy, in which only one of the compared items (typically, the comparee item A) is associated with (typically, the positive side of) the axis of comparison.

The three mapping operations are similar in that they all result in underlying structures which have the form of a sequence of propositions. Since such sequences of propositions which underlie comparatives must be seen as being modelled upon the underlying structures of temporal chains, underlying structures of comparatives must receive either a simultaneous or a consecutive interpretation. In one of the cases, namely, the *US-2.1–2.2* produced by the Ordered Strategy, a consecutive interpretation seems to be the most natural, since the mapping operation appears to involve a number of logically ordered substeps. In the other cases, the propositions in the US-sequence are read off independently, so that a simultaneous interpretation seems to be the most natural choice for them.

13

Grammatical Procedures in Comparative Formation

13.1 Introduction

In the preceding chapter, I have postulated a number of cognitive strategies by which the CS of comparison is assumed to be mapped onto the language system. The output of these cognitive strategies is in all cases a sequence of propositions, which must be viewed as being modelled on the codification of temporal chaining. Given that this analysis is acceptable, we can now turn to the second type of rules needed for the formal derivation of comparatives, viz. the *grammatical procedures*. The task of these rules is to map the underlying linguistic structures produced by the cognitive strategies onto the surface structures of comparative constructions in natural languages. Hence, the range of possible outputs of these grammatical procedures is empirically limited to the various types of comparatives established in chapter 2.

13.2 Functional aspects of grammatical procedures

Speaking from a functional point of view, one might say that grammatical procedures have to strike a balance between two different interests, which in some cases may be in conflict. On the one hand, grammatical procedures have to preserve underlying structure, so that the hearer will be able to decipher correctly the message contained in it. From this it follows that, whatever changes grammatical procedures may inflict upon the underlying structure, they must take care not to distort this underlying structure beyond recognition: they should always result in a surface structure which contains sufficient clues for the hearer to construct the intended interpretation. For this reason, it may happen that grammatical procedures generate surface structures which, from a strictly structural point of view, are to some extent redundant. Furthermore, grammatical procedures should not only guarantee that the interpretation of the message by the hearer can be made at all; they should also be helpful in ensuring that this interpretation can be performed by the hearer with a minimum of effort. Hence, we may expect that grammatical procedures will perform a number of operations whose primary function is that of some kind of service to the hearer: the main reason of existence of such operations is that they present the information in a linguistic surface form which is optimally easy to process.

However, opposed to operations which are primarily motivated as a kind of service to the hearer, grammatical procedures also perform tasks which primarily serve the interests of the speaker. Again, a minimalization of effort is the desired goal here. In the interest of fast and unproblematic communication, grammatical procedures must ensure that the hearer is presented with all the necessary information in an optimally accessible form, but they must also ensure that the speaker does not have to go to extraordinary lengths to achieve this communicative effect. Hence, grammatical procedures can also be assumed to function as a means by which the speaker can minimalize his own efforts, and hence we may expect to find some grammatical operations (such as the suppression of material which is predictable from the preceding linguistic context or the general real-world context) which are aimed at preventing the communication from being unnecessarily complicated and cumbersome to the speaker.

In a manner of speaking, then, we might say that the grammatical procedures (i.e., the rules of syntax) walk a thin line between the two evils of longwindedness and unintelligibility. These procedures can be conceived of as seeking a balance between the demands that are made on them from the part of the decoder and the encoder, sometimes giving in to one side, while in other cases the opposite interest prevails. As a matter of fact, it may be suggested that a fundamental respect in which languages differ from one another lies in the decisions which they make when faced with such conflicting interests; some languages are generally inclined to side with the hearer, whereas other languages generally prefer to sacrifice the interests of the hearer to the speaker's convenience.[1]

13.3   Deranking and identity deletion

Given the assumption that underlying structures of comparatives must be viewed as formal extensions of temporal chaining, it seems plausible to look for the relevant operations among those grammatical procedures which are pre-eminently applied in the linguistic formalization of consecutive and simultaneous chains. In what follows, I will propose two types of rules which I take to be operative in that area of syntax. Both of these operations may be subsumed under the general heading of *structure-reducing procedures*, since their main effect is to reduce, and hence to compress, underlying structures in the course of their transformation into surface structures.

The first of the structure-reducing operations which I propose for the grammatical treatment of chaining constructions has been dealt with extensively in the foregoing chapters, so that a few short remarks may suffice here. Throughout this book, we have employed a notion of *structural deranking*, i.e., a grammatical procedure by which predicates in a chain are downgraded in rank with respect to the remaining main predicate. In a certain sense, the procedure of deranking can be looked upon as an instance of a more general type of syntactic operation, viz. the procedure of subordination. However, as we have argued in chapter 4, deranking is a specific and limited case of subordination; while general subordination has the effect of downgrading a whole clause, deranking has the additional effect of robbing an erstwhile full clause of its sentential status by downgrading its predicate.

Functionally speaking, one might postulate that deranking is a type of grammatical procedure which is primarily aimed at making things easier for the hearer, at the expense of some additional effort for the speaker. By the application of deranking, the number of S-nodes in a chaining construction is reduced, and all the information contained in the chain gets structurally arranged under one S-node. Thus, looking at the deranking procedure from a specific angle, one might say that this procedure reduces the structural complexity of the structure at issue, in that it results in a 'pruning' of the original tree diagram by means of a minimalization of the number of rule cycles.[2]

As we have seen in chapter 4, languages may vary considerably in the extent to which they permit the procedure of deranking to apply in the encoding of their temporal chains. To be exact, we have found that, with respect to the applicability of deranking, languages can be divided into three categories, viz. languages which are *balancing*, languages which permit only *conditional deranking*, and languages which allow *absolute deranking*.

Now, in the preceding chapters we have tacitly assumed that the options which a language has in the deranking procedure constitute the only relevant determining factor in the prediction of the surface variation of comparatives across languages. At this point, however, we must introduce *a second grammatical procedure in the encoding of temporal chains*. As we will see below, the options which languages have in the applicability of this second procedure also have their effects upon the ways in which the choice for a particular comparative construction in a given language is made.

This second grammatical procedure may be referred to as *identity deletion*. The concept of identity deletion is meant to cover all those instances of chaining formation in which lexical material has been omitted or suppressed on the basis of the identity of that material with lexical material which is present elsewhere in the string. Using a somewhat different, but essentially equivalent terminology, we may say that identity deletion is meant to cover all those cases in which lexical material has been reduced to a null-anaphor under conditions of identity. Thus, the well-known phenomena of Coordination Reduction and Gapping, which have been discussed extensively in recent grammatical literature, are taken to be instances of a case in which (some specific variant of) identity deletion has applied to a string.

Concerning the concept of identity deletion, two remarks should be made immediately. First, we must stress that the concept of identity deletion which we employ here will be taken to apply only to those cases of string-reduction in which the omitted material bears a *formal relation* to some other element in the same string. In other words, a condition on the application of identity deletion is that the deleted material should be fully and unequivocally recoverable from the *linguistic* context. Hence, cases where lexical material is left out on the basis of recoverability from the general non-linguistic context will not be taken to constitute instances of identity deletion. For example, elliptical sentences like those in *(1)*, which have been discussed at length in Shopen (1973), do not fall under our definition of identity deletion. It will be clear that the suppressed lexical material in such sentences, whatever it may be, does not have to bear a relation of identity to previously mentioned material, but can only be supplied by invoking the extra-linguistic context:

(1)   ENGLISH:
a.   *Fire!*
b.   *One more beer, and I leave*
c.   *Into the dungeon with him!*

Also, cases of Pro-Drop are assumed to lie outside the scope of our notion of identity deletion. Thus, the fact that, in languages like Latin and Rumanian, there is no need for the overt expression of a subject by means of a non-stressed personal pronoun, as is illustrated in the following sentences:

(2) *LATIN:*
 In Asiam   transierunt
 in A.-ACC cross-PERF. 3PL
 '*They* crossed into Asia'

(3) *RUMANIAN:*
 Intelege   *piesa*
 understand-PRES. 3SG play-DET
 '*He* understands the play'

is not covered by our definition of identity deletion. Again it is clear that, in cases of Pro-Drop, unstressed lexical material may be omitted in any construction where the reference is recoverable from the general context,[3] and that this left-out material does not have to be subject to conditions of identity with previously mentioned material.

Secondly, we should make a short comment on the nature of the identity-relation which is fundamental to the deletion procedure at issue here. As the literature on various types of identity-deletion processes has shown conclusively, it is not just mere lexical identity which is required here. In addition, we need at least some further functional or configurational identity, to the effect that repeated material may be suppressed only if it occupies the same configurational position (c.q. has the same structural function) as the preceding element which 'triggers' the deletion. At present, it must be said that, despite considerable progress made in this area, the exact content of the notion of identity needed in this type of deletion procedure is not yet fully known. For our purposes, however, this does not have to be much of a problem, since we will apply the procedure of identity deletion only to very simple configurations, in which the combined requirements of lexical and configurational identity are met in a straightforward way.

If we compare the procedure of identity deletion to the procedure of deranking, we note considerable differences between the two. Identity deletion effectuates the elimination of lexical material, and hence it reduces the input string in length, but it does not alter the configuration of the underlying structure. That is, identity deletion has the effect of filling structural positions in the underlying configuration with lexically empty material, but – at least in general – it leaves the original structural configuration intact.[4] In opposition to this, deranking is a procedure which fundamentally affects the structural configuration of the input string, in that it changes the structural rank of some elements in that string. Unlike identity deletion, however, deranking normally does not result in the loss of lexical material from the string. That is, deranking alters the structural dependencies between elements of a string, but it generally keeps the original lexical content of the string intact.

This formal difference between the two structure-reducing procedures proposed here may be thought to have its reflection in a difference in functional status of these two procedures. As we suggested above, deranking may be thought of as a procedure which primarily serves the communicative interests of the hearer, in that it reduces the number of main clauses in a structure, and hence may lead to a reduction of the number of rule cycles which have to be applied to that structure. On the other hand, it is natural to assume that the application of identity deletion is mainly beneficial to the speaker; this procedure minimalizes the efforts made by the speaker, in that redundant material does not have to be repeated. Obviously, this will lead to some extra efforts on the part of the hearer, who is invited to fill in the gaps which the speaker has left open; however, since the type of redundancy reduction at issue here is governed by conditions of structural and lexical identity, the language system ensures that (at least to a significant degree) the implicit information can be recovered successfully from the preceding linguistic context.

13.4   Options in identity deletion

In the preceding section, we have delineated the grammatical procedure of identity deletion and commented upon its communicative function. Now we must take a closer look at the *options* which languages have in the application of this procedure in the derivation of the surface structures of temporal chains (and hence of comparatives). For our present purposes, we can confine ourselves to a rather limited range of input structures for this particular procedure. As will have become clear in section 2.3, the underlying structures which are the models of comparative constructions in natural languages typically consist of propositions which contain only a one-place predicate (such as BIG or SMALL) and its argument (*a* or *b*). Assuming that, in the linguistic encoding of such chains, these one-place predicates will be expressed by intransitive verbs or adjectives and that the arguments of these predicates will be expressed by a subject-NP, the typical underlying string to which identity deletion may apply in the derivation of comparative constructions will be a structure which has the general form of either *(4)* or *(5)*:

(4)   *(S V)*   *(S V)*
(5)   *(V S)*   *(V S)*

Given this situation, the only cases of identity deletion which are of relevance to us are cases in which *subjects* may or may not be deleted under identity, and cases in which *predicates* may or may not be deleted under identity.

Now, assuming that languages may vary in their possibilities of applying the procedure of identity deletion, we can first ask ourselves what the various options are with respect to the *conditionality* of this procedure. As it turns out, the typology of identity-deletion options parallels the typology of deranking options in an interesting way, in that both typologies can be shown to permit a *three-way variance*.

A first typological split in the options of identity deletion involves a simple yes–no decision. In the same way as there are languages which do not allow any deranking, we can find languages in our sample in which *no form of identity deletion at all* (i.e., neither subject-deletion nor verb-deletion) is permitted. In the ideal case of a language of this type, it is impossible to have null-anaphors which are bound by identity; these languages require that every configurational position be filled lexically, either by a full lexical constituent or by a pronominal element.

Opposed to languages with no identity deletion, we also find languages in which at least some form of this procedure can be documented. For languages which belong to this group, it will be clear that there are *three logical subtypes*, namely,

(a) languages which may delete subjects under identity, but which do not have the possibility to omit identical verbs;
(b) languages which may delete identical verbs, but which do not possess such an option for the suppression of identical subjects;
(c) languages in which both identical subjects and identical verbs may be reduced to null-anaphors.

However, if we look at the facts provided by the languages in the sample, we find that one of these categories, namely, the second one, does not occur in reality. That is, it appears that there are no natural languages in which verb-deletion is possible while at the same time deletion of identical subjects is forbidden. It seems that *the option of verb-deletion always automatically includes the option of subject-deletion*; in this respect, identity deletion presents an interesting parallel with the procedure of deranking, where – as we saw in section 4.4.3 – the option of absolute deranking always includes the option of deranking under identity of subjects.

Given the state of affairs outlined above, we can conclude that the typological options in the application of identity deletion allow for a three-way variance among languages, viz.:

(a) languages which have *no identity deletion*;
(b) languages which have *limited identity deletion* (i.e., subject-deletion only);
(c) languages which have *total identity deletion* (i.e., both subject-deletion and verb-deletion).

In addition to these remarks on the typological variation in the application of identity deletion across languages, we can also make a few comments on the *directionality* of this procedure. It can be observed that, within the class of languages that do have some form of identity deletion, there are some languages in which deletion of the first subject in the chain is required *(backward S-Deletion)*, while other languages prefer the deletion of the second subject *(forward S-Deletion)*. In a similar way, languages which permit the deletion of identical verbs in temporal chains may prefer either *backward V-Deletion* or *forward V-Deletion*. Now, the recent literature on deletion phenomena in chaining constructions (and, in particular, the literature on various processes of Coordination Deletion) has demonstrated that the choice for a particular direction of the deletion process is correlated to *the basic word-order type* of the language in question. Thus, we find once more a parallelism between the operation of deranking and the operation of identity deletion; with deranking, too, the directionality of the procedure is tied up with the word-order type to which a language belongs (see section 4.4.2).

The cross-linguistic investigation of the formal properties of identity deletion is at present still very much in progress, and has given rise to a steady flow of typological literature (Ross, 1970; Tai, 1969, 1971; Koutsoudas, 1971; Sanders and Tai, 1972; Sanders, 1976; Harries, 1978; Mallinson and Blake, 1981). Although it is too early to speak of any definitive results in this area, it appears that, at least as far as the directionality of identity deletion is concerned, a couple of general principles can be advanced with some confidence; for both of these principles, a motivation in functional terms readily presents itself.

The first of these principles, formulated in Sanders (1976) and Mallinson and Blake (1981), may be called the Forward Principle, and can be phrased as follows:

The Forward Principle of identity deletion:
The unmarked direction in which identity deletion operates is forward.

Thus, this principle states that, for both S-Deletion and V-Deletion, ellipsis of the second occurrence of the constituent at issue is the natural thing to do. The principle is confirmed *empirically* by the fact that, while there are languages with backward S-Deletion and languages with

backward V-Deletion, there are no languages in which both subjects and
verbs undergo backward deletion. In contrast to this, there are numerous
languages in which both S-Deletion and V-Deletion go forward. The
functional basis of the Forward Principle is neatly summed up in Sanders
(1976: 18–19), who writes:

The only way to recover an elliptical constituent is by determining what its
antecedent is, the constituent which governs or controls its ellipsis. When ellipsis
occurs in a following constituent, all of the possible antecedents of the elliptical
constituent have already been received and presumably understood, and they are
all available in prior memory when the site of the ellipsis is first encountered or
received. When an ellipsis site is encountered in a preceding conjunct, on the
other hand, none of its possible antecedents are available in memory at that time,
and the decoding process for the preceding conjunct must be suspended – with all
previously obtained result being held in storage – until an appropriate antecedent
is encountered in the following conjunct. Then it is necessary to go back and
complete the decoding of the preceding conjunct. Therefore, other things being
equal, the task of decoding will be much simpler and more efficient if ellipsis
occurs in following conjuncts rather than preceding ones.

Despite its functional naturalness, however, the Forward Principle is
not a blindly applicable law. The linguistic data clearly show that there
are languages in which this principle has been thwarted, in that backward deletion for subjects or predicates is permitted or even obligatory.
Accordingly, what we need is some principle by which the operation of
the Forward Principle can be constrained for specific cases. The relevant
research on this point is again due to Sanders (1976). His results can be
summarized in the following statement:

The Boundary Constraint on identity deletion:
Languages tend to avoid ellipsis of elements on sentence boundaries.

In effect, this constraint states that elements which are the first or the last
in a chaining construction are not likely to be omitted under identity. The
functional explanation for this constraint is, I think, a rather obvious
one. Since the sentence is the structural unit which serves as the frame for
the process of decoding and encoding, languages will attempt to make
sure that the boundaries of these units are clearly identifiable. One of the
mechanisms to achieve this is the imposition of demarcating intonation
contours on sentences, while another, related, mechanism provides for a
lexical filling of the positions which demarcate the boundaries of
sentences. Empirically, the Boundary Constraint leads to the prediction
that items which are initial in a sentence will be the items which are the
least likely to be deleted; omission of elements in this position would
violate both the Forward Principle and the Boundary Constraint. As

Sanders' results (1976: 17) show, this prediction is fully confirmed by the available linguistic facts.

Now, if we apply these two directionality principles to the operation of identity deletion in languages of different basic word-order types, we arrive at the following set of predictions. First, for SOV-languages which have some form of identity deletion, we can predict the following state of affairs:

(6) a. *If an SOV-language has S-Deletion, it will have forward S-Deletion.*

   b. *If an SOV-language has V-Deletion, it will have backward V-Deletion.*

Statements *(6a/b)* are based upon the operation of the Forward Principle and the Boundary Constraint on an underlying chaining structure of the form

(7) S_1 V_1 S_2 V_2

As will be seen, there is nothing which prevents identity deletion of S_2 in this structure, since this element occupies a medial position in the chain. On the other hand, the deletion of V_2, which might be predicted on the basis of the Forward Principle, is forbidden by the Boundary Constraint. Hence, the direction of V-Deletion has to be reversed, so that it can affect V_1, an element which is in a sentence-medial position and therefore more eligible as a possible ellipsis site.

The correctness of the statements in *(6)* can be illustrated by the facts from Japanese, an SOV-language with the option of total identity deletion. As sentence *(8)* shows, S-Deletion in Japanese goes forward. On the other hand, the sentences in *(9)* illustrate that at least some forms of V-Deletion in Japanese (viz. the elliptical procedure known as Gapping) applies in a backward direction. Cp.:

(8) JAPANESE:
   Sumie wa inu o   nadete neko o   tataita
   S.   TOP dog ACC pat-GER cat   ACC hit-PAST
   'Sumie patted the dog and hit the cat'

(9) JAPANESE:
a. *Sumie wa inu o   mita   , Norio wa ki   o   mita*
   S.   TOP dog ACC see-PAST N.   TOP tree ACC see-PAST
   'Sumie saw the dog and Norio saw the tree'

b. *Sumie wa inu o   , Norio wa ki   o   mita*
   S.   TOP dog ACC   N.   TOP tree ACC see-PAST
   'Sumie saw the dog, and Norio the tree'

Next, if we take a look at the direction of identity deletion in languages which have basic verb-initial word order, we find that a situation obtains which is diametrically opposed to the directionality in SOV-languages. For verb-initial languages, the following two statements turn out to be correct:

(10) a. *If a verb-initial language has S-Deletion, it will have backward S-Deletion.*
  b. *If a verb-initial language has V-Deletion, it will have forward V-Deletion.*

Given that verb-initial languages have underlying chaining structures of the following general form:

(11) V_1 S_1 V_2 S_2

it will be evident that forward deletion of identical verbs is not hampered by the Boundary Constraint, whereas forward deletion of identical subjects is. The statements in *(10)* can be illustrated by the following examples from Malagasy[5] and Jacaltec:[6]

(12) MALAGASY:
a. Misotro Rabe ary mihinam-bary Rabe
   drink   R.   and eat-rice   R.
   'Rabe is drinking and Rabe is eating rice'

b. Misotro sy   mihinam-bary Rabe
   drink   and eat-rice   R.
   'Rabe is drinking and eating rice'

(13) JACALTEC:
a. Slotoj ix hune' mancu wal naj hune' lahanẍeẍ slotoj naj
   eats   she one   mango but he one   orange   eats   he
   'She eats a mango, but he eats an orange'

b. Slotoj ix mancu wal naj hune' lahanẍeẍ
   eats   she mango but he one   orange
   'She eats a mango, but he an orange'

Finally, let us consider the direction of identity deletion in languages which have basic SVO order. Given that such languages have underlying chaining structures of the general form

(14) S_1 V_1 S_2 V_2

we can predict that, in such languages, S-Deletion, if it is permitted at all, will be able to apply *forward*. This prediction is borne out by the following examples from English:

(15) ENGLISH:
a.   *John came in, and John/he asked for a cup of tea*
b.   *John came in and asked for a cup of tea*

With respect to V-Deletion in SVO-languages, however, matters are a bit more complicated. From a structure like *(14)* we can predict that forward V-Deletion in these languages will be forbidden, due to the operation of the Boundary Constraint. As it turns out, this prediction is confirmed by the marginal acceptability of the English sentence *(16b)*, which has been derived from *(16a)* by means of Forward V-Deletion:

(16) ENGLISH:
a.   *My father drinks, and my mother drinks*
b. ? *My father drinks, and my mother*

A sentence like *(16b)* can be made passable only by imposing a highly marked intonation contour on the sentence, or by adding an adverb like *too* to the second conjunct (see sentence *(17a)*).[7] Both of these procedures have the effect of demarcating the sentence boundary which is left suspended by the null-anaphor in the second conjunct. Alternatively, SVO-languages may adopt the same solution as SOV-languages; they may reverse the direction of V-Deletion, so that the ellipsis site is removed from sentence-final position (see sentence *(17b)*). Cp.:

(17) ENGLISH:
a.   *My father drinks, and my mother, too*
b.   *My father and my mother drink*

It must be noted that a sentence like *(18b)*, in which a type of Forward V-Deletion (viz. Gapping) has been applied, is completely acceptable in English:

(18) ENGLISH:
a.   *My father drinks vodka and my mother drinks gin*
b.   *My father drinks vodka and my mother gin*

Within the framework adopted here the acceptability of Forward V-Deletion in *(18b)* as opposed to the marginal applicability of that same procedure in *(16b)* can be explained by the fact that, in SVO-languages, the verb of the second conjunct does not always appear in sentence-final position. As a result, SVO-languages are not as determined in their directionality of V-Deletion as SOV-languages are. In fact, we will see later on that the indeterminacy of the direction of V-Deletion in SVO-languages is often solved by not permitting V-Deletion at all; all the cases of limited identity deletion in our sample will turn out to be languages which have basic SVO word order.

13.5 Conclusion

In this chapter, we have discussed the two grammatical procedures which we claim to be crucial to the linguistic encoding of comparatives, viz. deranking and identity deletion. From a functional point of view, these two procedures may be looked upon as each other's opposites. Formally, however, the two procedures show a great deal of correspondence. Both procedures allow for a three-way variation; moreover, the three variants of both procedures exhibit striking parallels as to their conditionality. Lastly, we have seen that the directionality of application is in both cases connected with basic word-order type.

14

Optimal and Non-optimal Language Types

14.1 Introduction

With the discussion of the two grammatical procedures in chapter 13 we have concluded the specification of the various levels of structure and the various rule types which we assume to be needed in the description of the linguistic encoding of comparison in natural languages. Briefly summarizing our position, we can say that we have postulated a general model of linguistic description, in which a construction type is taken to be defined by three levels of structure, viz. the CS, the US and the SS. We have assumed that there is a universally valid CS of comparison of the type defined in section 11.4. In order to achieve the mapping of this CS of comparison onto the language system, we have postulated a set of three different cognitive strategies (see section 12.3), which result in three basic types of possible underlying structures for comparatives in natural languages. The mapping of these underlying structures onto the surface forms of comparatives is claimed to be effectuated by the operation of two crucially relevant grammatical procedures, viz. deranking and identity deletion (see section 13.3 and 13.4). Both of these grammatical procedures allow for a three-way variation in their application across natural languages.

Thus, in our analysis, the variation in surface manifestation of comparatives across languages is thought to result from the possibility that, starting from a universally valid CS, languages may vary in their application of cognitive strategies and grammatical procedures during the course of the mapping of this CS onto the various surface forms of comparatives. However, even if one accepts the general plausibility of this approach, it will be noted immediately that the analysis presented so far predicts a number of possible surface structures which is much larger than the number of comparative types which are actually attested in the cross-linguistic data. Our analysis assumes that there are at least three basic types of underlying structures which are possible candidates for the starting point of the operation of deranking and identity deletion. Furthermore, both deranking and identity deletion allow for a cross-linguistic variation into three categories, so that, logically, there are nine possible linguistic types in the application of grammatical procedures to the underlying structures of comparatives. Coupled with the three basic types of underlying structures, this will amount to the prediction of *twenty-seven possible surface types of comparative constructions* across languages. In reality, of course, the empirical data show that the actual number of attested comparative types is far more limited; there are only five major surface types of comparatives in the sample, plus a few minor ones, such as Particle Comparatives and cases of Mixed Comparison. In other words, our model of linguistic description is, as it stands, much too unconstrained to account for the empirical data; clearly, if our model is going to work at all, some principle (or set of principles) should be found by which the number of combinatory possibilities can be drastically limited.

In order to achieve this limitation, I will propose *two general principles* which I take to be applicable in the linguistic encoding of comparison, and in the operation of linguistic systems in general. The first of these principles is meant to delimit the ways in which the various options in grammatical procedures may be combined. The second principle, which will be discussed in section 14.3, has to do with the limitation on the possible combinations of procedure-types and strategy-types.

14.2   The Principle of Procedural Dependency

I take it to be self-evident that every natural language will have to make a choice for both one of the options in identity deletion and one of the options in deranking. That is, every natural language system will contain some pairing of a particular deletion variant and a particular deranking variant; if languages select a different pairing of these two types of variants, they will be said to belong to different *procedure types*. Now, up to the present point in the discussion we have more or less tacitly assumed that identity deletion and deranking are two grammatical procedures which operate independently of one another; hence, given the three-way variation which both procedures permit, one might conclude that languages can be divided into nine different procedure types. In reality, however, the combinatory possibilities of procedural variants turn out to be limited by the fact that there is a certain degree of interdependency between the two procedures at hand. To be specific, possible pairings of procedural variants turn out to be empirically restricted by the following universal principle:

The Principle of Procedural Dependency:
If a language has a deranking procedure, it must also have a procedure of identity deletion.

An alternative and equivalent formulation of this principle might be: 'If a language has no procedure of identity deletion, it cannot have a procedure of deranking'. In other words, the principle is meant to state that, out of the four logically possible combinations presented in the table below, the second combination (viz. deranking and no identity deletion) is empirically excluded:

	Deranking	*Identity deletion*
	+	+
	+	−
	−	+
	−	−

It should be stressed here that the Principle of Procedural Dependency (PPD) must be viewed as the statement of *an empirically attested cross-linguistic fact*; in other words, the PPD has the status of an implicational universal of language. In my sample, I have found no counterexample to this principle; that is, my sample does not contain any language which has deranking, but not some form of identity deletion. Conversely, there are no languages in my sample which lack identity deletion but have nonetheless the possibility to derank predicates in temporal chains. I hope I can be absolved from the obligation to present the full cross-linguistic evidence by which this principle is confirmed in my sample; a complete presentation of the relevant facts would fill at least 50 pages of text. Therefore, I must ask the reader to accept without further argumentation that the PPD embodies a valid restriction on the structural possibilities of natural languages.

It is, of course, natural to ask why a restriction like the PPD should be imposed on natural language systems. I can only offer some highly tentative speculations here. For one thing, the concept of explanation in general is still very unclear in Universal Grammar, and, moreover, in this particular case there are several plausible perspectives from which such an explanation might be developed. One of the approaches one might pursue on this point is an explanation on the basis of functional considerations. As we suggested in section 13.2, the procedures of identity deletion and deranking have a different functional status, in that deranking is mainly a service to the hearer, whereas identity deletion is primarily aimed at minimalizing the efforts of the speaker. Now, if we accept this suggestion, we can see that the pairing which is excluded by the PPD (viz. the pairing of deranking and no identity deletion) is the combination which puts all the efforts required for unproblematic communication on the shoulders of the speaker; in this pairing, the speaker has to make the effort of deranking predicates in temporal chains, but he is not compensated for this by a permission to omit redundant lexical material. In other words, the pairing which is excluded by the PPD demands maximal effort from the speaker while giving him nothing in return; and this 'unfairness' to the speaker may be the reason why natural languages try to avoid this particular pairing. It can be noted that in other possible pairings, which are permitted by the PPD, the efforts of communication are distributed more evenly over speaker and hearer. Thus, for instance, in the first pairing listed in the table the speaker must make the effort of deranking, but he is 'rewarded' for this by the permission to leave out redundant material. In the fourth pairing listed, speaker and hearer also strike an equal bargain: the speaker does not have to go through the trouble of deranking, but the hearer does not have to make the effort of recovering omitted material.

It goes without saying that such an explanation of the PPD in functional terms is at present nothing more than a speculative sketch. First of all, it will be necessary to support it by independent psycho-linguistic data. Furthermore, it should be observed that, even as it stands, the analysis outlined above leaves a number of questions unanswered. Thus, one may well ask why the third alternative in the table (viz. the pairing of no deranking and identity deletion) is not excluded as well, since in this pairing all the effort of communication is unloaded on the hearer. Now, we will see in the following sections that this particular pairing may indeed be viewed as less 'optimal' (in a sense to be defined below) than the other two pairings which are permitted by the PPD. However, even if we grant this, our analysis does not provide a principled account of the apparent fact that placing the whole burden of communication on the speaker will lead to the exclusion of the type in question, whereas placing that burden exclusively on the hearer is a permitted, albeit not optimal, possibility.

Alternative explanations of the PPD may seek the reason of its existence in considerations of a formal–structural nature. For example, one might argue that deranking is a procedure which has as its formal effect that a predicate gets turned into a non-finite, or at least morpho-logically impoverished, form. Now, there are indications that a minimal prerequisite for the transformation of a finite verb into a non-finite form is that the subject of the finite form can be deleted under identity. A clear example of a case in which the loss of a subject gradually leads to the non-finite status of a predicate is the serialization construction, which we discussed in section 8.2. We may also point to cases of Equi-NP-Deletion in Dutch and other languages; as can be seen from the examples in *(1)*, the complement of verbs like *willen* 'to want' in Dutch can be transformed into a non-finite form only if the subject in the complement clause is deleted under identity with the subject of the main verb:

(1)   DUTCH:
a.   *Ik wil   dat jij   danst*
     I   want that you dance-PRES. IND. 2SG
     '*lit.* I want that you dance: I want you to dance'

b. * *Ik wil   dat ik dans*
     I   want that I   dance-PRES. IND. 1SG
     '*lit.* I want that I dance'

c.   *Ik wil   dansen*
     I   want dance-INF
     'I want to dance'

In short, it may be true that, if a language is to have the possibility to derank predicates, it should at least have the minimal option in identity deletion, viz. S-Deletion. This is, of course, exactly what is stated by the PPD. Again, however, it should be admitted that there are several points in this analysis which are in need of independent confirmation, so that at present this analysis can be nothing more than a suggestion for future research.

Whatever the explanation for the existence of the PPD may be, we may conclude nonetheless that it formulates a valid linguistic universal, and that it can be employed to reduce the number of logically possible pairings of procedural options. Of the nine possible pairings listed below, the two pairings which have been boxed are excluded by the PPD, since they combine the option of no identity deletion (ID) with one of the two possible deranking options:

TOTAL – ABSOLUTE	LIMITED – ABSOLUTE	NO ID – ABSOLUTE
TOTAL – CONDITIONAL	LIMITED – CONDITIONAL	NO ID – CONDITIONAL
TOTAL – BALANCING	LIMITED – BALANCING	NO ID – BALANCING

14.3   The Principle of Optimal Harmony

In addition to the Principle of Procedural Dependency, which constitutes a restriction on the possible pairings of procedural variants, I propose a second general principle, which has the effect of *limiting the possible pairings of strategy types and procedure types*. This principle can, in its most general form, be formulated as follows:

The Principle of Optimal Harmony:
When confronted with a number of options in the choice of cognitive strategies, a natural language will select that strategy which leads to a US to which the grammatical procedures available to that language can be applied in an optimal fashion.

In other words, the Principle of Optimal Harmony (POH) claims that, in their combination of options for cognitive strategies and grammatical procedures, natural languages will tend to make such choices that their options with respect to these two rule types are maximally attuned to one another. Behind this principle lies the idea that systems in general will strive for the most economical and effective use of the means which they happen to have at their disposal; to state the matter somewhat informally, one might say that the POH is based upon the commonsense experience that there is no sense in acquiring a particular tool if you cannot find a way to use it. In linguistics, this general idea boils down to the choice of a particular cognitive strategy (and hence, the choice for a particular US) in the encoding of a given construction type. Since cognitive strategies and grammatical procedures are types of rules which, in principle, operate independently of each other, the level of underlying structure, where cognition and grammar meet, is constantly under pressure from two different sides. As I take it, the POH is the way in which natural language systems try to reconcile the demands made upon the system by both cognition and grammar; it is a principle by which possible conflicts in these demands are 'ironed out', in that it marks some logically possible pairings of strategies and procedural variants as *more optimal*, and hence more likely to be chosen, than others. Thus, the main function of the POH lies in the fact that it allows language systems to make optimal use of available means, and that it therefore reduces the efforts which the system has to make in order to generate its output.

As an illustration of the way in which the POH is supposed to operate in the linguistic encoding of comparatives, let us consider the way in which this principle may be used to limit the combinatory possibilities of cognitive strategies with the options for *identity deletion*. Since we have postulated three different cognitive strategies and three different options for identity deletion, the number of logically possible combinations of strategy types and deletion types amounts to nine. However, it can be shown that, by involving the POH, we can reduce this number of combinations to three, in that an optimal pairing of each cognitive strategy with one option in identity deletion can be established.

First, let us assume that a certain language L has the grammatical possibility of *total identity deletion*; that is, language L can delete not only identical subjects, but also identical predicates from underlying strings. Now, according to the POH, it is optimal for such a language to select a US for its comparative in which such an identity of predicates is indeed available; if language L were to choose a US in which the two predicates are non-identical, the language would be prevented from making optimal use of the grammatical possibilities which it possesses. Thus, assuming that the POH defines a viable line of conduct, we can state that a language with total identity deletion will tend to select the *Ordered Strategy*, rather than the Independent Strategy or the Relative Strategy, as its cognitive strategy for the mapping of the CS of comparison onto its linguistic system. As is shown by the formula in section 12.3, only the choice for the Ordered Strategy results in a US which contains identical predicates,[1] and which can therefore be subjects to total identity deletion.

In the same vein, there is also an optimal choice for those languages which can only delete identical subjects, but not identical predicates. For these languages, the optimal choice is a US in which the two propositions have the same subject; hence, languages which have only the syntactic option of S-Deletion will, according to the POH, prefer to select the *Relative Strategy*, since it is only this strategy which results in a US in which the requirement of identical subjects is met.

Finally, we can ask ourselves what the optimal choice of strategy may be for a language in which *no identity deletion* at all is possible. One might argue here that, since these languages do not have any deletion procedure at all, they do not impose any requirement of optimalization on the form of their underlying structures, and that they should therefore be free to select any cognitive strategy they like. However, it seems also plausible to assume that, in this case, the *Independent Strategy* is the option which, from the point of view of the POH, must be rated as the most optimal. Since languages with no identity deletion do not impose any identity requirements on their underlying structures, it is perfectly feasible for them to select a US in which both the subjects and the predicates in the two propositions are non-identical; if they were to choose another US, they could be expected to have some type of string-reducing procedure, which in fact they do not have. For this reason, I will assume that the most optimal or 'normal' choice of US for a language with no identity deletion is the US which is the result of the application of the Independent Strategy, since it is only this US which contains propositions with both non-identical subjects and non-identical predicates. As will be shown below, however, the choice of a different US for languages with no identity deletion is not completely excluded.

The Principle of Optimal Harmony can also be invoked in the establishment of optimal and non-optimal combinations between the various options of strategy choice and the options which languages have in *deranking*. First, let us consider the case of those languages in which predicates in chaining structures may undergo *absolute deranking*. In such languages, deranking of predicates in chains may take place regardless of the identity or non-identity of the subjects in the chain; as such, these languages are opposed to languages in which deranking may take place only under identity of subjects, and to languages in which deranking cannot take place at all. In other words, the unique feature of languages with absolute deranking is that they may employ the grammatical procedure of deranking in cases in which the subjects of the propositions in the US are non-identical. Given the POH, we may therefore expect that such languages will select a US in which this condition of non-identity of subjects is met. As a result, the possibility of having absolute deranking is optimally paired with the selection of either the *Independent Strategy* or the *Ordered Strategy*, since in these cases a US will be selected which has non-identical subjects. A choice for the Relative Strategy would be non-optimal for these languages, since this particular strategy leads to underlying structures in which the subjects of the propositions in the chain are identical.

Quite the opposite requirement on underlying structures can be predicted for languages in which predicates can be deranked only under identity of subjects. For languages with this *conditional deranking*, the US produced by the *Relative Strategy* is the obvious choice, since this is the only US which meets the demands made by the type of deranking available to these languages. Finally, for *balancing* languages (i.e., languages in which no deranking can take place at all), one might argue that they impose no conditions whatsoever on the selection of a US. Since these languages do not derank anyway, there appears to be no optimal selection of strategy to be derived for them by invoking the Principle of Optimal Harmony.

To sum up this section, we can state that the application of the POH to the problem of the pairing of strategy types and procedure types leads to two sets of tendencies. Concerning the procedure of identity deletion, we can state that

(a) languages with *total identity deletion* will tend to choose the Ordered Strategy in its mapping of the CS of comparison;
(b) languages with *limited identity deletion* will tend to choose the Relative Strategy; and
(c) languages with *no identity deletion* will tend to choose the Independent Strategy.

Application of the POH to the problem of strategy choice in relation to the options in deranking leads to the formulation of the following set of tendencies:

(a) languages with *absolute deranking* will tend to select either the Independent Strategy or the Ordered Strategy, and will tend to avoid the Relative Strategy in their mapping of the CS of comparison;
(b) languages with *conditional deranking* will tend to select the Relative Strategy; and
(c) *balancing* languages are, at least in principle, free to select any of the available cognitive strategies in their mapping of the CS of comparison onto their linguistic systems.

14.4   Optimal and non-optimal procedure types

In the preceding section, we have seen how the application of the Principle of Optimal Harmony enables us to cut down on the number of logically possible combinations of strategy types and the options for a particular variant of either of the two grammatical procedures which we assume to be relevant in the grammatical treatment of comparatives. We have summarized our results on this point by formulating two sets of tendencies, which state the preferred pairings of a particular strategy with the various options in identity deletion and deranking. Now we will proceed to combine these two sets of tendencies, and, as a result, we will establish a prediction as to what the optimal and non-optimal language types are for the linguistic encoding of comparative constructions.

Earlier on we stated that, since both identity deletion and deranking allow a three-way variation, the number of logically possible pairings of these procedural options amounts to nine. In other words, there are nine logically possible language types with regard to the syntactic derivation of comparative constructions across natural languages. However, as we saw in section 14.2, two of these nine possible language types (namely, those in which the option of no identity deletion is paired with the option of some variant of deranking) are excluded by the Principle of Procedural Dependency. Now, in what follows I will show that, by combining the requirements on strategy choice which the POH predicts for the various options in identity deletion and deranking, we can arrive at a further reduction of the seven remaining possible language types. In particular, it can be demonstrated that some of these pairings must be ruled out, on the grounds that the requirements which the POH imposes on them for the selection of a US are contradictory. On the other hand, we will also find that some of the logically possible pairings of procedural variants are optimal, in that these variants reinforce one another in the choice of one specific type of underlying structure.

One rather obvious example of a case in which the pairing of a deletion option with a deranking option leads to contradictory demands on the selection of a US is the following. Suppose that there were languages which have *limited* (i.e., subject-only) *identity deletion*, but which have also chosen the *absolute option in deranking*. For such languages the POH would predict, on the one hand, the selection of a US with identical subjects (thus optimalizing the possibilities of identity deletion in those languages), while on the other hand, the POH would require a US with different subjects (thus optimalizing the possibility of absolute deranking). Evidently, for such languages the POH would lead to contradictory results, since the two procedural variants selected here impose opposite and irreconcilable demands on the selection of an optimal US: one procedural option requires that the Relative Strategy be chosen, whereas the other procedural option demands that this Relative Strategy be avoided. For this reason, we may conclude that *the combination of limited identity deletion and absolute deranking is not an optimal pairing*, and hence we may predict that the languages in which this particular pairing has been chosen should be rated as a highly improbable, if not downright impossible, linguistic type.

A somewhat different kind of contradictoriness can be demonstrated for the logically possible language type in which a choice for *total identity deletion* would be combined with a choice for *conditional deranking*. The POH predicts that languages with total identity deletion will tend to choose a US with identical predicates; given our set of cognitive strategies, this will normally lead to the selection of the Ordered Strategy. On the other hand, the POH also predicts that a language with conditional deranking will opt for a US in which the subjects are identical, and hence the Relative Strategy should be the optimal choice for such a language. Now, if we combine these two requirements in a given language, we would arrive at an optimal choice for a US in which both the subjects and the predicates are identical. It will be clear that an underlying structure of this form will be ruled out immediately on semantic (or, if one prefers that, on pragmatic) grounds: it would amount to a US in which the same proposition appears twice in a sequence, and this would constitute a crass violation of the conversational maxims developed in Grice (1975). For this reason, it seems plausible to conclude that *the pairing of total identity deletion and conditional deranking will not result in an optimal selection of a US*, and hence we may again predict that this pairing will define an impossible language type.

Opposed to pairings which define improbable or even impossible language types, there are also combinations which lead to optimal results, in that both procedural variants lead to the same requirement on the choice of the US of the comparative construction. A clear case of such an optimal language type is constituted by those languages in which the options of *limited identity deletion* and *conditional deranking* have been combined. The POH requires for both of these procedural options that the US upon which they operate should have identical subjects. As a result, the Relative Strategy will be the optimal cognitive strategy for the mapping of the CS of comparison onto the syntactic systems of these languages. Thus, we may conclude that, given the correctness of the POH, *the pairing of limited identity deletion and conditional deranking defines a highly optimal linguistic type*, and hence we may expect that languages which possess this pairing will constitute a favoured category in the typology of comparatives.

Secondly, the combination of *total identity deletion and absolute deranking* can be predicted to be a favoured pairing, albeit for a more indirect reason. As we have seen, languages with total identity deletion are required by the POH to select a US with identical predicates. Given that, in underlying structures, subjects and predicates cannot both be identical, this requirement entails that the optimal US for a language with total identity deletion will have to have non-identical subjects. Now, the deranking option which also requires that the optimal US have non-identical subjects is the absolute variant; hence, *total identity deletion and absolute deranking are mutually reinforcing options* from the point of view of the POH. It will be clear that, for languages in which this pairing is present, the Ordered Strategy will be the most natural choice, since it is this cognitive strategy which produces underlying structures with identical predicates and non-identical subjects.

Thirdly, we must also rate the combination of *no identity deletion and balancing* as an optimal pairing of procedural variants. The reason for this is, quite simply, that for languages with no identity deletion no other pairing is available; the other two possible pairings are excluded by the

PPD (see section 14.2). As for the preferred cognitive strategy for balancing languages with no identity deletion, it will be recalled that the POH does not define an optimal strategy choice for the procedural option of balancing. However, we have also stated in section 14.3 that languages with no identity deletion must be assumed to have at least a slight preference for the Independent Strategy. As a result, we can assume that balancing languages which have no identity deletion will generally opt for a US produced by the Independent Strategy, although occasional instances for other strategies cannot be completely excluded for this language type.

Finally, we must discuss the two remaining possible pairings of procedural variants. In both of these cases, the option of *balancing* has been chosen, which is then combined with either the option of *total identity deletion* or the option of *limited identity deletion*. Now, as we have seen, the selection of a balancing option does not commit a language to the choice of a specific cognitive strategy. Since, however, the two deletion options with which the balancing option is paired in the language types at issue do define a favourite choice of cognitive strategy, we may expect that

(a) balancing languages with total identity deletion will tend to select the Ordered Strategy; and
(b) balancing languages with limited identity deletion will tend to select the Relative Strategy for their linguistic mapping of the CS of comparison.

Furthermore, we may state that these two pairings cannot be considered to be 'optimal'; the two options in these pairings do not reinforce one another, due to the fact that one of them is essentially neutral with respect to strategy choice. On the other hand, we must also remark that there is nothing in these pairings which leads to contradictoriness. Therefore, we will predict that these two pairings define language types for comparative-type choice which are *definitely possible, though not optimal*.

In summary, the application of our two restrictive principles (the PPD and the POH) to the nine logically possible pairings of procedural variants enables us to reduce this number to *a set of five (optimal or non-optimal) language types*. To each of these language types, a preferred cognitive mapping strategy (and hence a preferred US for its comparative) can be attributed, on the basis of the requirements made of that language type by the Principle of Optimal Harmony. Charting our predictions for the nine logically possible language types, we thus arrive at the following table:

Identity deletion	Deranking	Rating	Preferred strategy
Total	Absolute	Optimal	Ordered
Total	Conditional	Out by POH	–
Total	Balancing	Possible	Ordered
Limited	Absolute	Out by POH	–
Limited	Conditional	Optimal	Relative
Limited	Balancing	Possible	Relative
No	Absolute	Out by PPD	–
No	Conditional	Out by PPD	–
No	Balancing	Optimal	Independent (but maybe also others)

Surveying this list of permissible and excluded language types from a somewhat different perspective, we may describe the situation as follows. It appears that the optimal language types are those in which both procedural variants in the pairing are at the same level of 'extremism'. Thus, if a language does not have any deranking, it will tend to have no identity deletion, and vice versa. Opposed to this, we find that languages which have the most 'far-reaching' form of deranking (viz. absolute deranking) will tend to have the most extreme form of identity deletion as well. (It will be recalled that absolute deranking and total identity deletion properly include conditional deranking and limited identity deletion, respectively.) Lastly, it appears that languages which have the more 'moderate' form of deranking (viz. conditional deranking) will tend to pair this option with the more limited form of identity deletion. The two possible but non-optimal language types are a result of the fact that, apparently, balancing languages are free to choose any option of identity deletion. We have accounted for this by stipulating that the option of balancing, unlike all other procedural options, is not subject to requirements which derive from the Principle of Optimal Harmony.

Apart from this tendency of *parallelism in the conditionality* of identity deletion and deranking, we can also detect a *parallelism in the directionality* of these two procedures in a given language. As we saw in section 4.4.3, a language with anterior absolute consecutive deranking normally has SOV word order. If that language has also total identity deletion, it will (according to section 13.4) normally have backward V-Deletion. In other words, for languages of this optimal procedure type *the procedures of identity deletion and deranking tend to affect the same clause* (in this case, the anterior clause) in the underlying chaining structure. A similar situation can be observed for languages with absolute posterior consecutive deranking; these languages have typically verb-initial word order, which (given that the language has total identity deletion) will lead to forward V-Deletion. As for languages with conditional deranking, we have seen that they typically have posterior deranking and SVO word order (see section 4.4.3). If such languages pair their deranking option with the equally 'moderate' option of limited identity deletion, the subject which is deleted will be the subject of the posterior clause (see section 13.4). Thus, one might say that, in the optimal cases, the two grammatical procedures involved form a 'syntactic conspiracy'; they tend to adapt themselves to one another, both in the measure of 'extremism' of their conditionality, and in the direction in which they operate.

15

An Explanatory Model of Comparative-type Choice

15.1   Introduction

In the foregoing chapters of part three we have progressively developed a model by which we should be able to predict the attested occurrence and non-occurrence of comparative types in natural languages. The basic features of this model can now be summarized as follows. We have assumed that there is a language-independent cognitive representation of the concept of comparison. Furthermore, we take it that this CS of comparison is mapped onto the formal systems of natural languages by means of a number of different strategies; these strategies have in common that their mapping result is in all cases an underlying linguistic structure which has the form of a temporal chain of propositions. The selection of a particular mapping strategy (and hence, the possible US for a comparative) is taken to be determined by the formal–syntactic language type to which the language in question belongs; we have developed a general Principle of Optimal Harmony, which is meant to define the optimal (and the impossible) pairings of strategy types and formal–syntactic types in languages. The notion of 'language type' (or 'procedure type') which we have used in this context is defined by the specific pairing of the options which a language selects for the two grammatical procedures which we take to be essential to the formal–syntactic treatment of chaining constructions (and, therefore, of comparatives), viz. identity deletion and deranking. As it turns out, the pairing of options in these two procedures is in itself not entirely free; it is restricted by the general Principle of Procedural Dependency. The application of the two general principles mentioned above leads to a limited set of three optimal language types and two possible but non-optimal language types; each of these language types is associated with a preferred mapping strategy, and hence with a preferred underlying structure for comparative constructions. By applying the relevant grammatical procedures of the various language types to their preferred underlying structure, a range of different surface types of comparatives will be derived.

The model outlined above constitutes at present nothing more than a hypothetical framework. We should assess its empirical adequacy by checking whether the predictions which it makes conform to the facts found in the cross-linguistic data. As we have remarked before, these predictions concern two questions, viz. the question of whether the model correctly predicts all and only those types of comparatives which have been attested in the sample, and, secondly, the question of whether the new model can assign the correct set of languages to each of these types. To the extent that the new model can be shown to be successful in answering these two questions, it can be said that it constitutes at least a first approximation towards an explanation of comparative-type choice, in that it offers an account of the non-randomness involved in that choice.

15.2 The prediction of comparative-type occurrence

Since, in the end, the model outlined above leads to the derivation of a limited set of surface types for comparatives, the obvious way to assess the adequacy of this model is to check whether the set of comparative types which it generates is isomorphic to the set of comparative types which have been empirically attested. In other words, in order for our model to be adequate, it should be the case that it generates (i.e., predicts) all the types of comparatives established in chapter 2, and only those. In what follows, I will test the various predictions made by the model, by checking each of the language types permitted in the model for its corresponding comparative type (or types), and by establishing whether or not these predicted comparative types correspond to the 'real world' categories of comparatives found in the cross-linguistic data.

To start our investigation, let us consider the first of the three optimal language types established in section 14.4, viz. the set of languages which combine the options of *total identity deletion and absolute deranking*. Of the languages of this type, the first thing that can be noted is that their word order will be either SOV or VSO; SVO word order is excluded for these languages, since SVO-languages generally do not permit absolute deranking (see chapter 4). Furthermore, our model predicts that languages of this type will prefer the *Ordered Strategy* for their mapping of the CS of comparison. Accordingly, the preferred US for comparatives in languages of this type will be a sequence of propositions which has the form of one of the variants of US-2 (see section 12.3). For the moment, we will consider only the first two variants of this US, viz.

US 2.1   (*b* BIG)   &   (*a* BIG)
US 2.2   (*a* BIG)   &   (*b* BIG)

As will be recalled, the unmarked, or 'natural', temporal interpretation of a US of this kind is a consecutive interpretation.

Now, in the syntactic derivation of comparative constructions in the languages of this type, the following situation obtains. It can be observed that, depending on the word order of the relevant languages, it is either *US-2.1* or *US-2.2* which is preferred as the US of the comparative construction. To be specific, if a language of this type has SOV order, that language will select *US-2.1*, i.e., the variant in which the standard object is mentioned first in the underlying sequence. If a language of this type has VSO order, it will select *US-2.2*, the variant in which the comparee object is contained in the first proposition. In other words, VSO-languages which select the Ordered Strategy apparently take the comparee object as the starting point in the scanning strategy, and 'move' from there to the standard object; in contrast to this, SOV-languages which select the Ordered Strategy start their scanning with the standard object, moving from there to the comparee object. The situation can be illustrated by the following diagram:

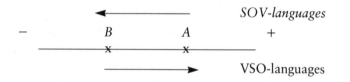

A putative explanation of this apparent opposition in scanning direction-ality might run as follows. It can be assumed that languages of this type (and, as a matter of fact, languages in general) will prefer to encode their comparatives in such a form that *the comparee NP can be the subject of the main verb* (c.q. one of the main verbs) in the construction. Since the comparee NP refers to the topic of the comparison, and since topics and subjects have the tendency to coincide in the syntax of natural languages,[1] construction of the comparee NP as a main subject seems to be the desirable thing to do. For languages with some kind of deranking procedure, this requirement on the surface structure of comparative entails that the underlying predicate which has the comparee NP as its subject cannot be the predicate which undergoes deranking; if it were, the comparee NP would never be able to turn up as a main subject in the SS. From this it follows that, for languages with some kind of deranking, it must be the other predicate in the underlying chain which has to undergo deranking; and, for languages which select the Ordered Strategy, this means that *the predicate which is going to be deranked has to be the predicate which has the standard NP as its subject.*

Given this, it will be clear that the languages under discussion here (viz. the languages with absolute consecutive deranking) are under the obligation to place the proposition which contains the standard NP in such a position in the US that the deranking procedure can actually operate on the predicate of that proposition. It is at this point that the difference between SOV-languages and VSO-languages becomes crucial. As we saw in chapter 4, absolute consecutive deranking in SOV-languages is anterior, that is, it affects the first predicates in a chain. As a result, for SOV-languages with absolute deranking the comparative construction needs a US in which the predicate that is going to be deranked (i.e., the predicate which has the standard NP as its subject) is placed in anterior position. The US in which this requirement is met is *US-2.1.* Opposed to this, VSO-languages with absolute consecutive deranking apply their deranking procedure to posterior predicates in temporal chains. Hence, for such languages the comparative construction requires a US in which the predicate to be deranked (i.e., the predicate which has the standard NP as its subject) occupies the second position in the chain. A US which meets this requirement is *US-2.2.*

It will be recalled, incidentally, that we have described both *US-2.1* and *US-2.2* as the product of one scanning strategy, which apparently allows for two opposite directionalities. Thus, if we accept the above explanation, we are automatically committed to the view that the directionality of scanning in a language with absolute deranking must be made dependent on the particular way in which the deranking procedure operates in that language. For example, since deranking SOV-languages require that the deranked predicate be the first predicate in the US, such languages must select a scanning strategy which ensures that the proposition which contains the standard NP is 'read off' first. The general idea that, in natural languages, strategy choice and procedural options must be attuned to each other was formulated in the previous chapter as the Principle of Optimal Harmony. Hence, it would be possible to conceive of the opposite directionality in the US-formation of comparatives in deranking SOV-languages and deranking VSO-languages as one more manifestation of this general principle.

Whatever the merits of the above explanation may be, the empirical fact remains that deranking SOV-languages and deranking VSO-languages select a US in which the two propositions are ordered in opposite successions. Given this situation, the derivation of a surface comparative for the languages of the type at issue proceeds as follows. If the language has SOV word order, it will have *US-2.1* as the underlying structure of its comparative. On this structure, the procedures of identity deletion and deranking will operate. I take it to be self-evident that, to underlying structures such as *US-2.1*, absolute deranking must apply before identity deletion is applied; if we were to order these procedures the other way round, identity deletion would delete the predicate on which deranking should have operated, so that the application of deranking would be made impossible. Thus, to *US-2.1* we will first apply absolute deranking; since the language at issue has SOV order, it will be the anterior predicate which will be affected. Following absolute deranking, total identity deletion will delete the identical predicate in the deranked clause. The result is a *Separative Comparative*. The various steps in this derivation can be represented in the following (quite informal) way:

US 2.1   (*b* BIG)   &   (*a* BIG) ⟶

absolute anterior deranking

b BIG-*deranked a* BIG-*main verb* ⟶

total identity deletion

b-from *a* BIG-*main verb*

If the language in question happens to have VSO word order, the opposite directionality of deranking and identity deletion will be chosen. Such a language will select *US-2.2* as the US for its comparative. On this structure, absolute consecutive deranking will operate, which in this case will affect the posterior predicate. Following this, total identity deletion will again delete the identical predicate in the deranked clause. The final result will be an *Allative Comparative*.

In addition to the Separative and the Allative Comparative, our model predicts that the languages of the type at issue (i.e., the languages with absolute deranking and total identity deletion) will have the option of forming a third type of surface comparative, viz. the *Locative Comparative*. This possibility stems from the fact that, while the USs produced by the Ordered Strategy normally receive a consecutive interpretation, it is nonetheless possible to interpret these USs as simultaneous chains. Now, as we saw in chapter 4, directionality does not play a role in the procedure of simultaneous deranking; this may be viewed as the 'neutral' case between anterior and posterior consecutive deranking, in that no 'temporal distance' between the two events in the chain is implied and hence no 'movement' from one event to the other. Thus, when interpreted as an S-chain, *US-2.1* and *US-2.2* are syntactically interchangeable. For both of these USs, absolute simultaneous deranking will derank the predicate which has the standard NP *(b)* as its subject, thus ensuring that the predicate which has the comparee NP *(a)* as its subject can become the main verb of the surface comparative. After deranking, total identity deletion will delete the deranked predicate under identity with the main predicate, thus deriving a Locative Comparative. As for word order, the model predicts that both SOV-languages and VSO-languages may be members of this class, since the factor which differentiates between these two word orders (viz. the directionality of the procedure of absolute consecutive deranking) is taken to be neutralized in absolute simultaneous deranking.

As a last remark on the languages of the type under discussion we should call attention to the following point. Our model predicts that languages which combine absolute deranking with total identity deletion will normally select the Ordered Strategy, since it is this strategy which produces USs with identical predicates and non-identical subjects. Now, the large majority of the languages at issue here do indeed conform to this prediction: they choose one of the variants of *US-2* as the underlying structure of their comparative, and hence they come up with an adverbial comparative. However, if we look at the list of possible underlying structures in section 12.3, we can notice that, in addition to the USs produced by the Ordered Strategy, there is at least one other US-variant which may (at least marginally) be considered as a suitable US-choice for the languages in question. To be specific, one of the variants which is produced by the Independent Strategy, viz.

US 1.2   *(a* BIG)   &   *(b* not-BIG)

is a US in which the subjects are non-identical, while at the same time the predicates might, from a certain point of view, be called at least partially identical. Given this, we can predict that it is at least possible that some languages which pair absolute deranking with total identity deletion will select *US-1.2* instead of one of the variants of *US-2*. We can also predict, however, that such languages are likely to be a definite minority within their language type, because of the fact that, in *US-1.2*, there is no full, and hence no optimal, identity between the predicates in the US.

In my opinion, the case of Telugu, which we commented upon in section 2.5, represents an examples of such a 'minority'-strategy. Since Telugu is a language with both absolute deranking and total identity deletion, it is definitely a member of the language type which is relevant here. Now, as will be recalled, the Telugu comparative has a form which is superficially similar to that of an adverbial comparative, the difference being that its standard NP is not marked by a spatial marker, but by a participial form of the negative copula *ka-du* 'not to be':

(1)   TELUGU:

I -pandu	a	-pandu-kanna			tipi	-ga	undi
this-fruit	that-fruit	-not	be-PCP.	PRES	sweet-one		is

'This fruit is sweeter than that fruit'

Within our proposed model, the deviant comparative in Telugu can receive a straightforward explanation. We can say that Telugu represents the rare, but definitely permissible case where a language with absolute deranking and total identity deletion has opted for *US-1.2*, instead of the regular choice of a variant of *US-2*. The syntactic derivation of the Telugu comparative exactly parallels that of the 'normal' languages of this type. Since *US-1.2* is normally interpreted as a simultaneous temporal chain, directionality of the deranking procedure does not come into play here. Absolute deranking will downgrade the predicate which has the standard NP as its subject, that is, the predicate which contains the negation. Following deranking, total identity deletion will delete that part of the deranked predicate which is identical to the predicate of the main verb, thus leaving behind a deranked form of the negative copula as a marker on the standard NP.

In conclusion, then, our model predicts that there will be a positive correlation between the option of an adverbial comparative and the possibility of combining the procedures of absolute deranking and total identity deletion, while allowing for a few isolated deviant cases such as the Telugu comparative. Having established this, we can now turn to the second language type with total identity deletion which is permitted by our model. In this type, *total identity deletion* has been paired with the option of *balancing*.

Regarding this second, non-optimal, language type, the first thing to note is that our model predicts that there will be *no preferred word order* here. The reason for this is that the choice of a balancing option is essentially independent of the word order of the language in question. Secondly, we have decided in section 14.4 that the languages of this type, like those of its optimal counterpart, will normally select the *Ordered Strategy*. Thus, the predicted range of underlying structures for the comparatives of the languages in this class consists of the variants of *US-2* presented in section 12.3. To all of these possible USs, the procedure of total identity deletion will apply, after the option of deranking one of the predicates in the chain has been foregone. In keeping with the general tendency noted above, total identity deletion will affect the predicate which has the standard NP as its subject; in this way, the comparee NP can turn up in surface structure as the subject of the main verb in the construction. Given this tendency, there is no need for us to consider those variants of *US-2* which differ from other variants only in the order in which the two predicates succeed one another. Hence, the relevant variants of *US-2* to which balancing and total identity deletion must be applied are the following three:

US 2.2   (*a* BIG)   &   (*b* BIG)
US 2.3   (*a* BIG-*x*)   &   (*b* BIG-*y*)
US 2.5   (*a* BIG-*x*)   &   (*b* not BIG-*x*)

Application of balancing and total identity deletion yields the following surface structures for the comparatives of the languages in this class:

SS 2.2   a big and B
SS 2.4   A big-*x* and B *y*
SS 2.5   A big-*x* and B not *x*

Given these surface structures, it will come as no surprise that I claim that the languages of the type which combine balancing and total identity deletion are those languages which have some kind of *Particle Comparative*. In chapter 9, and especially in section 9.4.3, I have argued that Particle Comparatives must be seen as cases of syntactization, a process which has as its necessary condition that the language in question possesses some form of Coordinate Ellipsis. Application of this string-reducing procedure may in itself be sufficient for the derivation of a structure to which syntactization can apply. However, it is often the case that, in addition to Coordination Ellipsis, the process of syntactization of a comparative construction will involve the incorporation of a negative element, or some form of relativization, or both. Now, I think that the various surface structures which have been derived from the variants of *US-2* by total identity deletion are just those types of structures which can, by means of the process mentioned above, be syntacticized into a Particle Comparative of some kind.

First, it is obvious that the SS which has been derived from *US-2.2*, viz. *SS-2.2*, is the kind of surface structure which is exhibited by those Particle Comparatives in which the comparative particle is identical to the elements *and, but* or *then/after that*. Thus, we claim that Javanese, Goajiro, Toba Batak, Ilocano, Basque and Bari form their (primary or secondary) comparatives by applying balancing and total identity deletion to *US-2.2*.

The second SS which results from the application of balancing and total identity deletion to a variant of *US-2*, viz. *US-2.4*, is a likely candidate for syntactization by means of relativization. For this to happen, we take it that the index on the deleted predicate *(y)* will be pronominalized, relativized and adverbialized into some locative or instrumental case; in other words, this index will be syntacticized into a pronominal adverbial item with the original meaning 'to/at/by which'. Languages in which this process seems to have taken place are Finnish, Russian and Albanian, and probably also French, Latin and Hungarian. For those languages in which the comparative particle has the meaning 'like', we will assume that the syntactization of the pronominal adverbial at issue has proceeded up to a point where the pronominal origin of the particle is no longer recognizable. Indications that there is some transition between a 'to-which'-particle and a 'like'-particle can be found in the data from Latin and Hungarian (see section 9.3).[2]

Thirdly, there are languages in which the comparative particle originates from a pronominal adverbial into which a negative element has been incorporated. Examples of languages in which such a 'to which not'-particle appears are Hungarian, and possibly also Dutch and English. For this type of Particle Comparative, we will assume that the grammatical procedures which are typical for all Particle languages (viz. balancing and total identity deletion) have applied to *US-2.5*. The SS which results from this application, viz. *SS-2.5*, then undergoes syntactization, in that the remaining index in the reduced clause is relativized into a pronominal adverbial item, while the residual negation in the reduced clause comes to be incorporated into that item.

By an analysis like the one given above, the occurrence of most of the attested types of Particle Comparatives can be accounted for. However, the reader will have noted that the analysis leaves out one attested category of Particle Comparatives, viz. those comparatives in which the comparative particle is a disjunctive element ('or') or a negative conjunction ('nor'). For this type of Particle Comparative (to be found in Gaelic, Latvian, Classical Greek and Gothic), we will claim a status which is similar to the position of the Telugu comparative within the class of adverbial comparatives. As was the case with languages which combine total identity deletion and absolute deranking, languages which combine balancing and total identity deletion will normally select the Ordered Strategy. There is, however, also a marginal possibility to select one of the variants of the Independent Strategy which meets the demands made by the language type at issue. The relevant US is *US-1.2*, which, by the application of total identity deletion and balancing, will have the following derivation:

US 1.2   (*a* BIG)   &   (*b* not BIG)   ——————————————→
SS 1.2   A big and B not

In our analysis, we will assume that *SS-1.2* will be syntacticized into a Particle Comparative, in that the conjunction *and* and the residual negative element melt together into a 'nor'-particle or an 'or'-particle.

In summary, our model predicts that there will be a positive correlation between the option of a Particle Comparative and the option of combining balancing and total identity deletion. In this way, our model describes the category of Particle Comparatives as a kind of 'intermediate' category between the 'optimal' categories of adverbial comparatives (which are correlated with the pairing of absolute deranking and total identity deletion) and conjoined comparatives (which, as we shall see shortly, correlate with the options of no identity deletion and no deranking). The (admittedly rather scanty) historical evidence which we have seems to suggest that most Particle languages are languages which used to belong to the first optimal type, but which gradually came to prefer the option of balancing to the option of deranking. Equivalently, one might say that, in the typical case, a language with a Particle Comparative is a language with total identity deletion, which, somewhere along the road, has lost the will to derank. As we noted in chapter 10, a considerable number of Particle languages have an adverbial comparative as their secondary option, and, in all the cases for which historical evidence is available, this adverbial comparative appears to be the elder of the two.

The two types of languages discussed so far are the most complex cases among the five language types listed in section 14.4; the predictions of comparative-type choice for the three remaining language types which our model allows can be dealt with relatively briefly.

First, let us consider the second optimal language type specified in the model, viz. the set of languages which combine the options of *limited identity deletion and conditional deranking*. For these languages, SVO word order is predicted, since the option of conditional deranking is restricted to languages of this word-order type. Furthermore, the model predicts that the languages of this type will preferably select the *Relative Strategy*, since the US produced by this strategy (viz. *US-3* in its several variants) is the only US available in which subjects are identical. Accordingly, we predict that the languages in the type under discussion will form their comparatives by deriving them from a US of one of the following forms:

US 3.1   (*a* BIG)   &   (*a* BEYOND *b*)
US 3.2   (*a* BEYOND *b*)   &   (*a* BIG)

As we stated in section 12.3, it is natural for USs of this type to receive a simultaneous interpretation. Therefore, we will expect that the procedure of conditional deranking applied to these USs will be the procedure which the language employs to derank its S-chains. A consecutive interpretation of these USs is not entirely excluded, but must definitely be rated as a secondary possibility here.

To these two variants of *US-3*, limited identity deletion (i.e., the deletion of a subject under identity) and conditional deranking will apply. Since there is no intrinsic ordering between the deletion of a subject and the deranking of a predicate,[3] we are, in principle, free to choose either ordering of application of these procedures; for the sake of illustration, I will adopt here the ordering in which limited identity deletion precedes the application of the deranking procedure. Furthermore, we must note that, in principle, the deletion of the subject might affect the first subject as well as the second subject in the chain, since the comparee NP will turn up in the SS as a main subject in any case, no matter what the directionality of the deletion procedure is. However, as we have established in section 13.4, general principles dictate that deletion of subjects in SVO-languages applies forward, i.e., always affects the second occurrence of the identical subject. Since, as we have seen in chapter 4, the deranking procedure in SVO-languages always affects the second predicate in the chain, we can conclude that the combined efforts of limited identity deletion and conditional deranking will be directed at the rightmost clause in the various versions of *US-3*.

Once we have made these decisions, it is fairly easy to sketch the syntactic derivation which leads to surface comparatives for the languages of this type. For those languages which select *US-3.1* as their starting point, the syntactic derivation outlined below leads to an *Exceed-1 Comparative*:

(*a* BIG) & (*a* BEYOND *b*) ————————————————→
                                 limited identity deletion

(*a* BIG) & (BEYOND *b*) ————————————————→
                                 conditional deranking

A big exceed-*deranked* B

If *US-3.2* is selected, the derivation will run along the following lines, eventually resulting in an *Exceed-2 Comparative*:

(*a* BEYOND *b*) & (*a* BIG) ————————————————→
                                 limited identity deletion

(*a* BEYOND *b*) & (BIG) ————————————————→
                                 conditional deranking

A exceeds B big-*deranked*

In short, our model predicts that there will be a strong positive correlation between the option of (some variant of) the Exceed Comparative and the possibility of combining limited identity deletion and conditional deranking in natural languages.

In addition to the second optimal language type discussed above, our model also allows for a non-optimal type of languages with limited identity deletion. In this latter type, *the option of limited identity deletion is coupled with the option of balancing*. For languages of this type our model will not specify a preferred word order, since the option of balancing is not restricted to languages of a particular word-order type. What our model does specify, however, is that languages of this type will select the *Relative Strategy*, and, as a consequence, some variant of *US-3* as the input of the syntactic derivation of their comparative constructions.

Given that languages of this type will delete the second subject in *US-3*, but will leave the second predicate balanced, the resulting surface structures will be the following:

A big-*main verb*   (and)   exceed-*main verb* B
A exceed-*main verb* B   (and)   big-*main verb*

It will be clear that the surface structures derived in this way are those which are exhibited by the so-called *Mixed Comparatives* which we discussed in section 2.5; we have seen there that languages like Acholi and Temne possess a (primary or secondary) comparative in which features of Conjoined Comparatives and Exceed Comparatives have been brought together. Cp.:

(2)   ACHOLI:
       Gwok mera dit ki   kato   meri
       dog   my   big and exceed your
       'My dog is bigger than yours'

In short, our model predicts a positive correlation between *the option of a Mixed Comparative (of the type exhibited by Acholi and Temne) and the possibility of combining limited identity deletion and balancing*. Thus, our model characterizes this type of Mixed Comparatives as being an intermediate category between the two optimal categories of Exceed Comparatives and Conjoined Comparatives. In the same way as Particle languages, languages with a Mixed Comparative can be rated as languages which have some form of identity deletion, but which have lost (or never have had) the ability to derank predicates in chaining constructions.

Finally, we arrive at the fifth language type which our model allows. The languages which belong to this set have a minimum of structure-reducing procedures, in that they have *neither deranking nor identity deletion*. For these languages, the model stipulates that there will be no preferred word order, due to the choice of the balancing option. Furthermore, we have argued in section 14.4 that the optimal strategy choice for languages of this type will be the *Independent Strategy*, and that therefore the favoured US for the comparative in these languages will be one of the variants of *US-1*, viz.

US 1.1   (*a* BIG)   &   (*b* SMALL)
US 1.2   (*a* BIG)   &   (*b* not BIG)

Since neither of the two relevant grammatical procedures will operate on these underlying chains, the surface result for the comparative in this language type will typically be a *Conjoined Comparative*, either in its antonymous variant (from *US-1.1*) or in its polar variant (from *US-1.2*). In short, our model predicts a positive correlation between the option of a Conjoined Comparative and the option of combining balancing with no identity deletion.

In this context it should be recalled that, although the Independent Strategy is preferred in this language type, other strategy choices are not completely excluded here. We can find occasional instances of comparatives where, apparently, a language with minimal structure-reducing procedures has opted for a different strategy. Clear examples of such a case are Fulani and Motu; in one of the comparatives of these languages, balancing and no identity deletion have been applied to a US which is the product of the Relative Strategy. The comparatives at issue have the following forms:

(3)   FULANI:
Samba mawi , o   buro   Amadu
S.   is-big , he exceeds A.
'Samba is bigger than Amadu'

(4)   MOTU:
Una na namo , ina herea-ia
this is good   that exceeds
'That is better than this'

It must be added, however, that examples like these from Motu and Fulani are very exceptional, and that the unmarked choice for minimally structure-reducing languages is a Conjoined Comparative of the polar or antonymous variety.

Summarizing the exposition in this chapter, we can say that we have argued for *the following new set of procedure-based universals of comparative-type choice:*

UNIVERSAL 1: *Languages with an adverbial comparative are languages with absolute deranking and total identity deletion.*

UNIVERSAL 2: *Languages with a Separative Comparative are languages with absolute anterior consecutive deranking and total identity deletion.*

UNIVERSAL 3: *Languages with an Allative Comparative are languages with absolute posterior consecutive deranking and total identity deletion.*

UNIVERSAL 4: *Languages with a Locative Comparative are languages with absolute simultaneous deranking and total identity deletion.*

UNIVERSAL 5: *Languages with an Exceed Comparative are languages with conditional deranking and limited identity deletion.*

UNIVERSAL 6: *Languages with a Conjoined Comparative, and the languages with a Mixed Comparative of the type encountered in Motu and Fulani, are languages with no identity deletion and no deranking.*

UNIVERSAL 7: *Languages with a Particle Comparative are languages with no deranking and total identity deletion.*

UNIVERSAL 8: *Languages with a Mixed Comparative of the type found in Acholi and Temne are languages with no deranking and limited identity deletion.*

If we look at our new model from the point of view of the prediction of the attested range of comparative types, we can conclude that it turns out to be adequate to a considerable degree. In our model, the range of possible comparative types in natural languages is conceived of as being a derivate of the possible combinations of identity deletion and deranking options. As the discussion in this section has shown, the range of comparative types predicted by our model matches exactly the range of comparative types established in the empirical investigation in chapter 2. In short, our model can be shown to fulfil the 'all-and-only'-requirement for the types of comparative choice: it predicts correctly that the types which are empirically attested are all possible options of comparative-type choice, and it does not predict any comparative type which is not attested in the data. Furthermore, our model accounts for the word-order preferences shown by some types of comparatives, in that it traces these preferences to the procedure types upon which these comparatives are assumed to be modelled.

It should be remarked here that, in its prediction of the range of comparative types, the model developed in this section is superior to a model which is based on a correlation of comparative types with deranking options alone. Unlike a model which takes deranking options to be the sole basis of predicting comparative types, the new model, which bases itself on the possible pairings of two procedural options, has a satisfying explanation for the existence of Particle Comparatives. Moreover, the new model is able to explain the occurrence of Mixed Comparatives and the Telugu comparative, cases which must appear as mere oddities in a model in which deranking is the only predictive factor.

15.3   The prediction of language distributions

In this section, we will consider the second general explanatory question, which regards the distribution of the various attested comparative types over the languages in the sample. Since the basic feature of our model is the claim that choice of comparative type is predictable from the procedure type to which a language belongs, we will have to check whether all the languages with a comparative of type X have the pairing of deranking and deletion options which the model predicts for them. Now, for the various options which languages select in the procedure of deranking, the chapters in part two have shown that, with only a small number of exceptions, the following correlations hold:

(a) languages with an adverbial comparative are languages with absolute deranking;

(b) languages with an Exceed Comparative are languages with conditional deranking;

(c) languages with a derived-case comparative (i.e., a Conjoined Comparative or a Particle Comparative) are languages which have chosen the option of balancing.

Since these correlations are exactly those which are predicted by the new model, we can conclude that this model is adequate as far as one of the factors which we claim to be predictive is concerned.

With respect to the other grammatical procedure which we claim to be a predictive factor in comparative-type choice, matters are considerably less clear. The new model predicts that, in the correlation of comparative types and types of identity deletion, the following three statements can be empirically confirmed:

(a) languages with either an adverbial comparative or a Particle Comparative are languages with total identity deletion;

(b) languages with an Exceed Comparative (including Mixed Comparatives of the Acholi type) are languages with limited identity deletion;

(c) languages with a Conjoined Comparative (including Mixed cases of the Fulani type) are languages with no identity deletion.

If we start out to check these predictions against the linguistic data, we will soon be confronted with the unfortunate fact that the sources on the languages in our sample usually fail to provide a clear statement of the conditions under which string-reduction is permitted or excluded. Identity deletion is a phenomenon which is very marginal to the average grammarian, even more so than the phenomenon of deranking; while deranking, if it takes place, gives rise to a distinct, new construction type, identity deletion will often escape the attention of grammarians, since its application does not, as a rule, create a specific construction type of its own. A further handicap is that it is often left unclear whether an example of a sentence in which a subject has been omitted is a case of genuine identity deletion or a case of Pro-Drop. That is, it is often impossible to decide from the presented data whether a given language can omit just any non-stressed subject, or only subjects which are bound by an identity condition. Thus, at the present state of our knowledge, we have no other choice than to admit that our predicted correlations between the options of identity deletion and the choice of comparative types are seriously underdetermined by the available linguistic data.

However, while we must concede that these predicted correlations are at present far from being confirmed, it must also be remarked that they do not seem to be seriously refuted by the available facts. In the limited set of languages for which I have been able to find explicit statements on the options of identity deletion, the facts appear to be in line with the tendencies contained in the above correlational statements. These facts (which are drawn from 42 languages, that is, almost 40 per cent of the sample) will be concisely enumerated below. For a large part, the relevant data stem from recent studies which deal explicitly with the phenomenon of ellipsis in coordinated structures; they are supplemented by data which I have gathered myself from grammatical descriptions which I have consulted.

Starting with those languages for which the possibility of *total identity deletion* is predicted, we can say that the crucial criterion for the positive identification of such a language lies in its ability to omit predicates or verbs from chains, under identity with another predicate or verb in the structure. Thus, the possibility of total identity deletion in a language can be demonstrated, among other things, by showing that this language has the possibility of VP-Deletion in coordinate structures (as illustrated by the French sentence *(5)*), or the possibility to reduce the predicate in answers under identity with the predicate in corresponding questions (as illustrated by the Dutch example *(6)*), or the ability to apply Gapping (as illustrated by the Japanese example *(7)*):

(5)   FRENCH:
    Mon frère   joue le piano, et   ma soeur aussi
    my   brother plays the piano and my sister too
    'My brother plays the piano, and my sister does, too'

(6)   DUTCH:
    Heeft Jan opgebeld? Nee, Henk.
    Has J. phoned No H.
    'Did Jan call? No, Henk did'

(7)   JAPANESE:
    Sumie wa inu o   , Norio wa ki o   mita
    S.   TOP dog ACC N.   TOP tree ACC see-PAST
    'Sumie saw the dog and Norio the tree'

Now, if we look at the languages for which the new model predicts a possibility of total identity deletion, we can attest the following facts. For the languages with a Separative Comparative, the possibility to apply Gapping has been documented for Finnish and Korean (Koutsoudas, 1971), for Japanese (Ross, 1967), for Turkish (Hankamer, 1979), for Quechua (Pulte, 1971) and for Amharic (Cohen, 1936: 348). In the set of languages with an Allative Comparative, we find positive evidence for Gapping and other verb-reducing procedures in Jacaltec (Craig, 1977: 38), Breton (Wojcik, 1976) and Maasai (Tucker and Mpaayi, 1955: 106). In the class of languages with a Locative Comparative, there is positive evidence for Gapping in Tamil (Asher, 1982: 75) and Latvian (Koutsoudas, 1971), while VP-Deletion can be attested for Mapuche (de Augusta, 1903: 230) and predicate-ellipsis in answers can be shown to exist in Cebuano (Wolff, 1967: 23). The category for which some form of total identity deletion can be identified most extensively is that of the languages with a Particle Comparative; various forms of verb-ellipsis, including Gapping, can be shown to operate in Dutch (own data), French (own data), English (Ross, 1967), Latin (Kühner–Gerth, 1955), Classical Greek (Kühner–Stegmann, 1963), Nahuatl (Andrews, 1975), Albanian (Hetzer, 1978), Malagasy (Keenan, 1976b), Hungarian and Russian (Harries, 1978), Gaelic (Mallinson and Blake, 1981) and Javanese (Kiliaan, 1919: 349ff.). Finally, Koutsoudas (1971) states that in Telugu the deletion of verbs under identity is a definite possibility. To sum up, the predicted correlation between, on the one hand, the option of total identity deletion and, on the other hand, the choice for an adverbial comparative or a Particle Comparative can be shown to hold for at least 27 out of the 71 relevant languages in the sample. Moreover, there is hardly any available evidence which contradicts this correlation. The only possible counterexample I know of is Toba Batak, a VOS-language with a Particle Comparative, for which Koutsoudas (1971) claims that verb-reduction is impossible. Opposed to this, however, are statements by Van der Tuuk (1867: 329ff.) to the effect that, in Toba Batak, all kinds of elliptical processes are a common occurrence.

In the second statement presented above, a correlation is predicted between the selection of an Exceed Comparative and the option of limited identity deletion. Thus, in order to confirm the correlation, we should be able to demonstrate that languages with an Exceed Comparative lack the ability to delete verbs under identity (that is, for instance, they should not be able to apply Gapping), while at the same time permitting the deletion of one of a pair of identical subjects. In this case, again, the set of data which we have at our disposal is far from optimal; of the 20 languages at issue, there are only eight for which an explicit statement as to their deletion options can be found. It is remarkable, however, that all of these eight languages provide straightforward corroboration of the correlation at issue. Thus, for instance, Mallinson and Blake (1981: 218) state explicitly that Mandarin and Thai are languages which 'totally resist deletion of verbs'. As a result, the following example from Thai is ungrammatical:

(8) THAI:
   * *Somchaj top Mali lae? Damrong Atcha*
   S.　　　slap M.　and D.　　　A.
   'Somchaj slapped Mali and Damrong Atcha'

On the other hand, it is quite clear that deletion of identical subjects is common in both Thai and Mandarin. The following examples bear witness to this fact·

(9) THAI:
   Somchaj top Mali lae? khâ: Damrong
   S.　　　slap M.　and kill D.
   'Somchaj slapped Mali and killed Damrong'

(10) MANDARIN:
   Wo na　hwo-penn wai-peul kiu
   I　carry stove　　outside　go
   'I carried the stove outside'

Apart from Mandarin and Thai, a resistance to verb-reducing processes such as Gapping has been noted for Yoruba, Igbo and other Kwa languages (George, 1975). Koutsoudas (1971) claims that Wolof and Hausa do not have any procedure for the elimination of identical verbs; moreover, he states that Swahili, at least in some of its dialects, lacks the option of verb-ellipsis. Finally, my own data on Fulani (taken from Taylor, 1921, and Labouret, 1952) show that this language is also resistant to the deletion of verbs. However, there is in this language, at least in some of the dialects, also a ban on the deletion of identical subjects, a fact which in our model is brought into connection with the Mixed Comparative that can be attested as one of the options for Fulani. In summary, the correlation under discussion here is confirmed by eight out of 20 relevant languages in the sample, while no data are as yet available which refute the validity of this correlation.

Lastly, we must consider the third correlational statement, which claims that the choice of a Conjoined Comparative is tied up with the inability to reduce both subjects and verbs under identity. Concerning this particular correlation, I am sorry to say that it has less support in the available data than the foregoing two correlations. Part of the difficulty here is that, in general, the grammatical descriptions of the languages at issue are of a poor quality anyhow, and that they occupy themselves mostly with morphology, to the exclusion of syntax. Another point, which we touched upon above, is that it is often hard to decide whether a case of apparent ellipsis in these languages is governed by conditions of structural identity, or whether it is rather a case of 'contextually recoverable' ellipsis, such as Pro-Drop. Up to now, I have been able to find pertinent data in only six of the 20 languages involved here. Of these six languages, Kobon (Davies, 1981: 75) and Yavapai (Kendall, 1976: 148) are clear confirmations of the correlation under discussion. The same may be claimed for Hixkaryana (Derbyshire, 1979), considering such non-reduced verbal sequences as the following:

(11) HIXKARYANA:
    Mawu   wono   Waraka   horoto   xarha
    howler-monkey he-shot-it W.   , spider-monkey also
    wono   Waraka
    he-shot-it W.
    'Waraka shot a howler-monkey and a spider-monkey'

As for Mangarayi, Merlan (1982: 36) notes that verb-ellipsis may take place in only a limited number of contexts, especially those in which specific sentential adverbs like *wadij* 'also' or *galayjmingan* 'in turn' are involved. In this context, it should be recalled that Mangarayi has an Allative Comparative as its secondary option (see section 10.3.2). Much the same observations can be made with regard to the two Polynesian languages in the sample: Maori and Samoan both have at least a limited possibility of total identity deletion, and they are both languages in which an adverbial comparative (in this case, a Locative Comparative) is possible in addition to the primary Conjoined Comparative.

Surveying our examination of the predictions which our model makes on the correlations between comparative types and deletion types, we have to accept the fact that, for the present, these predictions are underdetermined, and hence not confirmed, by the available data. On the positive side, however, it must also be recognized that there is as yet no reason to reject these predictions off-hand. On the contrary, what evidence is available seems to indicate that these correlations stand a good chance of being shown to be empirically valid, once the range of pertinent data has been extended to a satisfactory size.

15.4   The prediction of double options

In the preceding two sections, we have examined the empirical validity of the central claim which is incorporated in our model of comparative-type choice; that is, we have checked to what extent the correlations which our model claims exist between comparative type and procedure type are borne out by the cross-linguistic data. There is, however, also a more 'indirect' or 'circumstantial' respect in which our model can be confronted with linguistic reality. Thus, it may be the case that some linguistic support for the over-all validity of the model can be derived from an examination of *the attested and non-attested combinations of primary and secondary comparative-type choices* in the languages of the sample. In the remainder of this chapter, we will comment briefly on this phenomenon of 'double options' in comparative-type choice.

Given that we can attest six different types of comparatives in the sample, simple arithmetics tells us that there are 15 logically possible pairings into double options of comparative-type choice. However, the data on the attested combinations show that these 15 possible pairings are not distributed evenly over the languages with a double option for comparatives: there are certain pairings which are highly favoured, whereas others do not seem to occur at all. A classification of the cases of double options presents the following picture:

Separative–Particle:	*8 languages* (Albanian, Basque, French, Latin, Classical Greek, French, (Old) English, Russian)
Conjoined–Locative:	*7 languages* (Banda, Mapuche, Dakota, Maori, Gumbainggir, Samoan, Swahili)
Conjoined– Exceed:	*4 languages* (Banda, Sika, Swahili, Kirundi)
Separative–Locative:	*3 languages* (Basque, Nama, Tamil)
Allative–Locative:	*2 languages* (Tamil, Mandinka)
Conjoined–Allative:	*2 languages* (Nuer, Mangarayi)
Exceed–Allative:	*2 languages* (Maasai, Tamazight)
Exceed–Separative:	*2 languages* (Quechua, Aymara)
Exceed–Particle:	*2 languages* (Bari, Sranan)
Locative–Particle:	*2 languages* (Hungarian, Latvian)
Conjoined–Particle:	*2 languages* (Ilocano, Nahuatl)
Allative–Particle:	*0 languages*
Conjoined–Separative:	*0 languages*
Separative–Allative:	*0 languages*
Exceed–Locative:	*0 languages*

Given this distribution, it seems appropriate to assume that the phenomenon of double comparative-type choice is not a case of random pairing; it can be seen, for instance, that the first three pairs in the list, when taken together, cover more than half of the attested cases of double options. Therefore, we should be able to find a principled way to predict the apparent frequency of occurrence of certain combinations and the apparent exclusion of others. In my opinion, the model presented in this chapter can offer a framework for such predictions, provided that we are willing to accept some specific assumptions about the process of historical shift in the selection of comparative types.

First of all, we can note that, for at least three of the pairs listed, the model will immediately predict the fact that they are possible or excluded. For one thing, within our model it is perfectly natural to predict that the pairing *Separative–Allative* will be an improbable, if not impossible, option. As we have seen, these two comparative types presuppose mapping strategies which are diametrically opposed in directionality of scanning. Moreover, since this opposition in scanning directionality is apparently tied up with the opposition between SOV and VSO word order, a combination of these two comparative types would assume that a language can have these two diametrically opposed word orders at the same time. However, as is shown in the literature on word-order change and word-order variation (see, among others, Steele, 1978), a combination of SOV order and VSO order in one single language is highly untypical.

The fact that the pairing *Separative–Locative* and *Allative–Locative* are empirically attestable has also a straightforward explanation in our model. These combinations have as their only presupposition that languages can be undecided as to whether the US which they have selected for their comparative should be temporally interpreted as a consecutive or as a simultaneous chain; the relative indeterminacy of this temporal interpretation of underlying structures has been commented upon in section 12.2 and section 12.3. In any case, within these pairings no changes in the choice of strategy type or procedure type are implied.

As regards the remaining 12 possible pairings of comparative types, matters are considerably less straightforward. In order for our model to be able to account for at least some of these pairings, it will be necessary to adopt some specific views on the phenomenon of double comparative choice, which have their basis in some specific assumptions about *diachronic developments* in various classes of languages. To be specific, we will start from the idea that languages may undergo gradual shifts in the types of syntactic procedures which they possess, and that (at least some cases of) double options in comparative-type choice are a reflection of the fact that, in various groups of languages, this process of procedure-type shift has not yet been completed.

Given this basic conception of the phenomenon of double options, I propose the following analysis. As we saw in section 14.4, the five procedure types specified by our model can be rated according to their 'extremism' in the application or non-application of potentially available procedural options. On one end of the scale, we can place the optimal language type in which both relevant procedures are applied to a maximum; these languages combine total identity deletion and absolute deranking, thus giving rise to an adverbial comparative. On the opposite end of the 'extremism'-scale, we can place the optimal language type in which no use whatsoever is made of deranking and identity deletion; such languages will typically select a Conjoined Comparative. Now, given these two diametrically opposed language types, I claim that at least some of the frequencies in the list of double comparative options can be accounted for if we assume that these two opposed language types form the two starting points from which a gradual change in procedure type (and hence, a change in comparative type) can be set in motion. To be specific, I will assume that there are *two diachronic changes* which may lead to the adoption of a secondary comparative, viz.

(a) *languages with a deranking procedure may start to lose that procedure; and*
(b) *languages which have no deranking procedure may start to acquire such a procedure.*

In short, we claim that (at least some) double options derive from a historical shift in either the 'minimal' or the 'maximal' language type, and that this shift crucially involves a change of option in the deranking procedure.

As an illustration of the way in which these assumed historical developments may be instrumental in the acquisition of a 'new' comparative type, let us consider the case of the 'maximal' language type. As stated, these languages pair total identity deletion with absolute deranking, and typically select the Ordered Strategy, thus providing the US for an adverbial comparative. Now, suppose that some of the languages in this set undergo the first of the diachronic processes mentioned above, by which they gradually come to replace their option of absolute deranking by the option of balancing. It will be noted that our model predicts that such a change in the deranking procedure will not force these languages to select a new type of identity deletion; the Principle of Procedural Dependency, as stated in section 14.2, permits these languages to keep their option of total identity deletion intact. Hence, these languages do not have to change their strategy in the selection of a US: they can stick with the Ordered Strategy, and apply their only remaining procedure, viz. total identity deletion, to the US which is produced by this strategy. The new comparative construction which, according to our model, will result from this is some variant of the Particle Comparative.

Thus, we can conclude that our model, if supplemented by some specific assumptions about diachronic change, is able to account for the fact that *Separative–Particle, Locative–Particle* and *Allative–Particle* are empirically attested cases of double comparative choice. (The fact that, in our sample, Separative Comparatives occur almost three times as often as Locative Comparatives and almost five times as often as Allative Comparatives is reflected in the relative frequencies of these three double option types in the sample.) To summarize, the claim is that the languages in which these three types of double options can be attested are those languages in which the option of absolute deranking has gradually fallen out of favour; as a result of this, these languages have started to develop a Particle Comparative in addition to their adverbial comparative. In this context, it can be added that there are some (although, unfortunately, not very systematic) pieces of independent support for the analysis just given. These data, which are of a diachronic and of a geographical nature, will be briefly commented upon below.

First, it can be established that, for at least some of the languages with an Adverbial–Particle pairing, the adverbial comparative is the older of the two, and that it has come to be superseded by the newly developed Particle Comparative, which, as a rule, acquires a wider range of employ than the adverbial construction. The rise of such a 'rivalling' Particle Comparative has been documented for Latin, Classical Greek, Russian and several Germanic languages, including English. In English, and in Germanic languages in general, the process has led to the complete abolition of the older adverbial comparative, but traces of this comparative can be found as late as the fourteenth century. Completely in line with this change in comparative type is the fact that several of the languages at issue here can be shown to have undergone a gradual shift in their preference for deranked structures to balanced structures. For instance, the use of absolute constructions in modern English and French, as well as in modern Hungarian and Russian, has become very limited and stylistically marked, even to the point of bookishness.

As a further point, we must call attention to the fact that the Adverbial–Particle pair is clearly an areal phenomenon. All of the 10 languages in the sample which exhibit this pairing are (or were) spoken on the European continent. This fact may in itself lend a certain amount of credibility to the claim that the pairing of adverbial and particle comparatives is the result of a unified process. More to the point, the particular areal distribution of this double option type explains why some of the languages involved have SVO word order. Given the fact that languages with absolute deranking (and hence, with adverbial comparatives) prefer either SOV or VOS word order, the presence of SVO-languages in the group at issue is to some extent problematic for the analysis outlined above. However, if we take the European origin of this type of pairing into account, this occurrence of SVO-languages can be attributed to the well-known process of 'word-order drift' (see, among others, Vennemann, 1975), which has led to a change from SOV to SVO in European languages. (Whether this word-order drift is an independent phenomenon, or a process which is causally related to the loss of deranking in this group of languages, is a question that will remain unanswered here.)

Finally, the scarcity of Allative–Particle combinations (and hence, the scarcity of VSO-languages) in the group at issue is another fact that can be brought into connection with the areal limitation on the phenomenon involved. In the European Sprachbund, the only VSO-languages are the Celtic languages, and these are languages which, as a rule, have a Particle Comparative as their only option. Thus, one might venture the hypothesis that the Celtic languages have been very radical in their transition from deranking to balancing, and that they (just like modern English and other Western European languages) have chosen to discard their adverbial comparatives completely. That adverbial comparatives must have been an option for at least some members of the Celtic family is shown by the occurrence of an Allative Comparative in Breton. In section 7.2.3 we noticed that Breton is a deviant case, in that it has an Allative Comparative, but no (or very marginal) possibilities for deranking. If the analysis presented above is accepted, Breton can be accounted for as a language which has given up deranking but which, untypically, has retained its older adverbial construction as its only option in comparative-type choice.

Having dealt with the languages of the 'maximal' procedure type, we turn to the opposite case, viz. those languages which have neither identity deletion nor deranking. As we stated in section 14.4, languages of this type may, in principle, select any mapping strategy, and may therefore base their comparatives on any US. However, we have also seen that the selection of the Independent Strategy is the most natural for languages of this type, and that, as a result, they will normally opt for some variant of the Conjoined Comparative.

Now, we have claimed above that double options for languages with a Conjoined Comparative derive from a diachronic process by which these languages have gradually acquired some form of deranking. It will be recalled that our model implies that languages which acquire deranking must also acquire some form of identity deletion; the Principle of Procedural Dependency, which is incorporated in our model, states that a language cannot derank if it does not delete. In other words, if minimally structure-reducing languages start to acquire deranking, this change will necessarily involve a transition to a new optimal language type. This, in turn, presupposes the selection of a new mapping strategy and, consequently, a new US for the comparative in this languages. This, however, does not have to be a serious problem for the languages at issue, since, as we noted above, they have a certain amount of freedom anyway in the selection of their mapping strategies.

Reviewing the various cases of pairings in which a Conjoined Comparative is one of the options, we can note that, for one of these cases, the diachronic process outlined above can be supported by synchronic cross-linguistic observations. The *Conjoined–Exceed* pairing is attested synchronically in our data base in all the successive stages which we assume to figure in the diachronic development of this pairing; of special relevance in this context are the Mixed Comparatives in Fulani, Motu, Acholi and Temne. Thus, the process by which a Conjoined–Exceed pairing may come about can be reconstructed as follows. For a minimally structure-reducing language, the first step in changing its comparative involves the selection of a new mapping strategy and US instead of the normal Independent Strategy and *US-1*; for the languages which interest us here, this new strategy will be the Relative Strategy, and the new US will be *US-3*. Once this change has been made, it is quite possible that nothing further will happen; the comparative construction in Fulani (see sentence *(3)*) is an example of a case in which minimal structure-reduction is applied to *US-3*. However, languages which have opted for *US-3* instead of (or in addition to) *US-1* may proceed to develop the possibility of subject-reduction; the comparatives in Temne and Acholi are cases in point here. Having acquired some form of identity deletion, a language of this type may go as far as to derank the predicate in the clause which has been affected by S-Deletion; the result of this operation is a genuine Exceed Comparative. Thus, languages with a Conjoined–Exceed pairing are viewed here as languages which are synchronically undecided as to whether or not they should acquire the possibility of conditional deranking.

Again, it can be added that there is some independent evidence for the reality of the diachronic process assumed here. In particular, there is historical evidence that serializations (i.e., cases of conditional deranking of predicates) are the result of a gradual syntactization of balanced structures; references to literature dealing with this point have been given in section 8.2. Since one of the typical forms in which an Exceed Comparative may manifest itself is that of a serialization, it is obvious that this historical evidence on the development of serializations in general supports our specific claim that, in languages with a Conjoined–Exceed pairing, the Conjoined Comparative is the older of the two.

Turning now to the other possible pairings in which a Conjoined Comparative is present, we can state that our analysis predicts that languages with a *Conjoined–Adverbial* pairing are, in origin, minimally structure-reducing languages, which have chosen the Ordered Strategy, and consequently *US-2*, in addition to the more typical Independent Strategy. For these languages the claim is made that they have gradually acquired the possibility of absolute deranking; as we have seen, this process implies that such languages should also acquire the possibility of total identity deletion.

In this connection, it must be noted that our model definitely allows for the possibility that a minimally structure-reducing language may acquire total identity deletion *without* the additional acquisition of absolute deranking. For languages which have chosen *US-2* as an additional option, the acquisition of total identity deletion without the selection of absolute deranking will lead to the development of a secondary Particle Comparative, and hence to a *Conjoined–Particle* pairing. This process seems to have taken place in Ilocano and Classical Nahuatl (see section 10.2 for examples).

If we take a look at the cases of Conjoined–Adverbial pairing in the sample, we notice that the *Conjoined–Locative* pairing is by far the most popular of the three possible combinations. Despite the fact that Locative Comparatives are, as primary choices, far less frequent than Separative Comparatives, there are seven Conjoined–Locative cases against two Conjoined–Allative cases in the sample, while Conjoined–Separative is not attested at all. For this discrepancy in frequency, the following explanation presents itself. Minimally structure-reducing languages typically select a US which is temporally interpreted as a simultaneous chain, viz. *US-1*. If these languages select an additional US, they will tend to keep this temporal interpretation intact, and hence, when they select *US-2* as an additional option, they will typically derive that comparative which is based on a simultaneous interpretation of *US-2*, i.e., the Locative Comparative. In this context, it should be noted that the two attested cases of pairings in which a Conjoined Comparative is combined with a non-Locative Comparative (that is, the two cases of Conjoined–Allative) are of a dubious nature in any case. As we saw in section 4.7, Nuer is a deviant language, in that it is one of the very few cases where there is no procedural parallelism in the syntactic treatment of chaining constructions; Nuer has balanced S-chains, but absolute posterior de-ranking for C-chains. As for Mangarayi, we have noted in section 10.4 that this language is one of the very few cases in our sample where a comparative is not modelled on a temporal chain, but on a final construction. Given these considerations, we can safely say that the normal manifestation of a Conjoined–Adverbial pairing will be Conjoined–Locative, and that Conjoined–Allative and Conjoined–Separative are definitely secondary, if they are possible at all.

As a last remark on Conjoined–Adverbial pairings, let me point out that, here too, there is some fragmentary independent support for the historical process which we assume to have caused this type of double option. Authors on languages which have a Conjoined Comparative as one of their options often implicitly express the view that this option is very old and, in some way, 'characteristic' for the language in question. This feeling is made quite explicit in Merlan (1982: 68), who states that the Conjoined Comparative in Mangarayi is the most common construc-tion, while the Allative Comparative in this language is a 'less common (but nevertheless spontaneously produced) construction type'. Further-more, with regard to Maori and Samoan we may point out that various authors on Polynesian languages (e.g., Chung, 1978: Marsack, 1975) imply that the Locative Comparative in these languages is a relatively recent innovation and that the original 'Polynesian Comparative' is a Conjoined Comparative. It must be admitted, though, that historical evidence of this kind is very sporadic, due to the fact that the diachronic developments in the languages involved are very poorly documented in general.

As a last class of double options we must discuss the pairings in which an Exceed Comparative is combined with either an Adverbial Comparative or a Particle Comparative. From the listing of frequencies it can be seen that all these pairings define rather small classes in the sample: none of them contains more than two members. Moreover, from the word orders of the relevant languages it can be deduced that the Exceed Comparative in these pairings must be rated as secondary. None of the languages with an *Exceed–Adverbial* pairing has the SVO word order which might be expected if the Exceed Comparative were the primary option in the pair. Instead, the two languages with an *Exceed–Allative* pairing (Maasai and Tamazight) have the VSO order which is normal for languages with an Allative Comparative. In the same way, the two languages with an *Exceed–Separative* pairing (Quechua and Aymara) have the SOV order preferred by languages with a Separative Comparative. Thus, there are reasons for assuming that the Exceed Comparative in these pairs is an extra option, acquired by these languages as an addition to their basic comparative type. It should be added that, for at least one language at issue here (viz. Quechua), it can be established diachronically that the Exceed Comparative is a later addition, which is, moreover, restricted to certain dialects.[4]

Whatever the status of the Exceed Comparative in these pairs may be, however, it must be conceded that there is no elegant explanation for these pairings within the assumptions on which our analysis of double comparative choice is based. The problem which these pairings present can be elucidated by considering the following. It can be noted that, for all pairings discussed so far, our analysis has accounted for their occurrence or non-occurrence on the basis of the following general principle:

The Principle of Strategy Retention:
A secondary comparative in a language will be based upon the strategy which is required (or permitted) for the primary comparative in that language.

One might view this principle as another manifestation of a general principle of economy in the strategy choice and procedure choice of natural languages, on a par with the Principle of Optimal Harmony discussed in section 14.3. The Principle of Strategy Retention (PSR) is meant to stipulate that transitions and additions in comparative-type choice should involve changes which are as minimal as possible. When a language wants to add a secondary comparative, it will tend to be 'faithful' to its original strategy choice; changes and additions in comparative type do not involve a change or addition in mapping strategies, but are restricted to either

(a) a change in the *temporal interpretation* of the original US, while keeping the procedure type of the language intact; or
(b) a change in the *procedural option of deranking*, while keeping the temporal interpretation of the original US intact.

In this way, the PSR enables us to account for the occurrence of the Allative–Locative and Separative–Locative pairings; these are pairings in which the only change lies in the temporal interpretation of the US involved. Furthermore, the PSR accounts for the fact that Adverbial–Particle pairs are possible. These pairings occur in languages in which the Ordered Strategy, and hence *US-2*, is chosen as the basis for both the primary and the secondary comparative, but which have undergone a gradual change in their deranking option. On the opposite end, the PSR accounts for the fact that Conjoined–Exceed and Conjoined–Locative are possible pairings. Since for languages with a primary Conjoined Comparative all strategies are, at least in principle, available in any case, the double comparative choice in these languages does not involve a change in strategy; it can be attributed to a gradual change in the deranking option, while the original (simultaneous) interpretation of the US is kept intact. Finally, the PSR correctly predicts that Conjoined–Allative and Conjoined–Separative are minor, if not impossible, pairings, since they would involve both a change in deranking option and a change in temporal interpretation of the US.

Given that the plausibility of a principle like the PSR is accepted, it will be evident that the pairings Adverbial–Exceed and Particle–Exceed will always involve a violation of the PSR. No matter which direction one assumes for the diachronic transition in these pairs, the languages in which one of these pairs is present will always need the brute force to effectuate a change in mapping strategy. Hence, these pairings represent a serious difficulty for our analysis of double options in comparative-type choice, and, indirectly, for the validity of our model of comparative-type choice in general.

As I see it, there are several ways to evaluate this difficulty. First, one might rate the attested occurrence of Adverbial–Exceed and Exceed–Particle pairs as a genuine counterexample to the claims contained in our general model of comparative-type choice. Secondly, one might accept this model in its generality, but accept the occurrence of these pairings as a refutation of the PSR. As a consequence, one should allow languages to develop secondary comparatives which involve a change in mapping strategy. It must be remarked, however, that such a decision would diminish the value of our model for the prediction of possible comparative pairings almost to the point of vanishing; without a principle like the PSR (or some other restrictive principle), one essentially commits oneself to the view that, in the pairing of comparative types, practically anything goes. A third way to deal with these recalcitrant cases is to assign to them a status which differs from that of other pairings. Specifically, one might suggest that Exceed–Adverbial and Exceed–Particle pairings are not a case of a gradual structural shift in the languages themselves, but that they are the result of the extra-linguistic process of *linguistic borrowing*. Since the concept of borrowing is a notorious escape route for all kinds of problems in Universal Grammar, one should be very cautious in bringing up this possibility. However, if we look at the geographical and sociolinguistic position of the relevant languages, the notion of linguistic borrowing appears to be not completely implausible. Of the six languages at issue, the three African languages (viz. Tamazight, a Berber language, and Maasai and Bari, two Nilotic languages) are spoken by people who live either in or at the close periphery of the extensive linguistic area in Africa where the Exceed Comparative is the common and regular option. As for Sranan, this is an English-based creolization, which retained its Exceed Comparative from its African substratum, but which has, in modern times, largely discarded this comparative in favour of the *leki*-comparative, a direct borrowing from the English *like*-construction. Lastly, the Exceed Comparative in the two possibly related South-American languages Quechua and Aymara might also be a case of borrowing; there is some evidence that this Exceed Comparative is a later innovation in some dialects of Quechua, and that its rise may be connected with the fact that parts of the extensive area in which Quechua is spoken are heavily creolized. In short, we can say that the view of the Exceed–Adverbial and Exceed–Particle pairings as a non-structural, areal phenomenon is not completely refuted by the geographical and sociolinguistic data. It goes without saying, however, that the evidence for the borrowing-analysis of these pairings is extremely weak, as is generally the case with arguments in which the notion of linguistic borrowing is invoked.

Evaluating the discussion in this section, we may conclude the following. Our analysis of double comparative choice, which assumes processes of diachronic change which are constrained by the PSR, certainly has a number of strong points. In particular, this analysis is able to account for the fact that Adverbial–Particle, Separative–Locative and Conjoined–Locative are all combinations with a relatively high frequency, and that Conjoined–Separative, Conjoined–Allative and Separative–Allative are improbable, if not impossible, pairings. On the other hand, however, it must also be conceded that our analysis cannot be said to have been completely successful. In particular, the analysis fails to provide a principled account of a number of attested combinations in the sample, namely, the Exceed–Adverbial and Exceed–Particle pairings. In addition to this empirical inadequacy of the analysis, it must be admitted that the independent evidence for the reality of the diachronic processes postulated, as well as the evidence for the existence of the Principle of Strategy Retention, is far from conclusive, to put it mildly. Thus, while it can be maintained that our analysis may represent a first step in the explanation of double comparative choice, it must also be concluded that this curious phenomenon has aspects which, at least for the present, defy explanation.

15.5   An evaluation of the new model

In the foregoing sections of this chapter, we have examined the predictive value of the model of comparative-type choice which was progressively developed in the previous chapters of part three. Stripped to its essentials, this model claims that the range of attested comparative types in natural languages, and the distribution of these various types over natural languages, can be explained if we accept the correctness of the following statements:

> STATEMENT 1: *The linguistic expression of the concept of comparison is modelled on the linguistic expression of temporal sequencing. Therefore, the underlying structures of comparative constructions in natural languages have the form of temporal chains.*
> STATEMENT 2: *The relevant syntactic procedures in the derivation of surface structures of temporal chains (and hence, of comparative constructions) are deranking and identity deletion. These two procedures interact both with one another and with cognitive mapping strategies, to the effect that they define a restricted set of possible language types.*

The empirical content of this model of comparative-type choice has been laid down in section 15.1 in a set of *procedure-based universals*.

If we compare this new model of comparative-type choice with the earlier set of chaining-based universals (see chapter 5), we can conclude that the new model is superior in one important respect, namely, in its prediction of the attested range of comparative types. Since the new set of procedure-based universals fully incorporates the earlier set of chaining-based universals, the new model takes over all the correct predictions made by the earlier one. In addition, however, the new model also presents a principled account of cases like Particle Comparatives and Mixed Comparatives, which were to some extent problematic for the earlier model. Finally, we can observe that the word-order preferences of some of the comparative types find a systematic explanation in the new model, in that these preferences can be connected with the relevant procedure types on the basis of independently motivated directionality principles. Thus, we can conclude that the new model, in its prediction of the attested variation of comparative types among languages, achieves a remarkable degree of accuracy, and as such it can be said to provide an explanatory framework for the non-randomness in that variation.

Given this undeniably attractive feature of the new model, it is only fair to point out its potential weaknesses. For one thing, we must concede that the distribution of comparative types over the languages in the sample, as predicted by the new model, cannot be completely corroborated by the facts (see section 15.3); it remains to be seen whether this lack of confirmation will turn out to be a real weakness of the model, or rather just a matter of momentary absence of the relevant linguistic data. Secondly, we saw in section 15.4 that the prediction of double comparative choice, as specified by the new model, is not entirely conclusive, and that it is partially based on assumptions about diachronic developments for which there is only slight independent support. Lastly, a general criticism may be that the new model presupposes a number of cognitive and perceptual principles which have not, to my knowledge, been affirmed by research from outside the field of linguistics. At the present stage of our knowledge, I think it is hardly feasible to assess the extent to which these deficiencies are seriously damaging to the overall plausibility of the new model. Those who judge that the new set of procedure-based universals rests upon too many uncertainties should fall back upon our earlier, less comprehensive model of comparative-type choice; I trust that the data presented in part two of this essay show convincingly that the set of chaining-based universals formulated in chapter 5 is by and large in accordance with linguistic reality.

Notes

Chapter 1: Introduction

1 The concept of 'research programme' which is alluded to here should be taken in the technical methodological sense defined by Lakatos (1978).

2 Equi-NP-Deletion (see, among others, Rosenbaum, 1967) is the grammatical operation by which subjects of embedded clauses are reduced to null-anaphors if they are identical to some constituent (normally, the subject-NP) of the dominating main clause. A language which possesses this operation is Dutch. In this language, the complement of verbs like *willen* 'to wish, to want' is reduced to an infinitive if the subject of that complement is identical to the subject of *willen*:

> (i) DUTCH:
> *Ik wil   dat jij   weggaat*
> I   want that you leave-2SG
> 'I want you to leave'

> (ii) * *Ik wil   dat ik wegga*
> I   want that I leave-1SG
> 'I want that I leave'

> (iii) *Ik wil   weggaan*
> I   want leave-INF
> 'I want to leave'

In contrast, a language like Kabyl (Hanoteau, 1906) does not have Equi-NP-Deletion. The subject of the complement of verbs like *br'i-* 'to want' is always overtly expressed in surface structure, even if it is identical to the subject of *br'i-*:

> (iv) KABYL:
> *Br'ir   ad' iarou*
> want-1SG FUT write-3SG
> 'I want him to write'

(v) *Br'ir   ad' arour*
     want-1SG FUT write-1SG
     'I want to write'

3 Publications in which this localist position is defended more or less explicitly are Lyons (1968, 1977, 1979), Anderson (1971, 1977) and Halliday (1967, 1968).

4 Perkins (1980) contains a proposal for language sample stratification on the basis of an intersection of the two parameters of genetic independency and cultural independency between languages. Whether his proposed sample of 50 languages will turn out to be a satisfactory standardization of cross-linguistic samples is a question that will have to be decided by the results of the research which is based upon this sample. (I am grateful to Joan Bybee for calling Perkins' work to my attention.)

5 For collections of papers which elaborate on this point of view see Li (1975, 1977).

6 In its original context, this passage from Mallinson and Blake (1981) deals with the relation between active and passive sentences. Given its general methodological import, I have thought it fit to adapt this quote to my exposition of the way in which the term 'deletion' should be understood.

Chapter 2: The Typology of Comparative Constructions

1 It should be noted that, in some languages, the two available comparative constructions appear to be in a *complementary* rather than in an inclusive distributional relation. Thus, in Italian (Pieter Seuren, personal communication), cases of NP-comparison are characterized by the preposition *di* 'of, from' on the standard NP, whereas cases of clausal comparison require the particle *che* in front of the comparative clause:

(i) ITALIAN:
     Gianni è più   grande di   Piero
     G.   is more tall   from P.
     'Gianni is taller than Piero'

(ii) *Gianni è più   grande che non pensassi*
     G.   is more tall   than not think-PAST. 1SG
     'Gianni is taller than I thought'

In a sentence like *(ii)*, the comparative clause contains a negation. This phenomenon is not restricted to Italian; it can also be attested in French and Hungarian. A discussion of the relation between negation and comparison can be found in sections 9.4.3 and 15.2.

2 For a suggestion as to the etymological origin of this morphological comparative marking see chapter 15, n.2.

3 It should be pointed out that the formulation employed here has been chosen

for reasons of exposition only. I do not want to imply that the decision to encode this standard NP as a direct object is, in some functional or psychological sense, prior to the selection of an *exceed*-verb.

4 Among the wealth of publications devoted to the description of spatial relations in natural languages, I have been inspired particularly by Bierwisch (1967), Bennett (1970), Anderson (1971), E. Clark (1971), H. Clark (1973), Jessen (1974) and Traugott (1975).

5 For the relation between possessive structures and locative structures in natural languages see, among others, Lyons (1967, 1968), Asher (1968), Welmers (1973) and E. Clark (1978).

6 For an argumentation that at least some of these Particle Comparatives are diachronically derived from adversative conjunctions see sections 9.4.3 and 15.2.

7 My concept of the proportions of word-order type occurrence in a random sample has been borrowed from Greenberg (1963, 1966), who states that, in a random sample, there will be 50 per cent SOV-languages, about 40 per cent SVO-languages, and about 10 per cent VSO-languages. Obviously, this statement can itself be subjected to falsification, by checking it against word-order type occurrences in other random samples. For the present, however, I have assumed that Greenberg's statements provide a useful guide-line in assessing the degree in which word-order type occurrence in a given category deviates from the random norm.

8 English has a somewhat special status within this class, in that the particle *than* has gradually developed into a preposition. For detailed discussion of the English comparative see section 9.4.

9 Throughout the two grammars at issue, we can observe a systematic phonological variation, in that, for all kinds of words, Celedon records an *r* where Holmer records an *l*. It may be that this variation is due to geographical differences; the two grammarians describe different dialects of Goajiro.

Chapter 3: In Search of a Determinant Factor

1 For further elaboration of this point see section 8.2, where the notion of serialization is discussed in some detail.

2 The variation between the forms *baino* and *bainan* is probably due to dialectical differences (see N'Diaye, 1970; Rollo, 1925). However, Lafitte (1944: 176) rates these two forms as distinct lexical items. Further discussion of the Basque comparative particle will be given in chapter 9, n.1.

Chapter 4: Types of Syntactic Chaining

1 In some languages, the isomorphy between finite main verbs and finite verbs in subordinate clauses has been given up; those languages employ *a specific*

subordinative conjugation for verbs in subordinate clauses. Of course, it is rather difficult to decide whether such subordinative conjugational forms are instances of predicate deranking, or rather a concomitant phenomenon in the process of clause embedding. I have not adopted a generally applicable solution for these cases; the status of flexional forms which are marked for subordination will be decided upon for each individual case.

2 For further discussion of the notion of backgrounding see Givón (1979) and Hopper (1979).

3 For further discussion of the encoding of temporal chaining in Kanuri see section 7.2.3.

4 For the possibilities of deranking in Finnish see section 10.5. The (marginal) deranking options in English and French will also be discussed in that section.

Chapter 6: Testing the Set of Chaining-based Universals

1 In Lamutic, the elements *-du-k* and *-k* alternate as separative markers. See Benzing (1955).

2 The element *-aha* is the short form of *-iaha* 'since then, from then on'. Both items 'serve as markers of succession' (Landaburu, 1979: 253; my translation).

3 In addition to this, Swift remarks: 'Occasionally, in subordinate clausal constructions, there is no topic expressed in the subordinate clause, yet it would result in patent absurdity to interpret as "performer" of the action of the subordinate clause, the "performer" of the action of the ensuing one. This results from the meaning of the utterance and not from anything in the grammar, and in such cases the "performer" of the action of the subordinate clause is clearly someone to be clarified from the general context: *tekrar izah endince//anladim//* "Upon (someone's) explaining again, I understood" (where it is obvious that I did not myself do the explaining)' (Swift, 1963: 162).

4 The gerundial forms in Amharic present a case of neutralization between consecutive and simultaneous action; see section 4.1.

5 For a discussion of the basic word order in Cœur d'Alene see Keenan (1978).

6 I am grateful to Cees Versteegh and Wim Delsman, who provided me with the following examples from Arabic and Hebrew, respectively.

7 It may be the case that this suffix *-tsī* is etymologically related to the conjunction *tsî* 'and'. See Meinhof (1903: 35).

Chapter 7: The Allative and the Locative Comparative

1 Some languages in this class have VOS rather than VSO order. According to Keenan (1978), VOS order is a frequent alternative for languages in which the primary word order pattern is VSO.

2 As to the word order in Siuslawan, Frachtenberg (1922: 607) remarks: 'The successive order in which the parts of speech are arranged is arbitrary and

exempt from any well-defined rules. The subject may be placed at the beginning or at the end of the sentence, usage favoring its occurrence at the very end, especially in cases when the sentence contains a nominal subject and object'. Keenan (1978) counts Siuslawan among the languages with VOS word order.

3 Day (1973: 32) postulates that the aspect word *cat* is related to the suppletive imperative of the verb *tita* 'to come', which is *cata*.

4 For a discussion of this hypothesis on Middle Breton in a broader context see section 15.4.

5 Dumezil (1933: 89) mentions yet another suffix as a marker of standard NPs in Ubykh comparatives: cp.

> (i)　*UBYKH:*
> *Yi -gune wo -gune-ke　ca　-qasaqa-j*
> this-tree　that-tree　-PRT　more-tall　-3SG
> 'This tree is taller than that tree'

The element *-ke* must be seen as representing an opposition 'but', or 'only X and not Y'. Dumezil (1933: 90) remarks: 'Thus, I think that a phrase like [(i)] actually means 'This tree? That tree too, but it is taller' or 'that tree, yes (it is tall but) this tree is taller' (my translation). If we follow this analysis, the *ke*-comparative in Ubykh would be a specific variant of the Particle Comparative, viz. a Particle Comparative in which the comparative particle is an item with the meaning 'but'. A similar situation can be encountered in Bari, Basque and Ilocano (see section 3.3).

6 It may be added that the goal-marker *ug* is also employed as the conjunction 'and' between NPs and clauses. Cp.:

> (i)　*CEBUANO:*
> *Bir　ug　tubig*
> beer　and　water
> 'Beer and water' (Wolff, 1967: I, 164)

> (ii)　*Ningguway dayun　　ku dimaq-dimaq　ug*
> went out　immediately　I　there-and-then　and
> *nagpaqulan ku nga way*
> went to　I　to　rain
> 'I walked out there and then and went out in the rain' (Wolff, 1967: II, 261)

Furthermore, the element *ug* functions in the construction which represents our manner adverbials. In this case, the Abstract Form may also be used. Cp.:

> (iii)　*CEBUANO:*
> *Milakaw　siya ug　hinay*
> walked-away　he　PRT　did-slowly
> 'He slowly walked away'

(iv) *Milakaw   siya pag   -hinay*
walked-away he   ABSTR -do-slowly
'He slowly walked away'

Chapter 8: The Exceed Comparative

1 The literal German text is: 'Reihensätze sind Sätze die eine Geschehnisvorstellung aus mehreren aufbauen' (Dempwolff, 1939: 67). 'Die Vorstellung mehrerer Geschehnisse, meistens nur zweier, können zu einer neuen Vorstellung zusammengefasst werden, ähnlich wie im Deutschen durch Vorsilben Vorstellungen präzisiert werden in "weichen, ausweichen", "kommen, heraufkommen"' (ibid.: 28).
2 I am indebted to Pieter Seuren for this sentence, and for all other data on Sranan which are used in this essay.
3 See also George (1975) for an account of this neutralization in the serial constructions of Nupe and other Kwa languages.
4 Other languages in which the expression of manner adverbials is modelled directly on the encoding of some type of temporal chain are Navaho (section 7.3.2), Cebuano (chaper 7, n.6) and Mapuche. Manner adverbs in Mapuche consist of an infinitive which is governed by the postposition *meu*. Thus, this construction is formally identical to the simultaneous action construction illustrated by sentence *(34)*. Cp.:

(i)   MAPUCHE:
Ayuun   meu kupa -tu   -i
happy-INF on   return-PAST-3SG
'He returned happily'

Chapter 9: Derived-case Comparatives

1 The comparative particle in Basque is attested as *banon, bano* (N'Diaye, 1970: 236), as *bano, bane* (Rollo, 1925: 6V) and as *baino* (Lafitte, 1944: 176); it is possible that dialectical differences are at play here. N'Diaye and Rollo state that the comparative particle is identical to the conjunction 'but'. Against this opinion, Lafitte holds that there is a difference between the comparative particle *baino* and the element *bainan* 'but'.
    As for the etymology of the item *baino/bano/bane*, it is conceivable that this item has been derived from the element *bai*. This is the general affirmative particle 'yes', and is also employed as a coordinate marker:

(i)   BASQUE:
Hura bai , bainan ez   zu
he   yes but   not you
'He, not you'

> (ii) *Soldaddak bai gauaz bai egunaz hor zauden*
>   soldiers-ERG and day-MED and night-MED there were
>   'The soldiers stayed there day and night'

The suffix -*no* in *baino* might be identified as a limitative suffix, with a basic meaning of 'now that', 'if only'. Evidence for this analysis comes from the fact that the suffix -*no* also occurs in the Basque subordinate conjunction *de-no* 'now that (it is)', which consists of the form *de* 'it is' and the suffix under discussion. Cp.:

> (iii) BASQUE:
>   *Hemen   de -no dohatsu gira*
>   here-INESS he-is-PRT happy-PL we-are
>   'Now that he is here, we are happy'

In short, one might propose that the element *bai-no* is a subordinate form of a predicative stem *bai* 'it is, it is so', so that the comparative construction in Basque could have been modelled on a subordinate clause type with the meaning 'now that it is so'. Thus, a sentence like

> (iv) BASQUE:
>   *Jakes   baino lodi-ago da*
>   J.-NOM PRT fatter he-is
>   'He is fatter than Jakes'

would have as its original meaning: 'Now that Jakes is fat, he is fat', that is, the meaning of a *consecutive chain*.

   In this context, it might also be argued that the item *bainan*, which is given by Lafitte (1944: 176) as the element for 'but', is originally the Inessive case of the element *bai*, so that it would have the etymological meaning 'in its being, while it is'. If we accept this analysis, *bainan* 'but' would be the simultaneous counterpart of the essentially consecutive formation *baino* 'than'.

2 For this latter opinion, see in particular Weigand (1913: 49) and Kacori (1979: 153).

3 If the element *meer* 'more' is moved together with the *dan*-clause, these sentences are perhaps not very elegant Dutch, but they are certainly better than *(53b/c)*. Cp.:

> (i)   DUTCH:
>   *? Hij is meer dan je zou denken veranderd*
> (ii) *? Meer dan je zou denken is hij veranderd*

These facts suggest that, in Dutch, the comparative clause and the comparative marker *meer* form a constituent. However, such a conclusion will raise problems of its own, since in many Dutch comparatives the comparative marker (in this case, the morpheme -*er*) is morphologically bound to the predicate. Cp.:

(iii) DUTCH:

Hij is slimm-er dan je denkt
'He is smarter than you think'

In other words, we would have to assume that the Dutch comparative clause is in construction with an element which is (or can be) morphologically bound to another constituent. We will not pursue this matter further here.

4 For a thorough discussion of the rule of Gapping, and references to earlier work on this rule, see Neijt–Kappen (1979).

5 I am grateful to Wus van Lessen Kloeke for these facts of High German.

6 Bernard Comrie (personal communication) is of the opinion that, in present-day English, very few speakers actually control the system where the case of the NP after *than* is the same as that of the comparee NP. He suggests that speakers who use the Nominative after *than* generalize this nominative for both subject and object function; in other words, for these speakers, *than* is just a preposition which happens to take the Nominative. If this analysis is accepted, we have another piece of evidence for the claim that English is more 'radical' in its syntactization of the comparative construction than Dutch; there are numerous Dutch speakers (including myself) who spontaneously treat the comparative as a derived-case construction.

7 Classical Greek can be placed in this category if we assume that the meaning of the disjunctive element 'or' incorporates a negation, i.e., if we conceive of 'A or B' as being cognate to 'A, and *if not A, then B*'. Some evidence for such a position comes from Classical Arabic, where the element *wala* 'or' is etymologically a conditional phrase, with the meaning 'If it is not'.

Chapter 10: An Examination of Secondary Choices

1 The dative case of the participle in *-dams* is also, though rarely, used as a representation of absolute simultaneous predicates (Endzelin, 1922: 786). Cp.:

(i) LATVIAN:

Vilninu   verp-dam   -ai   , miedzins naca
wool-ACC spin-PCP. PRES -DAT   sleep   came
'While she was spinning the wool, she fell asleep'

2 Boas and Deloria (1941: 143) state: 'A considerable number of adverbs end in *p*. These are derived from verbs ending in *p'a*, most of which are obsolete. Some of these adverbs form new verbal themes with the ending *-tu*.' An example of this latter type of formation is the element *iwangkab-tu*, which appears in the following comparative, taken from Buechel (1939: 95):

(i)   DAKOTA:
Woilake ung king he   itangangye king he
servant PRT the the-one his-lord   the   the-one
iwangkab-tu   sni
superior/above   not
'The servant is not greater than his lord'

3 The indeterminacy of the structural function of constituents appears to be a general characteristic of Australian languages; these languages are to a large extent 'non-configurational' (see Hale, 1983).
4 I am indebted to Prof. Dr R. Veder for these Russian data.
5 The absolutive form in Albanian seems to be subject to considerable dialectical variation. In addition to the construction exemplified in *(56b)*, Hetzer (1978: 197) mentions an absolute construction in which the predicate has the form of the Perfect Participle, and is preceded by the particle chain *me te u.* Cp.:

(i)   ALBANIAN:
Me te u khtyer   . . .
ABS. PRT   return-PCP. PERF
'After he had returned . . .'

Chapter 11: Theoretical Background Assumptions

1 These word-order correlations have been formulated in sections 4.4.2 and 4.4.3.
2 I assume here that the scanning of linguistic structures proceeds in the order in which the elements of the structure are perceived; in our writing system, this order is matched by a left-to-right ordering. The reader will have noted that this assumption has already been tacitly adopted in the principles that were developed in sections 4.4.2 and 4.4.3.
3 It should be understood here that the directionality in this diagram (i.e., the placement of the negative side of the parameter to the left, and the placement of the positive side of the parameter to the right) is purely a matter of graphical convention, and that no claim for a particular ordering should be attached to it.

Chapter 12: Cognitive Strategies in Comparative Formation

1 As will have become clear from the CS of comparison, the extent x must also be understood to be defined in such a way that it envelops extent y.

Chapter 13: Grammatical Procedures in Comparative Formation

1 The distinction between 'configurational' and 'non-configurational' languages, which I alluded to in chapter 10, n.3, may be a structural manifestation of this functional split between languages.

2 I adopt here the 'classic' view of cyclicity, in which the *sentence* is taken to be the unit by which rules of encoding and decoding are bounded.

3 Or from other linguistic clues such as person-marking, which are present independently of the presence or absence of identity conditions.

4 In a number of cases, application of identity deletion leads to a further structural *regrouping* of the remaining constituents. See, among others, Tai (1969) and Harries (1978) for a discussion of this process.

5 After the application of S-Deletion, Malagasy requires that the two verbs in the sentence be regrouped into a verb phrase. Therefore, the connective *ary* 'and', which can only conjoin sentences, must be replaced by the phrasal conjunction *sy* (Keenan, 1976B). Alternatively, of course, one might hold that there is no procedural relation at all between the sentences in *(12)*, and that a sentence like *(12b)* is base-generated. With respect to this point, we should remind the reader that our approach is model-neutral. What the sentences in *(12)* are meant to illustrate is that, in a verb-initial language like Malagasy, the subject of conjoined verbs follows the second verb and not the first one. Thus, a sentence like *(i)* should be ungrammatical, which it is:

    (i)   MALAGASY:
        * Misotro Rabe ary/sy mihinam-bary

6 Sentences *(13a/b)* are taken from Craig (1977: 38). As will be noted from sentence *(13a)*, use of the conjunction *wal*, which signals an opposition, leads to a regrouping of the VSO word order in the second clause of such a conjunction. This, however, does not alter the fact that Gapping in this basic VSO-language applies forward. See Craig (1977: 35–9) for further discussion.

7 In addition, English has the possibility of formations such as

    (i)   ENGLISH:
        My father drinks, and my mother does, too
    (ii) *My father drinks, and so does my mother*

I take it that the element *do/do so* is the pronominal form for verb phrases in English. However, whatever the status of this element may turn out to be, it will be clear that both of these sentences offer additional evidence for the Boundary Constraint on identity deletion.

Chapter 14: Optimal and Non-optimal Language Types

1 This is not strictly true. *US-1.2*, which is produced by the Independent Strategy, also meets this requirement, at least to a certain degree. I will come back to this point in section 15.2.

Chapter 15: An Explanatory Model of Comparative-type Choice

1 For a further elucidation of this point see Keenan (1976a).

2 At this point, the reader may wonder where the second extent-index (i.e., the

index x) will end up in surface structure. I have no conclusive answer to this question. One possibility that suggests itself is that this index ends up as the morphological comparative marker on the predicate. Given this assumption, the fact that, in Dutch, this comparative marker seems to form a constituent with the following comparative clause can be explained; in the process of relativization which this type of Particle Comparative presupposes, the extent-index x functions as the antecedent, and hence as the head of the relative clause. Moreover, as we saw in section 2.4, it is a fact that morphological marking of comparative predicates is especially popular among languages with some kind of Particle Comparative. Needless to say, however, this suggested origin of the comparative marker is in need of further corroboration, especially with respect to the etymological status of the marking elements involved.

3 See, however, the discussion in section 14.2, where it is suggested that the deletion of a subject might be a minimal prerequisite for the start of a deranking process.

4 In this connection, it is also interesting to note that Quechua seems to be in a process of losing its ability for Backward Gapping. See Pulte (1971) for further discussion.

Appendix A
Alphabetical Listing of the Sample

Language	*Area*	*Source*
1 ABIPON	Gran Chaco, Paraguay	Dobrizhoffer (1902)
2 ALBANIAN	Albania	Weigand (1913), Lambertz (1959), Camaj (1969), Hetzer (1978), Kacori (1979)
3 AMHARIC	Ethiopia	Cohen (1936)
4 ANDOKE	Colombia	Landaburu (1979)
5 ARABIC (Classical)	Arabia	Yushmanov (1961), Nasr (1967)
6 ARANDA	New South Wales	Strehlow (1944)
7 AYMARA	Bolivia	de Torres Rubio (1966)
8 BANDA	Central African Republic	Tisserant (1930)
9 BARI	Sudan, Uganda	Spagnolo (1933)
10 BASQUE	Northern Spain, S.W. France	Rollo (1925), Gavel (1929), Lafitte (1944), N'Diaye (1970)
11 BEDAUYE	Ethiopia, Sudan	Conti Rossini (1912)
12 BILIN	Ethiopia, Eritrea	Reinisch (1882)
13 BRETON	Brittany	Ternes (1970)
14 BURMESE	Burma	Okell (1969)
15 BURUSHASKI	Northern Afghanistan	Lorimer (1935)
16 CAMBODIAN	Cambodia	Jacob (1968)
17 CARIB	Guyanas	de Goeje (1978), Hoff (1968)
18 CAYAPO	Southern and Central Brazil	Maria (1914)
19 CEBUANO	Cebu, Philippines	Wolff (1967)
20 CHUCKCHEE	North-East Siberia	Bogoras (1922)
21 CŒUR D'ALENE	Idaho	Reichard (1933)
22 DAGOMBA	Ghana, Togo	Fisch (1912)
23 DAKOTA	N. Dakota, S. Dakota, Montana	Buechel (1939), Boas and Deloria (1941)

Language	*Area*	*Source*
24 DUALA	Cameroon	Ittmann (1939)
25 DUTCH	The Netherlands, Northern Belgium	own data
26 EKAGI	New Guinea (West Highlands)	Drabbe (1952)
27 ENGLISH	British Isles, Northern America, Australia, New Zealand, South Africa	native speakers
28 ESKIMO	Alaska, Northern Canada, Greenland	Thalbitzer (1911), Hammerich (1970)
29 FINNISH	Finland	Fromm and Sadeniemi (1956)
30 FRENCH	France, Switzerland, Southern Belgium, Canada	native speakers
31 FULANI	Sahel territory	Gaden (1909), Taylor (1921), Leith–Ross (1922), Labouret (1952)
32 GAELIC	Scotland	McKinnon (1971)
33 GBEYA	Chad, Central African Republic, Zaire	Samarin (1966)
34 GOAJIRO	Northern Venezuela	Celedon (1878), Holmer (1949)
35 GREEK (Classical)	Greece	Kühner–Stegmann (1963)
36 GUARANI	Paraguay	Guasch (1956), Gregores and Suárez (1967)
37 GUMBAINGGIR	New South Wales	Smythe (1948), Eades (1979)
38 HAUSA	Northern Nigeria, Niger	Marré (1901), Mischlich (1911), Taylor (1923), Abraham (1941), Smirnova (1982)
39 HEBREW (Biblical)	Palestine	Brockelmann (1956)
40 HINDI	Northern and Central India	McGregor (1977)
41 HIXKARYANA	Northern Brazil	Derbyshire (1979)
42 HUNGARIAN	Hungary	Simonyi (1907), Nagy (1929), Sauvageot (1951), Tompa (1968)
43 IGBO	Nigeria	Welmers (1973)
44 ILOCANO	Luzon, Mindanao, Mindoro	Lopez (1928)
45 JABEM	North-East New Guinea	Dempwolff (1939)
46 JACALTEC	Guatemala	Day (1973), Craig (1977)

Language	*Area*	*Source*
47 JAPANESE	Japan	Kuno (1973, 1978)
48 JAVANESE	Java	Walbeehm (1915)
49 JURAK	Central-North Siberia	Hajdú (1963)
50 KANURI	Northern Nigeria, Niger	Lukas (1937)
51 KASHMIRI	Kashmir	Grierson (1919)
52 KHALKA	Mongolia	Street (1963)
53 KIRUNDI	Burundi	Menard (1908), Meeussen (1959)
54 KOBON	New Guinea (East Highlands)	Davies (1981)
55 KOREAN	Korea	Ramstedt (1939/1968), Pultr (1960)
56 LAMUTIC	Siberia	Benzing (1955)
57 LATIN (Classical)	Italy	Kühner–Gerth (1955)
58 LATVIAN	Latvia	Endzelin (1922), Dravins and Ruke (1958)
59 LAZ	Georgia (USSR)	Dirr (1928)
60 MALAGASY	Madagascar	Ferrand (1903)
61 MANCHU	Manchuria	Adam (1873), Haenisch (1961)
62 MANDARIN	Northern and Central China	Mullie (1947)
63 MANDINKA	Guinea, Sierra Leone	Delafosse (1929), Labouret (1934)
64 MANGARAYI	Northern Territory, Australia	Merlan (1982)
65 MAORI	New Zealand	Rere (1965)
66 MAPUCHE	Chile	de Augusta (1903)
67 MARGI	North-East Nigeria	Hoffmann (1963)
68 MASAI	Kenya, Tanzania	Tucker and Mpaayi (1955)
69 MENOMINI	Wisconsin	Bloomfield (1962)
70 MISKITO	Nicaragua, Honduras	Conzemius (1929)
71 MIWOK	California	Freeland (1951), Broadbent (1964)
72 MIXTEC	South Mexico	Alexander (1980)
73 MONUMBO	Central New Guinea	Vormann and Scharfenberger (1914)
74 MOTU	New Guinea (Port Moresby)	Lister-Turner and Clark (1930)
75 MUNDARI	Central India	Hoffmann (1903)
76 NAGA	India, Assam, Burma	Grierson (1903)
77 NAHUATL (Classical)	Central Mexico	Andrews (1975)

Language	*Area*	*Source*
78 NAMA	Namibia	Schils (1891), Meinhof (1903)
79 NAVAHO	Arizona, New Mexico, Utah, Colorado	Haile (1926, 1941), Pinnow (1964)
80 NGUNA	New Hebrides	Ray (1926)
81 NUER	Sudan, Ethiopia	Crazzolara (1933)
82 PALA	Southern New Ireland	Peekel (1909)
83 PIRO	Bolivia	Matteson (1965)
84 QUECHUA	Peru, Ecuador	von Tschudi (1884), Lastra (1968), Adelaar (1977), Cole (1981)
85 RUSSIAN	Soviet Union	Pulkina and Zakhava-Nekrasova (1974)
86 SALINAN	California	Mason (1918)
87 SAMOAN	Samoa	Marsack (1975)
88 SHIPIBO	Peru	Tessmann (1929)
89 SIKA	Flores Island	Arndt (1931)
90 SIUSLAWAN	Oregon	Frachtenberg (1922)
91 SRANAN	Surinam	Voorhoeve (1962)
92 SWAHILI	East Africa	Ashton (1947), Brauner and Bantu (1964), Loogman (1965)
93 TAJIK	Tajikistan	Rastorgueva (1963)
94 TAMAZIGHT	Central Sahara	Hanoteau (1896), Laoust (1918), Destaing (1920), Johnson (1966)
95 TAMIL	Southern India, Northern Sri Lanka	Arden (1942), Beythan (1943), Meile (1945), Asher (1982)
96 TARASCAN	Central Mexico	Foster (1969)
97 TELUGU	South India	Grierson (1906), Bhaskararao (1972)
98 THAI	Thailand	Noss (1964)
99 TIBETAN	Tibet	Jäschke (1929), Lalou (1950)
100 TOBA BATAK	Central Sumatra	van derr Tuuk (1867)
101 TUBU	Niger, Chad	Lukas (1953)
102 TUPI	Brazil, Paraguay, Argentina, Bolivia	Platzmann (1874)
103 TURKISH	Turkey	Swift (1963), Lewis (1967)
104 UBYKH	Black Sea Coast (USSR)	Dirr (1928)
105 VAYU	Nepal	Grierson (1909)
106 VIETNAMESE	Vietnam	Kim (1943), Jones and Thong (1960)

Language	*Area*	*Source*
107 WOLOF	Senegal	Rambaud (1903)
108 YAGAN	Tierra del Fuego	Adam (1885)
109 YAVAPAI	Northern and Central Arizona	Kendall (1976)
110 YORUBA	Nigeria	Bamgbose (1966), Awolobuyi (1973)

Appendix B

Genetic and Areal Stratification of the Sample

Eurasia

Indo-European	
Indic	HINDI
Dardic	KASHMIRI
Iranian	TAJIK
Hellenic	GREEK
Italic	LATIN
Baltic	LATVIAN
Slavic	RUSSIAN
Romanic	FRENCH
Germanic	DUTCH, ENGLISH
Celtic	BRETON, GAELIC
isolated	ALBANIAN
Caucasian	
North-West	UBYKH
Kartvelian	LAZ
Ural-Altaic	
Uralic	
Balto-Finnic	FINNISH
Ugric	HUNGARIAN
Samoyedic	JURAK
Altaic	
Tungus	LAMUTIC, MANCHU
Turkic	TURKISH
Mongol	KHALKA
Japanese	JAPANESE
isolated	KOREAN
Isolated	BASQUE

Asia

Sino-Tibetan	
Tibeto-Burmese	
Central	TIBETAN
Lolo-Burmese	BURMESE
Naga-Kuki-Chin	NAGA
Gyurung–Mishmi	VAYU
Sinitic	MANDARIN
Kam-Tai	THAI
Isolated	BURUSHASKI
Palaeo-Siberian	CHUCKCHEE
Dravidian	TAMIL, TELUGU
Munda	MUNDARI
Mon-Khmer	
Khmer	CAMBODIAN
Vietnamuong	VIETNAMESE

Africa and Middle East

Afroasiatic	
Berber	TAMAZIGHT
Chadic	HAUSA, MARGI
Cushitic	
Central	BILIN
Southern	BEDAUYE
Semitic	
South-West	ARABIC
Northern	HEBREW
Central African	AMHARIC
Niger-Congo	
West-Atlantic	FULANI, WOLOF
Kwa	IGBO, YORUBA
Gur	DAGOMBA
Mande	MANDINKA
Adamawa-Eastern	BANDA, GBEYA
Bantu	DUALA, KIRUNDI, SWAHILI
Nilo-Saharan	
Saharan	KANURI, TUBU
Nilotic	
Western	NUER
Eastern	BARI, MASAI
Khoisan	NAMA

America

Eskimo-Aleut	ESKIMO
Athapaskan	NAVAHO
Siouan	DAKOTA
Salishan	CŒUR D'ALENE
Algonquian	MENOMINI
Hokan	SALINAN, YAVAPAI
Oto-Manguean	MIXTEC
Uto-Aztecan	NAHUATL
Mayan	JACALTEC
Pano	SHIPIBO
Ge	CAYAPO
Araucan	MAPUCHE
Creolization	SRANAN
Isolated	TARASCAN
Penutian	
Miwok-Costanoan	MIWOK
Yakonan	SIUSLAWAN
Chibchan	MISKITO
Arawakan	GOAJIRO
Macro-Carib	
Carib	CARIB
	HIXKARYANA
Witotoan	ANDOKE
Tupi	TUPI, GUARANI
Guaycuru	ABIPON
Andes-Languages	QUECHUA
(affiliation unclear)	AYMARA, YAGAN

Indian Ocean and Pacific Ocean

Austronesian	
West-Indonesian	MALAGASY
	JAVANESE
	TOBA BATAK
Moluccan	SIKA
Philippine	CEBUANO
	ILOCANO
New Guinean	JABEM
	MOTU

Oceanic
  Polynesian   MAORI

                      SAMOAN
  Melanesian   NGUNA

                      PALA

Papuan
  Central   EKAGI
  Eastern   KOBON
  Bogia   MONUMBO

Pama-Nyungan
  Arandic   ARANDA
  Kumbainggaric   GUMBAINGGIR

Isolated   MANGARAYI

Bibliography

Superior figures after dates in the following list denote editions.

Abaev, V.I. 1964. *A grammatical sketch of Ossetic.* Bloomington/The Hague.
Abraham, R.C. 1941. *A modern grammar of spoken Hausa.* London.
Adam, L. 1873. *Grammaire de la langue mandchou.* Paris.
Adam, L. 1885. *Grammaire de la langue jagane.* Paris.
Adelaar, W.F.H. 1977. *Tarma Quechua. Grammar, texts, dictionary.* Lisse, The Netherlands.
Alexander, R.M. 1980. *Gramatica mixteca.* Mexico City.
Alexandre, C. 1880. *Dictionnaire gréco-français composé sur un nouveau plan.* Paris.
Anderson, J.M. 1971. *The grammar of case: towards a localistic theory.* London.
Anderson, J.M. 1977. *On case grammar: prolegomena to a theory of grammatical relations.* London.
Anderson, J.M. and Dubois-Charlier, F. (eds). 1975. *La grammaire des cas.* Paris.
Andrews, J.R. 1975. *Introduction to Classical Nahuatl.* Austin, Tex.
Annamalai, E. 1970. 'On moving from coordinate structures in Tamil', in: *Papers from the Sixth Regional Meeting of the Chicago Linguistic Society,* Chicago, Ill., 131–46.
Arden, A.H. 1942. *A progressive grammar of common Tamil.* Madras.
Arndt, P.P. 1931. *Grammatik der Sika-Sprache.* Ende, Flores.
Asher, R.E. 1968. 'Existential, possessive, locative and copulative sentences in Malayalam', in: J. Verhaar (ed.), *The verb 'be' and its synonyms, part 2,* Dordrecht, Holland, 88–111.
Asher, R.E. 1982. *Tamil.* Amsterdam.
Ashton, E.O. 1947[2]. *Swahili Grammar.* London, New York, Toronto.
de Augusta, F.J. 1903. *Gramatica araucana.* Valdivia, Chile.
Awolobuyi, O. 1973. 'The modifying serial construction: a critique', *Studies in African Linguistics,* 4, 87–111.
Bamgbose, A. 1966. *A grammar of Yoruba.* Cambridge, UK.
Bell, A. 1978. 'Language samples', in: J.H. Greenberg, C.A. Ferguson and E. Moravcsik (eds), part 1, 123–56.

Bennett, D.C. 1970. *Spatial and temporal uses of English prepositions*. Ann Arbor, Mich.

Benveniste, E. 1948. *Noms d'agent et noms d'action en Indo-européen*. Paris.

Benzing, J. 1955. *Lamutische Grammatik*. Wiesbaden.

Bergmans, L. 1982. 'Semantic aspects of comparison in Dutch, English and other languages'. Ph.D. Diss., Louvain.

Beythan, H. 1943. *Praktische Grammatik der Tamilsprache*. Leipzig.

Bhaskararao, P. 1972. 'On the syntax of Telugu existential and copulative predications', in: J. Verhaar (ed.), *The verb 'be' and its synonyms*. Dordrecht, Holland, 153–206.

Bierwisch, M. 1967. 'Some semantic universals of German adjectivals', *Foundations of Language*, 3, 1–36.

Bloomfield, L. 1962. *The Menomini language*. New Haven, Conn./London.

Boas, F. and Deloria, E. 1941. *Dakota Grammar*. Washington, DC.

Bogoras, W. 1922. 'Chuckchee', in: F. Boas (ed.), *Handbook of American Indian languages*, part 2, 631–903.

Brauner, S. and Bantu, J.K. 1964. *Lehrbuch des Swahili*. Leipzig.

Bresnan, J. 1971. 'On "a non-source of comparatives"', *Linguistic Inquiry*, 2, 117–25.

Bresnan, J. 1973. 'Syntax of the comparative clause construction in English', *Linguistic Inquiry*, 4 (3), 275–343.

Bresnan, J. 1975. 'Comparative deletion and constraints on transformations', *Linguistic Inquiry*, 7, 3–40.

Broadbent, S.M. 1964. *The Southern Sierra Miwok language*. Berkeley, Cal.

Brockelmann, C. 1956. *Hebräische Syntax*. Neukirchen (Kreis Moers).

Buechel, E. 1939. *A grammar of Lakota*. St Francis Mission.

Camaj, M. 1969. *Lehrbuch der albanischen Sprache*. Wiesbaden.

Campbell, A. 1959. *Old English grammar*. Oxford.

Cantrall, W.R. 1977. 'Comparison and beyond', in: *Papers of the Thirteenth Regional Meeting of the Chicago Linguistic Society*, Chicago, Ill., 69–81.

Celedon, R. 1878. *La lengua goajira*. Lima.

Chomsky, N.A. 1964. *Current issues in linguistic theory*. The Hague.

Chomsky, N.A. 1973. 'Conditions of transformations', in: S.R. Anderson and P. Kiparsky (eds), *A Festschrift for Morris Halle*, New York, 232–86.

Chomsky, N.A. 1980. 'On Binding', *Linguistic Inquiry*, 11, 1–46.

Chomsky, N.A. 1981. *Lectures on Government and Binding*. Dordrecht.

Chung, S. 1978. *Case marking and grammatical relations in Polynesian*. Austin, Tex.

Clark, E.V. 1971. 'On the acquisition of the meaning of *before* and *after*', *Journal of Verbal Learning and Verbal Behaviour*, 10, 260–75.

Clark, E.V. 1973. 'How children describe time and order', in: C.A. Ferguson and D.I. Slobin (eds), *Studies of child language development*, New York, 585–606.

Clark, E.V. 1975. 'Knowledge, context and strategy in the acquisition of meaning', in: D.P. (ed.), *Georgetown University Round Table on languages and linguistics. 1975. Developmental Psycholinguistics: Theory and Applications*. Washington, DC, 77–98.

Clark, E.V. 1978. 'Locationals: existential, locative and possessive constructions', in: J.H. Greenberg, C.A. Ferguson and E. Moravcsik (eds), part 4, 85–126.

Clark, H.H. 1970. 'Comprehending comparatives', in: G.B. Flores d'Arcais and W.J.M. Levelt (eds), *Advances in psycholinguistics*, Amsterdam/London, 194–206.

Clark, H.H. 1973. 'Space, time, semantics and the child', in: T.E. Moore (ed.), *Cognitive development and the acquisition of language*, New York, 28–64.

Cohen, M. 1936. *Traité de la langue amharique (Abyssinie)*. Paris.

Cole, P. 1981. *Imbabura Quechua*. Amsterdam.

Comrie, B. 1975. 'The syntax of causative constructions: cross-language similarities and divergences', in: M. Shibatani (ed.), 261–312.

Comrie, B. 1976. *Aspect. An introduction to the study of verbal aspect and related problems*. Cambridge, UK.

Comrie, B. 1978a. 'Ergativity', in: W.P. Lehmann (ed.), *Syntactic typology*, Hassocks, Sussex, UK, 329–94.

Comrie, B. 1978b. 'Linguistics is about languages', in: B.B. Kachru (ed.), *Linguistics in the seventies: directions and prospects*, Urbana, Ill., 221–36.

Comrie, B. 1981. *Language universals and linguistic typology*. Oxford.

Conti Rossini, C. 1912. *La langue des Kemant en Abyssinie*. Vienna.

Conzemius, E. 1929. 'Notes on the Miskito and Sumu languages of Eastern Nicaragua and Honduras', *International Journal of American Linguistics*, 5, 57–115.

Craig, C.G. 1977. *The Structures of Jacaltec*. Austin, Tex./London.

Crazzolara, J.P. 1933. *Outline of a Nuer grammar*. Vienna.

Cresswell, M.J. 1976. 'The semantics of degree', in: B. Partee (ed.), *Montague grammar*, New York, 261–92.

Curme, G.O. 1931. *A grammar of the English language*. Boston, Mass.

Davies, J. 1981. *Kobon*. Amsterdam.

Day, C. 1973. *The Jacaltec language*. Bloomington, Ind.

Delafosse, M. 1929. *La langue mandingue et ses dialectes*. Paris.

Dempwolff, O. 1939. *Grammatik der Jabem-Sprache auf Neuguinea*. Hamburg.

Derbyshire, D.C. 1979. *Hixkaryana*. Amsterdam.

Destaing, E. 1920. *Etude sur le dialecte berbère des Aït Seghrouchen (Moyen Atlas marocain)*. Paris.

Dik, S.C. 1968. *Coordination. Its implications for the theory of general linguistics*. Amsterdam.

Dirr, A. 1928. *Einführung in das Studium der kaukasischen Sprachen*. Leipzig.

Dobrizhoffer, M. 1902. *Auskunft über die abiponische Sprache*. Edited by Julius Platzmann. Leipzig.

Doherty, M. 1970. 'Zur Komparation antonymer Adjektive', *ASG-Bericht*, 6 (2), Berlin.

Doherty, P.C. and Schwartz, A. 1967. 'The syntax of the compared adjective in English', *Language*, 43, 903–36.

Dordillon, R.I. 1931. *Grammaire et dictionnaire de la langue des Iles Marquises*. Paris.

Downing, B. 1978. 'Some universals of relative clause structure', in: J.H. Greenberg, C.A. Ferguson and E. Moravcsik (eds), part 4, 375–418.

Drabbe, P. 1952. *Spraakkunst van het Ekagi*. The Hague.

Dravins, K. and Ruke, V. 1958. *Verbalformen und undeklinierbare Redeteile in der Mundart von Stenden*. Lund.

Dumezil, G. 1933. *Introduction à la grammaire comparée des langues caucasiennes du Nord*. Paris.

Eades, D. 1979. 'Gumbaynggir', in: R.M.W. Dixon and B.J. Blake (eds), *Handbook of Australian Languages, Vol. 1*. Amsterdam, 244–361.

Eliott, D., Legum, S. and Thompson, S.A. 1969. 'Syntactic variation as linguistic data', in: *Papers from the Fifth Regional Meeting of the Chicago Linguistic Society*, Chicago, Ill., 52–9.

Endzelin, J. 1922. *Lettische Grammatik*, Riga.

Erelt, M. 1973. 'Some remarks on comparative and superlative sentences in Estonian', in: F. Kiefer (ed.), *Trends in Soviet theoretical linguistics*. Dordrecht/Boston, Mass., 135–47.

Ernout, A. and Meillet, A. 1979[4]. *Dictionnaire étymologique de la langue latine: histoire des mots*. Paris.

Faltz, L.M. 1977. 'Reflexivization: a study in Universal Syntax'. Ph.D. Diss., Berkeley.

Ferguson, C.A. 1978. 'Historical background of universals research', in: J.H. Greenberg, C.A. Ferguson and E. Moravcsik (eds), part 1, 7–31.

Ferrand, G. 1903. *Essai de grammaire malgache*. Paris.

Fisch, R. 1912. *Grammatik der Dagomba-Sprache*. Berlin.

Fodor, J.A. 1976. *The language of thought*. Hassocks, Sussex, UK.

Fodor, J., Bever, T. and Garrett, M. 1974. *The psychology of language. An introduction to psycholinguistics and generative grammar*. New York.

Foster, M.L. 1969. *The Tarascan language*. Berkeley/Los Angeles, Cal.

Frachtenberg, L.J. 1922. 'Siuslawan (Lower Umpqua)', in: F. Boas (ed.), *Handbook of American Indian languages*, part 2, Washington, DC, 441–629.

Freeland, L.S. 1951. *Language of the Sierra Miwok*. Bloomington, Ind.

Fromm, H. and Sadeniemi, M. 1956. *Finnisches Elementarbuch*. Heidelberg.

Gaden, H. 1909. *Essai de grammaire de la langue baguirmienne*. Paris.

Gavel, H. 1929. *Grammaire basque*. Bayonne.

George, I. 1975. 'A grammar of Kwa-type verb serialization: its nature and significance in current generative theory' Ph.D. Diss., Ann Arbor, Mich.

Givón, T. 1975. 'Serial verbs and syntactic change: Niger-Congo', in: C.N. Li (ed.), *Word order and word order change*, Austin, Tex., 47–111.

Givón, T. 1979. *On understanding grammar*. New York.

de Goeje, C.H. 1978. *Etudes linguistiques caraïbes*. Wiesbaden (reprint from: Amsterdam, 1909).

Greenberg, J.H. 1963. 'Some universals of language, with particular reference to the order of meaningful elements', in: J.H. Greenberg (ed.), *Universals of language*, Cambridge, Mass., 73–113.

Greenberg, J.H. 1966. *Language universals, with specific reference to feature hierarchies*. The Hague.

Greenberg, J.H., Ferguson, C.A. and Moravcsik, E. (eds). 1978. *Universals of human language*. Vols 1–4. Stanford, Cal.

Gregores, E. and Suárez, J.A. 1967. *A description of colloquial Guarani*. The Hague.

Grice, H.P. 1975. 'Logic and conversation', in: P. Cole and J.L. Morgan (eds), *Syntax and semantics. Vol. III. Speech Acts*. New York etc., 41–58.

Grierson, G.A. (ed.). 1903. *Linguistic survey of India. Vol. III. Tibeto-Burman family. Part II. Specimens of the Bodo, Naga and Kachin groups*. Calcutta.

Grierson, G.A. (ed.). 1906. *Linguistic survey of India. Part IV. Munda and Dravidian languages*. Calcutta.

Grierson, G.A. (ed.). 1909. *Linguistic survey of India. Part III. Tibeto-Burman family. Part I. General introduction. Specimens of the Tibetan dialects, the Himalayan dialects and the North Assam Group*. Calcutta.

Grierson, G.A. (ed.). 1919. *Linguistic survey of India. Vol. VII. Part II. Specimens of the Dardic or Pisacha languages (including Kashmiri)*. Calcutta.

Guasch, P.A. 1956. *El idioma Guarani*. Asunción.

Haenisch, E. 1961. *Mandschu-Grammatik*. Leipzig.

Haile, B. 1926. *A manual of Navaho grammar*. St Michael's, Arizona.

Haile, B. 1941. *Learning Navaho. I–III*. St Michael's, Arizona.

Hajdú, P. 1963. *The Samoyed peoples and languages*. Bloomington, Ind.

Hale, K. 1976. 'The adjoined relative clause in Australia', in: R.M.W. Dixon (ed.), *Grammatical categories in Australian languages*, Canberra, 78–105.

Hale, K. 1983. 'Walpiri and the grammar of non-configurational languages', *Natural Language and Linguistic Theory*, 1, 5–47.

Halliday, M.A.K. 1967. 'Notes on transitivity and theme in English. I', *Journal of Linguistics*, 3, 37–81.

Halliday, M.A.K. 1968. 'Notes on transitivity and theme in English. II', *Journal of Linguistics*, 4, 179–216.

Hammerich, L.L. 1970. *The Eskimo language*. Oslo.

Hankamer, J. 1973. 'Why there are two *than's* in English', in: *Papers from the Ninth Regional Meeting of the Chicago Linguistic Society*, Chicago, Ill., 179–88.

Hankamer, J. 1977. 'Multiple analyses', in: C.N. Li (ed.), *Mechanisms of syntactic change*, Austin, Tex., 602–20.

Hankamer, J. 1979. *Deletion in coordinate structures*. New York.

Hanoteau, A. 1896[2]. *Essai de grammaire de la langue Tamachek'*. Algiers.

Hanoteau, A. 1906. *Essai de grammaire kabyle*. Algiers.

Harries, H. 1978. 'Coordination Reduction', in: J.H. Greenberg, C.A. Ferguson and E. Moravcsik (eds), Vol. 4, 515–83.

Hawkins, J.A. 1979. 'Implicational universals as predictors of word order change', *Language*, 55, 618–48.

Hawkins, J.A. 1980. 'On implicational and distributional universals of word order', *Journal of Linguistics*, 16, 193–235.

Hawkins, J.A. 1984. *Word order universals and their explanation*. New York.

Hellan, L. 1981. *Towards an integrated analysis of comparatives*. Tübingen.

Hendrick, R. 1978. 'The phrase structure of adjectives and comparatives', *Linguistic Analysis*, 4 (3), 255–99.

Hetzer, A. 1978. *Lehrbuch der vereinheitlichten albanischen Schriftsprache.* Hamburg.

Higgins, E.T. and Huttenlocher, J. 1971. 'Adjectives, comparatives and syllogisms', *Psychological Review*, 78, 487–504.

Hoeksema, J. 1983. 'Negative polarity and the comparative', *Natural Language and Linguistic Theory*, 1, 403–34.

Hoff, B.J. 1968. *The Carib language*. The Hague.

Hoffmann, C. 1963. *A grammar of the Margi language*. London.

Hoffmann, J. 1903. *Mundari grammar*. Calcutta.

Holmer, N.M. 1949. 'Goajiro (Arawak) III: verbs and associated morphemes', *International Journal of American Linguistics*, 15, 145–57.

Hopper, P.J. 1979. 'Aspect and foregrounding in discourse', in: T. Givón (ed.), *Syntax and semantics. Vol. 12. Discourse and syntax.* New York, 213–41.

Hopper, P.J. and Thompson, S.A. (eds). 1982. *Studies in transitivity. (Syntax and semantics, Vol. 15).* New York, etc.

Hyman, L. 1971. 'Consecutivization in Fe'fe', *Journal of African Linguistics*, 10 (2), 29–43.

Hyman, L. 1975. 'On the change from SOV to SVO: evidence from Niger-Congo', in: C.N. Li (ed.), *Word order and word order change*, Austin, Tex., 113–47.

Ittmann, J. 1939. *Grammatik des Duala (Kamerun)*. Berlin.

Jacob, J.M. 1968. *Introduction to Cambodian*. London.

Jäschke, H. 1929. *Tibetan grammar*. Berlin/Leipzig.

Jessen, M.J. 1974. 'A semantic study of spatial and temporal expressions'. Ph.D. Diss., Edinburgh.

Johnson, M.J. 1966. 'Syntactic structures of Tamazight'. Ph.D. Diss., UCLA.

Joly, A. 1967. *Negation and the comparative particle in English*. Quebec.

Jones, R.B. and Thong, H.S. 1960. *Introduction to spoken Vietnamese.* Washington, DC.

Kacori, T. 1979. *A handbook of Albanian*. Sofia.

Keenan, E.L. 1976a. 'Towards a universal definition of "subject"', in: C.N. Li (ed.), *Subject and topic*, New York, 303–33.

Keenan, E.L. 1976b, 'Remarkable subjects in Malagasy', in: C.N. Li (ed.), *Subject and topic*, New York, 247–301.

Keenan, E.L. 1978. 'The syntax of subject-final languages', in: W.P. Lehmann (ed.), *Syntactic typology*, Hassocks, Sussex, UK, 267–327.

Keenan, E.L. and Comrie, B. 1977. 'Noun Phrase Accessibility and Universal Grammar', *Linguistic Inquiry*, 8, 63–100.

Keenan, E.L. and Comrie, B. 1979. 'Data on the Noun Phrase Accessibility Hierarchy', *Language*, 55, 333–51.

Kendall, M.B. 1976. *Selected problems in Yavapai syntax*. New York/London.

Kiliaan, H.N. 1919. *Javaansche spraakkunst*. The Hague.

Kim, T.T. 1943^2. *Grammaire annamite*. Hanoi.

Klein, E. 1980. 'A semantics for positive and comparative adjectives', *Linguistics and Philosophy*, 4, 1–45.

Klooster, W. 1972. *The structure underlying measure phrase sentences.* Dordrecht.

Klooster, W. 1976. 'Adjektieven, neutraliteit en comparatieven', in: G. Koefoed and A. Evers (eds), *Lijnen van taaltheoretisch onderzoek*, Groningen, 229–59.

Klooster, W. 1978. 'Much in Dutch', in: *Papers from the Fourteenth Regional Meeting of the Chicago Linguistic Society*, Chicago, Ill., 217–28.

Klooster, W. 1979. 'Opmerkingen over de comparatief', in: *Handelingen van het XXXIIIe Vlaams Filologencongres*, Louvain, 197–206.

Koutsoudas, A. 1971. 'Gapping, conjunction reduction and coordination deletion', *Foundations of Language*, 7, 337–86.

Kühner, R. 1955. *Ausführliche Grammatik der lateinischen Sprache. Bearbeitet von B. Gerth.* Leverkusen.

Kühner, R. 1963. *Ausfuhrliche Grammatik der griechischen Sprache. Bearbeitet von C. Stegmann.* Darmstadt.

Kuno, S. 1973. *The structure of the Japanese language.* Cambridge, Mass.

Kuno, S. 1978. 'Japanese: a characteristic OV language', in: W.P. Lehmann (ed.), *Syntactic typology*, Hassocks, Sussex, UK, 57–138.

Kuno, S. 1981. 'The syntax of comparative clauses', in: *Papers from the Seventeenth Regional Meeting of the Chicago Linguistic Society*, Chicago, Ill., 136–55.

Labouret, H. 1934. *Les Manding et leur langue.* Paris.

Labouret, H. 1952. *La langue des Peuls ou Foulbé.* Ifan-Dakar.

Lafitte, P. 1944. *Grammaire basque (Navarro-Labourdin littéraire).* Bayonne.

Lakatos, I. 1978. *The methodology of scientific research programmes.* Edited by John Worrall and Gregory Currie. Cambridge, UK.

Lakoff, G. 1972. 'Linguistics and natural logic', in: D. Davidson and G. Harman (eds), *Semantics of natural language*, Dordrecht, 545–665.

Lalou, M. 1950. *Manuel élémentaire du Tibétain classique.* Paris.

Lambertz, M. 1959. *Lehrgang des Albanischen.* Halle (Saale).

Landaburu, J. 1979. *La langue des Andoke (Amazonie colombienne).* Paris.

Laoust, E. 1918. *Course de Berbère marocain.* Paris.

Larousse. 1970. *Grammaire Larousse du français contemporain. Par Jean-Claude Chevalier et autres.* Paris.

Lastra, Y. 1968. *Cochabamba Quechua syntax.* The Hague/Paris.

Lees, R.B. 1961. 'Grammatical analysis of the English comparative construction', *Word*, 17, 171–85.

Lehmann, C. 1984. *Der Relativsatz.* Tübingen.

Lehmann, W.P. 1973. 'A structural principle of language and its implications', *Language*, 49, 47–66.

Leith-Ross, S. 1922. *Fulani grammar.* Lagos.

Levin, N.B. 1964. *The Assiniboine language.* Bloomington, Ind./The Hague.

Lewis, G.L. 1967. *Turkish grammar.* Oxford.

Lewis, H. and Pedersen, H. 1974[3]. *A concise comparative Celtic grammar.* Göttingen.

Li, C.N. (ed.). 1975. *Word order and word order change*. Austin, Tex.

Li, C.N. (ed.). 1977. *Mechanisms of syntactic change*. Austin, Tex.

Li, C.N. and Thompson, S.A. 1973a. 'Serial verb constructions in Mandarin Chinese: subordination or coordination', in: C. Corum et al. (eds), *Papers from the Comparative Syntax Festival*, Chicago, Ill., 96–103.

Li, C.N. and Thompson, S.A. 1973b. 'Co-verbs in Mandarin Chinese: verbs or prepositions?', in: *Papers from the Sixth International Conference on Sino-Tibetan languages and linguistic studies*, La Jolla.

Li, C.N. and Thompson, S.A. 1975. 'The semantic function of word order: a case study in Mandarin', in: C.N. Li (ed.), *Word order and word order change*, Austin, Tex., 163–95.

Li, C.N. and Thompson, S.A. 1978. 'An exploration of Mandarin Chinese', in: W.P. Lehmann (ed.), *Syntactic typology*, Hassocks, Sussex, UK, 223–66.

Lister-Turner, R. and Clark, J.B. 1930. *Revised Motu grammar and vocabulary*. Port Moresby.

Loogman, A. 1965. *Swahili grammar and syntax*. Louvain.

Lopez, C. 1928. *Comparison of Tagalog and Iloko*. Ph.D. Diss., Hamburg.

Lorimer, D.L.R. 1935. *The Burushaski language. Vol. I. Introduction and grammar*. Oslo.

Lukas, J. 1937. *A study of the Kanuri language*. London.

Lukas, J. 1953. *Die Sprache der Tubu in der zentralen Sahara*. Berlin.

Lyons, J. 1967. 'A note on possessive, existential and locative sentences', *Foundations of Language*, 3, 390–6.

Lyons, J. 1968. 'Existence, location, possession and transitivity', in: B. van Rootselaar and J.F. Staal (eds), *Logic, methodology and philosophy of science III*, Los Angeles, Cal., 495–504.

Lyons, J. 1977. *Semantics*. Cambridge, UK.

Lyons, J. 1979. 'Knowledge and truth: a localistic approach', in: Allerton, D.J., Carney, E. and Holdcroft, D. (eds), *Function and control in linguistic analysis*. Cambridge, UK, 111–41.

McCawley, J.D. 1972. 'A program for logic', in: D. Davidson and G. Harman (eds), *Semantics of natural language*, Dordrecht, 498–544.

McGregor, R.S. 1977. *Outline of Hindi grammar*. Delhi.

McKinnon, R. 1971. *Teach yourself Gaelic*. London.

Mallinson, G. and Blake, B. 1981. *Language typology*. Amsterdam.

Maria, P.A. 1914. 'Essai de grammaire Kaiapó, langue des Indiens Kaiapó, Brésil', *Anthropos*, 9, 233–40.

Marré, E.C. 1901. *Die Sprache der Hausa*. Vienna/Budapest/Leipzig.

Marsack, C.C. 1975[4]. *Teach yourself Samoan*. London.

Mason, J.A. 1918. *The language of the Salinan Indians*. Berkeley, Cal.

Matteson, E. 1965. *The Piro (Arawakan) language*. Berkeley/Los Angeles, Cal.

Mätzner, E. 1880[3]. *Englische Grammatik*. Berlin.

Meeussen, A.E. 1959. *Essai de grammaire Kirundi*. Tervuren (Belgium).

Meile, P. 1945. *Introduction au Tamoul*. Paris.

Meinhof, C. 1909. *Lehrbuch der Nama-Sprache*. Berlin.

Menard, F. 1908. *Grammaire Kirundi*. Algiers.

Merlan, F. 1982. *Mangarayi*. Amsterdam.
Milner, G.B. 1956. *Fijian grammar*. Suva, Fiji.
Mischlich, A. 1911. *Lehrbuch der Hausa-Sprache*. Berlin.
Mittwoch, A. 1974. 'Is there an underlying negative element in comparative clauses?', *Linguistics*, 122, 39–45.
Mullie, J.L.M. 1947. *Korte Chinese Spraakkunst van de gesproken taal (Noord-Pekinees dialect)*. Brussels.
Nagy, A. 1929. *Ungarische Konversationsgrammatik*. Heidelberg.
Napoli, D.J. and Nespor, M. 1976. 'Negatives in comparatives', *Language*, 52, 811–38.
Nasr, R.T. 1967. *The structure of Arabic*. Beirut.
N'Diaye, G. 1970. *Structure du dialecte basque de Maya*. The Hague.
Neijt-Kappen, A.H. 1979. *Gapping. A contribution to sentence grammar*. Dordrecht.
Noss, R.B. 1964. *Thai reference grammar*. Washington, DC.
Okell, J. 1969. *A reference grammar of colloquial Burmese*. London.
Peekel, P.G. 1909. *Grammatik der neu-mecklenburgischen Sprache*. Berlin.
Perkins, R. 1980. 'The evolution of grammar and culture'. Ph.D. Diss., Buffalo, NY.
Pilch, H. 1965. 'Comparative constructions in English', *Language*, 41, 37–58.
Pinnow, H.-J. 1964. *Die nordamerikanischen Indianersprachen*. Wiesbaden.
Plank, F. (ed.). 1979. *Ergativity: towards a theory of grammatical relations*. London.
Platzmann, J. 1874. *Grammatik der brasilianischen Sprache*. Leipzig.
Popper, K. 1934. *Logik der Forschung*. Vienna.
Pulkina, I.M. and Zakhava-Nekrasova, E. 1974. *Russian. A practical grammar with exercises*. Moscow.
Pulte, W. 1971. 'Gapping and word order in Quechua', in: *Papers from the Seventh Regional Meeting of the Chicago Linguistic Society*, Chicago, Ill., 193–7.
Pultr, A. 1960. *Lehrbuch der koreanischen Sprache*. Halle.
Rambaud, J.-B. 1903. *La langue Wolof*. Paris.
Ramstedt, G.J. 1968. *A Korean grammar*. Oosterhout (Holland).
Rastorgueva, R.S. 1963. *A short sketch of Tajik grammar*. The Hague.
Ray, S.H. 1926. *A comparative study of the Melanesian island languages*. Cambridge, UK.
Reichard, G.A. 1933. 'Cœur d'Alene', in: F. Boas (ed.), *Handbook of American Indian languages, part 3*, Washington, DC, 515–707.
Reinisch, L. 1882. *Die Bilin-Sprache in Nordost-Afrika*. Vienna.
Rere, T. 1965. *Maori lessons for the Cook Islands*. Wellington.
Rollo, W. 1925. 'The Basque dialect of Marquina'. Ph.D. Diss., Leyden.
Rosenbaum, P.S. 1967. *The grammar of English predicate complement constructions*. Cambridge, Mass.
Ross, J.R. 1967. 'Constraints on variables in syntax'. Ph.D. Diss., Cambridge, Mass., MIT.
Ross, J.R. 1970. 'Gapping and the order of constituents', in: M. Bierwisch and K.

Heidolph (eds), *Progress in linguistics*, The Hague, 249–59.

Ross, J.R. 1972. 'The category squish: Endstation Hauptwort', in: *Papers from the Eighth Regional Meeting of the Chicago Linguistic Society*, Chicago, Ill., 316–28.

Samarin, W.J. 1966. *The Gbeya language*. Berkeley/Los Angeles, Cal.

Sanders, G.A. 1976. 'A functional typology of elliptical coordinations', Indiana University Linguistics Club, Bloomington, Ind.

Sanders, G.A. and Tai, J. 1972. 'Immediate dominance and identity deletion', *Foundations of language*, 8, 161–98.

Sauvageot, A. 1951. *Esquisse de la langue hongroise*. Paris.

Schachter, P. 1977. 'Reference-related and role-related properties of subjects', in: P. Cole and J.M. Sadock (eds), *Grammatical relations. Syntax and semantics*, Vol. 8. New York, 279–306.

Schils, G.H. 1891. *Grammaire complète de la langue des Namas*. Louvain.

Seuren, P.A.M. 1973. 'The comparative', in: F. Kiefer and N. Ruwet (eds), *Generative grammar in Europe*, Dordrecht, 528–64.

Seuren, P.A.M. 1978. 'The structure and selection of positive and negative gradable adjectives', in: *Papers from the Parasession on the Lexicon, Fourteenth Regional Meeting of the Chicago Linguistic Society*, Chicago, Ill., 336–46.

Seuren, P.A.M. 1984. 'The comparative revisited', *Journal of Semantics*, 3, 1/2, 109–141.

Sherman, M. 1969. 'Some effects of negation and adjectival marking on sentence comprehension'. Ph.D. Diss., Cambridge, Mass., Harvard.

Shibatani, M. (ed.). 1975. *Syntax and Semantics. Vol. 6. The grammar of causative constructions*. New York.

Shopen, T. 1973. 'Ellipsis as grammatical indeterminacy', *Foundations of Language*, 10, 65–77.

Simonyi, S. 1907. *Die ungarische Sprache. Geschichte und Charakteristik*. Strassbourg.

Skeat, W.W. 1901. *A concise etymological dictionary of the English language*. Oxford.

Small, G. 1923. *The comparison of inequality. The semantics and syntax of the comparative particle in English*. Baltimore.

Small, G. 1929. *The Germanic case of comparison with a special study of English*, in: Language Monographs, 4, Philadelphia, Penns.

Smirnova, M.A. 1982. *The Hausa language*. London, etc.

Smythe, W.E. 1948. *Elementary grammar of the Gumbainggar language (North Coast, N.S.W.)*. Sydney.

Spagnolo, L.M. 1933. *Bari grammar*. Verona.

von Stechow, A. 1984. 'Comparing semantic theories of comparison', *Journal of Semantics*, 3, 1/2, 1–77.

Steele, S. 1978. 'Word order variation: a typological study', in: J.H. Greenberg, C.A. Ferguson and E. Moravcsik (eds), part 4, 585–623.

Strachan, J. 1909. *An introduction to early Welsh*. Manchester, UK.

Street, J.C. 1963. *Khalka structure*. Bloomington, Ind.

Strehlow, T.G.M. 1944. *Aranda phonetics and grammar*. Sydney.

Swift, L.B. 1963. *A reference grammar of modern Turkish*. Bloomington, Ind.

Tai, J.H.-Y. 1969. 'Coordination Reduction'. Ph.D. Diss., Bloomington, Ind.

Tai, J.H.-Y. 1971. 'Identity deletion and regrouping in coordinate structures', in: *Papers from the Seventh Regional Meeting of Chicago Linguistic Society*, Chicago, Ill., 264–74.

Talmy, L. 1978. 'Relations between subordination and coordination', in: J.H. Greenberg, C.A. Ferguson and E. Moravcsik (eds), part 4, 487–513.

Taylor, F.W. 1921. *A first grammar of the Adamawa dialect of the Fulani language (Fulfulde)*. Oxford.

Taylor, F.W. 1949. *A practical Hausa grammar*. London.

Ternes, E. 1970. *Grammaire structurale du Breton de l'île de Croix (dialecte occidental)*. Heidelberg.

Tessmann, G. 1929. 'Die Tschama-Sprache', *Anthropos*, 24, 241–71.

Thalbitzer, W. 1911. 'Eskimo', in: F. Boas (ed.), *Handbook of American Indian languages, part 1*, Washington, DC, 967–1069.

Tisserant, Ch. 1930. *Essai sur la grammaire banda*. Paris.

Tompa, J. 1968. *Ungarische Grammatik*. The Hague.

de Torres Rubio, D. 1966. *Arte de la lengua aymara*. Lima.

Traugott, E.C. 1975. 'Spatial expressions of tense and temporal sequencing', *Semiotica*, 15, 207–30.

von Tschudi, J.J. 1884. *Organismus der Khetsua-Sprache*. Leipzig.

Tucker, A.N. and Mpaayi, J.T.O. 1955. *A Masai grammar*. London.

van der Tuuk, H.N. 1867. *Tobasche Spraakkunst*. Amsterdam.

Valin, R. 1952. *Esquisse d'une théorie des degrés de comparaison*. Quebec.

Vennemann, Th. 1974. 'Theoretical word order studies: results and problems', *Papiere zur Linguistik*, 7, 5–25.

Vennemann, Th. 1975. 'An explanation of drift', in: C.N. Li (ed.), *Word order and word order change*, Austin, Tex., 269–305.

Visser, F. Th. 1963. *A historical syntax of the English language*. Leyden.

Voegelin, C.F. and Voegelin, F.M. 1977. *Classification and index of the world's languages*. New York/Oxford/Amsterdam.

Vogt, H. 1940. *The Kalispel language*. Oslo.

Voorhoeve, J. 1962. *Sranan syntax*. Amsterdam.

Vormann, F. and Scharfenberger, W. 1914. *Die Monumbo-Sprache*. Vienna.

Walbeehm, A.H.J.G. 1915. *Javaansche Spraakkunst*. Leyden.

Walde, A. and Hoffmann, J.B. 1954³. *Lateinisches etymologisches Wörterbuch*. Heidelberg.

Weigand, G. 1913. *Albanesische Grammatik*. Leipzig.

Welmers, W. 1973. *African language structures*. Berkeley.

Whorf, B.L. 1956. *Language, thought and reality. Selected writings of Benjamin Lee Whorf*. Edited by John Carroll. New York.

Wojcik, R. 1976. 'The copula as auxiliary in a surface VSO-language', in: *Papers from the Twelfth Regional Meeting of the Chicago Linguistic Society*, Chicago, Ill., 666–75.

Wolff, J.V. 1967. *Beginning Cebuano*. New Haven, Conn./London.

Yushmanov, N.V. 1961. *The structure of the Arabic language*. Washington, DC.

Index of Topics

Index of Languages